Smoke and Mirrors

Smoke and Mirrors

The Politics and Culture of Air Pollution

EDITED BY

E. Melanie DuPuis

New York University Press

NEW YORK AND LONDON

NEW YORK UNIVERSITY PRESS
New York and London
www.nyupress.org

Library of Congress Cataloging-in-Publication Data
Smoke and mirrors : the politics and culture of air pollution /
edited by E. Melanie DuPuis.
p. cm.
Includes bibliographical references and index.
ISBN 0–8147–1960–0 (cloth: alk. paper) —
ISBN 0–8147–1961–9 (pbk.: alk. paper)
1. Air—Pollution—Political aspects.
2. Air—Pollution—Social aspects.   I. DuPuis,
E. Melanie (Erna Melanie), 1957– .
TD883.S635   2004
363.739'2—dc22   2003026720

New York University Press books are printed on acid-free paper,
and their binding materials are chosen for strength and durability.

Manufactured in the United States of America

c 10 9 8 7 6 5 4 3 2 1
p 10 9 8 7 6 5 4 3 2 1

Contents

Acknowledgments   vii

Introduction   I
    E. Melanie DuPuis

The Emergence of Air Pollution as a Problem

1   Perceptions and Effects of Late Victorian Air Pollution   15
    Peter Brimblecombe

2   "The Invisible Evil": Noxious Vapor and
   Public Health in Manchester during the Age of Industry   27
    Harold L. Platt

3   Public Perceptions of Smoke Pollution
   in Victorian Manchester   51
    Stephen Mosley

4   Uplands Downwind: Acidity and Ecological Change
   in the Southeast Lancashire Moorlands   77
    Matthew Osborn

5   The "Smoky City" between the Wars   100
    Angela Gugliotta

6   The Merits of the Precautionary Principle:
   Controlling Automobile Exhausts in Germany
   and the United States before 1945   119
    Frank Uekoetter

7   Interpreting the London Fog Disaster of 1952   154
    Peter Thorsheim

8   Localizing Smog:
     Transgressions in the Therapeutic Landscape   170
       Joshua Dunsby

   Air Pollution Policy Today

9   A Fine Balance:
     Automobile Pollution Control Strategies in California   203
       Sudhir Chella Rajan

10   Who Owns the Air? Clean Air Act Implementation
     as a Negotiation of Common Property Rights   223
       E. Melanie DuPuis

11   Air Pollution in Spain: A "Peripheral" Nation Transforms   241
       Alexander Farrell

12   Clearing the Air and Breathing Freely:
     The Health Politics of Air Pollution and Asthma   261
       Phil Brown, Stephen Zavestoski, Brian Mayer,
       Theo Luebke, Joshua Mandelbaum,
       and Sabrina McCormick

13   Invisible People, Invisible Places:
     Connecting Air Pollution and Pesticide Drift in California 288
       Jill Harrison

14   Notes from the Field:
     Air Pollution Engineering as Cultural Experience   305
       Roger K. Raufer

15   The Social and Political Construction of Air Pollution:
     Air Pollution Policies for Mexico City, 1979–1996   324
       José Luis Lezama

     Afterword   337
       Joel A. Tarr

     Contributors   343

     Index   349

Acknowledgments

This book came out of conversations. The first occurred during lunches with Paul Lubeck, director of the Center for Global, International and Regional Studies (CGIRS) at the University of California, Santa Cruz. Paul encourages scholars at UCSC to make their work available to a wider scholarly and policy audience. An inveterate strategist, he recommended (and funded) a conference to bring to Santa Cruz scholars and experts on the social aspects of air pollution. He also made available to me CGIRS's expert staff, Sarah Traxler and Lisa Nishioka, who provided invaluable assistance in organizing both the conference and the book.

Alex Farrell, then director of the Carnegie Mellon Electricity Industry Center, put me in contact with scholars from around the world. He was similarly encouraging about the prospects of a larger group conferring to talk about air pollution. Among those with whom Alex connected me were Joel Tarr and Peter Brimblecombe.

As I later learned, if you ask an urban environmental historian whether he or she was once a student of Joel Tarr's, the answer is either "Yes" or "No, but he was instrumental in my career." Joel has made urban pollution studies important as much by encouraging other scholars as through his own work. The care Joel puts into mentoring others is extraordinary. Although he was unable to attend the conference, his input from afar improved the quality of our conversation many times over. Peter Brimblecombe had a similar effect, taking an interest in the project in all its phases. During the conference itself, Marc Cioc, Brent Haddad, Carl Peckman, and Ravi Rajan all provided helpful, insightful comments on the paper presented.

The move from conference to book was also the result of conversation. At the end of the meeting, John Wirth laid out a plan of action that was irresistible. The plan included presenting revised chapters at the American

Society for Environmental History Conference, as a way to publicize a book under contract. Stephen Magro, my editor at New York University Press, convinced me to expand the scope of the book by adding more articles from a wide variety of disciplines and subjects. One of his ideas was to move the book away from a sole focus on Europe and the United States. Much of the work on air pollution in the industrializing countries has yet to be done, but I have tried to include some of the newest work to examine air pollution problems in the newly urbanized world. Editorial Assistant Jennifer Yoon did a great job with the day-to-day matters of manuscript preparation.

John Wirth's plan to bring our conversations into a book worked perfectly, exactly as he predicted. Unfortunately, John did not live to see his plan carried out. He died a few months later, on June 20, 2002. Without his energy—that plan of action—this book might not have come to pass. We dedicate this book to John.

Introduction

E. Melanie DuPuis

In air pollution policymaking today, the primary language spoken is that of science, engineering, and economics. This was exactly the language I did *not* speak when I began my career as an energy and environment policy analyst for the New York State Department of Economic Development in the early '90s. As a political sociologist, I had been trained to see policy as politics. Yet I learned to speak the idiom of numbers, percentages, and prices, of costs and benefits valued in dollars. Much like the typical definitions of "public policy" analysis, the academic literature we relied on in air pollution policy characterized problems and solutions in what Alain Lipietz calls the "eco*nomos*"—the language of management, of control.[1] Yet my politically trained eye could not help but see the numbers as mystifying a more important but unspoken reality: power contests between groups struggling for rights to use the air. City and country, commuter and industrialist, "downwind" and "upwind" states played the numbers game for a big stake: political dominance over a key resource.

There has always been an important, now growing, branch of air pollution studies that has looked at politics, most notably Matthew Crenson's 1971 work *The Un-Politics of Air Pollution.*[2] Nevertheless, the air pollution studies that gain and dominate policymakers' attention today have laid out the problem, and its solution, in terms of models and prices, that important but incomplete information that comes from quantitative assessments and markets.

A growing number of studies are looking at environmental issues as struggles over power and meaning. Political ecologists examine the contests over access to forest and water resources; environmental justice scholars show the political inequalities in the struggle to avoid pollution burdens. These studies speak in what Lipietz calls "eco*logos*"—the language of meaning. From this more cultural and political point of view, the frameworks used to answer the question "How do we solve the environmental problems caused by economic growth?" include attention to the political interests that gain the benefits and bear the costs of pollution, including the role that race, class, and gender have played in the distribution of environmental burdens. All these more meaning-*full* studies share the ambition of discovering how people make cultural and political sense of their environment—and each other—in the search for solutions to environmental degradation. In these studies, the solutions to environmental problems come from social interaction. Science and scientists are still important from this perspective. However, in the chapters in this volume by Peter Brimblecombe, Angela Gugliotta, Harold Platt, Joshua Dunsby, and Phil Brown and colleagues, scientists become part of the social context instead of the neutral source of "fact"; their questions come from the worlds in which they live.

These incisive but less attended-to scholars see air pollution through a social lens. Fortunately, I had the opportunity to invite several of these scholars to UCSC in 2002. From that original group, this book has expanded into a representation of some of the best current work in understanding air pollution as part of a more social and political picture of the environment. The chapters in this book emphasize the existence of air pollution—and air pollution abatement policies—not as scientific models and measurements or economic values but as social "artifacts": the products of social interactions and relationships, including inequalities, knowledge, power, and politics. While science and economics provide crucial and substantial information about air pollution, only in combination with studies of the meaning of air pollution is it possible to paint the full social "airscape" of air pollution policy.[3]

Numbers as a sole framework for understanding air pollution policy cannot paint a full picture of air pollution as our current reality. Whether the numbers describe air pollution implementation planning models or the benefits of a blue sky over the Grand Canyon, quantitative assessment assumes that rational decisionmaking will occur, and that that best decision can be discovered by putting values on projects and problems so that people know which decision to choose.

In addition, economists argue that the public motivation to create effective environmental abatement policies can be measured along what they call an "environmental Kuznet's curve": at a certain level of income, people decide to forfeit further material rewards of growth and instead invest in environmental quality through pollution control regulations. The chapters in this book show that the emergence of air pollution as a social problem in local contexts is not the product of some automatic formula based on per capita income. Instead, pollution as a problem emerges from the social and cultural context of human interactions.

The political landscape of current environmental policy shows us that, despite an avalanche of valuation studies, policy continues to follow its own path. Most often, environmental policy has not followed the recommendations of cost-benefit analyses. In addition, despite more than a decade of meta-cost-benefit "risk-ranking" projects that attempt to rationally guide policymaking resources toward the "next worst" unmitigated environmental risks,[4] environmental policies continue to be blown by the social and political winds.

The U.S. Republican Party shift in environmental strategies is a prime example of politics trumping rational decisionmaking in environmental policy. In previous decades, the Republicans had promoted rational decisionmaking through cost-benefit in the party's "Contract with America." Nevertheless, the current Republican administration has chosen to dismantle regulations without undertaking a rational assessment of the benefits and costs of these moves. One gets the overall impression that U.S. environmental policy is now swinging even more violently in the winds of party politics. How can the science of economic valuation and Kuznet's curves predict such political goings-on?

Even some economists have come to realize that simply putting prices on environmental benefits and burdens will not get us where we need to go. Some ecological economists argue that valuation studies must involve a "multicriteria" evaluative approach, which includes inputs from the political discourse of stakeholders.[5] These economists argue that not all "values" can be "valuated," that some values are incommensurable, that is, cannot be described in the universal calculus of the *nomos*.

This new turn in ecological economics certainly brightens the day for political sociologists such as myself, tutored in the intellectual history of environmental discourse, political ecology, pluralism, and studies of the "public sphere."[6] The turn also seems to be creating an intellectual space in which some ecological economists and some environmental historians and sociologists are beginning to talk to each other.[7] It remains to be seen, however, whether the idealistically rational scheme of multicriteria assessment will prevail against the realist vision of power and inequality, something even multiple criteria may not be able to take into account.

Yet the past tells us that, at certain times and in certain places, pollution control policies were formed and polluted environments became cleaner. There was a time, after all, when only the urban elite neighborhoods in the United States had access to running water in their homes. As the chapters in this book show, in certain places at certain times dirty air has become cleaner. In some places the air was so thick with smoke that not only did thousands die prematurely but everyday practices became transformed: residents abandoned any thought of wearing lighter clothing, architects simplified building ornament to prevent the visible effects of acid erosion, and writers invented the "mystery," wherein characters walked streets in search of answers behind a smoky veil. In a move that, in retrospect, looks (and smells) like progress, some places ended up with a fairer distribution of clean water and clean air, saving and improving many lives. Fighting against powerful forces, some places have made strong gains in environmental health—the health of forests and animals as well as the health of humans. What caused that change to happen, for the "fairer" and "healthier" option to be taken, in certain times and certain places?

Some of these chapters also show that "fairer" and "cleaner" options for some often imposed additional economic or pollution burdens on others. The in-depth views of pollution practices described here tell us that environmental cleanup is a conflictual and contradictory process. The conflicts are not just between citizen breathers and industrial polluters but also between various visions of the city. As chapters in this volume on Manchester, Cincinnati, and Los Angeles show, visions of the city as a feminine, middle-class, private "home," producing healthy people, conflicted with visions of the city as a masculine, public "workshop," producing wealth, including wages. For example, Joshua Dunsby's chapter on Los Angeles shows how a key, powerful group of eastern "healthseekers" challenged LA's growing smog problem based on their vision of the Los Angeles region as a place with a healing climate. José Luis Lezama's chapter shows how environmentalists', government regulators', and industrialists' conflicting views about Mexico City's air pollution mirror their conflicting visions of the future of that city.

The triumph of one or the other of these visions created victories for some but burdens for others. While workers were often aware of the price they paid in terms of their health and the health of their children, their economic dependence on polluting industries and activities meant that environmental cleanup exacted a high price. As Stephen Mosley shows, controlling coal smoke involved not just dealing with smokestacks but also with the cheerful open fireplace that sustained the otherwise dreary life of the industrial classes. Matthew Osborn shows that residents of the Lancashire countryside bore the brunt of the "invisible gases": the acidic emissions that increased with greater control of smoke and higher smokestacks. Jill Harrison shows that farmworkers bear the burdens of pesticide drift but also suffer economic losses if local residents ban chemical agriculture from their communities.

It is important to take these competing visions and unequal burdens into account. It helps us understand why environmental politics leads sometimes to odd, sometimes to effective, and sometimes to potentially disastrous choices about what a society chooses to put into and take out of its air. To understand these choices, it is necessary to look more closely at the social and political contexts in which they occur. The way in which a society pollutes—and cleans—its air tells us something about that society, its ideas about "fairness" and "health." In other words, the "smoke" a society produces is a "mirror" of the social relationships of that society.

To what extent do these "incommensurables" of culture and context determine what we do about air pollution? The scholars in this book, working in history, sociology, and political science, are asking that question, looking at the emergence of air pollution as a "problem" in a deeper way. Unlike cost-benefit analysts, who are interested in providing a quantitative basis for decisions, the main interest of the authors in this book is to describe how air pollution and air control policies have *actually happened* over time.

To some extent, these scholars' work has parallels to the "policy formation" studies in political science. However, most policy formation studies restrict themselves to the immediate interest groups or institutions concerned with the issue. Instead, the scholars in this book look at the entire social context in which these changes occurred, from media to markets, from poems to the dinner table. The story they tell brings in surprising aspects of these societies as data to ponder: the local garden club, John Wayne, cookstoves, deer hunting. Without seeing pollution as a mirror of society, these scholars argue, we miss what really happens in the formulation of pollution policies.

These works make the whole idea of global pollution control more complicated, but it is a necessary complication, one that cannot be avoided if we are going to deal with the problems that lie ahead. The *long duree*—long-term historical—perspective of this book enables us to recognize in sharper relief the shape of air pollution problems we face today. These complicated stories, covering many places and many decades, detail the confusions over what pollution was, where it came from, what it did, and how people tried to stop it. The story becomes even more complex when one realizes one is talking about not pollution but pollution*s*. Yet what seems like hopeless complication through careful attention to historical contingencies and local detail actually opens up political vision in ways that are not immediately evident in valuation studies. The complications also open up the array of "healths," "fairnesses," and "justices" involved in human and environmental deterioration, and the equally large array of "justices" involved in stopping that deterioration. Both the problem and the potential solutions affect people differently. An open-eyed view of how pollution—and its reform—has "mirrored" social inequalities means that we are more realistic when we forge ahead in the global fights over greenhouse gases and ozone depletion.

Because of the interest in local contexts, the chapters in this volume focus on particular urban and industrial regions. As a result, air stories also become the stories of cities or of industrial districts, such as California's Central Valley, one of the most industrialized agricultural regions in the world. These stories show us real people muddling through their increasingly sooty, smoggy, and pesticide drift–laden lives, trying to understand what is happening as their children cough, their walls darken, their public garden flowers die, their skies block out the light. In these stories, we see how understanding and commitment bloom or fade and how people privately adapt during decades of public inaction—darkening their clothes, simplifying their ornaments, or even celebrating smoke as healthful or as a source of beauty in art and literature. Smoke becomes part of them even as it wears away their lungs and their homes.

In the *long duree* view, darker dresses and simpler architecture are simply short-term solutions to problems that threaten eventually to spill back into the public arena. The *long duree* looks at the many times these short-term solutions have hidden the long-term problem, such as the centuries-long deforestation process in the Middle East and Europe, an environmental apocalypse that was avoided by the eventual discovery of coal as a source of energy to replace wood.[8] Yet Peter Brimblecombe, Harold Platt, Stephen Mosley, Matthew Osborn, Angela Gugliotta, and Peter Thorsheim address the fact that coal, in turn, created its own form of environmental deterioration. The ability to control the negative environmental effects of coal became a topic of wide conversation over the industrializing world. As later chapters by Roger Raufer and Alexander Farrell show, this conversation about coal "smoke" continues today in the countries that are currently choosing the industrial and "modern" path.

As nearly all the chapters in this book illustrate, the conversation to control pollution has itself been controlled to a great extent by those who benefited from the enormous productivity of highly polluting industries. So the story of economic growth and environmental deterioration has also been a struggle within the confines of the capitalist production system that industrialization—particularly coal-based industrial production—set loose. The chapters by Phil Brown and colleagues and Jill Harrison emphasize that the inequalities involved in this struggle go beyond class. Working from an environmental justice perspective, these authors show that people of color, often considered the pollution and detritus of society, are the ones who are most exposed to the detritus society creates. This racial hierarchy of pollution exposure appears to be "natural" or "invisible" to the public as a whole, and it is only through civil rights–style activism that the everyday exposures of these groups to toxics, particulates, and the rest emerges as "pollution."[9]

The Faustian bargain of fossil fuels still tempts and punishes us, and the contradictions surrounding the harnessing of this enormously productive source of power have only multiplied. Yet Mosley's chapter on the positive meanings of smoke for the working class in terms of work and the cheerful open fireplace and Sudhir Chella Rajan's chapter on the attractiveness of "automobility" show that the Faustian bargain is not that simple. In fact, the ruling pollution regimes tend to include valuable amenities for their masses—warmth and fast movement, in these cases. These amenities, once won, become tenures that are strongly defended by exactly the people exposed to the harm.

Brimblecombe, Platt, and Gugliotta show that the public conversation about pollution that began in the nineteenth-century English coal districts grew increasingly professionalized. Raufer and Farrell show that this professional conversation continues today, although this talk is now often situated in national agencies such as the U.S. Environmental Protection Agency and in international organizations such as the United Nations Environment Program.

These past and current conversations involve issues of knowledge as power, geopolitical and economic, as well as cultural imperialism and elite privilege. The questions "Who gets to breathe clean air?" and "Who benefits from the cheaper products produced with dirty air?" are still with us, although the answers are as gray as the air itself. For example, as the chapter by Raufer shows, cleaning China's air must include a focus on the family cookstove. Controlling cookstoves, however, has serious implications for poor Chinese families who cannot afford the cleaner fuels or more efficient equipment. Similarly, controlling smoke in Manchester, Pittsburgh, and elsewhere was intrinsically entangled with working-class struggles for employment and workplace control. The high stack billowing smoke meant that work was available, work that sometimes had positive attributes cleaner options did not share. The solutions—moving industries away from the cities, more automated technologies, electrifying train lines—meant cleaner air but less, or less satisfying, employment.

Today, the air pollution conversation is also part of what seems to be a new debate over the benefits or detriments of going the "neoliberal" way to global environmental governance. The chapters by Thorsheim, Farrell, Frank Uekoetter, and Brown and his colleagues show how conversations over the proper role of government are intrinsically intertwined with conversations about the authority of science, especially when choices need to be made in the face of uncertain knowledge about the effects of pollution and about the effectiveness of certain controls. These debates echo those of earlier periods described in a number of chapters in the book.

Today, those who are not ideologically wedded to the idea of less government and "free" markets as the universal solution are looking for ways to specify the proper role of government. As the social and environmental wreckage of free trade ideology accumulates, there is increasing attention to the idea that public action must play a role. Yet, as chapters by Raufer and Lezama show, government policies are not always relevant to the specific cases at hand. In the China case described by Raufer, international pressures to impose controls that diffuse the regulatory models of the West will simply exacerbate the problem. In the case of Mexico City described by Lezama, government actors define the problem in ways that negate their own responsibilities. As a result, solutions to long-term and wider problems such as urban smog and global warming may exacerbate short-term local inequalities.

The chapters are organized into two sections. The first section deals with the emergence of public perceptions of pollution as a problem and the earliest ways in which scientists, growing local governments, and the public began to deal with that problem. Gugliotta's, Mosley's, and Brimblecombe's chapters look at influences on, and of, air pollution in arenas not commonly considered, including song, art, poetry, and film. Their studies also look intensely at the individual scientists involved in making sense of the air in their cities, and particularly at how the technical and political contexts in which they worked affected how and what they could know. Yet, in contrast to triumphalist historical studies of science and its emphasis on individual "discovery" as the source of solutions to environmental problems, these studies do not celebrate individuals as harbingers of progress. Instead, their contributions, while indisputably real, are seen as products of the times in which they lived and worked.

Similarly, a number of chapters, including those by Platt, Gugliotta, and Dunsby, look at middle-class reform groups and their ways of discovering the effects of air pollution, such as the death of city garden flowers. Platt, for example, shows that the determination of air pollution as unhealthy required a reassessment of popular notions of physical health and relationships between body and environment. Dunsby shows that LA's growing smog forced middle-class resident "healthseekers" to abandon the idea of Southern California as healthful and edenic.

If, indeed, smoke is a "mirror," if societies do pollute their air in ways that reflect their culture and politics, what does that say about current attempts to improve air pollution policy? The studies in the second section deal with current air pollution problems, taking a broad analytical look at the emergence of new regulatory policies. Using the analytical tools of sociology, history, political science, and anthropology, the authors examine today's attempts to regulate regional air pollution through local policies, transnational agreements, and/or market-based incentives. The contemporary cases described by Harrison, Lezama, Rajan, and Brown and colleagues illustrate that the emergence of air pollution as a "problem" is still a work-in-progress. The political stories here parallel earlier stories in this volume, in which struggles over knowledge of pollution melded with struggles over who would bear the brunt of what is—or is not—done about it. Both DuPuis and Raufer look closely at the social and political context in which a new, market-based approach to air regulation has become salient and has moved toward implementation. DuPuis shows that the process of designing an air credits trading system in New York State prompted various interest groups to open up the "black box" of U.S. property institutions. Raufer and Farrell show that what is commonly understood as the fair international regulatory option—the "harmonization" of laws—can have unequal and possibly unfair impacts on nations in differing cultural and economic circumstances. Nevertheless, these studies show that the alternative to harmonization does not mean less stringent rules, just different ones.

The scholars in this volume consciously attempt to escape the conceptual limitations that the *nomos* imposes in its lack of attention to issues of historical context, cultural specificity, equity, politics, and culture. These alternative analytical approaches come from many disciplines, including environmental history, political science, sociology, political ecology, political economy, and business history. By taking an analytical tack that differs from cost-benefit analysis, these approaches ask different questions, such as *why* regulatory decisions get made, including the role of awareness, social perception of air pollution, and the rise of an interventionist public and environmental consciousness(es). They also get to ask *how* particular regulatory policies happen, as in the debates over cooperative versus coerced regulatory solutions, over the role of experts, and over the geographic scale of governance. Even the more traditional cost-benefit study question of *which* regulatory decisions *should* be made is asked in a different way, with more sensitivity to the social and cultural contexts of these decisions. Moreover, the studies look at the contending knowledges that are part of decisionmaking controversies, including the role of technical and science work and of expert versus lay knowledge. These studies also help us understand *how long* it took for public action to take place.

This deeper look into the mirror of pollution shows that understanding what is in our air—and how to get it out—requires understanding ourselves, our livelihoods, and our entanglement in the Faustian fossil-fuel bargain. How we renegotiate that bargain so that our souls and bodies are not at risk is a subject worthy of close study, the kind of work done in this volume.

NOTES

1. Alain Lipietz, *Green Hopes: The Future of Political Ecology,* Cambridge, MA: Polity Press, 1995.

2. Some examples of work done to date from this perspective are S. H. Dewey, *Don't Breathe the Air: Air Pollution and U.S. Environmental Politics, 1945–70,* College Station, TX: A&M University Press, 2000; D. Stradling, *Smokestacks and Progressives,* Baltimore: Johns Hopkins University Press, 1999; J. Tarr, *The Search for the Ultimate Sink: Urban Pollution in Historical Perspective,* Akron, OH: University of Akron Press, 1996.

3. I am not an innocent party in the move toward quantification in environmental policy analysis. As part of an interagency workgroup convened by the New York State Governor's Office of Regulatory Reform, I helped create a set of procedures for implementing cost-benefit analysis in regulatory policymaking in that state. I am not against cost-benefit per se. In fact, I think the procedure provides valuable information to assist in decisionmaking. As an environmental policy analyst, I was in fact surprised how often regulations were put into place without any analysis of the costs, especially the burdensome costs to small businesses. In this regard, I was also a co-author of a cost analysis of new dry-cleaning regulations in the state and their impact on small business owners. My concern about cost-benefit analysis is the associated, implied idea that numerical results, often reliant on complex but unexamined assumptions, enable policymakers to avoid difficult political choices.

4. See, for example, *Unfinished Business: A Comparative Assessment of Environmental Problems Overview Report,* U.S. EPA, Office of Policy, Planning, and Evaluation, Feb. 1987.

5. See, for example, J. Martinez-Alier, G. Munda, and J. O'Neill, Theories and methods in ecological economics: a tentative classification, in C. J. Cleveland, D. I. Stern, R. Costanza (eds.), *Economics of Nature and the Nature of Economics,* 34–56, Northampton, MA: Edward Elgar Publishing, 2001.

6. See, for example, J. Dryzek, *The Politics of the Earth: Environmental Discourses,* New York: Oxford University Press, 1997; E. M. DuPuis and P. Vandergeest, *Creating the Countryside: The Politics of Rural and Environmental Discourse,* Philadelphia: Temple University Press, 1995.

7. The journal *Ecological Economics* is an example of this new conversation. The journal includes authors from a number of disciplines.

8. P. Brimblecombe and C. Pfister (eds.), *The Silent Countdown: Essays in European Environmental History,* Heidelberg: Springer Verlag, 1990.

9. For an analysis of race and pollution, see philosopher Charles Mills's "Black Trash," in Laura Westra and Peter S. Wenz (eds.), *Facing Environmental Racism,* Lanham, MD: Rowman & Littlefield, 1995, 73–91.

The Emergence of
Air Pollution as a Problem

Perceptions and Effects
of Late Victorian Air Pollution

Peter Brimblecombe

A general problem of environmental history is to understand the relationship between the effects of environmental pollution and its social perception. Some have argued that environmentalism arises as a response to environmental stress (e.g., Pfister's 1950s syndrome), while others have felt that pollution is probably a necessary disposition but not a sufficient reason for changing perceptions of the environment. The subtitle to this book reminds us that we cannot ignore that the perception of pollution takes place within the broadest social context.

This chapter examines the air pollution in late Victorian cities and explores both its effects and its social and administrative perceptions. These perceptions affected the way in which the earliest coherent legislation began to develop and may ultimately have affected the strength of the response to air pollution in English cities. A historical look at the emergence of air pollution as a "problem" draws attention to the complexity of our environmental perceptions.

Air Pollution during Industrialization

Air pollution has been recognized from the earliest of times, with perceptible odor an issue in the cities of ancient Egypt and smoke of concern to Roman administrators and lawyers. However, this recognition tended to lead to *ad hoc* responses rather than a strategic and coherent approach to the regulation of early air pollution problems. Indeed, Mieck (1990) has argued that the numerous pollution decrees from the Middle Ages are essentially a response to single sources of what he terms *pollution artisanale,* as distinct from the later and broader *pollution industrielle* that characterized an industrializing world.

The need for strategic approaches to urban air pollution grew in late-eighteenth-century Britain in cities such as Manchester, where the steam engine had been adopted with great enthusiasm. The first steam-powered cotton mill in Manchester was constructed by Richard Arkwright in 1782 and occupied a building five stories high and two hundred feet long. By 1800 there were many more, along with furnaces and refineries, which created air pollution problems and aroused administrative concern.

From medieval times, smoke and other nuisance offenses in English cities were usually addressed through the Court Leet. By the 1790s the Manchester Court Leet ceased to exercise effective controls over the growing sanitary problems of the city. Even contemporary writers saw this as an outmoded form of government, and it was especially weakened by the growth of industry beyond the jurisdiction of parish boundaries. This limited options for enforcement and difficulties over defining what reasonably constituted a nuisance. The problem Mieck terms *pollution artisanale* had been replaced by *pollution industrielle.*

Manchester was an example of a city that benefited from improvement acts (e.g., 32 Geo III of 1792), which allowed it to set up a new body, the Police Commissioners. The commission rapidly grew in importance from late 1799, as it began to respond to urban sanitary issues. It soon added smoke from steam engines as an issue of concern. Using the powers of the 1792 act, a Nuisance Committee with standardized procedures began addressing the issue of smoky chimneys. Central legislation regarding nuisances from steam engines developed in an act of 1821 (1+2 Geo IV c.41), which led to the Manchester Police Commissioners immediately giving notice to all owners of steam engines that they meet the provisions of the new act. Despite their enthusiasm to abate smoke, the commission's resolve proved weak.

One important action of the Manchester Police Commissioners was the development of the office of Inspector of Nuisance. In 1799 the commission appointed a constable to inspect the streets and report on nuisances and offenses contrary to the act of Parliament. By the 1820s these duties fell to Nuisance Inspectors, who reported to the Nuisance Committee. This post became increasingly a part of improving the environment of English towns and cities of the nineteenth century.

Public Health Act of 1875

The notion of sanitary reform formed an important element in the changes of civic administration in the nineteenth century. This is often seen as deriving from the work of individuals such as Chadwick in England but was in fact much broader. Smoke abatement cannot be separated from sanitary reform in the nineteenth century, because so much of the legislation about smoke abatement occurs within UK sanitary legislation. In Britain, legislation on this matter abounds in Public Health Acts (e.g., 1848, 1875), Sanitary Acts (e.g., 1866) and other acts, such as the Towns Improvements Clauses Act (1847). A further connection between sanitary reform and smoke is seen in the development of Nuisance Inspectors, who investigated urban smoke, among other things. They were often seen as an aid to the Medical Officer of Health. Early Medical Officers came from the medical profession, but there was at first no formal training for Inspectors of Nuisance. However, by 1876 the Sanitary Institute set about certifying inspectors and developing professional competence. Such qualifications were not compulsory, but by the late 1880s many urban districts had highly qualified inspectors and professionalism rapidly became desirable in applicants for posts.

The work of the Sanitary Inspector was directed by the Medical Officer of Health, who often focused on disease and thus viable entities in the air. Medical officers often worried about smells, effluvia, and general aspects of domestic sanitation. In general, they were less concerned about the inorganic constituents of smoke; indeed, these, especially sulfur dioxide, were frequently perceived to be disinfectants.

There was a further problem for the inspectors. The activity and agitation over smoke in English cities in the earliest decades of the nineteenth century appear not to have lessened its spread. This is true even of a city such as Manchester, which had tried to reform the way in which it approached this nuisance. There were economic forces that constrained councils to bend to the will of industrialists, but administrative and technical difficulties were also important.

It was not until the Public Health Act of 1872/1875 that there was a more uniform approach to the smoke problem throughout England. The transitions of the 1870s were thus very important. Sanitary officials and, importantly, the Medical Officer of Health became compulsory positions. The appointment of these officials was not regarded as a trivial matter, and the city of York was chastised for attempting to appoint the Chief Constable (rumored to have vested interests in local industry) as the Inspector of Nuisance.

A growing group of talented and enthusiastic professionals began to emerge in towns and cities throughout the country. They addressed a wide range of public health issues, from adulteration of food, to the state of the sewers, to working conditions in factories, to air pollution matters. The profession began to include women, to some extent prompted by the need for access to domestic premises and factories dominated by women. The earliest appointment of women provoked considerable discourse between the civic administrators, the Local Government Board, and professional organizations. The involvement of women in the profession had the potential to bring new perceptions of smoke to bear. Most particularly, women were seen as guardians of morality in Victorian society, which often led to an equation between sooty deposits in the city and "moral dirt." Domestic activities such as cleaning and washing had to confront the realities of smoky air on a daily basis.

The activities of Sanitary Officers and Nuisance Inspectors failed to stop a profound deterioration in the environment of many cities through the late nineteenth century. However, it would be wrong see no value in their work. They can be seen pursuing the most difficult of cases against large and powerful industries. The daily logs of these inspectors and the reports in *Council Minutes* indicate in many cases considerable effort in difficult circumstances and a developing sense of professionalism.

Air Pollution in the Late Nineteenth Century

It is difficult to get an objective picture of air pollution in late-nineteenth-century cities. There are many vivid descriptions from writers, but the lack of measurements is an important issue. In particular, it creates a problem among both contemporary administrators and historians in assessing the impact of regulation. It was not that nineteenth-century inspectors didn't wish to analyze progress; rather, they had little understanding of how this would be done. Urban air pollution monitoring networks did not really begin until the development of deposit gauges, inspired by work of *The Lancet* in 1910. In the documents left by early inspectors, they seem keen to assess progress by counting the number of times smoke was observed each year (see Figure 1.1). Such observations tend to relate to activities initiated

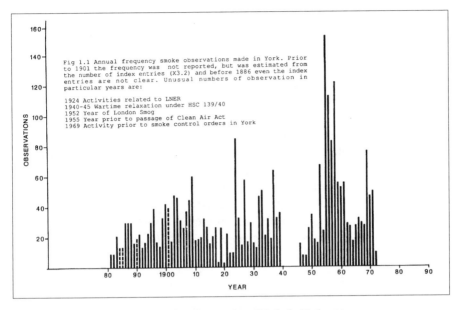

Fig 1.1 Annual frequency smoke observations made in York. Prior to 1901 the frequency was not reported, but was estimated from the number of index entries (X3.2) and before 1886 even the index entries are not clear. Unusual numbers of observation in particular years are:

1924 Activities related to LNER
1940-45 Wartime relaxation under HSC 139/40
1952 Year of London Smog
1955 Year prior to passage of Clean Air Act
1969 Activity prior to smoke control orders in York

FIGURE 1.1. Number of Smoke Observations Made in York, 1880–1972

by the administrators, but the administrators did not seem to confront the fact that this did not reflect the amount of pollution.

Thus sanitary inspectors did not take measurements of the concentration of air pollutants and relied on visual observations. They did not possess the skills to undertake analyses of the atmosphere, and textbooks of the time show that it was not part of their training. Nevertheless, the paucity of air pollution measurements is somewhat surprising given the importance governments gave to scientific approaches to some pollution issues, such as contamination of rainfall and river water and even compliance with the Alkali Acts of 1863. The Alkali Acts required manufacturers of sulfuric acid to limit their emissions, which were to be measured through chemical analysis. Britain was fortunate in its choice of the first Chief Alkali Inspector, Robert Angus Smith. He was responsible for many early chemical analyses of the air and rain, and his interests always went far beyond the requirements of the act. A few others, notably W. J. Russell, privately undertook analyses in London in the 1880s. The accuracy of measurements of urban air quality of the nineteenth century is difficult to assess, however, and measurements frequently appear to be unreasonably high.

It is also possible to estimate the concentration of air pollutants through modeling. This has been done using only the simplest of models, but it suggests that air pollution concentrations were high at the end of the nineteenth century. This is supported by a strong similarity between fog frequency observed in London and modeled pollution load. This is expected, as the pollutants from coal burning can enhance formation of fogs.

There is evidence that fog frequency declined in London from the early part of the twentieth century, and crude models would agree that the total load of pollutant smoke and sulfur dioxide may also have been on decline. As difficult as the early London monitoring data is to interpret, it doesn't discount the idea that air pollution load may have been highest about 1900 (see Figure 1.2). It is more difficult to establish such patterns for other cities, where there are less data. In all probability the maximum in air pollution occurred later.

Fin de Siècle Cities

In spite of a developing body of legislation, there was considerable gloom about improvements in the sanitary state of cities by the end of the nineteenth century. Estimates of the pollution from modeling work suggest that it could well have been at its worst in Victorian London. Sanitary inspection had developed as a profession, yet there was a lack of a central power to help force improvements. A fragmented local structure characterized an administration very different from the national sway exerted by the Alkali Inspectorate. This meant the centrally administered Alkali Act may have had more force than the localized approach to regulating general urban air pollution matters.

Despite a sense of ineffectiveness to the control of urban smoke, the individual Sanitary Inspectors' hard work sometimes led to a perception that they must be having an effect. There was no doubt a certain amount of posturing in local claims that things were getting better or worse. In some areas of Manchester it was said there had been so much local improvement that it was smoke drifting in from industries of neighboring authorities that was becoming a problem. In another case it was claimed that while a "steady improvement in the diminution of factory smoke is undoubtedly being obtained . . . there is considerable room for improvement. . . . What is greatly wanted in this matter is a higher public con-

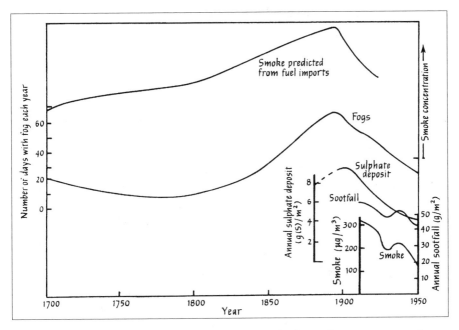

FIGURE 1.2. Predicted Smoke Concentration and Observed Fog Frequency for London, 1700-1950, Compared with Shorter-Term Measurements of Sulphate and Soot Deposit and Smoke Concentration

science; it is difficult otherwise to obtain improvement, as repeated prosecutions are burdensome and sufficiently heavy penalties appear to be impracticable." Recognizable achievements in the short term tended to be small or rather specific, so a gloomy prognosis was understandable.

Improvements appear not to have come swiftly through the adoption of a given piece of legislation. They seem more an outcome of continual pressure on industry, which gradually caused it to: (1) modernize boilers (especially the adoption of mechanical stoking), (2) make more careful choice of fuel, (3) improve training of stokers, and (4) relocate industries. Wohl has argued that Victorian legislation laid the groundwork for twentieth-century activity but managed only to turn the urban skies of Britain from a gritty black to a dull gray. Mosley argues that this gradualist view of the development of air quality regulation fails to recognize that government could have done more to press for rapid improvements. This is a reasonable view, although the lack of atmospheric measurements makes it unclear if changes in air quality were already underway at the start of the twentieth century.

Effects

In many larger cities of Britain, smoke may have been close to its worst at the end of the nineteenth century. We have few doubts that this had severe effects on the health of the population, but it is not easy to decide how air pollution affected mortality and morbidity. During severe incidents of London fog, increasing death rates give a clue to the effects of London's air pollution on mortality increase above the expected norm. This was widely recognized in Victorian times and received comment well beyond medical circles; the public knew that death rates increased during fogs. Concern went beyond human health effects, and many lamented the suffering of livestock in Smithfield Market during periods of high pollution. Parallel to these effects, the vegetation of large cities was damaged by pollution. Although this had been recognized in the seventeenth century, there were scholarly investigations deriving from the Victorian interests. Smoke disfigured buildings, but its effects were more than superficial. The acidic gases released during coal combustion were seen as a major cause of the rapid weathering of limestone buildings.

Social and Artistic Implications

Smoke pollution had a much wider impact on life in Victorian cities than can be encompassed by its direct physical and medical effects. Although social effects of air pollution are to be expected, they seem to have drawn little comment in the academic literature, and the source materials are often anecdotal.

The Victorian use of language reveals many references to air pollution and even indicates affection for the smoke at times. London was popularly called "the big smoke," and getting confused was termed *being fogged*. Indoor gathering around the coal fire became an important aspect of English life. The soot and fogs of cities had made walking less pleasurable (as seen in the writings of Swift or Gay) from the late eighteenth century onward. By Victorian times this had led to a vision of gardens as the lungs of a city and, more broadly, to the notion of "garden cities" (Ebenezer

TABLE 1.1
Important Fogs in Victorian London

Year	Month	Duration/days	Excess deaths
1873	December	3	270–700
1880	January	4	700–1100
1882	February		
1891	December		
1892	December	3	~1000

Howard, *Garden Cities* 1898), as well as to calls for a return to nature, often epitomized by the aspirations of William Morris and his followers.

The choice of clothes or even furnishings became affected by pollution. Umbrellas were black to ward off inky, soot-laden rain; hangings vanished from English houses; wallpapers and furnishings were dark in color; and women preferred not to wear white dresses. The cleaning of clothes became an increasingly burdensome task for women.

The Victorian period showed a growing belief in the potential for an urban apocalypse. Macaulay's essay on the history of the popes of Rome[1] uses as a metaphor the vision of a future when "some traveller from New Zealand, in the midst of vast solitude, takes his stand on a broken arch of London bridge to sketch the ruins of St Paul's." This inspired the engraver Gustav Doré to capture an eerie image of London's twilight. In such visions, London's end was often related to poison gases, an element in a succession of stories such as Richard Jeffries's "After London" (1885), Robert Barr's "The Doom of London" (1892), M. P. Sheil's *The Purple Cloud* (1901), and Arthur Conan Doyle's *The Poison Belt* (1913).

In the visual arts we also see changes. Claude Monet, André Derain, and Yoshio Markino came to London to capture its fogs. Choosing its light to engage in particular styles, Monet made London warm-colored and abstract, Derain gave the city a Fauvist look, and Markino employed the notion of atmospheric perspective always so important in Eastern painting. Such ideas had a long-lasting impact on some schools of twentieth-century painting. Photographers also captured the fog, and the blue sensitivity of early photographic emulsions gave London's atmosphere an excessive opacity.

The Victorians believed that coal smoke was imparting a "new color" to towns, but aesthetic opinions about this were divided. Some felt Time and Nature effected a "softening" appearance on urban buildings and accepted the smoke, while others claimed that all that was required to bring color back to London was to wash buildings regularly with water. Yet others argued that architects should aim at designs that would become "beautifully colored by Nature charged with smoke."

Architects recognized problems in cities, so that by late Victorian times the air pollution issue encompassed many aspects of the design of urban buildings. The architects recognized a wide range of environmental factors—over-crowding, decreased access to light, air pollution, stone discoloration, indoor pollution, and inappropriate building styles for harsh urban environments—as a significant aspect of their designs. At the end of the nineteenth century, the range of responses included:

> abandonment of the gothic and promotion of less detailed classical styles not so susceptible to air pollutants;
> careful choice of pollution-resistant stone and glazed materials;
> extensive provision of clear window glass to let in more light;
> adoption of electric light and air filtration to lower pollution indoors;
> development of dust-excluding interior fittings to protect books and other items.

Conclusions

The air pollution of Victorian cities such as London may have been the worst it ever became in terms of total pollution loading. The problems of air pollution had been recognized before, and the industrialization of cities and an interest in sanitary reform triggered frequent legislation. Economic, administrative, and technical issues prevented this legislation from having an immediately perceptible impact, but a lack of monitoring data restricts our understanding of the amount of pollutants in the air of Victorian cities. On the positive side, local inspectors played increasing roles in local government, and into the twentieth century industry slowly moved to adopt more modern furnaces. The total pollutant load in London and other cities declined throughout the twentieth century, albeit to be replaced by pollutants from automobiles. The pollution concentrations in the late Victorian city damaged human health, livestock, vegetation, and the fabric of buildings. However, in more subtle ways it affected social behavior and the creations of artists and designers.

So, what of the relation between environment and environmental reaction, or between air pollution and its perception? In late Victorian London, pollution-generated fogs were at their most frequent, which certainly affected social perceptions. This is reflected in language, literature, and art. However, the intensity of the experience did not necessarily translate into a rapid advancement or application of smoke-abatement legislation. Perhaps it was a matter of priorities. The energy of policy makers went into limiting the spread of disease and improving sanitation and housing. They recognized the air pollution problem, and although there were advocates for smoke abatement, other issues seem to have dominated the attention of Sanitary Inspectors and Medical Officers of Health.

Nevertheless, the perceptions of air pollution created in this period are especially strong. Images of *fin de siècle* London fogs, found in stories about Sherlock Holmes and Mr. Hyde, persist in a city that has a now come to possess a very different summer photochemical pollution.

NOTES

1. T. B. Macaulay, "The Ecclesiastical and Political History of the Popes of Rome during the Sixteenth and Seventeenth Centuries," *Edinburgh Review*, Oct. 1840.

REFERENCES

Bowler, C. & Brimblecombe, P. 1990. The difficulties of abating smoke in late Victorian York. *Atmospheric Environment*, 24B:49–45.

———. 2000a. Control of air pollution in Manchester prior to the Public Health Act, 1875. *Environment and History*, 6:71–98.

———. 2000b. Environmental pressures on the design of Manchester's John Rylands Library. *Journal of Design History*, 131:175–191.

Brimblecombe, P. 1987. *The Big Smoke*. London: Methuen.

———. 1990. Air pollution in York 1850–1900. In *The Silent Countdown*, ed. P. Brimblecombe & C. Pfister. Heidelberg: Springer-Verlag, 1990, pp. 182–195.

———. 1992. A brief history of grime: accumulation and removal of soot deposits on buildings since the seventeenth century. In *Stone Cleaning*, ed. R. G. M. Webster. London: Donhead Publishing, 1992, pp. 53–62.

———. 1998. History of Urban Air Pollution. In *Urban Air Pollution—European Aspects*, ed. J. Fenger, O. Hertel, & F. Palmgren. Dordrecht, Netherlands: Kluwer, 1998, pp. 7–20.

———. 2003. Emergence of the sanitary inspector in Victorian Britain. *Journal of the Royal Society for the Promotion of Health*: 182–195.

Crowther, C. & Ruston, A. G. 1911. The nature, distribution and effects upon vegetation of atmospheric impurities in and near an industrial town. *Journal of Agricultural Science*, 4:25–55.

Diederiks, H. & Jeurgens, C. 1990. Environmental policy in nineteenth century Leiden. In *The Silent Countdown*, ed. P. Brimblecombe & C. Pfister. Berlin: Springer-Verlag, 1990, pp. 167–181.

Kupper, P. 2001. Environmental pollution and social perception: how do they relate? From the "1950s syndrome" to the "1970s diagnose." In *European Society for Environmental History First International Conference*. St. Andrews, Scotland, UK, 5–9 September: Abstracts: http://www.eseh.org/programme.htm.

Marsh, J. 1982. *Back to the Land*. London: Quartet Books.

Mieck, I. 1990. Reflections on a typology of historical pollution: complementary conceptions. In *The Silent Countdown*, ed. P. Brimblecombe & C. Pfister. Berlin: Springer-Verlag, 1990, pp. 73–80.

Mosley, S. 2001. *The Chimney of the World*. Cambridge: White Horse Press.

Redford, A. & Russell, T. S. 1939. *The History of Local Government in Manchester*. Volume 1: *Manor and Township*. London: Longmans Green and Co.

Ricardo, H. 1896. *Art and Life and the Building and Decoration of Cities*. London: Rivington, Percival and Co.

Smith, E. M. 1909. *Annual Report of the Medical Officer of Health for the Year 1908*. City of York.

Voelcker, A. 1864. On the injurious effects of smoke on certain building stones and vegetation. *Journal of the Society of Arts*, 12:146–151.

Wohl, A. S. 1983. *Endangered Lives*. London: Dent and Sons.

2

"The Invisible Evil"

Noxious Vapor and Public Health in Manchester during the Age of Industry

Harold L. Platt

In a pioneering essay on European efforts to identify and reduce the environmental impacts of acid rain, E. Schramm draws a sharp distinction between town and country. Dating the inauguration of the city's campaign against air pollution in the early 1880s, he argues that "its political imagination, however, only extended to technological solutions, especially smoke prevention measures, such as better fuel economy, use of improved smokestacks and ovens, electrification, etc. In contrast to that of the urban movement, the foresters and biologists saw the limits of a technical solution to the smoke problem." Only these scientists understood the paradox that reform measures to reduce the visible black soot belching out of coal-burning home and factory chimneys would increase public toleration of the invisible noxious gases spreading into the atmosphere. Although Schramm admits that policy makers largely ignored or suppressed the impressive findings of the plant researchers, he still champions their broad ecological perspective against the myopic vision of the smoke-abatement crusaders.[1]

This environmental retrospective, however, ignores the contemporary perceptions of smoke reformers in relation to the appalling human and social costs resulting from urban air pollution. Missing is an accounting of Victorians' concerns about not only horrendous mortality rates from respiratory diseases among the inner-city poor but also stilted lives, self-destructive behavior, class conflict, and even race degeneracy. Urban reformers—at least those in England—were not so much unaware of the limits of their campaigns for clean air as willing to trade them off for improvements in the public health and welfare. To these Victorian environmentalists, the wide diffusion of harmful emissions into the countryside seemed preferable to their current heavy concentrations in the most densely populated areas of the city, especially during recurring episodes of deadly fog. Faced with the emergence of an energy-intensive consumer society, they could logically hope only to mitigate the effects of a bad situation and keep it from getting far worse. Even if the Smokeless City remained a futuristic ideal, the influence of urban reformers in shaping the formation of public policy on air quality standards deserves careful reconsideration.[2]

A close examination of air pollution reform in Manchester reveals a civic arena within which elite groups realistically confronted the modern dilemma between the rising consumption of energy and the declining quality of daily life. During the mid-1830s, it became the first Shock City of the age of industry and remained a classic Dickensian Coketown a century later. As local historian Shenna Simon lamented in 1938, "We cannot say that [first Medical Officer of Health] Dr. John Leigh's 'dark canopy which hangs as a pall over the city' is a thing of the past, or something dimly remembered by the very old. Sometimes it has been the overhead darkness, which requires complete lighting-up for houses, business premises, and vehicles at midday, when the city has literally been under a roof of soot, but without mist, visibility at street level being the same as at night. Other times the city has been wrapped in choking sulphurous (SO_3) fog, composed of mist, a natural phenomenon met with in the open country and at sea, but here laden with soot."[3]

Despite the ultimate defeat of Manchester's battle to replace bad air with good, its leaders never retreated from the front lines of the nation's assault on this seemingly intractable problem. Some of the industrial center's most eminent scientists, doctors, and engineers enlisted their professional expertise to secure victory over the original causes of environmental pollution. In addition, its amateur botanists and town gardeners volunteered in the early 1890s to launch a bold mission in unknown territory to advance understanding of the linkage between acid rain and public health. Contrary to Schramm's depiction of urban reformers, Mancunians helped identify many of the most chronic, unintended consequences of the industrialization of the natural world, including the impacts on its single most important organic resource, human beings.[4]

Gas, Grates, and Grime

Contemporaries of the age of industry might doubt Schramm's priorities of trees over people, but they would probably agree with him about the timing of a new phase in the battle for clean air. In England, the Smoke Abatement Exposition of 1881–1882 marked a propitious moment in urban environmental reform. Mounted by housing and open spaces activist Octavia Hill and Dr. Ernest Hart of the National Health Society, it drew over 115,000 visitors in London and another 31,000 in Manchester. Reformers had three important reasons for believing that they were turning a historic corner in making substantial gains in improving the quality of urban life. Technological innovations offered one promising avenue for significantly replacing innumerable smoke-producing devices with a few relatively clean, large-scale gas and electric central stations. Second, the emerging field of bacteriology was opening a new era of medicine and public health by helping doctors draw causal connections between respiratory disease and air quality. A crescendo of distressing great fogs in London over the previous decade signaled that a third sea change had been reached in the social perception of the smoke evil and the political will to do something about it. Taken together, the technological, scientific, and civic directions of change raised expectations among city dwellers that the tide of environmental reform was now moving in the right direction.[5]

If exceptional killer fogs galvanized public opinion in favor of remedial action in London, the ordinary daily weather was sufficient in Manchester to mobilize civic attention on behalf of smoke abatement. The environmental setting of "Cottonopolis" created just the right conditions to maximize the deleterious impacts of air pollution caused by burning fossil fuels. The city was situated at the bottom of a crescent-shaped amphitheater of coal-laden hills facing southwest toward the Atlantic Ocean. At the center of perhaps the world's first great conurbation of factory towns, Manchester and its sister city, Salford, were subject to the full effects of this industrial ecology. Dr. Leigh vividly described the nearly constant smog that resulted. "On the finest day," he wrote during the year after the exhibit, "the vista is obscured by a column of haze, the accumulated density of which terminates the view by an apparent wall of fog. The smoky envelope of the town is very well seen from a distance of four or five miles in the country, particularly on the approach of evening, when the slanting rays of the sun give a remarkable definition to the black, cloudy covering, and indicate very distinctly the site and general boundaries of Manchester." The burdens of a valley location were greatly exacerbated by climatic conditions that made it one of the wettest places in the kingdom. With rain on average every other day, Manchester had roughly twice as much precipitation as London. The rain coming down combined with the discharges going up to produce what Mancunians aptly called "the blacks."[6]

Local perceptions of the downside of technology paralleled the earliest adaptation of the steam engine to the factory. With the installation of the first Boulton and Watts engine in Peter Drinkwater's cotton mill in 1789, Mancunians began tinkering to attain more complete combustion and hence reductions in the amount of unburned carbon escaping up the stack as soot. But like so many would-be improvements that followed, the price paid in lost power and/or fuel costs soon led to their rejection. By the turn of the century, local authorities were complaining "that the increase of . . . steam engines, as well as the smoak issuing from chimnies used over Stoves, Foundraries, Dressers, Dyehouses, and Bakehouses, are become a great Nuisance to the town unless so constructed as to burn the Smoke arising from them which might be done at moderate expense." Needless to say, very little was done to impede the growth of industry during the next four decades of extraordinary expansion and prosperity. By then, Manchester/Salford mills had over two hundred engines generating 10,000 hp and consuming a million tons of coal a year.[7]

The record success of its merchants and manufacturers that made the "textile district" the horror and wonder of the world also made it the center of urban reform. Manchester's town council and its scientific community became leaders in the battle against the bad air. Smoke-abatement reform groups and city ordinances date to the early 1840s, when the central city had 250,000 inhabitants crammed in the shadows of its mills and warehouses. But against the fractures within the medical community over the role played by coal smoke in causing diseases of the lungs, the sanitary crusade led by Edwin Chadwick captured the attention of policy makers and medicine men alike into a narrow public discourse on the hardware of water management. Instead of mainstream protest against coal smoke, the battle against urban air pollution established a beachhead of scientific research on a fringe of public health concerns, the chemical industry. And even here, the link to lung disease was rather indirect, a deductive inference from the inescapable conclusion that the noxious fumes from alkali and other acid-spewing factories were toxic to plant life in the immediate vicinity.[8]

In the 1850s–60s, Manchester became the center of this area of study for two reasons. The country's largest concentration of alkali manufacturing was located nearby in Merseyside towns such as Widnes and St. Helens. Robert Angus Smith, the preeminent student of what he would soon be calling the science of "chemical climatology," also happened to live in the city. In 1852, Angus Smith had inaugurated this study with a report on atmospheric levels of acidity and organic contamination at different distances from the center. He had collected rain from the upwind edge of the suburbs at Greenheys fields on the southwest side and comparable samples about a mile and a half away from a location close to the Royal Exchange building. Finding three times more pollution in the inner city than the outskirts, Angus Smith concluded that "the rain was found to contain sulphuric acid (H_2SO_4) in proportion as it approached the town and with the increase of acid the increase also of organic matter."[9]

Five years later, in 1857, fellow member of the Manchester Literary and Philosophical Society Peter Spence took up the investigation and pushed it forward toward a logical conclusion. He asserted that the invisible gases of fossil fuels were harmful to living organisms such as plants and animals. Few were better qualified to make the pronouncement: the chemical manufacturer had invented a process to recycle the waste by-products of coal mining and gas making to produce alum, a mordant treatment used in dyeing and printing textiles. He had also been convicted under the air pollution regulations, forcing him to move his factory farther out of town. The chemical manufacturer conducted a careful analysis of the composition of the smoke of the two million tons of coal annually consumed within a two-mile radius of the city center. There was a "mass of atmospheric poisons," he declared, ". . . slowly rising from our firegrates, and wending their way quite deliberately up the chimney, preparatory to pouring themselves down the throat of the first pedestrian they meet in the street." He was upset by the complete absence of attention in the smoke-abatement movement to the hidden dangers lurking in the black fumes.[10]

A keen appreciation of the paradox of reform amplified his distress. *"But the invisible evil is completely ignored,"* Spence exclaimed. "'Burn your smoke!' is the united cry of the Sanitary Association, the public and the law. . . . [F]or in this case not only does the cure of the visible not effect the cure of the invisible evil, but every effort to effect the cure of the one only increases the noxiousness of the other. Perfect freedom from smoke would, if accomplished, only increase the evil arising from the purely gaseous result of combustion."[11]

Although further discussion of the subject in the "Lit and Phil" was suspended during an interval of relatively clean air caused by the "cotton famine" of the American Civil War, a renewal of the investigation paralleled the return of the factories to full blast. Spence, for instance, delivered a paper to this intellectual oasis of the social elite that reinforced previous reports. He combined Angus Smith's geographic approach with his own work on acid rain by exposing litmus paper for twelve-hour periods at various locations. Like Angus Smith, he found tremendous differences between his home in Smedley, two miles downwind of the inner city, and Gilda Brook on the opposite side of town. After his earlier study, he had also planted twenty camellias in his backyard to test the effects of high levels of sulphurous compounds in the air on living things. "I have full proof at Smedley," he stated in dire Darwinian terms, that "vegetable life on the whole of that side of town is a mere struggle for existence." Eight years later, only four "miserable specimens" survived, which he had transplanted on the south side. Over the past season, they recovered and bloomed with beautiful flowers. The chairman of the session was Robert Angus Smith, who now appears to have been convinced that both the visible smoke and the acidic gases were harmful to organic life.[12]

In 1868, Dr. Leigh drew out the implications of these studies on human health. The doctor made air pollution a keynote in his inaugural report as Manchester's first Medical Officer of Health (MOH). His appointment finally brought the city into conformity with national policy, twenty years after Parliament empowered local governments to establish this important position. The town council promoted him from a job as chemical analyst for the municipal gas works because he was willing to defend its decision to deny the working classes access to indoor plumbing. For the next two decades, the MOH would faithfully uphold the position that outdoor privies were not only better for the environment but also all that the mass of inner-city residents deserved. At the same time, this restrictive quid pro quo on water management appears to have freed him to become outspoken on the issue of air pollution. "The normal condition of the working man of middle age in Manchester is bronchitic," he found, and "all observation tends to establish the fact that an impure atmosphere increases enormously the tendency to consumption. Ozone is never found in the air in Manchester, whilst the solid particles constantly floating in the atmosphere from our factory chimneys and other sources, keep up a constant irritation in the air tubes, producing ultimately chronic bronchitis and emphysema of the lungs."[13]

By the late 1860s, Manchester's professional and amateur circle of science had been able to show a relationship between factory emissions and living organisms. Angus Smith, Spence, Leigh, and others had also made a compelling case that the unseen gases released in the industrial city posed a health hazard at least equal to the black smoke from the incomplete combustion of coal. By now, moreover, the microscope was beginning to reveal a previously imperceptible world of "germs" that added yet another layer of scientific controversy over the cause of human disease. Even under the most favorable light of public opinion, microbes played a still mysterious role in bringing about sickness and death. Louis Pasteur in France and J. B. Dancer in Manchester helped initiate a gradual change in the emphasis of medicine from chemistry to biology. The discovery of invisible toxic gases and dangerous microorganisms in the air ironically had the further effect of shifting sensory priorities from a centuries-old reliance on the nose to the eye. Closely related was the power shift in authority from the bodily senses of the common man in the street to the official reports of the trained scientists in the municipal laboratory. During the transitional decade of the 1870s leading up to Koch's major advance, however, urban reformers had to continue to use traditional indicators, arguments, and tactics in their long-running battle to replace bad air with good.[14]

Vapors, Violators, and Vice

Manchester's men of science, technology, and medicine laid the groundwork for its reformers to launch a new campaign against air pollution. Spearheaded by the Manchester and Salford Sanitary Association (MSSA), urban environmentalists turned from investigation to instigation of public prosecutions of the smoke-abatement laws. In 1873, the MSSA set up the Subcommittee on Noxious Vapours from Chemical and Other Works, composed of two doctors and a scientist. Two years later, they admitted difficulty in establishing "reliable statistics as the effect of such vapours on human life."[15]

Still, they had no doubt about the need for stronger enforcement of the "smoke clauses" against blatant violators. To convince policy makers of the "continued prevalence of ordinary smoke nuisances," they hired a "practical man" to observe violations of the current legal standards, which prohibited the emission of "dense black smoke" for more than three minutes in a half-hour period. While he recorded sixty-nine offenses in a week, the two official inspectors reported only four. To bolster their case that the inspectors were not doing an adequate job, the subcommittee hired a second observer who found thirty-five infringements of the law in a week. His list of worst offenders included, for example, J. Smethurts's factory in the heart of the central business district, where "dense smoke [poured out] for eleven minutes. . . . Standing in the street you were smothered in dirt from it."[16]

In addition to petitioning Town Hall for more forceful remedial action, the MSSA lobbied the medical societies to fill in the gaps on the human toll paid for public acquiescence in an urban condition of suffocating smoke and toxic gases. They responded with a report that showed a death rate from respiratory diseases in the inner city (Manchester township) three times greater than in rural areas and twice the national average. The costs of bad air in terms of lives lost and bodies diminished by chronic illness were indeed high. It was this disturbing realization that drove the under-funded, small group of moral crusaders to undertake the Herculean task of moving the Smoke Abatement Exhibition from London to Lancashire.[17]

In affording the reform movement an opportunity to pause for reflection, the exposition of 1882 also generated enthusiasm to launch new initiatives based on a reordering of tactical priorities and long-term goals. A Manchester industrialist, Herbert Philips, took the lead in turning the MSSA committee into a full-fledged organization, the Manchester and Salford Noxious Vapours Abatement Association (MSNVAA). It became the main vehicle of reform to infuse into civic discourse a powerful array of fresh ideas about energy technologies, public health, town planning, and environmental justice. The group also strove to build class-bridging alliances by highlighting novel conceptual links between body, city, and nature. For the most part, however, working-class political mobilization after 1880 remained effectively channeled into an interrelated campaign for better housing, slum clearance, and indoor plumbing.[18]

Bad air took on new political meaning as a potent source of class conflict by driving all who could afford it to move beyond municipal borders to less polluted havens at the city's edges. "The estrangement thus created between the cultured classes and those compelled to live in depressing surroundings," MSNVAA secretary Fred Scott feared, "has been frequently pointed out as productive of many evils." Chief among them, he believed, was male intemperance caused by the futile efforts of the suffering housewife to transform dingy, sad surroundings into bright, welcoming refuges for family life. Moreover, "the blacks" raining down on the neighborhoods kept the women from opening the windows, contributing further to a lack of wholesome ventilation inside the home. "All who can afford to escape from the polluted atmosphere of the town for their leisure hours naturally do so," Scott affirmed.[19]

While commonsense notions linking interior air circulation to good health were standard tropes of miasmatic medicine, they were given added authority by the new discoveries of bacteriology. As historian Peter Thorsheim points out, germ theories tended to reinforce, not undercut, traditional concepts of disease causation. Scientific research demonstrating that sunlight killed infection-spreading microbes strengthened the position of smoke-abatement advocates, who stood in favor of strict enforcement of air pollution standards. Dark canopies of choking smog, punctuated by eerie, blinding fogs, created troublesome images of civilization sinking underground into the depths of moral depravity and race degeneracy. Londoners voiced concerns about the effect of stunted bodies and minds on the fate of the global empire. In contrast, Mancunians worried about their impacts on the future of the urban economy, which appeared in the late 1870s to go into permanent decline. Rallying labor-class support behind a grandiose solution—a ship canal to by-pass Liverpool—the business elite began to pay greater attention to grass-roots demands of inner-city residents for social and environmental justice.[20]

By the end of the eighties, the MSNVAA had gained enough experience to lay out a significantly different agenda of urban environmental reform. Announced in a series of published lectures, the agenda was marked by a much tighter focus on the impacts of air pollution on human well-being. Linking noxious vapors and public health, in turn, encouraged reformers to take a more militant, confrontational posture toward the town council. Dr. Henry Simpson of the Manchester Royal Infirmary, for instance, took a strong stand that good air actually represented the number-one priority of public health reform. And he exploited recent concerns about city fogs to assert that the harmful effects of "the blacks" and the acid rain on humans were no longer a subject of scientific doubt. He further bolstered his case by repeating the findings of Angus Smith that coal soot was not pure carbon but a spongy material impregnated with sulphurous acid.[21]

Marshaling the authority of official experts, the reformers' platform also called upon the City Analyst, Charles Estcourt, to identify the sources of Manchester's bad air. After pointing a finger at the emissions belching out of the factories, he reported that chemical tests of their fuels estab-lished an average content of 1.5 percent of sulfur. "It is disagreeable to breathe," he declared, "and in fog is often productive of pain and a feeling of tightness in the chest, very oppressive indeed. . . . It is patent to all ob-servers that although mechanical stokers and proper stoking and firing may keep back the black particles from the smoke as emitted from the chimneys, still that invisible demon, sulphurous acid gas, which becomes sulphuric, is emitted exactly as before."[22]

One additional position paper warrants careful consideration because of its contribution to a better understanding of the dilemma of reform. As Estcourt realized, gains in smoke abatement would tend to encourage greater energy consumption, with the unintended consequence of produc-ing more and more noxious, albeit invisible, gases. In this case, the MSNVAA drew upon the scientific expertise of plant biologist Robert Holland. He spoke with special authority on acid rain from his experience as the forester of a large estate outside Swansea, a center of cooper smelt-ing and its sulfurous emissions. Holland fought a losing battle; he help-lessly watched the destruction of a ten-thousand-tree woodland. Warning that all vegetation in England was suffering the toxic effects of this insidi-ous process, Holland outlined a bleak prognosis for nature by drawing at-tention to his work for the town council's Park Committee. Manchester's "fine open spaces," he complained, had been ". . . rendered hideous by the blackness of everything within them—trees stunted, dying—flowers struggling to bloom, and sometimes their special scent[?] scarcely recog-nisable. It is no exaggeration; and as long as the surrounding chimneys send out volumes of sulphurous acid and of carbon, there can be no im-provement."[23]

The new platform provided the MSNVAA with a foundation of scien-tific and medical authority on which to mount a different kind of political movement. Between 1890 and 1892, the outlines of its agenda of urban en-vironmental reform emerged. Although the nuisance-abatement cam-paign had become a frustrating uphill struggle in the courts, it would be a mistake to write off this tactical approach as a complete failure. On the contrary, it was keenly felt by Manchester's manufacturers, prompting the formation of self-defense organizations such as the Society of the Chemi-cal Industry. In response, the now-seasoned reformers not only turned up the heat on the innumerable producers of smoke but also turned to solu-tions that could be achieved by more centralized, regional-scale institu-tions of government. They also argued that the standards of air quality should be raised. The problematic prohibition of "dense black smoke" should be replaced with a more encompassing intolerance of "moderate" emissions.[24]

The centerpiece of their new agenda, however, represented a more radical departure from previous political objectives. Initiating a cross-class movement, the MSNVAA demanded that the town council cut the gas rates. The municipally owned utility had long been a source of lucrative profits, which acted as a subsidy from its customers to the property owners in the form of lower tax bills. While the shopkeepers had protested the inequity of this financial burden in the past, now the reformers appealed to a much broader, more inclusive concept of social and environmental justice. They envisioned a universal distribution of gas to every type of energy consumer, from efficient central stations at prices competitive with coal. In the nineties, parallel efforts by the larger MSSA included a brief flirtation with getting directly involved in organizing the poor into neighborhood political clubs under such rubrics as the Healthy Homes Society and the Workingman's Sanitary Association. Quickly dropping this risky venture in partisan politics, the genteel reformers probably felt safer in backing demonstration-scale suburban housing projects for working-class families and insisting that the health inspectors fully enforce the law.[25]

During the 1880s, rapid advances in the manufacture of relatively cheap "water gas" and the invention of the incandescent illuminating mantle had completely transformed the final product from a light-bearing to a heat-generating fuel. Furthermore, the introduction of penny slot-meters supplied a flexible, pay-as-you-go mechanism to bring gas lighting and cooking within reach of the mass of city residents. The reformers discussed several other means of distributing energy such as electricity, compressed air, and pressurized water from central stations. But these remained on the horizon in 1890, compared to a proven technology that was already in place throughout the metropolitan area.[26]

To strengthen the case for a major change in the municipal corporation's energy and environmental policies as public health reform, the MSNVAA promoted additional research on the harm acid rain caused plant life. Such a strategy served the dual purpose of drawing stronger links between invisible gases and the well-being of human bodies and of forcing elected officials to take remedial action to restore nature in the public parks. Joining hands with the Manchester Field Naturalist Society (MFNS), the reformers petitioned the Local Government Board to expand its jurisdiction under the Alkali Act of 1881 to inspect all factories releasing effluents bad for the public health and welfare. The memorial declared that "it is scarcely possible for them [the urban naturalists] to work to any purpose so long as the present excessive pollution of the air, especially acid vapours, is permitted."[27]

Fumes, Flowers, and Flasks

In 1891–92, the Town Gardening Section of the MFNS undertook a series of air quality experiments that represented the climax of Manchester's reform effort to prove the interdependency of the health of the body, the city, and the environment. Conducted by professional and amateur scientists, the research broke new ground in both methodology and findings. The goal was to demonstrate that the adoption of energy policies that promoted the best use of technology could reduce the suffering of the town's human population as well as the waste and degradation of the nation's natural resources. The logical implications of the study pointed toward a greater reliance on central-station service and gave priority to people over trees. But these conscious choices do not mean that the members of the gardening society were unaware of the larger ecological ramifications of their proposals. A central focus of their experiments was the toxic gases of coal combustion, "the invisible evil" that was the known enemy of urban horticulture. This indicates that garden society reformers were willing to make the practical trade-offs necessary in bucolic scenery to improve the quality of daily existence in city neighborhoods.[28]

The transformation of the garden society into the shock troops of the battle for urban environmental reform began with an absolute rout in their first skirmish with bad air. Perhaps with naive expectations, these would-be botanists volunteered in 1891 to undertake the civic mission of giving the city a face-lift. The obvious choice for a makeover was the pride and joy of Manchester liberalism, the Town Hall and its adjoining Albert Square. The amateur horticulturists were perfect candidates for archetypes of the well-heeled, club men and women with an interest of some kind or other in the "city beautiful" movement. The MFNS normally sponsored events such as a slide lecture on the life cycle of the coral polyp or an exhibit of Chinese snuff bottles. By the time of their Autumn Soirée, however, their experience in bedecking the spacious civic plaza with flowers had, according to chairman Charles Bailey, "given us a valuable object-lesson on the atmospheric conditions of Manchester. . . . Those plants were seen to suffer, and had to be carted away as failures. He hoped [no one] would forget that lesson."[29]

Abused but not disheartened, the society turned to a professional chemist, Dr. G. H. Bailey of Owens College (now the University of Manchester), for expert advice in devising a counterattack against the poisoning of the air. Lecturing his rapt audience in the language of popular science, the professor used the extreme and hence convincing case of winter fogs to deliver his message on the public health crisis of atmospheric pollution. He proposed that a series of sub-district experimental stations be set up throughout the metropolitan area to test for microorganisms, acid rain, and natural sunlight. Manchester's Medical Officer of Health, Dr. John F. W. Tatham, stood up to voice his approval for this strategy because "of the many factors which went to make the frightful death rate of the city, the fog plus smoke must be regarded as the (single) most important element." He pledged the support of his office to help correlate the disease and mortality statistics of the sub-districts with the three air quality indicators.[30]

Despite the elite makeup of the garden club, its report underscored the environmental injustice of Manchester's sharp class divisions, which resulted in rigid patterns of spatial segregation. The most politically potent expression of municipal reform was a comparison of mortality rates in the suburbs and in Ancoats, the oldest and worst slum just north of the central business district. The MFNS study made the jam-packed district ground zero of the council's failed policies on energy and pollution control. The correlation of public health and air quality statistics hammered home the point with compelling authority (see Tables 2.1 and 2.2).

Mancunians forced by poverty to live in Ancoats were dying from pulmonary diseases at a rate "at least fourfold what it should be under anything like favourable conditions, and which in times of continued fog . . . rise to double even this excessive rate." The bottom line, they reported, "has been to show that pollution of the atmosphere by organic matter and by gaseous emanations must be regarded as one of the most fertile sources

TABLE 2.1
Comparison of Mortality Rates in Ancoats and Suburban Districts, 1891–1892

LOCALITY	Zymotic Diseases	Pulmonary Diseases	All Other Diseases	Total
Suburbs 1891	241	534	954	1,729
Ancoats 1891	510	1,549	1,698	3,752
Suburbs 1892	175	429	904	1,508
Ancoats 1892	455	1,166	1,630	3,251

TABLE 2.2

Comparison of Sunlight Levels in Ancoats and Didsbury, 1891–1892

LOCALITY	1891				1892							
	Sept.	Oct.	Nov.	Dec.	Jan.	Feb.	Mar.	April	May	June	July	Aug.
Didsbury Weekdays	39.6	24.7	10.4	9.5	7.2	15.4	25.9	38.7	51.0	55.3	44.2	36.8
Ancoats Weekdays	25.4	12.8	4.7	3.2	2.3	12.1	13.6	24.3	32.7	25.5	26.3	21.3
Didsbury Sundays	32.0	30.0	11.0	11.0	15.6	11.1	22.6	55.0	52.6	60.5	32.6	39.0
Ancoats Sundays	19.8	17.6	6.0	3.4	4.7	10.0	20.8	38.5	34.8	36.0	20.6	23.2

Source: Town Gardening Committee, "The Atmosphere of Manchester and Salford—Second Report of the Air Analysis Committee," in Reports and Proceedings of the Manchester Field Naturalists and Archaeologists' Society (1893), 81, 91.

of disease and of the lowering of tone which are invariably associated with overcrowded districts."[31]

The science of the garden club seemed to strengthen the resolve of the leaders of the smoke-abatement movement to press their agenda of reform with more forceful action. Over the remainder of the nineties, small but significant advances were made in reaching these goals. In 1895, for example, the council finally made a concession to insistent demands for lower gas rates by shaving 3d. off the base price of 2s. 6d. per thousand cubic feet (mcf) and dropping rental charges for simple cooking burners. The MFNS research also persuaded urban reformers to move forward in adopting regional perspectives on the enforcement of smoke-abatement regulations. The metropolitan scope of the study helped in 1894 to kickstart stalled proposals to consolidate the scattered local groups into a single organization, the Lancashire Smoke Abatement League (LSAL). The culmination of this lobby campaign came in 1899, when the LSAL gained a meeting with the president of the Local Government Board. He was swayed to take its brief to the Home Secretary, who rejected it outright. Without the evolution of air pollution control to a regional scale analogous to that being established over river conservancy, the limits of urban environmental reform had been reached. As Dr. William Graham, the MOH of Middleton, observed, "It is surprising how action has lagged behind knowledge in dealing with smoke prevention, and especially in the face of the great sanitary sin and the injustice inflicted on the industrial population forced to live amongst it."[32]

Conclusions: Energy, Effluvia, and Environment

In November 1911, Manchester held another smoke-abatement exposition. Coming thirty years after the first, it gave environmental reformers an opportunity to take stock of their movement to replace bad air with good. The promise of science, technology, and medicine had made impressive advances toward the goal of raising standards of living and reducing rates of mortality. Without question, bacteriology had achieved the biggest gains by appearing to bring some of the most deadly epidemic diseases under control. Central-station gas and electric service, too, had accomplished much in supplying energy more efficiently than previous methods. And fear of fog had retained its potency in mobilizing political support for more effective pollution controls.[33]

But, paradoxically, reformers had very little to show for all of their hard work in terms of realizing an ideal of the Smokeless City. At best, they could claim that the dark canopies still enveloping urban England would be much worse without their dedication to the cause of pure, natural air for both town and country. As Sarah Wilmont demonstrates, the chemical industry in Manchester bore the full brunt of the reformers' assault on bad air (and poisoned water). "Although contemporary commentators castigated public opinion for its weak opposition to air pollution," she states, "my investigations suggest both that this opposition was well organized after 1870, and that the manufacturing sector did feel under pressure as a result. This pressure was felt not withstanding the lack of a truly 'popular' anti-pollution movement, and the extreme variation in the enforcement of pollution controls locally."[34]

But the reformers faced an impossible task because whatever incremental improvements they scored in air quality were more than overwhelmed by exponential gains in the consumption of fossil fuels in the city. The promise of bacteriology in the hands of the medical profession had undoubtedly become seen as the single most important weapon in the battle to improve the quality of urban life. To be sure, the doctors were scoring their greatest victories in the conquest of water-borne diseases rather than respiratory diseases, which seemed affected by air quality. The overall death rate in the inner city had dropped from thirty to twenty-five per thousand inhabitants since the first smoke abatement convention. "Manchester, however," according to a later MOH, Dr. James Niven, "is still conspicuous for its high mortality, and it is especially conspicuous for its excessive death rate from phthisis [tuberculosis], from pneumonia, from bronchitis, and from heart disease." In this regard, little had changed in cleaning up the air to dispute Dr. Tatham's estimation that the black soot and noxious vapors cut ten years off the lives of the working classes living in the city center.[35]

As with medical science, the hope environmental reformers had placed in technology for a breakthrough in smoke-eating devices had been only partially fulfilled. Gas and electric utility managers were making solid headway by installing equipment that reduced the emission of particulates, building chimneys higher to diffuse the invisible gases, and locating their central stations farther away from populated areas. In Manchester, for example, fifty-four thousand homes had gas cookers, which cut the amount of coal burned in its residential neighborhoods by sixty thousand tons a year. Similarly, the municipal electric works had 10,500 customers who used the equivalent of over four hundred thousand gaslights. Its generators provided another 50,000 horsepower that replaced steam engines. Five years earlier, in 1906, the first all-electric textile mill had been built in the metropolitan area. Though still powered by an on-site, self-contained steam plant, the factory represented a prototype that could easily become smokeless by plugging it into the grid of remote networks of power.[36]

Nevertheless, this type of step-by-step advance was offset by urban society's even faster acceleration in the rate of energy consumption. As the chairman of the Smoke Abatement League of Great Britain, John W. Graham, rather awkwardly explained, "We are, even as it is, less the victims of Smoke and Fog than were a generation ago[. If it were not for] the phenomenal increase of manufacturers and of population during this wonderful but ugly era of development, we should see more clearly the effect which gas and electricity, mechanical stokers, hot blasts, combustion chambers, artificial draught, and slow combustion grates have caused." An emerging culture of consumption for the masses would keep these idealized visions of a bright future in the realm of dreams, not reality.[37]

The most problematic aspect of expectations from the first expo turned out to be public opinion. One does not have to accept Stephen Mosley's thesis that working people were convinced by their bosses to equate pollution in positive terms with jobs and prosperity in order to agree with his conclusion that "protests and campaigns against the 'smoke nuisance' failed to attract widespread public support." At least in Manchester, working-class activism after 1880 stayed pragmatically focused on more physical, bricks-and-mortar types of municipal reform. As we have seen, the city's genteel reformers tried to use the gas rate issue to bridge the socio-political gap between the classes. But given the crying needs of the slum, each water closet hooked up, social housing unit constructed, and substandard dwelling demolished represented a tangible reward for the neighborhood. In contrast, each victory in the battle against air pollution was difficult to discern, let alone measure in some concrete way.[38]

A more plausible explanation of why the movement for clean air only partially reached its goals rests on the paradox of reform that literally made achievements impossible to see. On the one hand, the reformers faced the "problem of the commons." For the fisherman, this timeless dilemma gave him a counterproductive disincentive to conserve the remaining stock. If he didn't catch what was left, then someone else would, until there were none left. The polluter had to deal with an analogous quandary of paying extra to eliminate his relatively small contribution of bad air to the "ultimate sink" of the larger atmosphere while everyone else continued to add theirs without penalty or cost. In other words, there was no practical way to make smoke producers pay their fair share of the social costs of the degradation of the environment and the consequent deterioration of the public health and welfare.[39]

On the other hand, reformers confronted the equally baffling challenge that every gain in abating the visible particulates of smoke undercut their related efforts to reduce its unseen, albeit poisonous, gases. Here the problem can be restated as the old adage "out of sight, out of mind." For example, one of the primary responses of the manufacturers was to build higher smokestacks. Such technological strategies placated local critics while depriving reformers of specific targets to attack for the environmental harm caused by acid rain to entire regional ecologies. As David Nye has brilliantly shown, the electric dynamo became a key icon of the "technological sublime" in the Machine Age, a dazzling symbol of power and modernity. The 1911 convention's scale model of the Smokeless City of tomorrow was emblematic of this cultural definition of the engines of progress. Yet a fascination with energy technologies further obscured the long-term repercussions of burning fossil fuels on the health of the human body and the natural world.[40]

The utopian fantasy of the Smokeless City offered comforting reassurances that engineers could design such an ultimate, energy-intensive community without cost to the public health or the environment. A quarter century later, little had changed to shake blind faith in this worship of high technology. At the World's Fair of 1939 in New York City, the largest diorama ever built, by Henry Dryfuss for Consolidated Edison, and the most popular display, Futurama, created by Norman Bell Geddes for General Motors, envisioned a pollution-free metropolis of giant generator stations, superhighway networks, and gasoline-powered automobiles. Instead, an increasing reliance on the technological fix would only engender the rise of a mass society of conspicuous consumption.[41]

In this cultural context, the organizers of the smoke-abatement exposition of 1911 deserve praise for making ethical choices to save the townspeople at a cost of knowingly sacrificing the country's trees. Given a restricted range of politically viable alternatives, they were justified in the belief that they were making a difference in reducing the suffering of Mancunians from bad air. In the fashionable language of social environmentalism, their final report concluded that "[f]ew will deny that a large proportion of the evils of slums, the dreariness of towns, and high death rates are evils fostered by the thick black pall of Smoke which hangs over practically all our Cities, shutting out the sunshine and corrupting a health-giving breeze into a wave of swirling black soot, fog, and grime into the innermost recesses of the Home and the Office. Good health and a higher moral tone will follow as an inevitable result when the value of a Smokeless City has been properly realized."[42] We are still trying to get there.

NOTES

1. E. Schramm, "Experts in the Smelter Smoke Debate," in P. Brimblecombe and C. Pfister (eds.), *The Silent Countdown—Essays in European Environmental History* (Berlin and London: Springer-Verlag, 1990), 207, for the quotation; ibid., 196–209. Also F. J. Bruggmeier, "Waldsterben: The Construction and Deconstruction of an Environmental Problem," in C. Bernhardt and G. Massard-Guilbaud (eds.), *The Modern Demon: Pollution in Urban and Industrial European Societies* (Clermont-Ferrand, France: Presses Universitaires Blaise Pascal, 2002), for further insight on German forestry as well as a cautionary tale of the historical interpretation of science.

2. Bill Luckin, "The Social and Cultural Repercussions of Environmental Crisis: The Great London Smoke Fogs of the Late Nineteenth and Early Twentieth Centuries," in *The Modern Demon,* and Anthony S. Wohl, *Endangered Lives: Public Health in Victorian Britain* (London: Dent & Sons, 1983).

3. Shenna Simon, *A Century of City Government, Manchester, 1838–1933* (London: Allen and Unwin, 1938), 207–8, for the quotation. Also see Harold L. Platt, *Shock Cities: The Environmental Transformation and Reform of Manchester, UK and Chicago, USA* (Chicago: University of Chicago Press, forthcoming 2004).

4. In the 1990s, a national report on air quality still showed Manchester dead last in the nation. See Stephen Mosley, "The 'Smoke Nuisance' and Environmental Reformers in Late Victorian Manchester," *Manchester Regional History Review* 10 (1996): 40–47. Manchester has a long tradition of both professional and amateur science. For an introduction, see R. H. Kargon, *Science in Victorian Manchester* (Manchester: University of Manchester Press, 1977); and Anne Secord, "Science in the Pub: Artisan Botanists in Early Nineteenth-Century Lancashire," *History of Science* 32 (September 1994): 269–315.

5. Smoke Abatement Committee, *Report of the Smoke Abatement Committee 1882* (London: Smith Elder, 1883). For technological innovation, see ibid.; Harold L. Platt, *The Electric City: Energy and the Growth of the Chicago Area, 1880–1930* (Chicago: University of Chicago Press, 1991). For medicine, see Bruno Latour, *The Pasteurization of France* (Cambridge: Harvard University Press, 1988); and Nancy Tomes, *The Gospel of Germs—Men, Women, and the Microbe in American Life*

(Cambridge: Harvard University Press, 1998). For the London fogs, see Luckin, "Environmental Crisis."

6. John Leigh, *Coal-Smoke: Its Nature, and Suggestions for Its Abatement* (London: John Heywood, 1883), 4–5. On politics of water management and sanitation policy, see Harold L. Platt, "'The Hardest Worked River': The Manchester Floods and the Industrialization of Nature," in Genevieve Massard-Guilbaud, Harold L. Platt, and Dieter Schott (eds.), *Cities and Catastrophe: Coping with Emergency in European History* (Frankfurt, Germany: Peter Lang, 2002), 163–84.

7. Manchester, *Police Commissioners' Report* (1800), as quoted in Daphine de-Jersey Gemmill, "Manchester in the Victorian Age: Factors Influencing the Design and Implementation of Smoke Abatement Policy" (Ph.D. diss., Yale University, 1972), 3, for the quotation. For energy history, see R. L. Hills, *Power in the Industrial Revolution* (New York: Kelly, 1970); and Mike Williams and D. A. Farnie, *Cotton Mills in Greater Manchester* (Preston: Carnegie, 1992).

8. See William Graham, *Smoke Abatement in Lancashire—A Paper Read before the Public Medicine Section of the British Medical Association (London, 2 August 1895)* (Manchester: Cornish, 1896), for the most complete account of early reform efforts in Manchester. Also see Gemmill, "Manchester in the Victorian Age"; Ann Beck, "Some Aspects of the History of Anti-Pollution Legislation in England, 1819–1954," *Journal of the History of Medicine* 14 (October 1959): 475–89; Catherine Bowler and Peter Brimblecombe, "Control of Air Pollution in Manchester Prior to the Public Health Act of 1875," *Environment and History* 6 (2000): 71–98; and Sarah Wilmont, "Pollution and Public Concern: The Response of the Chemical Industry in Britain to Emerging Environmental Issues, 1860–1901," in Ernst Homberg, Anthony S. Travis, and Harm G. Schroter (eds.), *The Chemical Industry in Europe, 1850–1914: Industrial Growth, Pollution, and Professionalization* (Chemists and Chemistry Series, no. 17; Drodrect, Netherlands: Kluwer Academic Publishers, 1998), 121–48.

9. Robert Angus Smith, "On the Air and Rain of Manchester," *Literary and Philosophical Society of Manchester, Memoirs,* 2nd ser., 10 (1852): 207–17. For context, see Roy M. Macleod, "The Alkali Acts Administration, 1863–84: The Emergence of the Civil Scientist," *Victorian Studies* 9 (December 1965): 81–112; and John M. Eyler, "The Conversion of Angus Smith: The Changing Role of Chemistry and Biology in Sanitary Science, 1850–1880," *Bulletin of the History of Medicine* 54 (Summer 1980): 216–34. The industry trade name for hydrochloric acid was muriatic acid. The process of making alkali also generated significant amounts of sulfur.

10. Peter Spence, *Coal, Smoke, and Sewage—Scientifically and Practically Considered; with Suggestions for the Sanitary Improvement of Towns, and the Beneficial Application of the Sewage, a Paper Read before the Literary and Philosophical Society of Manchester* (Manchester: Cave and Sever, 1857) 21, for the quotation. Also see

"Peter Spence," in C. S. Nicholls (ed.), *The Dictionary of National Biography.* *"Missing Persons,"* (Oxford: Oxford University Press, 1993), 627.

11. Spence, *Coal, Smoke,* 4, for the quotations, with emphasis added. Spence proposed a solution unique in the annals of urban sanitary reform. He called for the adoption of the infrastructure of sewer pipes to carry the city's exhaust fumes to a gigantic chimney at least six hundred feet high. The draft created would cause a vacuum, which he believed would suck both these emissions and sewer gases away from harm to people in buildings and on the streets.

12. Peter Spence, "On Sulphurous Acid in the Air of Manchester," *Literary and Philosophical Society of Manchester, Proceedings* 8 (1869): 137–39; Robert Angus Smith, as reported in ibid., 139. Also see J. B. Dancer, "Microscopical Examination of the Solid Particles from the Air of Manchester," ibid., 7 (1868): 157–61.

13. John Leigh, *Report of the Medical Officer of Health for Manchester* (1868), 1, for the quotation. Also see ibid., (1872), 35–36; A. Wilson, "Technology and Municipal Decision-Making: Sanitary Systems in Manchester 1868–1910" (Ph.D. diss., University of Manchester, 1990); and John V. Pickstone, *Medicine and Industrial Society—A History of Hospital Development in Manchester and Its Region, 1752–1946* (Manchester: University of Manchester, 1985).

14. Latour, *Pasteurization of France,* 1–150; Wilmont, "Pollution and Public Concern," 121–48; John V. Pickstone, "Ways of Knowing: Toward a Historical Sociology of Science, Technology and Medicine," *British Journal for the History of Science* 26 (December 1993): 433–58; and Michael Worboys, *Spreading Germs—Disease Theories and Medical Practice in Britain, 1865–1900* (Cambridge: Cambridge University Press, 2000).

15. Manchester and Salford Sanitary Association, *Annual Report* (1875), 7. Hereafter cited as MSSA, *Annual Report.*

16. Ibid., Appendix A, 19, 20, for the quotations; ibid., (1873–75), passim. They referred to the Public Health Act of 1866 as the legislative foundation for prosecutions. Also see Gemmill, "Manchester in the Victorian Age," 64–78; and Mosley, "'Smoke Nuisance.'" The pressure was clearly felt by the chemical industry in Manchester. See Wilmont, "Pollution and Public Concern," 121–48.

17. MSSA, *Annual Report* (1873–76). Also see Graham Mooney and Simon Szreter, "Urbanization, Mortality, and the Standard of Living Debate: New Estimates of the Expectation of Life at Birth in Nineteenth-Century British Cities," *Economic History Review,* no. 1 (1998): 84–112.

18. See MSAA, *Annual Report* (1882–1892), passim, for the history of the organization's activities.

19. Fred Scott, "The Need for Better Organization of Benevolent Effort in Manchester and Salford," *Manchester Statistical Society, Transactions* (1884–85), 143, as quoted in Mosley, "'Smoke Nuisance,'" 41; also see Mosley for background on the leaders of the MSNVAA.

20. Peter Thorsheim, "Miasma, Smoke, and Germs: Air Pollution and Health in Nineteenth-Century Britain" (paper presented to a meeting of the American Society for Environmental History, Baltimore, March 1997); Luckin, "Environmental Crisis"; Rosalind H. Williams, *Notes on the Underground: An Essay on Technology, Society, and Imagination* (Cambridge: M.I.T. Press, 1990); G. S. Jones, *Outcast London: A Study of the Relationship between Classes in Victorian London* (Oxford: Clarendon Press, 1971); I. Harford, *Manchester and Its Ship Canal Movement: Class, Work, and Politics in Late Victorian England* (Halifax: Ryburn, 1994); and P. F. Clarke, *Lancashire and the New Liberalism* (Cambridge: Cambridge University Press, 1971). Also see M. Harrison, "Social Reform in Late Victorian and Edwardian Manchester, with Special Reference to T. C. Horsfall" (Ph.D. diss., University of Manchester, 1988). Harrison shows a close interconnection between the membership of the various urban reform movements and associations. Horsfall, for example, was not only a decrier of race degeneracy but also a leader in housing reform, a supporter of the smoke-abatement crusade, and a member of the Field Naturalist Society and several other, similar causes.

21. Henry Simpson, "The Pollution of Air, as Affecting Health," in Manchester and Salford Noxious Vapours Abatement Association (MSNVAA), *Lectures on Air Pollution* (Manchester: Manchester and Salford Noxious Vapours Abatement Association, 1888), no. 8, 97–107. Dr. Simpson was a physician who practiced in the Manchester Royal Infirmary and the Manchester Hospital for Consumption and Diseases of the Throat.

22. Charles Estcourt, "Why the Air of Manchester Is So Impure," in MSNVAA, *Lectures on Air Pollution,* no. 4, 44, for the quotation; ibid., 39–51.

23. Robert Holland, "Air Pollution as Affecting Plant Life," in MSNVAA, *Lectures on Air Pollution,* no. 9, 122, 121, for the quotations; ibid., 110–25. Holland concluded in terms similar to Estcourt on the dilemma of reform: "The burning of carbon, so as to render the smoke invisible," he stated, "does not in the slightest degree lessen the quantity of the invisible sulphurous acid" (125). Cf. Schramm, "Experts in the Smelter Smoke Debate."

24. MSNVAA, *Annual Report* (1890), as reported in MSSA, *Annual Report* (1890): 70–79. Also see Wilmont, "Pollution and Public Concern," 141–48, for industry responses with a focus on Manchester.

25. MSNVAA, *Annual Report* (1888–1895).

26. Ibid. (1892): 60–62; and Harry Grimshaw, "Note on the Presence of Sulphur in Illuminating Gas," *Literary and Philosophical Society of Manchester, Proceedings* 20 (1880): 51–54. Also Estcourt, "Why the Air of Manchester Is So Impure," for a discussion of alternative, central station technologies.

27. MSNVAA, *Annual Report* (1890), as reported in MSSA, *Annual Report* (1890): 79, for the quotation; ibid. (1892): 66–70. On the parks, also see Theresa Wyborn, "Parks for the People: The Development of Public Parks in Victorian Manchester," *Manchester Regional History Review* 9 (1995): 3–14. On working-class

adoption of gas lighting, see Bill Luckin, *Questions of Power: Electricity and Environment in Inter-War Britain* (Manchester and New York: Manchester University Press, 1990).

28. The work of the MFNS is contained in three reports: Town Gardening Committee, "The Atmosphere of Manchester—Preliminary Report of the Air Analysis Committee," *Reports and Proceedings of the Manchester Field Naturalists and Archaeologists' Society* (1891): 1–10; Town Gardening Committee, "The Work of the Air Analysis Committee," ibid., 66–72; and Town Gardening Committee, "The Atmosphere of Manchester and Salford—Second Report of the Air Analysis Committee," ibid. (1893): 73–98. Also see G. H. Bailey, "Some Aspects of Town Air as Contrasted with That of the Country," *Literary and Philosophical Society of Manchester, Memoirs,* 4th ser., 8 (1893): 11–17. For an ideal example of the history of science "from the bottom up," see Secord, "Science in the Pub."

29. Town Gardening Committee, "The Autumn Soirée: Air Pollution and Fog in Manchester," in *Reports and Proceedings of the Manchester Field Naturalists and Archaeologists' Society* (1891), 41, for the quotation; and "The Owens College Museum: Corals and Their Allies," in ibid., 40–41, for a previous, more typical meeting.

30. Town Gardening Committee, "Autumn Soirée," 42, for the quotation; ibid., 41–43; and "Second Report," in *Reports and Proceedings* (1893), 73–98, for the full details of the study

31. "Second Report," 81, for the quotation. For reform in Ancoats, see J. H. Crosfield, *The 'Bitter Cry' of Ancoats and of Impoverished Manchester: Being a Series of Letters on Municipal Topics* (Manchester: Ireland, 1887); and Charles Rowley, *Fifty Years Work without Wages* (2d ed.; London: Hodder and Stoughton, n.d. [1911]).

32. Graham, *Smoke Abatement in Lancashire,* 11, for the quotation; MSSA, *Annual Report* (1893–1901), passim; and Wilson, "Technology and Municipal Decision-Making" on the Local Government Board's exertion of authority over Manchester's sewage disposal policy.

33. Manchester and District Smoke Abatement Society, *The Manchester and Salford Smoke Abatement Exhibition, 10–25 Nov. 1911, City Exhibition Hall* (Manchester: n.p. [Manchester], n.d. [1912]). Also see Latour, *Pasteurization of France;* and Mooney and Szreter, "Urbanization, Mortality, and the Standard of Living Debate." Thanks to Angela Gugliotta for reminding me that the exact reasons for the mortality decline at the end of the nineteenth century remain undefined.

34. Wilmont, "Pollution and Public Concern," 146.

35. James Niven, "The Relation of Smoke and Health," in Manchester and District Smoke Abatement Society, A*batement Exhibition,* 116, for the quotation; ibid., 115–24, for his full paper, including mortality statistics; and "Introduction," in Manchester and District Smoke Abatement Society, *Abatement Exhibition,* 9, for reference to the statement of Niven's predecessor.

36. Manchester and District Smoke Abatement Society, *Abatement Exhibition,* 25–30 for utility statistics; and Williams and Farnie, *Cotton Mills,* 134, for the electrification of the Acme Mill in Pendleton. Also see Roy Frost, *Electricity in Manchester* (Manchester: Richardson, 1993); and Thomas P. Hughes, *Networks of Power: Electrification in Western Society, 1880–1930* (Baltimore: Johns Hopkins University Press, 1983).

37. Manchester and District Smoke Abatement Society, *Abatement Exhibition,* 19, for the quotation.

38. Mosley, "'Smoke Nuisance,'" 46, for the quotation; Stephen Mosley, "Public Perceptions of Smoke Pollution in Victorian Manchester," in David E. Nye (ed.), *Technologies of Landscape—From Reaping to Recycling* (Amherst: University of Massachusetts Press, 1999), 161–86.

39. For the term, see Joel Tarr, *The Search for the Ultimate Sink—Urban Pollution in Historical Perspective* (Akron: University of Akron Press, 1996). For additional insight, also see Arthur F. McEvoy, *The Fisherman's Problem—Ecology and Law in the California Fisheries, 1850–1980* (Cambridge: Cambridge University Press, 1986); and Theodore Steinberg, *Nature Incorporated: Industrialization and the Waters of New England* (New York: Cambridge University Press, 2003), 199.

40. David E. Nye, *American Technological Sublime* (Cambridge: M.I.T. Press, 1994).

41. Helen A. Harrison (ed.), *Dawn of a New Day—The New York World's Fair, 1939/40* (New York: New York University Press for the Queens Museum, 1980).

42. Manchester and District Smoke Abatement Society, *Abatement Exhibition,* 113, for the quotation.

3

Public Perceptions of Smoke Pollution in Victorian Manchester

Stephen Mosley

Unlike many of today's environmental dilemmas, such as climate change and the thinning of the ozone layer, the smoke of Victorian Manchester did not elude the sensory perceptions of contemporaries. Coal smoke characterized the nineteenth-century urban atmosphere and affected the lives of all city dwellers, rich and poor alike. People lived and worked beneath lowering coal-black skies and imbibed the sulphurous, smoke-filled air with every breath they took. At the inaugural meeting of the Manchester Association for the Prevention of Smoke (MAPS) on 26 May 1842, the Reverend John Molesworth, the association's chairman, vehemently denounced a nuisance that "polluted our garments and persons" and that all the town's inhabitants "saw, tasted, and felt."[1] Despite the tangible nature of this form of air pollution, however, most contemporaries endured living in the midst of the city's "eternal smoke-cloud" without much outward sign of complaint. No popular mass movement against smoke developed in the city during the nineteenth century, even though its damaging effects were widely recognized.

How can we account for this seeming indifference toward smoke pollution? In this chapter, I examine the dominant images and narratives that gave meaning to and created common understandings of a concrete environmental pollution issue in Victorian Manchester, the "smoke nuisance." Urban environmental degradation was rationalized and naturalized by the stories contemporaries told about air pollution, and, as William Cronon has recently argued, "to recover the narratives people tell themselves about the meanings of their lives is to learn a great deal about their past actions and about the way they *understand* those actions. Stripped of the story, we lose track of understanding itself."[2]

Environmental discourse about smoke in Manchester, England, was a bewildering stream of contested and contradictory claims and concerns. By analyzing how a variety of actors framed the phenomenon and investigating the context in which stories about the city's smoke unfolded, we can enrich our insights into how people defined, thought, and made choices about the local environmental conditions in which they lived. Thus far, Victorian urban dwellers have been portrayed mainly as being uninterested in environmental issues. However, as I shall show, the citizens of nineteenth-century Manchester were much more than apathetic spectators where smoke pollution was concerned. To bring the main story lines about smoke pollution into sharper relief, I shall draw on a diverse range of texts, from newspaper stories, novels, and working-class autobiographies to postcards, poems, and popular songs. After briefly sketching the background to the problem, I focus on a "wealth" story line, assembling the components of a narrative that consistently emphasized the "inevitable" correlation between smoke, well-being, and economic prosperity. I then knit together the threads of a narrative that accentuated "waste" and constantly emphasized the unnecessary peril to the health of the urban workforce, the damage to the natural and built environment, and the uneconomic and willful misuse of Britain's finite natural resources. Finally, I suggest reasons why the concept of smoke control did not readily capture the public's imagination.

In the nineteenth century, Manchester was one of the world's most important cities as a result of the success of its cotton trade and associated industries. The first real industrial city, Manchester attracted visitors from all parts of the globe to wonder at the new "cityscape" of massive textile factories and warehouses and its forest of smoking chimneys. In the early 1780s the predominantly verdant and countrified town of Manchester had boasted just one solitary tall industrial chimney; by the early 1840s, the "shock city" of the Industrial Revolution had sprouted some five hundred factory chimneys, growing to around twelve hundred chimneys by 1898.[3] Coal consumption in the city had also increased substantially, from around 737,000 tons per year in 1834 to more than three million tons a year by 1876.[4] With people attracted by its mushrooming industries, the population of Manchester grew apace, increasing from around 40,000 to more than 76,000 inhabitants between 1780 and the first census of 1801. Sustained, dynamic urban growth saw Manchester's population more than treble to reach 242,000 in 1841, and only thirty years later the city had a population of some 351,000.[5] The sight of black sulphurous smoke billowing out from the new factories and domestic hearths prompted Leon Faucher to compare Manchester to an active volcano in the 1840s, and Major General Sir Charles Napier, appointed commander of the troops of the Northern District in 1839, called Manchester "the chimney of the world . . . the entrance to hell realised."[6] From the turn of the nineteenth century the city's ever-deepening smoke cloud was a constant element of the urban environment. By the 1880s, after a century of rapid urban and industrial growth, Manchester, once "the symbol of a new age," had come to epitomize the smoke-begrimed, polluted industrial city. However, at the same time a positive utilitarian image of Manchester's blackened physical environment had evolved, drawing on cultural values and beliefs that reflected its citizens' definition of themselves as an urban industrial workforce. For the steam-powered mills had brought material wealth as well as environmental problems for many of the city's inhabitants.

The first of the story lines that dominated the public's understanding of the production of smoke in Victorian Manchester contended that a factory chimney and, for that matter, a domestic chimney belching out black smoke symbolized the creation of wealth and personal well-being. Most of Manchester's manufacturers, its magistrates and councillors, members of its trade associations and chamber of commerce (with two or more of these positions of authority often held by one and the same person), and its substantial workforce seemed to subscribe wholeheartedly to this narrative. The smoke was represented as a necessary by-product of industry: "the inevitable and innocuous accompaniment of the meritorious act of manufacturing."[7] The production of smoke warranted no apologies from most industrialists, who pointed to their smoking chimneys as a barometer of economic success and social progress.

The city's booming industries, especially cotton, provided numerous job opportunities and produced rising living standards for an ever-increasing number of Manchester's working class—particularly after 1850. Nevertheless, there were periodic slumps in the cotton trade, most notably the trade depression of 1837–1843, the Cotton Famine of the early 1860s, and the cyclical pattern of slumps known as the Great Depression of the

1870s to 1890s, as well as the challenge of German and American competition looming on the horizon, Traveling around the cotton towns of Lancashire during the very lean year of 1842 and finding the factories of Bolton, near Manchester, hard at work, William Cooke Taylor of Trinity College, Dublin, exclaimed: "Thank God, smoke is rising from the lofty chimneys of most of them! for I have not travelled thus far without learning, by many a painful illustration, that the absence of smoke from the factory-chimney indicates the quenching of the fire on many a domestic hearth, want of employment to many a willing labourer, and want of bread to many an honest family."[8] The image of thousands of smokeless chimneys, as envisioned by the smoke reformers of the period, was almost certain to cause alarm and anxiety among Manchester's working classes. Concerns about the absence of smoke in the industrial city found expression in popular culture's representations of the dilemma. During the Cotton Famine, a cyclical slump exacerbated by the American Civil War, a poem entitled "The Smokeless Chimney" sold well, chiefly at Britain's railway stations, in aid of the Relief Fund for Lancashire's unemployed textile workers. Written in 1862 by Mrs. E. J. Bellasis, under the pseudonym of "A Lancashire Lady," it mirrors Taylor's earlier personal narration of the meaning of smoke:

> Traveller on the Northern Railway!
> Look and learn, as on you speed;
> See the hundred smokeless chimneys,
> Learn their tale of cheerless need.
>
> "How much prettier is this country!"
> Says the careless passer-by.
> "Clouds of smoke we see no longer.
> What's the reason?—Tell me why.
>
> "Better far it were, most surely,
> Never more such clouds to see,
> Bringing taint o'er nature's beauty,
> With their foul obscurity."
>
> Thoughtless fair one! from yon chimney
> Floats the golden breath of life.

Stop that current at your pleasure!
Stop! and starve the child,—the wife!

Ah! to them each smokeless chimney
Is a signal of despair.
They see hunger, sickness, ruin,
Written in that pure, bright air.

"Mother! mother! see! 'twas truly
Said last week the mill would stop!
Mark yon chimney,—nought is going,—
There's no smoke from 'out o'th top!'

Weeks roll on, and still yon chimney
Gives of better times no sign;
Men by thousands cry for labour,—
Daily cry, and daily pine.

Let no more the smokeless chimneys
Draw from you one word of praise.
Think, oh, think! upon the thousands
Who are moaning out their days.

Rather pray that, Peace soon bringing
Work and plenty in her train,
We may see these smokeless chimneys
Blackening all the land again.[9]

Bellasis's paean to air pollution (here much abridged) contains many of the cultural messages that were essential for the propagation of the myth that smoke was inextricably linked to health, happiness, and prosperity. Workers wait despondently for smoke to issue from the lifeless factory chimneys; and it is smoke, the "golden breath of life," and not clean air, that would bring the urban masses employment, comfort, and plenty. The importance of coal and the cotton textile industry for growth and prosperity in Manchester was also widely recognized in the lyrics of the popular songs of the period. In the 1840s and 1850s, for example, the comic song "Manchester's Improving Daily," composed by Richard Baines, became a great favorite with the city's working inhabitants. The first verse went as follows:

> In Manchester, this famous town,
> What great improvements have been made, sirs;
> In fifty years 'tis mighty grown,
> All owing to success in trade, sirs;
> For we see what mighty buildings rising,
> To all beholders how surprising;
> The plough and harrow are now forgot, sirs;
> 'Tis coals and cotton boil the pot, sirs.
> Sing Ned, sing Joe, and Frank so gaily,
> Manchester's improving daily.[10]

While coals and cotton provided the workers' daily bread, this act was not usually accomplished without the "inevitable" production of large volumes of black smoke from the city's industrial chimneys. This view of coal and smoke was widespread and is reproduced in the following verse about Glasgow:

> There's coal underground,
> There's coal in the air,
> There's coal in folk's faces,
> There's coal—everywhere;
> But—there's money in Glasgow![11]

In an "age of smoke," popular poems and songs generated associations that helped naturalize and rationalize the relationship between wealth and air pollution in the industrial towns and cities of Britain. By the end of the nineteenth century, the image of a smoking factory chimney had become indivisible from employment and a full stomach in the minds of the urban masses.

On a more modest scale, a generous amount of smoke seen freely issuing from any one of the city's many thousands of domestic chimneys signified a working family's continued good fortune. Mrs. A. Romley Wright, who taught domestic economy classes in Manchester, illustrates the symbolic power of the smoke emitted from "the popular British institution" of the open coal fire: "The kitchen fireplace is filled with coal—large pieces, of course, for roasting. A volume of smoke rushes up the chimney, and the admiring neighbours may ejaculate 'Oh, *what* a dinner Mr. so and so must be having.'[12] An extravagantly smoking chimney pot visibly demonstrated to onlookers that a family was doing well economically, and might even have enhanced their social status in the community. The smokeless fuel coke, although relatively inexpensive, was unpopular among the city's inhabitants. Coke did not make a good blaze in the hearth and was widely perceived as "a fuel of poverty."[13]

Domestic life revolved around the fireplace, especially during the cold, damp, and dreary winter months. A blazing fire imparted much more than an agreeable degree of heat. The domestic hearth was closely associated with the notion of human warmth, signifying love, friendliness, and a sympathetic, comfortable environment. There are innumerable popular images, both visual and literary, extolling the pleasures of hearth and home that date from the Victorian period. The popular culture of the day often depicts a family and friends seated around a roaring fire, swapping stories, enjoying eating and drinking together, singing songs, reading aloud, or simply watching the shapes made by the flames. A verse from the Lancashire dialect writer Edwin Waugh's short poem "Toddlin' Whoam" encapsulates the powerful attractions of the domestic hearth:

> Toddlin' whoam, for th' fireside bliss,
> Toddlin' whoam, for th' childer's kiss;
> God bless yon bit o' curlin' smooke;
> God bless yon cosy chimbley nook!
> I'm fain to be toddlin' whoam.[14]

Although such representations of hearth and home were often overly romanticized, it would be extremely pessimistic to suppose that such pleasant activities were not experienced by most working-class families, at least from time to time. Smoke spouting from chimney pots and cheerful open coal fires were, then, symbols that were commonly employed by contemporaries to indicate that times were relatively good. The other side of the coin—the cold, fireless grate—was an image that was used by novelists of the period, from national figures such as Charlotte Brontë, Mrs. Gaskell, and Charles Dickens to local working-class dialect authors such as Waugh and Ben Brierly, to denote want and poverty. And when, for example, Waugh wrote of "fireless hearths, an' cupboards bare" in the song

"Hard Weather" (penned during the acute recession of 1878–1879), he would without question have sent a pang of anxious recognition through many of those who heard or sang it.[15]

The existence of bad trade conditions was not a prerequisite for the success of the story line that smoke was inevitable and denoted economic prosperity. At mid-century, for example, a time of neither boom nor bust in the city, the journalist Angus Reach wrote in the *Morning Chronicle,* "Purify the air of Manchester by quenching its furnaces, and you simply stop the dinners of the inhabitants. The grim machine must either go on, or hundreds of thousands must starve."[16] This message was repeated unremittingly by Manchester's employers, who were increasingly worried about the squeeze on profit margins and market share in the face of foreign competition. Their views, closely associating smoke with continued economic growth, were regularly reported at length in the *Manchester Guardian* and other local newspapers. Reginald Le Neve Foster, an influential director of Manchester's Chamber of Commerce, countered one of the City Council's many attempts to enforce the law against smoke pollution by declaring that if it succeeded, "they would drive away all their industries, . . . and Manchester would soon become one of the 'dead cities' of the world."[17] This was a narrative that was to a large extent shamelessly predicated on negative images of smokeless chimneys. It played constantly and effectively on immediately intelligible fears about what life in the industrial city would be like *without* its familiar and reassuring smoke cloud. Just as today, the issue of pollution control was often viewed in simplistic terms, with the manufacturers presenting a stark choice between smoky prosperity or economic stagnation if environmental safeguards were proposed.

The Victorian's well-documented abhorrence of dirt and filth did not always extend to coal smoke, which was often portrayed as good, honest dirt and not as "matter out of place."[18] Indeed, that Manchester's smoking chimneys came to be widely interpreted as benign signs of progress and prosperity is also indicated by a northern expression that has survived to this day: "Where there's muck, there's brass." As a result, the unsightly black face that the hard-working city of Manchester presented to the world could be viewed uncritically by some contemporaries. In 1887, for example, a contributor to the *Manchester Guardian* wrote, "Physically, we must admit that Manchester does not make a good show, except of dirt; but it is only work-day dirt after all—the grime of a collier who has to deal with coal, the dust of a miller who has to apologise for his floury propor-

FIGURE 3.1. Beautiful Manchester, Early Twentieth Century. Postcard in the Collection of Stephen Mosley.

tions."[19] Smoke was represented as beneficial and innocuous, a form of dirt that constituted no great threat to life and health. By the turn of the twentieth century, affectionate, tongue-in-cheek images of the city's smoking factory chimneys were appearing on postcards bearing the legend "Beautiful Manchester" (Figure 3.1.) The image of a smoking industrial chimney had become as comforting psychologically as that of the domestic hearth. The production of smoke was commonly understood and hailed as an infallible sign that Manchester was a flourishing and enterprising city. Throughout the nineteenth century and beyond, the story line continued to resonate with meaning, with the local businessman Reuben Spencer writing of Manchester in 1897, "The factories are still there, the 'incense of industry' still floats in clouds above the tops of countless towering chimneys, the throngs of busy workers are more numerous than ever, and the whirr of gearing and the hum of machinery resounds in a hundred streets, whence emanate a thousand different wares for the use and benefit of the peoples of the earth."[20]

As late as 1913, *Black's Guide to Manchester* told of the city's "thick cloud of smoke that turns to invisible gold."[21] The narrative of wealth was imparted through a great variety of texts in Victorian Manchester, all of which bracketed smoking chimneys with healthy trade conditions, stable or rising living standards, and personal well-being. Charles Dickens sardonically captures the spirit of the age when he has Josiah Bounderby of Coketown say, "First of all, you see our smoke. That's meat and drink to us. It's the healthiest thing in the world in all respects, and particularly for the lungs."[22] But despite the willingness of the majority of Manchester's manufacturers, politicians, and workers to endure polluted air in the name of growth and prosperity, an active minority of influential reformers questioned the popular belief that smoke was synonymous with economic and social progress and countered with a compelling story line of their own.

The second of the story lines that conferred symbolic meaning to the production of smoke reflected the values and beliefs of a largely middle-class, educated, and professional elite, who, rather than viewing smoke as signifying prosperity and progress, saw the columns of sulphurous black smoke as "barbarous" signs of waste and inefficiency. Doctors, scientists, lawyers, clerics, architects, and others from the burgeoning professional ranks, along with several of Manchester's leading merchants and manufacturers, all promoted this skeptical alternative narrative. From the 1840s on, many reformers banded together to form antismoke societies in the city, among which were MAPS and the Manchester and Salford Noxious Vapours Abatement Association (MSNVAA), founded in 1876. The antipollution activists challenged entrenched cultural values and beliefs about Manchester's "productive" smoke by holding public meetings against air pollution; by regularly inviting leading "experts" to lecture on the subject; by testing and exhibiting smoke-abatement technology; and by publishing articles and letters in newspapers, magazines, and journals.[23] Coal smoke, according to this story line, meant a failure to make profitable use of valuable and finite natural resources and a reckless waste of irrecoverable energy. Smoke meant the needless defacement and destruction of the city's buildings and green spaces; it caused a needless and preventable loss of life and health; and, finally, it represented a serious threat to Manchester, Britain, and empire. The narrative that smoke was synonymous with waste was a denser, more complex response to the dilemma posed by smoke pollution and was conveyed in considerably fewer, and often less accessible, texts. However, although much of what follows was reconstructed from sources that did not enjoy an extensive popular readership, these narratives *were* widely disseminated in both the local and national presses.

The towering factory chimneys of the new industrial towns conveyed coal smoke quickly and cheaply into the "vast atmospheric ocean" overhead, where it was thought the unburned products of combustion would be harmlessly diluted and dispersed to a "safe distance" from urban areas.[24] However, as the number of smoky industrial towns mushroomed in southeast Lancashire and elsewhere, this system of pollution removal had the unwanted effect of displacing the problem from one municipality to the next. An appeal to economic rationality was the initial response to this galling situation, with smoke reformers portraying the destructive results of air pollution as nothing less than a burdensome local tax.[25] In 1842 the manufacturer Henry Houldsworth, a prominent member of MAPS, calculated the financial cost to Manchester's inhabitants in "washing, cleansing, and keeping clean persons, garments, furniture and houses" to be "not less than £100,000 per annum"—undoubtedly one of the first of the many attempts by Victorian environmental reformers to use cost-benefit analysis in trying to persuade people to reduce air pollution in urban areas.[26] The meteorologist Rollo Russell listed some twenty-four different forms of loss or damage caused by smoke in London in his cost-benefit exercise of 1889, including the extra gas used for lighting all year round because of the loss of sunlight; reduced capacity for work due to ill health; and the destruction of trees, plants, shrubs, flowers, vegetables, and fruits. Although he did not include "uncertain items," such as the effects of the residence outside the metropolis by all those wealthy enough to avoid the smoke, the total cost still reached £5,200,500.[27] By the early years of the twentieth century, Manchester's Air Pollution Advisory Board reported that the city's smoke was costing its householders no less than £242,705 per annum in extra washing alone. The report continued, "Not only does black smoke mean waste in itself, but it causes further waste. Everybody knows how much it disfigures, but it is not generally known how much it destroys. It levies what may be called the Black Smoke Tax, and everybody living in Manchester pays this tax. . . . Black smoke means not only an aesthetic but also an economic loss."[28]

Coal smoke was also depicted as the visible failure of manufacturers to capitalize economically on the nation's coal stocks by burning their fuel efficiently. Smoke control was ceaselessly posited as a valuable business proposition for industrialists, with Manchester's antismoke campaigners claiming that improved, mechanized fuel technology or even "ordinary care" taken in the operation of hand-fired furnaces could mean substantial financial savings. Clouds of black smoke, according to the narrative of waste, denoted nothing less than pounds sterling hemorrhaging needlessly from Manchester's chimneys into the skies above. At mid-century the smoke-filled urban air was depicted as a vast unused "aërial coalfield" by *The Times*.[29]

Economic concerns over wasted fuel were augmented after mid-century by severe criticisms of the irresponsible depletion of limited natural resources. The noted sanitary reformer Dr. Neil Arnott mournfully denounced the thriftless squandering of Britain's coal reserves: "Coal is a part of our national wealth, of which, whatever is once used can never, like corn or any produce of industry, be renewed or replaced. . . . To consume coal wastefully or unnecessarily, then, is not merely improvidence, but is a serious crime committed against future generations."[30] In 1850, the German physicist Rudolph Clausius had formulated the second law of thermodynamics, developing the concept that all energy becomes disorganized and dissipates over time, eventually being lost forever.[31] As ideas concerning entropy filtered down to the public domain, industrialists, who treated the nation's coal reserves as if they were an inexhaustible asset, were constantly urged by reformers to conserve what were now recognized to be finite fuel reserves. Nor did the inefficiency of the smoky domestic hearth escape censure by contemporaries, with John Percy estimating in 1866 that "in common domestic fires . . . seven-eighths, and even more, of the heat capable of being evolved from the coal pass up the chimney unapplied."[32] Russell went so far as to advocate that local authorities should levy a punitive tax on the open kitchen range of the "wasteful householder."[33] By the early 1860s, serious concerns were being voiced as to just how long coal supplies in Britain would last, with Sir William Armstrong, in his presidential address to the British Association, calculating that stocks would last only for another 212 years. In 1865 the economist W. Stanley Jevons heightened these concerns when he estimated that Britain's coal reserves would be exhausted in no more than a century.[34] The question of a threat to Britain's future power and prosperity was frequently highlighted, and featured prominently in Jevons's work. "When our main-spring is here run down, our fires burnt out," he wrote, "Britain may contract to her former littleness, and her people be again distinguished for homely and hardy virtues . . . rather than for brilliant accomplishments and indomitable power."[35] It was argued that without the conservation of coal, a major source of industrial and imperial power, Britain and Manchester had nothing to look forward to but a gradual decline into mediocrity.

Ideas that connected smoke with wasted resources were common in the popular press of Britain in the last quarter of the century. In 1889 a *Manchester Guardian* account of a crowded public meeting against smoke pollution, held at Manchester Town Hall, voiced the main themes of this strand of the story line. Lord Egerton of Tatton, who chaired the meeting, is reported as declaring that the "consumption of smoke" would result in "pecuniary gain" to the city's manufacturers, who needed to be "enlighten[ed] . . . as to their own interests, to show them that the emission of smoke into the air was a waste of valuable carbon which ought to be in the furnace." Sir W. H. Houldsworth, M.P. for Manchester N.W., proclaimed to the large and influential gathering that "he himself believed that the consumption and prevention of smoke was economical . . . because the black smoke which they wanted to stop was actual force and energy going into the air."[36] Air pollution was increasingly vilified as "barbarous and unscientific," and readers were regularly bombarded by representations of the smoking chimney as indicative of wasted money, energy, and natural resources.

The damage smoke caused to the health of Manchester's inhabitants was an important component of the narrative of waste, and one that acquired an increasingly apocalyptic edge as the century progressed. The detrimental effects of local smoke on the human respiratory system had been pointed out as early as 1659 by John Evelyn in his pamphlet *A character of England,* where he observed that "pestilential smoak . . . fatally seiz[es] on the lungs of the inhabitants [of London], so that the cough and the consumption spares no man."[37] However, at Manchester concerns about the smoky atmospheric conditions causing ill health did not surface conspicuously until 1842, when MAPS was formed. The Reverend John Molesworth, for example, told the Select Committee on Smoke Prevention of 1843 that the smoke-drenched air of the city was "no doubt unhealthy" and "must tend to disease."[38] The smoke-abatement movement emerged at a time when the "condition of England" question was attracting great attention, with public health reformers gathering damning statistical evidence regarding the dangers of unhealthy water supplies and inadequate drainage and sewer systems in Britain's towns and cities.[39] Numerical data were used to link air pollution to the increased incidence of chronic respiratory diseases, especially bronchitis, in poor urban areas, with one report showing that the average death rate from respiratory diseases between the years 1868 and 1873 was just 2.27 per thousand in Westmoreland, 3.54 per thousand for the whole of England and Wales, 5.12 per thousand for Salford, and 6.10 per thousand for Manchester. In 1874 the death rate from these causes had risen to 7.70 per thousand in Manchester, leading the report's author to conclude "that Manchester suffers more from diseases of respiratory organs than any town or city in England."[40] In 1882, Dr. Arthur Ransome, president of the Manchester and Salford Sanitary Association, calculated that in the preceding decade some thirty-four thousand people had died from "diseases of the lungs" in Manchester and Salford. Ransome argued that smoke pollution was a significant—and preventable—cause of this mortality and that its abatement "would save many useful lives in the next generation."[41] Concerns about the health risks posed by smoke were often expressed in terms similar to those that communicated the negligent misuse of mineral resources.

Then, as now, reformers consistently used the burgeoning death rates from respiratory diseases to keep the issue of air pollution in the public eye. But while considerable progress was made in improving sanitation and lowering death rates from "dirt diseases" such as cholera and typhoid during the nineteenth century, mortality statistics could not conclusively prove the relationship between ill health and the burgeoning smoke cloud. Increasing death rates from respiratory diseases were also associated with other environmental sources of illness, such as damp, overcrowded housing. Frustration at the ineffectiveness of "reform by numbers" in the case of air pollution saw a growing number of impassioned appeals to the public's moral sensibilities, with, for example, the socialist Edward Carpenter writing emotively that "any one who has witnessed . . . the smoke resting over such towns as Sheffield or Manchester on a calm fine day—the hideous black impenetrable cloud blotting out the sunlight, in which the very birds cease to sing,—will have wondered how it was possible for human beings to live under such conditions. It is probable, in fact, that they do not live. . . . The workers, producers of the nation's riches, dying by thousands and thousands, choked in the reek of their own toil."[42]

By the last quarter of the nineteenth century, the notion that smoke was contributing markedly to ill health and mortality in the city had reached beyond medical circles to acquire a wider resonance. The idea had become an important part of public discourse concerning urban air pollution, as this letter to the *Manchester Guardian* illustrates:

FIGURE 3.2. The Smoke Demon, 1893. From Robert Barr, "The Doom of London," *The Idler* 2 (1893): 7.

The great city of Manchester stands in the unenviable position of being one of the unhealthiest cities in the kingdom, with an appalling death-rate behind it. The evils are not far to seek. They are, in my opinion, mainly due to . . . the smoke demon and noxious vapours. So much has been written and said on this nuisance that I can add nothing fresh, only to hope that they who are charged with guarding the public health will be alive to their duties and enforce their power to abate the evil, which is killing downright our boys and girls—the men and women of the future—and let them breathe pure air and not poison . . . it is high time that something practical were done to make it what it ought to be—the second city in the Empire, healthy and cheerful, instead of what it is, insanitary and gloomy.[43]

The smoke pollution that veiled Manchester and other coal-fired cities, rather than being a cause for celebration, was represented to the public as nothing less than a funereal pall (Figure 3.2). By the latter decades of the century, however, concerns about the putative effects of smoke on health were not limited solely to an increase in death-dealing respiratory diseases.

The smoke-laden atmosphere of the city obscured the sun, and this "destruction of daylight" led to fears that smoke pollution was contributing to the general physical and moral deterioration of the urban workforce—a much-debated concern throughout the century. As early as 1876, Dr. Thomas Andrews, president of the British Association for the Advancement of Science, stated, "There can be no doubt that the prevalence of smoke in the atmosphere of our large towns tends to deteriorate the physical condition of our people." Arthur Ransome argued in 1882 that the absence of sunlight in urban areas was contributing to "the pallid and unhealthy and stunted appearance of our town populations." In an article entitled "Smoke, and Its Effects on Health," the pseudonymous "Lucretia" discussed yet another dimension to the narrative: that the degeneration of the urban populace, caused directly by Manchester's smoking chimneys, threatened the very survival of the city itself:

> A stunted, scrofulous, and ricketty working population has been raised up in our midst . . . The present existing facts of physical and moral deterioration of the human type which apparently lives, eats, and has its being amongst the lower classes of this large city, certainly shakes to its foundation Darwin's theory of the "survival of the fittest" . . . the smoky atmosphere of Manchester is not *all* that can be desired. . . . The clearing of the atmosphere is one of the greatest necessities of the age; and we should consider it so, . . . the proof of the great dangers existing to the prosperity of Manchester, socially, physically, and commercially, is the apathy of the general mass of its inhabitants with regard to the "smoke nuisance."[44]

The narrative also strongly emphasized the perceived moral degeneration of the urban masses. It was claimed that "hundreds of thousands of English children are now growing up into men and women . . . with no sign of a green field, with no knowledge of flowers or forest, the blue heavens themselves dirtied by soot—amid objects all mean and hideous, with no entertainment but the music hall, no pleasure but in the drink shop."[45] It was argued that to compensate for the grim local environmental conditions—the lack of daylight, natural color, and vegetation in the drab industrial city—many of the working classes simply wasted their scant financial resources on "vulgar" entertainment, gambling, and drinking excessively, which was, in the memorable phrase of Mr. Justice Day, "the shortest way out of Manchester."[46]

This story line gained currency in 1899, when of eleven thousand men in Manchester who volunteered for military service in the Boer War, eight thousand "were found to be physically unfit to carry a rifle and stand the fatigues of discipline." Concern did not end there, however, as of the three thousand who were accepted to serve in the army, only twelve hundred were found to be even "moderately" fit.[47] After the Boer War, during which Britain's urban-raised soldiers were thought to have performed poorly in comparison with their country-bred opponents, Fred Scott, secretary of the Manchester and Salford branch of the Smoke Abatement League, warned that the "smoke nuisance" was seriously undermining the health of the nation, "sapping the virility of our people—that grand heritage which has made the British the greatest colonising and conquering race the world has known."[48] The ethos of imperialism was based on virility, and smoke pollution was thought to seriously impair the development of "a manly, vigorous, enterprising, healthy race which will hold its own against all foreign competition."[49] The colonies were depicted by the reformers as healthy limbs on a decaying body, and the wisdom of the state in continuing to allow the air to be polluted by coal smoke was seriously questioned. From the 1880s on, the smoke reformers' narrative repeatedly emphasized the degeneration of the lower classes of the city, aiming to shake the public's confidence in a viable future for Manchester, Britain, and empire. This grim vision of the future for the smoky city was intended to countervail the doom-laden story line that had been constructed for a smoke-free Manchester.

The skeptical story line concerning smoke production also vigorously attacked the serious damage being caused to Manchester's recently erected "architectural beauties" and the wholesale destruction of vegetation in the city. The 1840s and 1850s had seen the flowering of a competitive form of civic pride in Britain that produced, in the second half of the century, not only an abundance of monumental town halls, public libraries, and municipal art galleries but also a large crop of new public parks, where plants from every corner of a growing empire could be displayed. Whether in art, architecture, parks, or ornamental gardens, the emphasis was on spectacle, and the lofty aspirations of Manchester's manufacturing and commercial middle class found expression in public buildings such as Alfred Waterhouse's neo-Gothic town hall, which took nine years to construct at the cost of £1 million. However, the architecture of the city dubbed "the Florence of the North" by the architect Thomas Worthington, which was designed to reflect the sophistication, power, and status of its urban "aristocracy" ad infinitum, rapidly began to blacken, and its elaborately carved stonework to crumble, as a result of the corrosive action of the viscid, sulphurous smoke cloud. Furthermore, trees, shrubs, flowers, and grass all struggled for survival in Manchester's parks and gardens due to the problem of acid rain, and paintings were placed behind glass to protect them from the smoke-laden air. Discontent regarding the grimy condition of the city and the harmful effects of smoke on the natural environment was already evident in the early 1840s, when an editorial in the *Manchester Guardian* complained about the city's dying trees and shrubs and stated that smoke pollution "has for years been the standing reproach of the town."[50] The "unloveliness" of Victorian Manchester was a sensitive issue for many contemporaries, since from an aesthetic perspective Manchester was thought to compare poorly to other great cities of the world, such as London, Paris, Rome, or, indeed, Florence.

Discolored, decaying buildings and stunted vegetation were a recurring motif of the skeptical narrative regarding smoke, as the murky conditions were thought to effectively advertise "the waste which goes along with these aesthetic and hygienic backslidings." If medical statistics were unable to prove the link between smoke and ill health, this component of the story line frequently highlighted the visibly damaging effects of smoke on the city's masonry and vegetation as important indicators of what air pollution might be doing to human health. The high acidity of the city's rain, a direct consequence of the ever-expanding smoke cloud, was eroding the headstones in Manchester's cemeteries. This led the town clerk of Manchester, Sir Joseph Heron, to ask, "If the gravestones were suffering, what would be the effects on those above?"[51] It was but a small step for some contemporaries to use imagery of deteriorating, etiolated vegetation as a commonsense analogy to illustrate what they thought was happening to the urban populace. Ernest Hart, chairman of the National Smoke Abatement Institution and editor of the *British Medical Journal,* took "very carefully" the counsel of the leading medical authorities of the day, including Sir Andrew Clark, Sir William Gull, Sir James Paget, Dr. Alfred Carpenter, and Manchester's Ransome, concerning the effects of smoke on health, before giving the following evidence to the Select Committee investigating Smoke Nuisance Abatement in 1887:

> The increase in the volume of smoke emitted in London, within the last 20 years, has produced perceptible differences in the health of the people, diff-

erences which you can measure pretty accurately by certain biological standards. For instance, Mr. Stansfield was telling me that not very many years
ago roses could be grown successfully. . . . at Prince's Gate, but that now it is
impossible to grow roses there . . . At the present moment the very last
conifer, I believe, is dying, or dead, in Kensington Gardens . . . all the vital
processes of healthy life are allowed to droop for lack of the actinic rays of
the sun: they are struck down by the increasing volume of smoke, which
means a general deterioration of the health of the children, and grown-up
people also.[52]

The reformers asserted that if smoke was abated and something of nature restored to the city, the results would include a happier, healthier, and
more civilized urban workforce; an increase in artistic creativity and industrial output; higher standards of production; and, ultimately, the
maintenance of Manchester's and Britain's standing in the world. They
continually stressed that an investment in the regeneration of the urban
environment—in clean air, dirt-free architecture, and flourishing green
spaces—was also a way to increase the public wealth of a city. However,
despite widespread and favorable press coverage, the narrative of "waste"
failed to overturn the dominant cultural myth that smoke equaled prosperity.

By the 1880s, a century's experience of living with smoking chimneys
had given a cultural permanence to the notion that coal smoke denoted
wealth. The correlation between smoke and prosperity had become so
deeply embedded in the culture of northern industrial society that many
city dwellers did not often think to complain about the murky atmospheric conditions. The journalist and socialist Allen Clarke wrote of his
working-class upbringing in Bolton: "Living there, I had grown familiar
with its ugliness, and familiarity oftener breeds toleration than contempt;
I had accepted the drab streets, the smoky skies, the foul river, the mass
of mills, the sickly workers, as inevitable and usual—nay, natural, and did
not notice them in any probing, critical way."[53] Indeed, the gloomy city
conditions helped to form, and strengthen, the British urban dweller's
legendary attachment to the bright and cheerful open coal fire. Professor
William Bone wrote of the national preference for coal fires: "An English-
man, oppressed as he is [by] . . . dreary sunless skies . . . seeks relief in his
home at nights by his radiant fireside, and disregards with characteristic
disrespect the vapourings of scientific cranks who condemn it as wasteful."[54]

Coal was one of life's necessities as far as the working classes were concerned, and finding a lump of coal in the street was looked upon as a sure sign of good luck. Robert Roberts considered that obtaining food and warmth was the greatest worry of the slum dwellers of Salford and set down the views of a regular customer to his father's shop: "'A full belly and a warm backside', Mrs. Carey would announce, 'that's all our lot want! I got a sheep's head boiling on the hob and a hundredweight o' nuts [coal] in the backyard. What more could folks wish for in winter?'"[55] The answer to Mrs. Carey's question is "regular employment," and this is where the potency of the "wealth" story line really comes into its own. We must not forget that the only occasions on which urban dwellers had experienced clean city air were in times of hardship, such as a trade depression or a strike. Their encounters with a smoke-free urban environment had been uniformly wretched, and under these circumstances it is not difficult to understand why most of Manchester's citizens accepted the polluters' customary story line; they preferred to cling to what they knew to be true. When the city's workers saw a smoking industrial chimney, they did see wealth being created, and smoke issuing freely from their domestic chimneys did signify their prosperity. Although both main story lines were at times grossly exaggerated, they carried many different kinds of truth concerning smoke pollution that the city's inhabitants could readily identify with. However, the narrative of "wealth" was by far the most credible in the eyes of the urban workforce, who knew, from bitter, lived experience, that a smokeless chimney signified enforced idleness, hunger, and poverty.

The views of the mass of workers have been largely absent from discussions about urban environmental conditions. Working people, however, held strong opinions about air pollution, and glimpses of their perceptions of the "smoke nuisance" in the industrial towns of northern Britain occasionally come to light—and not only in popular poems and songs. In conclusion, I suggest that the workers of Manchester employed an evaluative hierarchy where these story lines were concerned. There is ample evidence to suggest that substantial numbers of working-class people complained about the harmful effects of smoke pollution, with Captain A. W. Sleigh, former assistant commissioner of police at Manchester, telling the Select Committee on Smoke Prevention of 1843 that "the poor people themselves consider it a very great nuisance. . . . The whole population do. Lord Ashley was at Manchester some time before I left there, and he did me the honour of asking me to go round with him, to look at the condition of the poor people, together with other matters. We visited all the localities minutely, and they all complained of the smoke."[56]

Ill health; the Sisyphean task of attempting to keep homes, furnishings, and clothes free from soot; and the destruction of vegetation in the barren, smoky city were all issues that attracted laborers' criticism. But the working classes unquestionably afforded a higher priority to the manufacturers' claims that they would be worse off *without* the industrial smoke with which they had come to associate jobs and economic well-being. That there was little active support for the smoke-abatement movement among the working classes can be exemplified by an account in the *Manchester Guardian* of a public meeting against smoke, convened by the NVAA, at Broughton Town Hall on 11 December 1882. The meeting was planned with a view to putting pressure on Salford Corporation to prevent "the needless emission of black smoke . . . in the neighbourhood." The *Manchester Guardian* reported that there "was a large attendance of working men" at the meeting, and their hostility to the aims of the reformers soon became apparent. Despite an earnest appeal to the "vital importance to themselves and their families that their health be sustained in order that they might continue to earn that income upon which both they and their family depended," the NVAA's various arguments concerning the deleterious effects of smoke made little impression on the assembled throng. A resolution rebuking the Salford Corporation, on being put to the meeting, "was lost by a very large majority, only four people in the body of the room voting for it." Directly after the vote had been taken, Thomas Horsfall, on behalf of the NVAA, asked, "Whose voice was it that ordered that no hand be raised up in favour of the resolution? Was it that of a manager or overlooker?" The angry crowd immediately shouted Horsfall down. An opposing speaker, George Jones, a member of the Health Committee of the Salford Corporation, found great favor with the audience when he protested that he "did not think there was much to complain of in Broughton, and he would be sorry to see a persecution commenced against the manufacturers, for if they were driven from the borough, where would the bread of the working man come from?"[57]

The reformers claimed later that "it was evident from the opening of the meeting that a large number of workmen who entered the hall . . .

had been sent to defeat the objects of the Association."[58] It is impossible to know whether these workers had been coerced by their employers into attending the meeting at Broughton, but it is likely that any use of coercion was minimal, as many working men undoubtedly saw their own interests as being intimately linked to those of their employers in this respect.

No single view of air pollution dominated to the exclusion of all others. The story lines of "wealth" and "waste" are two sides of the same coin, with smoke simultaneously existing as good and evil in the minds of contemporaries in urban industrial areas. But the strong foothold that the straightforward, cohesive narrative of "wealth" had obtained in popular culture gave it great influence and staying power. The more fragmentary and scientific story line of "waste" was not as readily intelligible to the working classes and failed to duplicate or seriously undermine the former's authority. Trust in the purveyors of these different knowledge claims also influenced the ways people made decisions about smoke in their uncertain day-to-day lives. Against the backdrop of cyclical depressions, especially during the Great Depression years, it is likely that both employers and employees came to share a sense of increased vulnerability and feared change and the unknown. The growing foreign challenge to Britain's commercial supremacy also eroded confidence in Manchester's future, as cotton prices fell and production expanded less rapidly.[59] "Sun doesn't pay hereabout," one worker stated flatly to a reformer in 1890. "More smoke more work hereabout, at least, that's wot my master says."[60] The working classes were suspicious of and did not support the reformers' questionable initiatives that might limit industrial growth and endanger their often precarious livelihoods.

Most of Manchester's citizens were not indifferent to smoke, which they had come to view primarily as the "incense of industry" and only to a subordinate degree as a symbol of waste. Despite the palpability of the coal smoke, this nineteenth-century environmental issue was no less socially constructed or complex than today's intangible air pollutants. The "waste" narrative attracted widespread public attention but failed to break the hold of the enduring cultural myth that smoke equaled prosperity. Had they been asked about their goals in life, most working people in Victorian Manchester would have had a clear and definite answer: a blazing coal fire in the hearth, a good meal, and the aim of raising—or at least not worsening—their material standard of living. At the end of the nineteenth century, as at the beginning, people still looked to the city's thousands of chimneys to gauge the condition of their world.

NOTES

I am indebted to Greg Myers, Paulo Palladino, Thomas Rohkrämer, and John Walton for their helpful comments on a draft of this essay.

1. "Prevention or Abatement of Smoke? Public Meeting at the Victoria Gallery," *Manchester Guardian,* 28 May 1842.

2. William Cronon, "A Place for Stories: Nature, History, and Narrative," *Journal of American History* 78 (1992): 1369. Maarten Hajer's recent study of environmental discourse in Great Britain and The Netherlands (*The Politics of Environmental Discourse: Ecological Modernisation and the Policy Process* [Oxford: Clarendon Press, 1995]) was also an influence on this essay.

3. See Stephen Mosley, "The 'Smoke Nuisance'" and Environmental Reformers in Late Victorian Manchester," *Manchester Region History Review* 10 (1996): 43.

4. *Manchester as It Is* (Manchester: Love and Barton, 1839), 26; Robert Angus Smith, "What Amendments Are Required in the Legislation Necessary to Prevent the Evils Arising from Noxious Vapours and Smoke?" *Transactions of the National Association for the Promotion of Social Science* (1876): 518.

5. See Alan Kidd, *Manchester* (Keele, England: Keele University Press, 1993).

6. Leon Faucher, *Manchester in 1844: Its Present Condition and Future Prospects* (Manchester: Abel Heywood, 1844), 16; Napier quoted in Steven Marcus, *Engels, Manchester, and the Working Class* (London: Weidenfield and Nicolson, 1974), 46.

7. Thomas C. Horsfall, "The Government of Manchester," *Transactions of the Manchester Statistical Society* (1895–96): 19.

8. William Cooke Taylor, *Notes of a Tour in the Manufacturing Districts of Lancashire* (London: Duncan and Malcolm, 1842), 22.

9. John Harland, ed., *Lancashire Lyrics: Modern Songs and Ballads of the County Palatine* (London: Whittaker, 1866), 289–292.

10. Richard Wright Procter, *Memorials of Manchester Streets* (Manchester: Thos. Sutcliffe, 1874), 40–42.

11. Peter Fyfe, "The Pollution of the Air: Its Causes, Effects, and Cure," in Smoke Abatement League of Great Britain, *Lectures Delivered in the Technical College, Glasgow 1910–1911* (Glasgow: Corporation of Glasgow, 1912), 77.

12. A. Romley Wright, "Cooking by Gas," *Exhibition Review, no.* 5 (April 1882): 3.

13. Robert Roberts, *A Ragged Schooling: Growing Up in the Classic Slum* (Manchester: Manchester University Press, 1976), 73.

14. George Milner, ed., *Poems and Songs by Edwin Waugh* (Manchester: John Heywood, n.d.), 34–35.

15. Ibid., 107–109.

16. J. Ginswick, ed., *Labour and the Poor in England and Wales, 1849–1851: The Letters to the Morning Chronicle from the Correspondents in the Manufacturing and Mining Districts, the Towns of Liverpool and Birmingham, and the Rural Districts*, vol. 1: *Lancashire, Cheshire, Yorkshire* (London: Frank Cass, 1983), 5.

17. *Manchester Guardian*, 20 June 1891.

18. The work of Mary Douglas provides a good starting point concerning human understandings of dirt and disorder. See especially Mary Douglas, *Purity and Danger: An Analysis of Concepts of Pollution and Taboo* (London: Routledge and Kegan Paul, 1966).

19. "The Ugliness of Manchester," *Manchester Guardian*, 17 August 1887.

20. Reuben Spencer, *A Survey of the History, Commerce and Manufactures of Lancashire* (London: Biographical Publishing, 1897), 48.

21. *Black's Guide to Manchester* (London: A. C. Black, 1913), 1.

22. Charles Dickens, *Hard Times* (Oxford: Oxford University Press, 1989), 166.

23. For a summary, see Mosley, "Smoke Nuisance," 44–45.

24. See, for example, Peter Spence, *Coal, Smoke, and Sewage, Scientifically and Practically Considered* (Manchester: Cave and Sever, 1857), 21–22.

25. "The Smoke Nuisance," *Manchester Guardian*, 7 June 1843.

26. "Prevention or Abatement of Smoke? Public Meeting at the Victoria Gallery," *Manchester Guardian*, 28 May 1842.

27. Rollo Russell, *Smoke in Relation to Fogs in London* (London: National Smoke Abatement Institution, 1889), 22–26.

28. Manchester Air Pollution Advisory Board, *The Black Smoke Tax* (Manchester: Henry Blacklock, 1920), 1–2.

29. "London Smoke," *The Times*, 2 January 1855.

30. Neil Arnott, "On a New Smoke-Consuming and Fuel-Saving Fireplace," *Journal of the Society of Arts* 2 (1854): 428.

31. David Pepper, *Modern Environmentalism: An Introduction* (London: Routledge, 1996), 230–233.

32. John Percy, "Coal and Smoke," *Quarterly Review* 119 (1866): 451.

33. Russell, *Smoke*, 27.

34. Brian W. Clapp, *An Environmental History of Britain since the Industrial Revolution* (London: Longman, 1994), 152–156.

35. W. Stanley Jevons, *The Coal Question*, 3d ed. (1906; reprint, New York: Augustus M. Kelley, 1965), 459.

36. "The Prevention of Smoke in Towns: Meeting in Manchester," *Manchester Guardian*, 9 November 1889.

37. John Evelyn, *Fumifugium* (1661; reprint, Exeter: Rota, 1976), prefatory notes.

38. *Parliamentary Papers* (House of Commons), 1843 (583) VII, qs. 680 and 686.

39. See Anthony S. Wohl, *Endangered Lives: Public Health in Victorian Britain* (London: Methuen, 1984).

40. *Manchester and Salford Sanitary Association Annual Report 1876* (Manchester: Powlson and Sons, 1877), 9.

41. Arthur Ransome, "The Smoke Nuisance: A Sanitarian's View," *Exhibition Review*, no. 1 (April 1882): 3.

42. Edward Carpenter, "The Smoke-Plague and Its Remedy," *Macmillan's* 62 (1890): 204–206.

43. "The Manchester Death-Rate," *Manchester Guardian*, 25 June 1888.

44. Andrews quoted in Smith, "What Amendments," 537; Ransome, "Smoke Nuisance," 3; Lucretia, "Smoke, and Its Effects on Health," *Exhibition Review*, no. 5 (April 1882): 2–3.

45. Fred Scott, "The Case for a Ministry of Health," *Transactions of the Manchester Statistical Society* (1902–3): 100.

46. Quoted in *Parliamentary Papers* (House of Commons), 1904 (Cd.2175) XXXII.I, 20.

47. Carl Chinn, *Poverty amidst Prosperity: The Urban Poor in England, 1834–1914* (Manchester: Manchester University Press, 1995), 114.

48. Scott, "Case," 99.

49. Sir James Barr, "The Advantages, from a National Standpoint, of Compulsory Physical Training of the Youth of This Country," in *Manchester and Salford Sanitary Association Annual Report 1914* (Manchester: Sherratt and Hughes, 1915), 22.

50. "The Smoke Nuisance," *Manchester Guardian*, 28 May 1842.

51. "The Smoke Nuisance," *Manchester Guardian*, 19 September 1888 and 3 November 1876.

52. *Parliamentary Papers* (House of Lords), 1887 (321) XII, q. 338.

53. Allen Clarke, *The Effects of the Factory System* (1899; reprint, Littleborough: George Kelsall, 1985), 38.

54. William A. Bone, *Coal and Health* (London, 1919), 15.

55. Roberts, *Ragged Schooling*, 71.

56. *Parliamentary Papers* (House of Commons), 1843 (583) VII, qs. 1553 and 1554.

57. "The Smoke Nuisance in Broughton: Lively Public Meeting," *Manchester Guardian*, 12 December 1882.

58. *Manchester and Salford Noxious Vapours Abatement Association Annual Report 1883,* in *Manchester and Salford Sanitary Association Annual Report 1883* (Manchester: John Heywood, 1884), 82.

59. John Walton, *Lancashire: A Social History, 1558–1939* (Manchester: Manchester University Press, 1987), chap. 10.

60. Hardwicke, D. Rawnsley, "Sunlight or Smoke?" *Contemporary Review* 57 (1890): 523.

4

Uplands Downwind
Acidity and Ecological Change
in the Southeast Lancashire Moorlands

Matthew Osborn

The Moorland Sink

The High Moorlands zone of the Pennines is among the most desolate and uninhabited regions of Britain. Even with the population densities of the present day, there are a few areas of up to twenty square miles without a house, fence, tree, road, or even a path. In the midst of these open spaces, it is still possible to travel for miles without seeing humans or evidence of their passing. Heavy rainfall cuts deep channels through the blanket peat, known locally as *groughs,* right down to the solid rock or the hard clay. Each section of moor is a mini-watershed, with countless tributary streams running in places over five feet deep and twenty feet wide. If you walk for half a mile in a straight line, you may have to cross a hundred of these deep gullies. Deep-brown-colored peat can be seen on the exposed sides of these channels, and on the intervening little plateaus peat is carpeted with its own complex of plants. Most of this plateau is unfit even for less-discriminating livestock such as sheep. The High Moorlands were difficult to integrate into the agrarian and pastoral economies in times of agricultural and population growth, and they were also left unsettled and unexploited by industry.[1]

There is no precise definition for the term *moor,* and there is no exact definition, scientific or popular, that can be used for every type of moorland. It is commonly used in the Pennines to mean any large area of land without either trees or cultivation. Moors can range from a great expanse miles across to a tiny pocket of soil hardly bigger than a front lawn set in the midst of a forest or field; they may be dry or studded with pools of water. Even in plant biology the word *moor* is vaguely defined. The zone known as the High Moorlands in southeast Lancashire is located in the central Pennine area separating Lancashire from the West Riding of York-shire. In this area the botanical definition of a moor applies best: a specific colony of acid-loving (acidophilus), peat-forming plants. This part of the Pennines is an uneven plateau, rising to heights between fifteen hundred and two thousand feet above sea level.[2]

Contrary to its appearance as an undeveloped and unchanged natural area, the ecology of the High Moorlands has been greatly degraded through human activity. For over two hundred years the Pennines have been the main sink for industrial and urban Lancashire's acidity. This area, as part of the hinterland of industrial Lancashire, was a sacrifice zone that was intimately connected through air pollution to the prosperous down-wind sites of its production. Deindustrialization and better pollution con-trols have decreased sulphur dioxide pollution, but these gains have been offset by increases in other forms of acid deposition and by increased acid precipitation in other regions.[3]

In the last fifty years, the regulation of smoke pollution has mitigated some of the more noxious impacts on human health. The anti-smoke campaigns and the development of anti-smoke legislation were pro-foundly linked to concerns about human health impacts and were given a great boost by one of the worst and most deadly smog events in British history, in December 1952. The resulting 1956 Clean Air Act led to marked reductions in soot, particulate, and smoke pollution in general. However, the regulation of smoke did not solve the problem of acidity, as many thought it would. Emissions of acid-forming sulphur dioxide (SO_2) and oxides of nitrogen (NOx) continued. Removal of acid-forming com-pounds from emissions is much more complicated and costly than re-moval of smoke. This technological difficulty, acidity's invisibility, the less obvious impacts on human health, and acidic pollution's ability to travel far from where it was produced combined to keep it from being properly regulated. But this form of air, water, and land pollution has had an enor-mous impact on the ecology of downwind areas, especially if they also had high rates of precipitation. Downwind from Manchester, in the area sur-rounding Oldham, acidity in freshwater ecosystems was even worse due to drainage from coal mines and other associated run-off. In the more recent past, attempts to regulate acidity have been based on a much more complex understanding of atmospheric chemistry and the long-range transport of pollutants, of ecology, and of our role in transforming environments through our actions. This understanding has been considerably advanced through the study of acidification in the human and natural communities of the Pennines.[4]

Acid Deposition

Rainwater is naturally acidic. Water in equilibrium with carbon dioxide (CO_2) in the atmosphere forms a dilute carbonic acid with a pH of about 5.6; below this level is what is considered to be acid rain. The pH scale is a measure of the hydrogen ion concentration in water, with 7 being neutral and levels below that being progressively more acidic. As this is a logarithmic scale, a pH of 3.6 is one hundred times more acidic than a pH of 5.6. Even small drops in pH can have significant impacts in natural ecosystems. Rain can have a lower pH than 5.6 through natural processes such as volcanic eruptions, and in some areas sea salt adds sulphur to the air and can increase natural acidity. However, these natural forms of acidity are distributed fairly evenly, while most of the human-induced acidity (90 percent of the total) has been historically concentrated in northern Europe and northeastern North America (in some smaller localities within these regions it is concentrated still further). Though there have been significant reductions in sulfur emissions since 1956, by the late 1990s the rainfall averages were still lower than pH 4.3 to 4.4 in eastern Britain.[5]

Acid deposition can take place in two ways. Dry deposition is a more localized phenomenon, with acidity being directly deposited through a gaseous exchange with plants and soils, or through settling onto the land as aerosols or particulates. This kind of deposition was responsible for the earliest recognized damage to natural systems by high acidity in areas downwind of alkali production in southwest Lancashire. Dry deposition easily fit with the prevailing view of pollution as a local phenomenon and was an early target of regulation. Wet deposition is much more significant as a mechanism for transporting the acids over distance, and this is done through rain and snow or fog and low clouds. Acids of greatest environmental concern have been sulphuric acid and, to a lesser degree, nitric acid. In the atmosphere, these acids exist in aerosol droplets and move under the influence of turbulence and global circulation patterns. This transport allows for acid deposition in areas far from their production, and in combination with a slow process of oxidation it is a significant factor in the prevalence of high acidity in areas of high rainfall. While acidity from nitric acid is less of a factor in the history of acid deposition, in the last fifty years it has become much more important due to its generation in the high temperatures of internal combustion engines.

As Harold Platt demonstrates in this volume, the threat of acid rain to natural systems has been a subject of concern in the scientific community from R. A. Smith's coining of the term *acid rain* in the 1850s right up to today. Combustion of coal and other fossil fuels has always resulted in the production of the primary pollutants sulphur dioxide and oxides of nitrogen. These, in turn, react with water in the atmosphere to produce the secondary pollutants, sulphates and sulphuric acids and nitrogen compounds and nitric acid. The transformation from primary to secondary pollutant, particularly of sulphur, can take several days, during which it may be blown a great distance. That this was a problem separate from the smoke nuisance was not well known or readily apparent until well after the passage of the 1956 act. Before this, it was thought that the reduction of smoke would address the problem of increased acidity. In a 1984 Nature Conservancy Report by G. L. A. Fry and A. S. Cooke, this was highlighted: "We were well aware of effects of air pollution from industry on organisms such as lichens, mosses and trees, but in the main these seemed to have been caused by the 'black rains' and smogs of the past rather than being changes that could be seen to be in progress now." By the 1980s the extent and complexity of this problem were recognized by the international scientific and political communities.[6]

Two Centuries of Smoke and Acid

Referring to Manchester and its surroundings, Robert Angus Smith noted in his 1872 volume *Air and Rain*, "I do not mean to say that all rain is acid; but in general, I think, the acid prevails in this town."[7] By the turn of the century, the smoke spewing from textile mills, canal barges, mine pumps, breweries, brick kilns, machine works, and, perhaps most important, domestic chimneys was a thick and sooty mixture of deadly gases and particulates. Grime and dirt quickly became a part of life in this region. Peter Brimblecombe has reported that in London, where human health and agriculture were subordinated to heating and industrial needs earlier than in Lancashire, sulfur dioxide levels rose to the mean of 150 micrograms per cubic meter as early as the end of the seventeenth century. These levels remained at least this high into the twentieth century. To put this in perspective, annual means of less than 80 micrograms per cubic meter are considered the maximum tolerable level in modern cities.[8] This subordination of health concerns, both human and natural, was repeated throughout industrializing Britain, especially in southeast Lancashire. Pollution and environmental degradation aided industrialization and urbanization in this area, and they were self-feeding phenomena in the uplands downwind of Manchester. By decreasing agricultural yields, killing aquatic, riverine life, and depleting forest and other plant cover, pollution further marginalized the already poor agricultural land in the upland parishes and helped push the landless and the jobless into degraded urban environments where wage labor was the only recourse.[9]

The influence of coal smoke upon rainfall was substantial in the upland parish of Oldham, which is six miles outside Manchester and about seven hundred feet higher in altitude. As the prevailing winds blow across the Irish Sea and gain altitude in the Pennines, they drop a substantial portion of their moisture on Oldham and the moors above. In 1901, C. E. Moss described the view from a western escarpment of the Pennines: "Deadly suburban fields form the most extensive element of the background; but what rivets the eye are the scores, and scores again, of mill chimneys, tall, straight and lank, belching forth volumes of black, dense smoke, straight at the rocks on which we stand!"[10] These thick drifts of black smoke from south and east Lancashire crossed the Pennine moorlands and then mingled with the smokes of the West Riding of Yorkshire. There is a rapidly changing and close relationship between the amount of rainfall and the topography of this area. As this is a rainfall-rich area, much of the pollution was wrung out of these clouds as they ascended from the plains. A steep precipitation gradient varies from thirty-two to thirty-six inches of rain per year on the plains to sixty to seventy inches per year near the summits. The highest point of Oldham borough and the lowest are 1,250 feet apart, with corresponding differences in rainfall and temperature. The hillier areas of Oldham receive from 46.9 (Brushes Clough) to 57.4 inches of rain annually (Greenfield). Not far from Oldham, on Rishworth and Rippondon Moors, over one hundred inches of rain can fall in a year.[11]

In addition to rain, fog or low cloud droplets also contained high concentrations of pollution, and when blown by the wind over hills and mountains, this pollution was deposited on the soils and vegetation. Even in the eighteenth century, one stood a good chance of being soaked in a soot-laden shower or engulfed by an "obnoxious mist." As early as 1739 there were complaints in this area about the stifling "smoke-pall." Streets were coated with soot and clothes were constantly dirtied. At the dawn of the nineteenth century these conditions worsened, and the growing Manchester conurbation sent tons of its soot and grime up and over the Pennines. This soot precipitated out in greater quantities as it increased in altitude, with Oldham and Manchester's other satellite towns adding to the burden.[12]

With increasing industrialization, and before the air pollution control laws of the 1950s, the number of clear days per year was diminished as the urban area spread over the countryside. In early-nineteenth-century Manchester the duration of sunshine in winter months was reduced to less than half that of the rural areas. The difference between central Manchester and the Cheshire fringe of development was three hundred hours per year of sunshine. It was even worse as one ascended the Pennines. The deepest town- and smoke-choked valleys of the moors served as natural smog traps. On the relatively rare clear nights, cold air would pour into these cloughs and trap smoke. In mid-winter there was often no sign of dawn, and sometimes even the noonday sun was obscured. In Oldham, reckoned as one of the least sunny places in England, the addition of local coal smoke and that of other towns could make for very long dark periods. A 1914 investigation of polluted rainwater in several towns and cities showed that air pollution in Oldham was more severe than in Manchester, and of all the towns tested Oldham came in dead last (twenty-nine metric tons of soot, tar, and dust per square kilometer for the month of October). Oldham was more polluted than such major cities as Birmingham (twenty-three metric tons), Sheffield (twenty-two), Manchester (twenty), and even London (twenty-two).[13]

Acidity through Mine Drainage and Run-Off

Obviously, the smoke pollution burden in this area was immense. However, as a key coal producer for the regional markets in the nineteenth century, Oldham was not only affected by the burning of coal; it was also affected by coal production and associated acidic run-off. In the early coal mines a persistent problem was drainage. The farther down a mine shaft went, the more seepage it experienced. In the hilly areas of Oldham, laterally cut adits and soughs were commonly used to drain shallow mines through gravity. Rarely more than four feet high or wide, these outlets required a nearby area that was naturally drained and lower than the pit sump. As these sites were quickly exhausted and the demand for coal increased, mine owners resorted to various types of water pumps. Initially, horse-powered pumps were used, but any mine below ninety to one hundred feet was too deep for these pumps to work. After 1712 the Newcomen steam engine began to be used. On the average, the Newcomen engines consumed twenty-five pounds of coal per horsepower per hour. It has been estimated that one engine consumed thirty tons of coal a year. The disadvantages of the enormous appetite of this machine were offset by its use at the pit-head, which eliminated transportation costs, and the drainage ability it afforded led to deeper and more productive mines. Though producing an enormous amount of smoke and soot, these engines only worked well on anthracite coal, which burned cleaner, was less sulfuric, and clogged the pumping mechanism more slowly than bituminous coal.[14] This technology was clumsy but cheap (at the pit-head) and effective. Before the expiration of Newcomen's patent in 1733, only one of these engines was in use in Lancashire. Later it was more widely adopted, and the switch to the more efficient, and more complicated, Boulton-Watt engine was resisted by the mine owners.[15]

In 1776 the first Boulton-Watt steam engine was used for mine drainage. By this time, twenty Newcomen engines were in operation in Lancashire. The Boulton-Watt engines used coal at little more than half the Newcomen rate, and an additional advantage was the ability to use the cheaper and more sulfuric bituminous coal. This coal was plentiful in southeast Lancashire and was not as coveted for home heating. Though the Boulton-Watt engine was more efficient in its use of coal, use of bituminous coal led to greater acidity and a more noisome odor. By 1800, steam engines of all kinds amounted to about 14 percent of coal consumption in this region.[16]

Widespread use of the Boulton-Watt engine, combined with the ability to burn bituminous coal, added greatly to the amount of SO_2 released into the atmosphere. But acidity was not only produced through the combustion of coal; it was also produced through the operation of draining these mines. This polluted water reached people in a direct manner, as they often tapped water from the colliery workings themselves or drank run-off deposited in local watercourses. Mines regularly flooded at the bottom of the shaft and served as plentiful and easily accessed wells.[17] A mining commission report of 1850 reported that the ordinary supply of water from springs was interfered with by mines, and the population was too large to be properly supplied with potable water unless new water works were constructed. There were also indirect impacts on human health from mine run-off and from the rain and groundwater that ran over slag heaps or through mines. In general, the extension of the coal industry caused a serious dislocation of the local water supply. Health hazards from use of this tainted water may seem obvious enough, but we now know in some detail the subtler dangers that were present.[18]

As water passed through collieries and colliery waste, its character was drastically degraded. Effects of this drainage included increased acidity, release of suspended solids (particulates), deposition of iron and iron compounds into the streams and river beds, and higher heavy metal concentrations due to heavy metal solubility in highly acidic conditions.[19] Coal itself is a discolorant, and its phenolic content can be very damaging. Phenols are corrosive crystalline acidic compounds that are considered carcinogenic. In Newcastle, which had a much older and more extensive mining industry, it was reported in 1620 that the meadowlands were at times so degraded by colliery-tainted water that "there groweth no grass thereon," and elsewhere animals refused to drink the filthy water or to eat the grass tainted by it.[20] Suspended solids also interfere with natural self-purification in streams and rivers by diminishing light penetration by up to 50 percent, which decreases photosynthetic activity. They negatively impact on fisheries through the silting over of food organisms and the loss of plant life associated with the lack of a light source. Many of these solids are also abrasive, and just their presence can damage fish and plants.[21]

Even more damaging to aquatic life is the highly acidic nature of this run-off. Fish populations are severely reduced or are eliminated altogether from freshwater habitats when the pH falls below 4.8. This damage is primarily due to reproductive failure resulting from high egg mortality and the death of the more sensitive young fish. With a sudden inflow of low pH water, either through the introduction of a new drainage adit or from substantial run-off after a storm, large numbers of mature fish can also be killed.[22] Some of the first casualties of high acidity are the insect species that break down organic matter, such as leaves or dead plants that fall into or grow in streams. The loss of these invertebrates often results in an increase of plant biomass, decreasing available oxygen for other life. The extraction of oxygen from the stream, combined with the effects of iron oxidation (iron is a product of acidic mine run-off), can also be fatal to stream life.[23]

For plants and animals and the people who eat them, concentrations of heavy metals in river sediments can be dangerous. These metals and metalloids occur naturally but are leached from the earth by acidic run-off in excessive amounts and are highly toxic to most plants and animals when liberated from their natural context. The surface feeders (flies and larvae) tend to have high concentrations through bioconcentration, and the animals that feed on these surface feeders will develop even higher levels through the process of bioaccumulation (concentration increasing up the trophic levels). Surveys of rivers and streams contaminated by mine run-off, when compared with unpolluted rivers, show that these rivers are seriously depleted in species variety. Generally, the more advanced the organism, the more susceptible it is to heavy metal pollution, with obvious implications for humans.[24]

The impact of these toxic metals on humans and animals in southeast Lancashire is conjecture, but their presence in the environment is a certainty. It is likely that heavy metal contamination due to high acidity did occur, but to what extent we will never know. Fish once served as a protein source and as an important supplement to the Oldhamer's grain-based diet, as evidenced by a number of entries in the weaver William Rowbottom's diary. "John Ogden of Busk commited to the New Bailey July 6th [1791] for fishing in the Grounds of Mr. Hopwood of Hopwood. . . . Thomas his son Comitted for the Same ofence . . . July 12th."[25] The Ogdens were later released from prison on condition of paying a fine of ten pounds. In 1794, "Joseph Lee of Chadderton and his two sons were apprehended for stealing fish of Sir Watts Horton when Joseph was committed to Lancaster and his 2 sons suffered to enlist."[26] These entries, and most of the others that mention fishing, are included only because the gentry prosecuted the poachers. It is likely that fishing was a more important dietary supplement than existing records show.

More serious than the consumption of heavy metals are the toxic threats to health associated with the production of polycyclic aromatic hydrocarbons (PAHs). Produced and released by coal combustion or through run-off, several PAHs are potent carcinogens and are known to cause a variety of skin tumors in cases of extensive, prolonged exposure. The most famous and one of the earliest documented instances of these effects was the discovery of scrofula (scrotum cancer) in chimney sweeps and briquette makers in the late eighteenth century. In industrialized areas, PAHs are found in air and soil and on plant surfaces, and in the moorlands they are well integrated into the peat record. PAHs also play a key role in the production of acid rain. Hydrocarbons are essential precursors to oxidants formed photochemically in the atmosphere. The oxidization rates of both SO_2 and NOx in the air are strongly dependent on the concentrations of these precursors and constitute another reason why the regulation of vehicle emissions is so critical in the production of acidity. Internal combustion engines widely distribute both NOx and hydrocarbons throughout the biosphere.[27]

PAHs taken into the body through water usually pass through the system. However, those inhaled (the major vector of PAH accumulation) and eaten accumulate in the body. An increase in PAH concentration leads to increased disease and a higher incidence of malignant tumors. Also associated with inhalation is the presence of arsenic and chromium in fly ash particles (which often contain the toxic heavy metals cadmium, cobalt, copper, mercury, and nickel) that are the result of the incomplete combustion of coal, which was common up to the mid–nineteenth century. Among nine countries studied by Michael Chadwick, the arsenic in British coal was the highest. With a mean value of 16.8 micrograms of arsenic per gram, British coal in general was far worse than the next highest country, France, at 14.5 micrograms per gram. Burning high-arsenic coal contaminates plants and soils downwind, and the danger of transfer to humans through the consumption of contaminated water and livestock is high.[28]

While PAHs represent a considerable danger to health in and of themselves, combined with sulphur dioxide (as they often were) they are much more dangerous. A highly soluble gas, sulfur dioxide dissolves rapidly into the lining of the respiratory tract during inhalation, and acute exposure to sulfur dioxide has been shown to cause bronchoconstriction and symptoms of asthma. This effect is rapid in its onset, and susceptible people, including the very old and the very young, as well as asthmatics, are hit almost immediately. During the 1952 London smog episode, SO_2 levels increased sevenfold, and the peak levels of SO_2 coincided with the highest levels of mortality. Chronic bronchitis is correlated with heavily industrialized and polluted areas and is also associated with sulfur dioxide levels. Rural areas escape it almost completely. Lung, bronchus, and stomach cancer (which is also linked to the drinking of coal-tainted water) are associated with high sulfur dioxide levels as well. Sulfur dioxide reduces the clearance of particles from the alveoli, the areas of the lungs responsible

TABLE 4.1

Region	Coal Type	% Sulfur
Lancashire	Bituminous	1.38
Nottinghamshire	Bituminous	0.45
Yorkshire	Bituminous	1.20
Durham	Bituminous	1.00
Scotland	Anthracite	0.10
S. Wales	Anthracite	0.70

for oxygenating the blood, and this accumulation of insoluble particles acts as a cofactor in bronchial carcinoma. Chronic exposure to sulfates also increases the incidence of acute respiratory infection in children, and this, in turn, leads to an increase of chronic heart and respiratory disease in adults. This has been estimated to shorten the average life span of humans by five to fifteen years.[29]

In 1851, Angus Smith estimated that in one year, two million tons of coal were consumed by Manchester and its satellites. In addition to these immense quantities, the quality of Lancashire coal contributed to the acid burden. Lancashire coal had one of the highest sulfur contents of any coal in the British Isles.[30] These high sulphur contents translated to high levels of acidity in the downwind precipitation. Using Smith's own data, pH values of Manchester's rainwater in the mid–nineteenth century were as low as 3.5, more than one hundred times more acidic than naturally occurring rainwater.[31]

Coal mining and coal combustion contaminated soils and vegetation, polluted water and adversely affected the health of humans, animals, and other organisms. The degree of damage was determined by the concentration of particles and the characteristics of the region affected. At the same time that Angus Smith was making his observations, the term *moorgrime* in the dialects of Yorkshire and eastern Lancashire, which had probably been in use for half a century, became common. This referred to the dark, oily accumulations in the wool of sheep grazing on upland pastures.[32] Due to primitive and incomplete combustion methods employed in the nineteenth and early twentieth centuries, especially in the open hearths of people's homes, it is almost certain that the damage was considerable in the upland Pennine communities. Peat profiles in the Pennines show widespread accumulation of soot and heavy metals, such as lead, within the peat formed since the early 1800s, and sediment records in the Galloway lakes of southwest Scotland have shown that acidification has been a continuous process since the mid–nineteenth century. Pre-acidification, the pH values of these lakes were constant between 5.5 and 6.1, but by the 1980s all four lakes had been acidified by 0.5 to 1.3 pH. This long history of acid deposition on these uplands has transformed them tremendously, and despite our growing and ever more complex understanding of how acid affects these systems, it may take another two hundred years of "normal" precipitation to reduce their acidity to pre-industrial levels.[33]

Acid-Induced Change in the Ecology of the High Moorlands

Where the regional urban demand justified the effort, moorland agriculture experienced quick improvement during industrialization, but elsewhere it was less cost effective and this spared those areas from the improvers. The "weeping climate" of the High Moorlands was an almost insuperable obstacle to arable farming and grain production. Slopes that were not too steep for the plow were usually too wet. At lower altitudes the agriculture nearer the towns was seriously damaged by the accumulation of pit waste from the coal mines and by mine subsidence. These moors were mainly used for grazing, but other resources were exploited. Peat was dug for fuel; bracken was cut for the bedding of livestock, for floor covering, and for thatch; and heather and furze were also gathered for fuel. Naturally occurring soil acidity was also a serious obstacle to the agricultural improvers. The moorland's high precipitation resulted in the rapid loss of lime, and the poor drainage encouraged the formation of acid peat. Most of the soils in these areas were base-poor long before the widespread combustion of coal. On the highest uplands, some of the soils were shallow and stony, and others were immature *rankers,* a thin layer of acid organic matter overlying base-poor rock. As was the case for the growth of the coal industry, communications were key to what little agriculture existed on the moorlands. They not only encouraged regional specialization, but they also permitted intensification by allowing the cheap transportation of sewage, marl, and lime to enhance soil fertility.[34]

However, rain was an important part of life in the Pennines, and water has been one of its most important resources for almost two hundred years. The trans-Pennine canals were a key component of the early industrialization of this region, and without a ready supply of water they would not have been possible. Of the fifty to sixty inches a year that fall on Oldham, as much as 60 percent becomes run-off due to the steep slopes, impermeable rocks, and lack of trees. At times this could lead to water shortages in an area that was generally rainfall rich. By the time the coal and cotton industries breathed their last gasp, the uplands of the Lancashire Pennines were the most fully exploited hydrological area in England. Over 21 percent of the available rainfall was gathered in upland reservoirs—which slowly released the catchment's water. Just north and east of the town center, the Strinesdale reservoirs have served Oldham for over 150 years. The upper reservoir was completed in 1832 and was visible on the 1842 Ordinance Survey; the lower one was completed eighteen years later. The open Pennine foothills and large areas of grassland form the catchment of these reservoirs, through which the river Medlock once flowed.[35]

The clouds generated over this area by the rise in altitude contain a higher concentration of ions, as they are formed in the boundary layer where the pollution is emitted. These low, hill-topping, and altitude-dependent clouds are known as orographic clouds. In the Pennines, precipitation from higher "seeder" clouds washes out the lower orographic "feeder" clouds, increasing both the rainfall amount and the concentrations of ions reaching the ground. This process is known as seeder-feeder enhancement of rainfall, and it has played a key role in the acidification of the moors.[36]

By itself, this seeder-feeder process would lead to the deposition of large amounts of acidity in the uplands, but this was further enhanced in the nineteenth century by the quality of the local coal. The sulfur dioxide in these emissions is transformed to sulfuric acid when oxidized (picking up an oxygen molecule) in polluted fog droplets in the orographic clouds or absorbed from the surface of other materials. The high humidity of the Oldham area greatly facilitated this process.[37] Due to widespread urbanization and the long history of this kind of atmospheric pollution, little of the pre-industrial natural vegetation in southeast Lancashire now survives. In the 1870s, R. A. Smith noted that "there is no hope for vegetation in a climate such as we have in the northern parts of the country."[38] There are remnants that have been protected from human activity, and others that were difficult to exploit economically, but even in these areas profound changes have occurred.

As the High Moorlands is largely a treeless zone, the main impacts of acidity are evident in the loss of certain mosses and of most lichens. Lichens are an excellent biological indicator of atmospheric pollution, and specifically of atmospheric SO_2. Shrubby lichens are found only where SO_2 levels are very low, and leafy species can withstand somewhat higher levels.[39] In the 1850s, L. H. Grindon noted that the quantity of lichens was "much lessened of late years through the cutting down of old woods and the influx of factory smoke."[40] Over the last two hundred years there has been a dramatic change in the lichen flora of the Pennines, and even with smoke reduction the losses continued due to acid precipitation. The lichen *Lobaria scrobiculata* was completely absent from the Pennines in surveys after 1960, but it was well documented in earlier records. While this species and others have successfully recolonized some urban areas over the last fifty years, in more remote upland areas lichens continue to lose ground. More important than lichens in the ecology of this area is the impact of acid rain on mosses.[41]

In the southern Pennines, particularly in the blanket bogs, there has been a large and widespread vegetation change in the last two hundred years. The sulfur dioxide in the rain and run-off of the southern Pennines has resulted in the almost complete disappearance of blanket bogs, due to the reduction in growth of six separate sphagnum species. Peat is formed when partly decomposed plant remains accumulate over a minerally deficient rock or soil base and this combination is waterlogged by persistent rainfall. These conditions are fairly uniform on the summit plateau. The subsequent low soil temperatures and the lack of oxygen preclude strong bacterial activity. The result of this is an over-lapping and acidic layer of organic matter that is unmixed with its base matter. Peat mosses are found generally above twelve hundred feet but in some places extend down to one thousand feet or even lower. In this part of the Pennines, the peat is largely composed of sphagnum remains that have been accumulating since about 5000 B.C.E.

In much of this area, the effects of acid deposition are severer due to the higher amount of rainfall and the low buffering capacity of the soil. By the early twentieth century, a number of associated peat-loving species in the Peak District had disappeared: bog myrtle (*Myrica gale*), sundew (*Drosera intermedia*), white beak sedge (*Rhyncospora alba*), and lesser twayblade (*Listera cordata*). Others were observed to have diminished populations, such as bog rosemary (*Andromeda polifolia*) and even one of the most well known moorland plants, heather (*Calluna vulgaris*). Also, the grasslands that are so prevalent on the upper Pennine moors not only have been made aesthetically less pleasing but ecologically have been severely impaired and simplified due to increased acidity.[42] Chlorophyll in the grass is reduced, and this leaves these ecosystems extremely susceptible to disturbances such as fire, drought, or over-grazing.[43] This change is chronicled in the peat and is clearly correlated with the appearance of soot in the peat profile. The long-term selective pressures in this area have led to the dominance of only a few acid-resistant species: the sphagnum species *recurvum,* in the peaty areas, and cotton grass (*Eeriophorum angustifolium*). Cotton grasses are now the exclusive dominants over many thousands of hectares.[44]

It might be assumed that the blanket peats, already naturally acidic, would be well adapted to acid precipitation, but there is a fundamentally different nature to this acidity. The sphagnum species of the high moorland has evolved with acidity in the groundwater and in soils, but not with such high levels in precipitation. Bryophytes (non-flowering plants comprising mosses, liverworts, and hornworts) are most at risk from atmospheric pollutants, as they are adapted to draw their water from rain, clouds, and fog due to the acidity in the soils and water. In this very wet and rain-rich area, these plants have evolved as if it were water-poor. For this reason, they tend to cluster in areas of high precipitation, and in the case of southeast Lancashire, this puts them at risk. The increased acidity of their water supply is not *per se* what harms these mosses; it is the inhibition of photosynthesis caused by the SO_2. In addition, smoke pollution was at its worst in the winter, and this corresponded with many of the mosses' growing seasons. Over two hundred years, a tolerance for SO_2 was selected for in these Pennine populations, and experiments have shown that sphagnum from unpolluted moors will be killed by concentrations of bisulphate ions, whereas in the same concentrations sphagnum from the south Pennines will survive and even grow a little. These species are at a competitive disadvantage in cleaner air, and the evolution of acid tolerance may have led to a loss of other favorable genetic traits.[45]

Progress and Retrogression

A growing recognition of the dangers of dry deposition to nearby areas, and a belief that a policy of "dilute and disperse" would end this problem, led to even greater international damage and the resultant recognition of the widespread problems of acid deposition. As a solution to the problem of acid deposition, tall stacks were advocated by a number of pollution experts in the 1950s and 1960s.[46] Smoke pollution could be controlled, but it was deemed economically impracticable to remove sulphur dioxide from emissions. Since air pollution was conceived of as a local problem, the Clean Air Act of 1968 adopted the use of tall chimneys for industries burning coal and liquid or gaseous fuels. Tall stacks were much cheaper, and the higher the chimney (some over one hundred meters tall), the better the dispersal of the air pollution. This dramatically reduced ground-level concentrations locally but increased long-range transport of SO_2 by approximately 10 to 15 percent (increasing distance of deposition by about fifty kilometers). This may not seem like a large difference, but it is a significant enhancement of the abilities of these gases to travel long distances, which they already do quite well. Currently, tall stacks contribute 80 percent of the United Kingdom's total emissions. Perhaps without the development of tall stacks, our present-day understanding of acid precipitation would be much less, as much of the groundbreaking work was done where these emissions were deposited: in Scandinavia.[47]

Nationally, as industrial coal burning has almost ceased and domestic combustion has been controlled, acid rain air pollution is no longer the serious problem it once was in this region. This has allowed acid-sensitive species such as heather to return to the higher moors, particularly in better-drained areas along railway lines and on reclaimed areas such as Oldham Edge. However, a typical problem in pollution control is that the regulation of one vector often leads to the substitution of another. The adoption of tall stacks may have stemmed the problem of local dry deposition, but it led to even greater acid deposition in the uplands and greatly increased the international exportation of acid wastes. By 1979, the United Kingdom was still the single greatest emitter of SO_2 in Europe after the former Soviet Union.[48] In the case of the Medlock River in Oldham, the introduction of smokeless zones since the 1950s hurt the river, as materials such as unwanted food and sanitary towels, which were often burned in domestic fireplaces, were flushed down toilets and into the sewage system (which was antiquated and could not handle a lot of solid waste). When this system became blocked, as was often the case in heavy rains, the backup poured into the river through the 150 storm overflows in the valley.[49]

Some damaged freshwater lakes and streams are showing signs of recovery due to a 50 percent cut in sulphur dioxide emissions, but now nitrogen oxides and ammonia are the main air pollutants and causes of acid deposition. The increasing popularity of the car in the United Kingdom makes this a serious and growing problem. Just as the step-by-step advances in emission controls of the late nineteenth and early twentieth centuries were offset by an even greater growth in energy consumption and industry, so the current developments are being partially offset by the increases in car ownership per capita and the sprawl of auto-dependent development. Car ownership has risen steadily over the last thirty years, with the 1980s recording the steepest increase. The proportion of households with access to a car rose from 52 percent in 1972 to 59 percent in 1981, rising to 68 percent in 1991, and then to 73 percent in 2000. The proportion of households with two or more cars tripled, from 9 percent in 1972 to 28 percent in 2000. In recent years there has also been an increase in three-car households, the proportion rising from 4 percent in 1996 to 6 percent in 2000. Trends in trip lengths in the United Kingdom, Denmark, and Belgium show how urban sprawl has contributed to vehicle emissions in recent decades, as people are driving farther and spending more time in stop-and-go traffic.[50]

Vehicles can contribute to acid rain in two ways. First, well over one-third of NOx emissions in Britain are from their exhaust, which is then oxidized in the atmosphere to NO_2 and nitric acid. These are then efficiently scavenged in rain systems and present in collected precipitation. Second, vehicles contribute both oxides of nitrogen and hydrocarbons to the ambient air on a widely distributed basis, and the oxidation rates of both NO and SO_2 are strongly dependent on the concentrations of hydrocarbons. In addition to the effects caused by the deposition of nitric acid, nitrates have been shown to reduce growth in south Pennine plant communities.[51] In the more recent past (1995 to 1997), areas that exceeded the critical load of acidity extended to 71 percent of the sensitive ecosystems in the United Kingdom. This is projected to decline to 41 percent by 2010, but the deposition of nitrogen is a major part of this exceedance and will become the dominant component by that same date.[52]

Conclusion

Acidity in the form of wet and dry deposition and drainage and run-off from mines has had an enormous impact on freshwater ecosystems and on the High Moorlands over the last two centuries. Despite the decline in industrial activity and our increased understanding of the sources and consequences of increased acidity, recovery has been uneven. Changes in technology have merely shifted the pollution burden elsewhere, and the growing use of the automobile is resulting in the substitution of nitric acids for sulphuric acids. Common to both the past and the present is the combination of acid-forming compounds with hydrocarbons, and in spite of national and international regulation of acid-forming emissions, the ecology of the High Moorlands zone will be slow to recover as precipitation continues to be acidic.

Initially red-flagged in Scandinavia, in the 1950s, 1960s, and 1970s acid rain was increasingly recognized as having a negative effect on the ecology of lakes and forests and their plant and animal communities. By 1972, acidity was acknowledged as an international and global issue at the UN Conference on the Human Environment in Stockholm. International and national political pressure eventually led to the United Kingdom's adoption of programs to reduce long-range air pollution, and by extension acid rain. In 1979 the Convention on Long-Range Transboundary Air Pollution was agreed to by the world's leading economic nations.[53] Despite the retrenchment of the Thatcher administration in the 1980s (in conjunction with the Reagan administration in the United States), the combination of public pressure and overwhelming scientific evidence of damage caused by acid rain led to further regulation and legislation. In 1999 the United Kingdom signed the Gothenburg protocol ("Protocol to Abate Acidification, Eutrophication and Ground-Level Ozone"), agreeing to annual emission ceilings of sulphur dioxide, nitrogen oxides, ammonia, and volatile organic compounds to be achieved by 2010. Another important development was the mandating in 1993 of catalytic converters in all vehicles sold in the United Kingdom, predating the Gothenburg protocol's call for reductions in SO_2 and NO emissions from large power stations and vehicle emissions.

The debate over acid rain in the 1970s and 1980s is very similar to the present debate over another invisible by-product of fossil fuel combustion: carbon dioxide (CO_2). With respect to both of these debates, the precautionary principle can serve as a guide. If the scientific evidence is incomplete, one should not do anything to make the situation worse. The above actions, taken on the basis of compelling but incomplete scientific evidence, have had a major impact on acid rain. The National Expert Group on Transboundary Air Pollution (NEGTAP) reported a 50 percent cut in emissions over the past twelve years (from 1979 to 2001). For the first time, there were signs that some freshwater ecosystems were slowly recovering, and there was evidence of an increasing diversity of plant life in areas across the United Kingdom. Deposition of non-sea-salt sulphur in the United Kingdom declined by 52 percent between 1986 and 1997, during which emissions declined by 57 percent. Between 1986 and 1997, the wet deposition of sulphur declined by 42 percent, while dry deposition declined by 62 percent. There has been a substantial decrease (between 30 and 50 percent) in rainfall acidity recorded in the United Kingdom between 1986 and 1997, but the potential acidification from nitrogen deposition now substantially exceeds that of sulphur.[54]

Our understanding of the impacts of SO_2 emissions and acid precipitation has been greatly furthered by work done in Lancashire. By 1914, the important first step of a systematic placement of deposition gauges was accomplished in a number of sites in the Manchester and Sheffield areas. The Greater Manchester Acid Deposition Survey (GMADS) in the northwest of England has provided the only long-term continuous monitoring of acid deposition in the United Kingdom. The area covered is approximately 2,000 km^2 and supports a population in excess of 2.8 million.[55]

Despite the enormous advances in our knowledge and the substantial cuts in emissions, recovery in the upland acid sink has been uneven at best. The term *non-linearity* has been used to illustrate the fact that as emissions decline, the rates of reductions in concentrations and deposition vary in time and place. In some areas, the 50 percent reduction in emissions has meant a 70 percent reduction in deposition (generally in the east), and in others only 30 percent (generally in the west). Clearly, the recovery process is not uniform, and in some places there is no recovery. The chemical and biological recovery of these damaged systems will happen very slowly, if at all.[56]

The invisible gases associated with fossil fuel combustion are now receiving the attention they merit. Despite our considerable knowledge about the causes and effects of acid deposition, the transformations wrought by over two hundred years of high acidity may require another two hundred years of relatively normal acidity to restore the diversity and resiliency of the pre-industrial ecology. This is why global climate change is often referred to as a "supertanker" issue. Like a supertanker, the change in direction was initiated long before we clearly saw where we were going, and now that we are pointed in this direction, it will be slow to stop, and slow to return to our earlier course.

NOTES

1. Tom Williamson, *The Transformation of Rural England: Farming and the Landscape 1700–1870* (Exeter: University of Exeter Press, 2002), 116; David Hey,

"Moorlands," in Joan Thirsk, ed., *The English Rural Landscape* (Oxford: Oxford University Press, 2000), 189.

2. Oldham Local Studies Center (OLSC), Fred J. Stubbs, *The Natural History of Moorlands,* Nature Study, 1.

3. As Joel Tarr points out in *The Search for the Ultimate Sink—Urban Pollution in Historical Perspective* (Akron: Akron University Press, 1996), the progress in one area (the moorlands and Britain generally) was matched by retrogression in another (Scandinavia).

4. For a less localized short survey of acid rain and its effects, see Peter Brimblecombe, "Acid Drops," *New Scientist,* Inside Science, 150, May 18, 2002.

5. National Environmental Group on Transboundary Air Pollution (NEGTAP), available: http://www.nbu.ac.uk/negtap/docs/finalrep_web/NEGTAP_C3ConcDep.pdf; G. L. A. Fry and A. S. Cooke, *Acid Deposition and Its Implications for Nature Conservation in Britain* (Peterborough [U.K.]: Joint Nature Conservation Committee, 1984), 1, 2.

6. Harold Platt, "'The Invisible Evil': Noxious Vapour and Public Health in Manchester during the Age of Industry," chapter 2 in this volume; The Watt Committee on Energy, *Acid Rain,* report #14 (Aug. 1984), v; Fry and Cooke, 1.

7. Robert Angus Smith, "On the Air and Rain of Manchester," *Literary and Philosophical Society of Manchester, Memoirs,* 2d series, 10 (1852), 207–217; Robert Angus Smith, *Air and Rain* (London: Longmans, Green and Co., 1872), 227.

8. Peter Brimblecombe, "London Air Pollution," *Atmospheric Environment* 11 (1977), 1158.

9. Robert Challinor, *The Lancashire and Cheshire Miners* (Newcastle: Frank Graham, 1972), 242.

10. C. E. Moss, "Changes in the Halifax Flora during the Last Century and a Quarter," *The Naturalist* 26 (1901), 99–107.

11. T. W. Freeman, H. B. Rodgers, and R. H. Kinvig, *Lancashire, Cheshire, and the Isle of Man* (London: Thomas Nelson, 1966), 22–23; Leonard Kidd, *Oldham's Natural History* (Oldham: Oldham Libraries, Art Galleries and Museums, 1977), 8.

12. Stephen Mosley explores this in great detail in *The Chimney of the World: A History of Smoke Pollution in Victorian and Edwardian Manchester* (Cambridge: White Horse Press, 2001); See also Watt Committee on Energy, 3–4; Alfred Wadsworth and Julia De Lacy Mann, *The Cotton Trade and Industrial Lancashire: 1600–1780* (Manchester: Manchester University Press, 1965), 241.

13. Kidd, 8; H. H. Lamb, *Climate, History, and the Modern World* (London: Methuen and Co., 1982), 333; Mosley, 33, 65. One indicator of a lack of sunlight is the incidence of rickets. Rickets is a deficiency disease that affects the young during the period of skeletal growth, is characterized by soft and deformed bones, and is caused by failure to assimilate and use calcium and phosphorus due to inadequate sunlight or vitamin D. A 1902 survey of Leeds, which is located on the lee-

ward side of the Pennines and receives less rain and more sun than Oldham, found that one-half of the children in the poorer districts were suffering from rickets. It is probable that rickets was partly attributable to coal combustion, in combination with already dark and dank weather conditions in Lancashire. G. M. Howe, *Man, Environment and Disease in Britain* (New York: Barnes and Noble Books, 1972), 57; Freeman, Rodgers, and Kinvig, 22.

14. Michael W. Flinn, *The History of the British Coal Industry,* vol. 2 (Oxford: Clarendon Press, 1984), 247; Peter Brimblecombe, *The Big Smoke* (London: Methuen, 1987), 98.

15. Flinn, 114.

16. Ibid., 247.

17. Kidd, 8; John Benson, *British Coalminers in the Nineteenth Century* (New York: Holmes and Meier, 1980), 98. In the Orrell coalfield of southwest Lancashire, approximately 1,250 tons of water seeped through each acre of land each year. With the prodigious rainfall of the Oldham area (in places, twice as much as the Orrell field), it would not be an exaggeration to expect even greater seepage. Flinn, 109.

18. Benson, 98.

19. Roger Gemmell, *Colonization of an Industrial Wasteland* (London: Edward Arnold, 1977), 6; C. G. Down, *Environmental Impact of Mining* (New York: John Wiley and Sons, 1977), 112.

20. Quoted in David Levine and Keith Wrightson, *The Making of an Industrial Society: Whickham, 1560–1765* (Oxford: Clarendon Press, 1991), 115. From Public Record Office, Durham, 7/19, pt. I.

21. Down, 109.

22. Michael Chadwick, *Environmental Impacts of Coal Mining and Utilization* (Oxford: Pergamon Press, 1987), 308.

23. David Shriner, ed., *Atmospheric Sulfur Deposition* (Ann Arbor: Butterworth Group, 1980), 449.

24. K. Martyn, *Mining and the Freshwater Environment* (London: Elsevier Applied Science, 1988), 56; Down, 115.

25. Manchester Central Reference Library (MCRL), *Annals . . . Rowbottom,* vol. 1 (1791), 10.

26. MCRL, *Annals . . . Rowbottom,* vol. 2 (1794), 3.

27. Watt Committee on Energy, 6.

28. Chadwick, 235, 239, 177, 193.

29. Shriner, 70, 91; Peter Brimblecombe, "Acid Drops," *New Scientist,* Inside Science, May 18, 2002, 150; Howe, 232; Chadwick, 247.

30. Smith, *Air and Rain,* 228; Brimblecombe, *Big Smoke,* 66.

31. Mosley, 34.

32. Peter Brimblecombe, "Nineteenth Century Black Scottish Showers," *Atmospheric Environment* 20 (1986), 1057.

33. Watt Committee on Energy, 16, 37; Fry, 9.

34. The need for lime on these acidic soils led to the development of a large-scale lime industry. In the late eighteenth and early nineteenth centuries, large industrial complexes were developed to produce lime for agriculture and for the building industry. The large kilns used in the production of lime consumed a considerable amount of fuel, and as coal production expanded and costs dropped, this industry experienced a major boost. Improvements in the transportation network—better roads, canals, and eventually the development of railroads—lowered costs substantially. This allowed ever larger quantities of lime to be applied to offset the natural and human-induced acidity, while simultaneously adding to the already considerable amount of SO_2 in the upland precipitation. Williamson, 119, 121, 124–125; Freeman, Rodgers, and Kinvig, 26, 103, 105, 109.

35. Freeman, Rodgers, and Kinvig, 184.

36. D. Fowler, I. D. Leith, J. Binnie, A. Crossley, D. W. F. Inglis, T. W. Choularton, M. Gay, J. W. S. Longhurst, and D. E. Conland, "The Influence of Altitude on Rainfall Composition at Great Dun Fell," *Atmospheric Environment* 22 (1988), 1355–1362; T. W. Choularton, M. J. Gay, A. Jones, D. Fowler, J. N. Cape, and I. D. Leith, "The Influence of Altitude on Wet Deposition," *Atmospheric Environment* 22 (1988), 1363–1371; D. W. F. Inglis, T. W. Choularton, A. J. Wicks, D. Fowler, I. D. Leith, B. Werkman, and J. Binnie, "Orographic Enhancement of Wet Deposition in the United Kingdom: Case Studies and Modeling," *Water Air and Soil Pollution* 85 (1995), 2119–2124; Dore et al., "An Improved Wet Deposition Map of the United Kingdom Incorporating the Seeder-Feeder Effect over Mountainous Terrain," *Atmospheric Environment* 26A (1992), 1375–1381.

37. Howe, 34.

38. Smith, *Air and Rain,* quoted in J. A. Lee, M. C. Press, C. Studholme, and S. J. Woodin, "Effects of Acidic Deposition on Wetlands," in M. Ashmore, N. Bell, and C. Garretty, eds., *Acid Rain and Britain's Natural Ecosystems* (London, 1988), 29.

39. Watt Committee on Energy, 28–29.

40. L. H. Grindon, *The Manchester Flora* (London, 1859), quoted in J. H. Looney, and P. W. James, "Effects on Lichens," in Ashmore, Bell, and Garretty, 14.

41. Looney and James, 16.

42. M. Press, P. Ferguson, and J. Lee, "Two Hundred Years of Acid Rain," *The Naturalist* 108 (1983), 125–129.

43. OLSC Stubbs, 2; Chadwick, 302; Shriner, 428.

44. Watt Committee on Energy, 17.

45. Lee, Press, Studholme, and Woodin, "Effects of Acidic Deposition on Wetlands," in Ashmore, Bell, and Garretty, 28–29, 32.

46. Tarr, 18.

47. Watt Committee on Energy, 12; NEGTAP, "Transboundary Air Pollution: Acidification, Eurtrophication and Ground-Level Ozone in the UK," Dec. 10, 2001,

Concentrations and Deposition of Sulphur, Nitrogen, Ozone and Acidity in the UK.

48. Fry, 3.

49. Geoffrey H. Peake, "Recreation and Environment in the Medlock Valley: The Role and Interaction of Statutory and Voluntary Bodies" (diss. for Manchester Polytechnic Certificate in Environmental Studies, June 1983), 42.

50. NEGTAP; Platt; Department of the Environment, Transport and the Regions (United Kingdom), "National Statistics: Living in Britain," available: http://www.statistics.gov.uk/lib/Section69.html.

51. Watt Committee on Energy, 6; Lee et al., 33.

52. NEGTAP, Recovery.

53. Brimblecombe, "Acid Drops."

54. NEGTAP, Recovery.

55. Acid Rain Information Centre (ARIC), Manchester Metropolitan University, available: http://www.ace.mmu.ac.uk/Resources/Fact_Sheets/Key_Stage_4/Air_Pollution/contents.html.

56. NEGTAP, Concentrations and Deposition of Sulphur, Nitrogen, Ozone and Acidity in the UK.

5

The "Smoky City" between the Wars

Angela Gugliotta

Stories of Pittsburgh from the First to the Second World War are self-conscious narratives of transformation.[1] Residents, observers, and critics of the city sifted through competing claims of change accomplished, change expected, and change endured. What kind of change this was to be, which aspects of the city's identity were to be treated as foundational and which as alterable, and who would benefit from proposed changes were subjects of local conflict. Smoke, through assertions of its reduction, persistence, or painful absence, was also the subject of transformation stories. Questions about civic identity in this time of change were often worked out through consideration of the relationship of smoke to industries, worker populations, natural features, and technologies that had long defined the city. This period has been characterized as Pittsburgh's smoky Dark Age before its subsequent Renaissance. Yet these years witnessed the remaking of both the science of smoke/air pollution and the relation of environment and industry to important aspects of urban identity.

Between the 1910s and the 1940s, talk about smoke in Pittsburgh alternated between claims of success and calls for control.[2] On the eve of the First World War, many of Pittsburgh's heavy industries had already improved combustion technologies in ways that reduced smoke. Local mills, for their own reasons, had converted from heavily polluting beehive coke ovens to waste-reclaiming by-product coke ovens, and the largest mills saved fuel using automatic stokers. Pittsburgh's smoke ordinance was expanded in 1917 to include the city's mills only in the context of such accomplished facts.[3] During World War I, transportation difficulties and coal strikes turned the hopes of the federal government, industries, and cultural critics toward other fuels and toward greater efficiency in coal use.[4]

The decline of coal shifted the foundations of the city built upon it. By the 1920s, younger steel cities, closer to iron mines and reservoirs of cheap labor, had already begun to eclipse Pittsburgh, just as other fuels threatened coal. Local and national writers reflected on these threats through examination of the contradictory meanings of nature to the city. In the 1924 short story "How Pittsburgh Returned to the Jungle," written by Carnegie Tech professor Haniel Long and published in *The Nation,* industry and pollution are driven from the city by a conspiracy to over-grow it with lush vegetation. The mere presence of the flowers is enough to drive out heavy industry already beset by competition from "Gary, Pueblo and Birmingham," "young Titans who proved too strong for their giant father." The story provides a caricature of the motives for environmental change in Pittsburgh as crassly economic, but it is also a testament to the power of nature in shaping human affairs. Just as coal and water had made the industrial city what it was, plant life, initially deployed in service of capitalist gain but soon spreading under its own natural power, could de-industrialize it.[5] Another story by a Pittsburgher, from the same year, *The Pittsburgh Owl,* moved beyond the simple opposition of nature and industry. The story's protagonist works to convince her husband that the hooting sound she hears some mornings is an owl and not a truck's horn—that wild nature can live in the midst of a city of heavy industry. *The Pittsburgh Owl* endorsed the pervasive view of Pittsburgh in which the mixing of nature and technology gives the city its unique strength and staying power.[6]

As Pittsburgh struggled with threats to its industries built on local natural abundance, and writers claimed contradictory relations between nature and the city's decline, those interested in smoke abatement cast historical discontinuity in a positive light. They claimed that the city had already been remade through their own efforts. In 1924, Pittsburgh's smoke inspector and Mellon Institute of Industrial Research air pollution investigator Herbert Meller claimed that his Bureau of Smoke Regulation had reduced smoke by 80 percent since 1914. Pittsburgh newspapers reiterated Meller's claim of smoky-day reduction, but more often they emphasized that air quality in other cities was just as bad as in Pittsburgh.[7] Claims to success found an interested audience. In the 1920s, it was less politically contentious to oppose smoke than it had been at any previous time in Pittsburgh history. To oppose smoke was no longer to oppose industry, since visible smoke from industry was regulated by the 1917 ordinance, and many industries had installed economically attractive new technologies that also abated smoke. The mills in these years were portrayed as setting a good example for domestic consumers—at least in terms of the reduction of visible smoke.[8]

Claims of success continued through the 1920s in the face of ambiguous scientific results from the Mellon Institute. In 1923–24, the institute published results of its second soot-fall study. Celebrated by institute director Edward Weidlein as evidence of the efficacy of Mellon's scientific leadership in smoke abatement, the study reported a significant decrease in tar deposited.[9] The total weight of particulates deposited, however, exceeded the level identified in the 1912–13 soot-fall study. Tar was quickly interpreted as the single component representing visible smoke. The reduction in tar was taken to show that the ordinance had worked. Yet the increase in total solids and the persistence of complaints during the ten-year period between the soot-fall studies pointed to a continuing problem.[10] The ambiguous results of the 1923–24 study proved to be a flexible tool in the hands of both those who wanted to celebrate Pittsburgh's success in smoke abatement and those who were troubled by its persistent failures.[11]

Soot-fall studies had long been the bulwark of smoke research at the Mellon Institute. After the 1923–24 study, Mellon researchers began both to examine critically the method of soot-fall study and to look beyond it. They complained of the discrepancy between pollution regulated and pollution measured: while soot-fall studies looked at all solid deposits, smoke ordinances regulated only dense smoke.[12] After the 1923–24 study, Mellon investigators began to turn their attention toward the broader problem of air pollution—particulate and gaseous, visible and invisible. Researchers at Mellon took up the task of correlating various measures of air pollution but were, in reality, operationally defining air pollution itself. They clearly agreed that air pollution was not simply tar. Was air pollution what was measured in total soot-fall? No, soot-fall measured both not enough and too much. While the 1912–13 study took total soot-fall as the sole measure of smoke, it had been clear from the earliest Mellon studies that gases, along with particulates, were responsible for much of the damage attributed to smoke. Soot-fall did not even catch all particulates. It primarily caught heavy particles that fell close to the source. These were neither those most likely to cause fog nor those that—as new evidence from occupational medicine suggested—were most likely to injure human health. In addition, dust from many non-combustion sources made its way into soot-fall collection containers. The degree to which the atmosphere should or should not be particulate-free became the central conceptual issue for Mellon investigators through the 1930s.

Attempts to address this issue became an exercise in determining the limits of pollution regulation. Beginning in April 1931, Meller promoted the notion of "hygienically pure air"[13]—air as pure as the food and water supplies regulated and controlled by Progressive legislation and public health infrastructure. To be hygienically pure, air needed to be pure enough to be healthful but not absolutely particulate-free.[14] Meller's 1930s research sought to base pollution regulation on health consequences and focused on the idea of maximum exposure standards as developed in industrial hygiene.[15] Throughout the 1930s, Meller tried to mobilize medical resources for the setting of these standards.[16] Unfortunately, the continuing depression interrupted the funding necessary for technologically sophisticated research, on which the correlation of measurement techniques and the setting of health standards depended.

To fill gaps in Mellon funding, Meller turned to industry. Yet, with industry underwriting, experimentation and observation were replaced with cheaper public relations work or with intermittently funded corporate projects that sometimes weakened rather than strengthened the case for pollution control. Meller and L. B. Sisson, a public relations specialist brought to Mellon Institute by the Anthracite Institute, were charged with popularizing smoke abatement so that cities "in anthracite territory" would be more likely to adopt stricter smoke regulations, favoring anthracite, when the depression was over. In December 1933, Meller and Sisson described their mission to the officials of the Anthracite Institute. It was to "re-lay scientific foundations for the air pollution campaign" and, in so doing, to provide anthracite with an unprecedented opportunity to gain market share. Sisson proclaimed: "Here is anthracite's epochal chance."[17]

Under the sponsorship of the Anthracite Institute, public relations outstripped research at Mellon. At the same time, Mellon researchers turned to the intensified work in occupational health and safety conducted under the auspices of the U.S. Bureau of Mines in the 1930s for knowledge about air quality standards. In 1935 the Air Hygiene Foundation was established, with corporate funding, at Mellon Institute, with Meller as managing director. Its stated mission was to eliminate or reduce to safe concentrations injurious dust and fumes, but its focus was on "separating fact from speculation" and on establishing the limits of employer liability. The foundation would treat the problems both of industrial dust exposure and of municipal air pollution.[18] The formation of the Air Hygiene Foundation, like the work for the Anthracite Institute, was an expression of the instrumentalization of air pollution research by corporate interests at Mellon Institute. Its work would make clear that *no* standard of particulate-free air would be upheld for indoor air, much less for the air of polluted cities. Occupational health researchers were interested in specific damage from particles of particular chemical composition, size, and shape. The particles for which health danger had been established were found in much higher concentrations in the occupational setting than in municipal air. In addition, the Air Hygiene Foundation actually worked to limit corporate liability for air pollution by measuring ambient pollution levels in industrial cities. Smelter company executives employing Meller, under the foundation's auspices in 1936, were delighted to learn that Pittsburgh air contained more sulphur dioxide than the federal government was prepared to allow in the air around their plant. They regarded the acquisition of this information alone as having provided them with satisfactory return on their investment in air pollution research.[19]

Problematic features of the Mellon Institute investigations noted above—pandering to specific financial interests and the instrumentalization of political ideology—resonated with more general social criticism of contemporary Pittsburgh culture. Pittsburgh in the 1930s was, by consensus, ripe for change. There are three not entirely independent perspectives from which this period can be seen as a watershed in Pittsburgh's history. One is the sense that Pittsburgh's special industrial prominence, and hence the city itself, was threatened, coupled with the notion that threats could be resisted by means of the city's special relationship to nature through technology and work. Illustrated in national magazine and newspaper articles,[20] this perspective is nonetheless most clearly exemplified in the short stories discussed above, as well as in a poem from depression-era Pittsburgh to be discussed below. It is linked to the expectation of imminent transformation through the rise of a more regulated economy and the recognition of the dignity of labor embodied in the New Deal. This second perspective, the transformation of Pittsburgh along the lines set out by the radical New Deal, is most clearly enunciated in a 1930 *Harper's* article, "Is Pittsburgh Civilized?" and in the Federal Theater Project's drama *The Cradle Will Rock,* to be discussed below.[21] The third perspective, in many ways opposed to the first two, treats technological transformation as a mark of civilizational change. This perspective was enunciated in Lewis Mumford's 1934 *Technics and Civilization,* embodied in the mission of Mellon Institute, and expressed in the architectural design of Mellon Institute's new building, completed in 1937.[22]

The sense of Pittsburgh as a problem to be solved and as ripe for change is common in sources from the period. The 1930 *Harper's* article "Is Pittsburgh Civilized?" scathingly criticized Pittsburgh's social structure and looked toward ethnic and religious transition to remake the city. According to the article, Pittsburgh's main problem was domination by an irresponsible hereditary elite: a Scotch-Irish Presbyterian cadre hand-picked by the Mellons. It characterized the group as without social conscience and as taking a purely instrumentalist view of the city. It argued that Pittsburgh's elites, for instance, would not bring about the economic diversification needed to stave off the city's industrial decline because they were doing well enough as things were. The article characterized the city's impressive efforts in industrial research—including Mellon work on smoke abatement—as exercises in improving these elites' capacity to extract profit from the city.[23] Social critics took the instrumentalization of civic improvement by Mellon air pollution researchers as typical of Pittsburgh's culture. Nonetheless, while the article scathingly criticized the declining state of the city, it predicted that Pittsburgh would survive because of the power of local nature and of the new ethnics who would replace Scotch-Irish Calvinists as the city's leaders.[24] The 1937 Federal Theater Project drama *The Cradle Will Rock*—while not explicitly about Pittsburgh—echoed the criticisms of "Is Pittsburgh Civilized?" It portrayed a fictional "Steeltown" under the control of Mr. Mister—an obvious Mellon type. In the play, all elements of society make their living only by prostituting themselves to Mr. Mister in one way or another. The play ends with a union leader finally refusing to take a bribe from Mr. Mister and thereby rocking the cradle of power in the city. As he stands up to Mr. Mister, he describes the solidarity and Americanism of his followers and the amenity-rich community he and his union plan to build.[25] The poem "Pittsburgh 1932," by local poet Eleanor Graham,[26] emphasized similar, but subtly contradictory, themes. It equated the city's lack of smoke during the Great Depression with its age and senility. According to the poem, Pittsburgh would rise again not because of "the Chamber of Commerce and Mellon Bank" but because of nature—the rivers, "its belly full of coal"—and because of nature's laws, reflected in the rising of steam from a cigarette dropped by a bum in the river.[27] Local nature and local workers provided one source of vitality in Pittsburgh's future.

Standing in contrast to visions of the transformation of Pittsburgh and American industrial society based on longstanding relations of particular places to nature and labor is the vision outlined in Lewis Mumford's *Technics and Civilization* (1934). Mumford understood the nascent transformation as a civilizational change both driven by and expressed in technology. He saw industrial society as engaged in a transition from a "paleotechnic" technological regime to a "neotechnic" one. Mumford's paleotechnic era rested on iron and coal and on steam power, while his neotechnic era rested on "new alloys, rare earths, lighter metals," as well as on electricity and synthetic chemicals, especially coal by-products. For Mumford, aluminum—light, highly conductive, globally dispersed in small quantities, and dependent for its refining on large amounts of electricity—was the most characteristically neotechnic metal.[28] The importance of minute quantities of materials like aluminum, scattered around the globe, would bring a new emphasis on conservation of minute quantities of any previously wasted industrial materials. The neotechnic also often transmuted such wastes into new synthetic substitutes for raw materials whose abundance had previously underpinned local processing industries.[29] Mumford saw synthetics, such as those made from coal tar, as offering "greater freedom from local conditions." Rayon, for instance, could free the clothing industry from vulnerability to a plague striking silkworms. The use of widely dispersed materials and the re-use of wastes meant that the neotechnic marked the end of the dependence of industry on local raw materials. The consequences of neotechnic ideology for Pittsburgh were clear: the city that owed its existence to local natural resources was to be vulnerable to global industrial competition.[30]

Some on-going technological trends in Pittsburgh fit well with neotechnic ideology, among them smoke abatement. Close association with electricity, efficiency, and the re-use of industrial wastes linked neotechnics with the control of air pollution from paleotechnic coal. Smoke regulators had long looked toward electricity production from central plants as an important contributor to smoke-abatement progress.[31] For Mumford, the kind of energy used determined the prominence of the certain materials. Electricity challenged coal (as used in steam generation), and so aluminum challenged steel.[32] Mumford also took the utilization of coal tar through by-product coke ovens, an important local technological transformation after World War I, to be "one of the greatest neo-technic advances." Since coal by-products were condensed from combustion emissions, by-product ovens combined two of the hallmarks of the neotechnic: the efficient re-use of waste and the production of synthetic substitutes for natural products. They also reduced smoke emissions.

The Mellons and Mellon Institute were both heavily involved in neotechnic enterprises. Investments in Alcoa aluminum, Gulf Oil, and Koppers by-product coke ovens would become, by some estimations, more important to the Mellons than their banking business.[33] Even before World War I, Mellon Institute was engaged in numerous synthetic chemical research projects; by the 1930s and 1940s, a great number of these focused on coal by-products.[34] A 1957 history of the institute saw the production of synthetics from coal and petroleum as the most valuable type of research that had been conducted there.[35]

The neotechnic ideology embodied in the work of the institute was expressed in the design of its new building, the Temple of Science, dedicated in 1937. The building's design made alchemy a prominent metaphor for the institute's chemical work in the manufacture of synthetics. While decorating aluminum elevator doors with alchemical symbols, architects reserved wooden panels in the library for carvings that represented the natural sources of the artificial products made at the institute. Coal and iron, the materials most closely associated with local industrial identity—and with the paleotechnic—were conspicuously absent from the decoration of the new building.[36]

Both Mumford and the Mellon building promotional materials recognized the problems of worker displacement and the disruption of traditional industries inherent in the development of synthetics. They identified the problem as one of the unsynchronized pace of cultural and technological evolution.[37] Yet both Mumford and Mellon Institute materials gave only lip-service to the unintended consequences of rapid technological change. Tensions around this issue are evident from the discussion in Mellon Institute promotional material of some of the building's ornamentation. The new building featured quotations from important figures in world history, Aristotle prominent among them: "If there is one way better than another, it is the way of nature." Pamphlets written for the dedication and about the history of the building recognized the contradiction between this pronouncement and the concentration of the institute's work in the manufacture of the artificial. These pamphlets reinterpreted the phrase to mean that "nature teems with great things" from which the artificial could be made. Mumford used similar language in his discussion of the relationship of the new synthetic chemicals to nature.

Threats of the dislocations promised by the neotechnic were particularly apparent in the sorry state of Western Pennsylvania's coal industry. The rise and fall of the idea of Pittsburgh's "natural" dependence on local bituminous coal modeled changing expectations about the character and basis of Pittsburgh's anticipated transformation. Herbert Meller, writing in 1926, had espoused the idea that any efforts at smoke control must make use of an area's "natural fuel."[38] Yet, by July 1929, Meller took oil and natural gas as desirable modern methods for home heating,[39] and by April 1931 he had predicted that Pittsburgh would eventually become a gas- and electric-powered White City.[40] In a talk in 1934 entitled "Air Hygiene," Meller consciously revised the idea of the "logical" or natural fuel to that which could be burned cheaply *and* smokelessly.

By 1939, on the eve of the city's Renaissance, the air pollution control recommendations Meller was able to make would fall short of the expectations he held ten years earlier.[41] This was largely due to failures at Mellon Institute to provide a scientific grounding, based in well-understood health effects, for smoke regulation.[42] In 1939, after Meller had moved from work on smoke to work in industrial hygiene, the Bureau of Smoke Regulation he had headed was closed as an end-of-depression gesture intended to welcome the return of prosperity. In the same year, Pittsburgh civic leaders began to look toward St. Louis's experiment with air pollution control. In 1941 the Pittsburgh City Council passed a St. Louis–style smoke ordinance that, because of the war, would be implemented piecemeal over the course of the decade. Conflict raged in the years of smoke control's final implementation about whether the problems of the coal industry and of miners were due to John L. Lewis and the United Mineworkers or to the smoke control law itself.[43]

While *The Cradle Will Rock* had portrayed similarly oppositional relationships between various interests in New Deal Pittsburgh, the 1942 movie *Pittsburgh* presents a vision of such conflicts resolved—melted in the crucible of the Second World War. The story follows two young coal miners, "Pittsburgh" (John Wayne) and "Cash" (Randolph Scott), in their rivalry over a coal miner's daughter made good, "Hunky" (Marlene Dietrich), and in their involvement with a local physician, "Doc" Powers (Frank Craven), who is experimenting with coal-tar products. Pittsburgh, at Hunky's urging and through ruthless behavior toward his friends, business associates, and the workers in his employ, rises from coal miner to steel boss.

All three views of the expected transformation of Pittsburgh as it emerged from the Great Depression were harmonized in the movie. *Pittsburgh* unfolds as a flashback from the early 1940s war-production context under the voiceover of Doc Powers. Powers says that coal in the 1920s was an unrecognized treasure and coal tar, as a waste product, presented a challenge to science. Powers's rhetoric is in perfect accord with points Mumford makes about the importance of minute quantities in the neotechnic regime encouraging greater attention to efficiency and the re-use of waste in characteristically paleotechnic industries. Much of the movie focuses on contradictory meanings of coal: is it the source of future profits through coal-tar research and an escape from the degradation of the miner's life, or is it necessarily connected only with mining catastrophes and smoke?

When Pittsburgh betrays and is estranged from his friends, it is by refusing to fund their research and by turning his back on his own union workers. This reflects historical criticisms of the behavior of the city's elites. After a violent confrontation with his workers, in which Hunky is incidentally injured, Pittsburgh re-evaluates his life. When philanthropy fails him, he finds his answer in war work. The war transforms the man and, we are led to infer, the city. "As weapons of war were forged so were you as a human being," Doc Powers's voiceover says to Pittsburgh. After the crisis, Pittsburgh vows to reform and, as an anonymous workman, pulls together with his old friends in a glorious orgy of over-the-top war production and union democracy. Local labor and local nature, transformed by neotechnic means, remake the city.[44]

The smoke-control movement predicted a similar happy coincidence in the immediate post-war period. Processed smokeless fuel from local coal, coal-tar products, and coal gasification were to allow the coal industry to recover lost market share while eliminating smoke. They were to provide—but, as Joel Tarr has argued, in fact failed to provide—a no-cost solution.[45] Proponents of smoke control argued that it would create rather than eliminate industrial and mining jobs through the development of new coal-processing industries.[46] Yet, during 1946–47, local commentators blamed John L. Lewis and the United Mineworkers for coal's loss of the local domestic fuel market to fuel oil and natural gas. Between 1947 and 1949, as controversy continued over the shift to natural gas, newspapers promised miners salvation through coal gasification. Plans for the new industry were, however, abandoned as unprofitable by local corporations by 1950. The *Pittsburgh Press* blamed Lewis for this development as well and proclaimed that coal had lost out to "laborless fuels."[47] The newspapers saw the shift from what Meller in the 1920s had called Pittsburgh's "natural fuel" to "laborless fuels" as simply rational.

Pittsburgh industry was never *saved* by neotechnics. Lack of diversification and old technology continued to plague the city until the final decline of steel in the 1980s. Yet neotechnic ideology was operative among Pittsburgh's business leaders, who continued to turn their investments away from iron, steel, local labor, and local nature and toward global outlets. Nonetheless, the effort behind the Pittsburgh Renaissance speaks to an uncharacteristically non-neotechnic attachment of the Mellons to a particular place. The Mellon family and the others who orchestrated the Pittsburgh Renaissance put the effort they did into this particular city because of the power of local history. Generations of Presbyterian steel masters in Pittsburgh had been criticized for lack of public spirit. Here at last was an opportunity to act on this criticism without fundamentally threatening their business interests. This was true for three reasons. First, many of their most important business interests were primarily elsewhere—global, diversified, and neotechnic. Second, local banking and corporate headquarters, in the competitive post-war climate, required smoke control in order to attract professional staff to the city. Third, the neotechnic had already transformed even the local steel industry to rely on the re-use of its own wastes. By-product collection had been the standard in mills since just before the First World War. When the new smoke ordinance was passed in 1941, industrial users were the first class of smoke producers asked to comply. Smoke abatement for industry—to the level required by the ordinance—was nearly a done deal, of a piece with expected neotechnic standards.

An additional irony about the Pittsburgh Renaissance remains. In the years between the wars, Pittsburgh's smoke problem had been scientifically redefined as an air pollution problem. Nonetheless, those charged to study and regulate air pollution in this era faced numerous difficulties in defining it, measuring it, and justifying action against it. In examining claims to success, both during this period and in the city's subsequent Renaissance, it is important to ask what happened to these difficulties and ambiguities. While, by several measures, Pittsburgh's air pollution was significantly reduced by the new ordinance, the improvement was nowhere near what Meller had hoped for in the 1930s. The difficult questions Meller asked about the measurement and definition of air pollution and about health standards for regulation were never answered, and the ordinance as it was passed had very little to do with them. Invisible air pollution, especially fly-ash from the mills, remained a problem. The number of days of heavy smoke declined, but the number of days on which any smoke was observed stayed at a very high level.[48] Without the answers to Meller's questions from the 1930s, it is difficult to assess the significance of such findings. The happy coincidence of Dietrich and Wayne and of the 1941 ordinance—plenty of jobs, neotechnic industry, and clean air—never came to pass in Pittsburgh; not in the 1950s, and certainly not after the final decline of steel three decades later.

NOTES

1. Images of Pittsburgh as a city undergoing, enduring, or expecting major transformation are constantly reiterated by local writers and in the national press in the years between the wars. The stories, poems, and articles herein all put forward such views. The text of this chapter discusses only a few of the most significant examples among them. Haniel Long, "How Pittsburgh Returned to the Jungle" *The Nation* 116, June 20, 1923, 717–18; Frances Lester Warner, *The Pittsburgh Owl* (Pittsburgh: n.p., 1925); "No Mean Cities of the Middle West," *New York Times,* November 4, 1923; French Strother, "What Kind of a Pittsburgh Is Detroit?" *World's Work* 52 (October 1926): 633–39; "The Mighty Symphony," *New York Times,* October 14, 1927; "A Tower of Inspiration to a Busy City," *New York Times,* June 17, 1928. George Seibel, "Pittsburgh Peeps at the Stars," *American Mercury* 11 (July 1927): 300–306; R. L. Duffus, "Our Changing Cities: Fiery Pittsburgh," *New York Times,* February 13, 1927; C. W. Simpson, G. L. Ralston (illustrator), "Pittsburgh," *Ladies Home Journal* 46, October 1929, 6–7; R. L. Duffus, "Our Cities in a Census Mirror," *New York Times,* June 29, 1930; R. L. Duffus, "Is Pittsburgh Civilized?" *Harper's Monthly* 161, October 1930, 537–45; G. Seibel, "Pittsburgh: The City That Might Have Been," *American Mercury* 28 (March 1933): 326–29; Haniel Long, "Pittsburgh Memoranda," *Survey Graphic* 24 (March–April 1935): 119–23, 181–85; D. Macdonald, "Pittsburgh: What a City Shouldn't Be," *Forum* 100 (October 1938): supplement 7; M. F. Byington, "Pittsburgh Studies Itself," *Survey Graphic* 27 (February 1938): 75–79+; R. L. Duffus, "American Industry: Many-Headed Giant," *New York Times,* March 13, 1938; "Pittsburgh's Cleanup Campaign Began in 1935," *American City* 53 (March 1938): 15; "What Pittsburgh Suggests," *Journal of Home Economics* 30 (April 1938): 246–47; Glenn E. McLaughlin and Ralph J. Watkins, "The Problem of Industrial Growth in a Mature Economy," *American Economic Review* 29 (March 1939): 1, supplement, Papers and Proceedings of the Fifty-first Annual

Meeting of the American Economic Association, 1–14; "Pittsburgh Begins to Rebuild," *American City* 54 (March 1939): 49; "Report: Pittsburgh at Capacity" *Fortune* 24, December 1941, 38+.

2. "Smoky Days in City Cut to Seven for Year," *Pittsburgh Dispatch*, December 14, 1920; "The War against Smoke," *Pittsburgh Sun*, July 15, 1920; "Pittsburgh's Cleanliness," *Pittsburgh Gazette Times*, July 23, 1920; "News Is Colorless—Smoke Here and Abroad," *Pittsburgh Post*, July 27, 1922; "Pittsburgh Model of Spotlessness," *Pittsburgh Gazette Times*, December 7, 1922; "Smoke Bureau Has Been Successful—Miller [*sic*] Says Department Has Reduced Smoke 80 Per Cent since 1914--Few Violations Are Seen," *Pittsburgh Chronicle Telegraph*, January 29, 1923; "Know Your City," *Pittsburgh Sun*, February 19, 1924; "King Smoke Losing Grip on Pittsburgh, Research Reveals—Tar Content Removal Is Great, Inquiry Shows—City's Record Beats London," *Pittsburgh Post*, October 1, 1924; "The Smokiest Cities," *Literary Digest*, April 24, 1927; "Pittsburgh World's Best Example of What Smoke Regulation Will Do," *Greater Pittsburgh*, August 27, 1927 (reprint from the *New York Sun*); "Smoke Abatement," *Pittsburgh Post Gazette*, September 1, 1927; "Pittsburgh and Collars," *New York Times*, October 21, 1927; "Find More Soot Here Than in Pittsburgh," *New York Times*, April 1, 1928; "Pittsburgh No Longer Smokiest City in U.S.," *Pittsburgh Sun Telegraph*, April 31, 1928; "Pittsburgh Model of Spotlessness," *Pittsburgh Gazette Times*, December 7, 1928; "Officers Told 'To Go Limit' in Smoke War," *Pittsburgh Press*, January 12, 1929; "Pittsburgh's Fight on Smoke," *Greater Pittsburgh*, March 23, 1929; "Authority of Experience," *New York Times*, February 18, 1929; "Six Carloads of Dirt in Pittsburgh Air Daily," *Pittsburgh Post Gazette*, July 12, 1929; "City Bureau Begins Drive against Many Violators of Smoke Laws—Railroad Firemen Held Chief Offenders—Ordinance to Be Enforced," *Pittsburgh Post*, July 11, 1929; "Pittsburgh Air Found Cleaner," *Pittsburgh Press*, March 20, 1930; Henry Obermeyer, *Stop That Smoke!* (New York and London: Harper and Brothers, 1933); "Progress against Smoke," *Pittsburgh Post Gazette*, January 16, 1934; "Pittsburgh Loses 'Smokiest' Title," *Pittsburgh Sun Telegraph*, November 27, 1934; "What Pittsburgh Suggests," *Journal of Home Economics* 30 (April 1938): 246–47; D. Macdonald, "Pittsburgh: What a City Shouldn't Be," *Forum* 100 (October 1938): supplement 7.

3. Joel A. Tarr, "Searching for a Sink for an Industrial Waste: Iron-Making Fuels and the Environment," *Environmental History Review* 18 (Spring 1994): 9–34.

4. John G. Clark, "The Energy Crisis of 1919–1924: A Comparative Analysis of Federal Energy Policies," *Energy Systems and Policy* 4, no. 4 (1980): 239–71.

5. Haniel Long, "How Pittsburgh Returned to the Jungle," *The Nation*, June 20, 1923.

6. Frances Lester Warner, *The Pittsburgh Owl* (Pittsburgh: n.p., 1925).

7. "Smoky Days in City Cut to Seven for Year," *Pittsburgh Dispatch*, December 14, 1920; "Pittsburgh's Cleanliness," *Pittsburgh Gazette Times*, July 23, 1920; "The War against Smoke," *Pittsburgh Sun*, July 15, 1920; "News Is Colorless—Smoke

Here and Abroad," *Pittsburgh Post*, July 27, 1922; "Smoke Bureau Has Been Successful—Miller [*sic*] Says Department Has Reduced Smoke 80 Per Cent since 1914—Few Violations Are Seen," *Pittsburgh Chronicle Telegraph*, January 29, 1923; "Know Your City," *Pittsburgh Sun*, February 19, 1924.

8. H. B. Meller, "Smoke Abatement, Its Effects and Its Limitations," *Mechanical Engineering*, mid-November 1926; H. B. Meller, "Memorandum" (Mellon Institute of Industrial Research, Pittsburgh, 1923). In 1924 the Elliot Nursery won a suit against Duquesne Light for damage to plants from air pollution. The judge in the case refused to apply the balancing reasoning that had been introduced in Huckenstine's appeal (70 Pa. 102) against the claim of similar damages. Huckenstine's appeal is discussed in Christine Rosen, "Differing Perceptions of the Value of Pollution Abatement across Time and Place: Balancing Doctrine in Pollution Nuisance Law, 1840–1906," *Law and History Review* 11 (1993): 303–81. The local cultural significance of the rhetoric of the judicial opinion is discussed in Angela Gugliotta, "Class, Gender and Coal Smoke: Gender Ideology and Environmental Injustice in Pittsburgh, 1868–1914." *Environmental History* 2 (2000): 165–93, discussion on 168. This decision was a major departure from the ethos that saw the desire to prevent damage to vegetation as the expression of a taste for a non-economic luxury. Looking back from the 1930s, Herbert Meller took 1924 as the peak of anti-smoke activism in Pittsburgh.

9. "King Smoke Losing Grip on Pittsburgh, Research Reveals—Tar Content Removal Is Great, Inquiry Shows—City's Record Beats London," *Pittsburgh Post*, October 1, 1924.

10. Meller pointed out that ash was a major subject of public complaint and that it was as yet unregulated. Smoke-abatement technologies adopted in the wake of initial Mellon surveys actually contributed to the ash problem. To increase the likelihood of complete combustion, Mellon Institute and the smoke inspector's office had urged the introduction of more air into furnaces, yet the resulting higher wind velocities carried up the chimney more and more particulate matter that, in a lower draft situation, would have remained in the furnace.

11. H. B. Meller, "Smoke Report: Air Pollution Problem of Pittsburgh" (draft) (Mellon Institute of Industrial Research, Pittsburgh, 1924).

12. H. B. Meller, "The Air Pollution Problem of Pittsburgh" (draft) (1924); Meller was interested in understanding the nature of the many components of pollution, in hopes of regulating them eventually. Yet, in 1924 ,Meller asserted that it was not possible to regulate smoke and other pollution components more strongly than did the current ordinance because the equipment that would allow such ordinance requirements was not yet available. The adequacy of the current ordinance was nonetheless clearly at issue during the second half of the 1920s. Meller searched for sources of smoke not governed by the ordinance for which improved control might not be limited by the capabilities of currently available technology, and that had not contributed to the rising components of the most

recent soot-fall study. The relatively light suspended particles that outlying areas contributed to Pittsburgh's pollution load could not have been measured as soot-fall. In 1925, Meller called for the formation of a "metropolitan smoke district" encompassing all those municipalities whose emissions contributed to the pall hanging over Pittsburgh ("Smoke Nuisances of the Suburbs," *Pittsburgh Post,* September 26, 1925).

While seeking to broaden legal control where technologically possible, Meller chafed against the demands placed on smoke inspectors to eliminate all air pollution, when many of its kinds and sources were not regulated by current ordinances. In spite of Meller's efforts and the persistent claims of progress, in 1926 the Pittsburgh City Council called on Meller's bureau for more aggressive action against smoke. Again, in 1928, in the face of inefficient operation of plants due to industrial slowdown, City Council members complained about increased pollution. According to Meller, these complaints focused on the kinds of pollution unregulated by the ordinance: chiefly smog due to winter domestic heating, pollution from mills outside the municipality, and railroad cinder. Meller complained in 1929 that smoke inspectors were ignored in good times and blamed for the weather in bad. He was pleased with the progress in industry and proud that his office had secured industrial cooperation without driving a single plant from the city. This set of circumstances led Meller to the view that, in winter, domestic smoke—unregulated by Pittsburgh's ordinances—was the city's biggest problem. In the midst of this period of complaint, regulators and newspapers continually reasserted claims to progress. Despite his efforts to justify the narrowness of existing smoke regulations, all of Meller's scientific energies were focused on identifying and publicizing the broader problem of air pollution.

At an air pollution symposium in 1928, Meller and others discussed broadening of the scope of air pollution policy, with explicit reference to possible new technologies to be employed. They noted that some dust collectors were available on the market but agreed that they needed to be improved before they could become required equipment. Participants in the symposium also exhibited a new awareness of the kinds of distinctions to be made in evaluating different components of the air pollution threat and basing control policy on these evaluations. In particular, they noted that fine dust was the most dangerous to health yet hardest to catch in pollution control equipment. (H. B. Meller, "Damage due to Smoke—Enormity of the Destruction and Defacement Caused by Air Pollution Owing to the Unrestrained Products of Combustion," *Transactions of the American Society of Mechanical Engineers* 50, no. 33 [1928]: 213–21.)

13. H. B. Meller, "What Smoke Does and What to Do about It," *American City* (April 1931).

14. Meller had already begun connecting his work on air pollution at Mellon with the industrial dust studies of the Bureau of Mines in 1930–31 (H. B. Meller, "Progress Report for the Week Ended February 11, 1930, Smoke Abatement Indus-

trial Fellowship No. 3," Archives of Industrial Society, Mellon Institute of Industrial Research, Series 1, Box 2, F 24, 1930).

15. Other researchers moved in this direction as well. In 1933 the Metropolitan Life insurance company undertook a study of pneumonia and anthracosis that aimed to determine a safe carbon load for the lungs (H. B. Meller, "The Proposed Pneumonia Studies of the Metropolitan Life Insurance Company," Archives of Industrial Society, Mellon Institute of Industrial Research, Series 2, Box 2, F 1, 1933).

16. Despite Meller's insistence on the centrality of health claims in the justification of air pollution control, connections between smoke and health remained persistently tenuous. Meller throughout the 1920s and 1930s requested greater physician participation, and indeed physician leadership, in the campaign against air pollution. In 1928, Meller spoke of his wishes for stronger smoke and health evidence and asked physicians to lead the way in establishing it. Again, in November 1931, Meller spoke of the need for physician leadership, and in August 1933 he targeted physicians for anti–air pollution education.

17. L. B. Sisson, "Annual Report: Anthracite Institute Fellowship, Dec. 1, 1931 to Dec. 31, 1933," Archives of Industrial Society, Mellon Institute of Industrial Research, Series 1, Box 2, FF 28. In their 1932 correspondence with officials at the Anthracite Institute, Meller and Sisson argued that New Deal rehabilitation must include smoke abatement and that they would work for stricter ordinances in anthracite territory. They looked toward the New Deal focus on housing improvement and slum clearance to provide a new opening for the promotion of smoke abatement. They hoped to gratify their Anthracite Institute sponsors by getting the new automatic stoking anthracite furnace, the "anthramatic," into federal housing programs. H. B. Meller, "City Air Pollution in a Period of Industrial Depression," Archives of Industrial Society, Mellon Institute of Industrial Research, Series 2, Box 3, 1934; L. B. Sisson, "Summary Report for the Anthracite Institute," Archives of Industrial Society, Mellon Institute of Industrial Research, Series 1, Box 2, FF 28. Meller promoted the connection between slum renovation and smoke control in an article in *Collier's* magazine in the same year (1934). He argued that it was in fact impossible to wipe out slums without controlling air pollution. "Smoke Review," *Bulletin Index,* January 25, 1934.

18. H. B. Meller, "Science and Industry Combine in Campaign to Control Dust Diseases," *American Mutual Magazine,* Spring 1936; *History of Industrial Hygiene Foundation: A Research Association of Industries for Advancing Industrial Health and Improving Working Conditions* (Pittsburgh: Mellon Institute, 1956).

19. George R. Hill, "Letter of George R. Hill to H. B. Meller" (1936), Joel Tarr, personal files.

20. "No Mean Cities of the Middle West," *New York Times,* November 4, 1923; R. L. Duffus, "Our Changing Cities: Fiery Pittsburgh," *New York Times,* February 13, 1927; C. W. Simpson, G. L. Ralston (illustrator), "Pittsburgh," *Ladies Home Journal* 46, October 1929, 6–7; G. Seibel, "Pittsburgh: The City That Might Have Been,"

American Mercury 28 (March 1933): 326–29; Haniel Long, "Pittsburgh Memoranda," *Survey Graphic* 24 (March–April 1935): 119–23, 181–85; D. Macdonald, "Pittsburgh: What a City Shouldn't Be," *Forum* 100 (October 1938): supplement 7; M. F. Byington, "Pittsburgh Studies Itself," *Survey Graphic* 27 (February 1938): 75–79+.

21. This perspective is also exhibited in other national magazine and newspaper articles: D. Macdonald, "Pittsburgh: What a City Shouldn't Be," *Forum* 100 (October 1938): supplement 7; Glenn E. McLaughlin and Ralph J. Watkins, "The Problem of Industrial Growth in a Mature Economy," *American Economic Review* 29 (March 1939): 1, supplement, Papers and Proceedings of the Fifty-first Annual Meeting of the American Economic Association, 1–14; "Report: Pittsburgh at Capacity," *Fortune* 24, December 1941, 38+; "What's Itching Labor? Survey of Opinion of Workers In Pittsburgh Area" *Fortune* 26, November 1942, 100–102+.

22. The Mellons had long been interested in research on new uses for coal. "Fuel Men to Confer on Soft Coal Uses," *New York Times,* November 24, 1926; "Says Coal and Wood Assure Us Food," *New York Times,* November 18, 1926.

23. R. L. Duffus, "Is Pittsburgh Civilized?" *Harper's Monthly* 161, October 1930, 537–45.

24. R. L. Duffus, "Is Pittsburgh Civilized?" *Harper's Monthly* 161, October 1930, 537–45.

25. Mark Blitzstein, *The Cradle Will Rock* (New York: Random House, 1938).

26. Clipping file, "Pittsburgh, Poems about Pittsburgh," Pennsylvania Department, Carnegie Library of Pittsburgh, Pittsburgh, Pa. Eleanor Graham was a Pittsburgh poet who published verse in the *Saturday Evening Post,* the *New Yorker, Good Housekeeping,* and *Ladies Home Journal,* along with three books of poetry, *For These Moments* (1939), *Store in Your Heart* (1950), and *It Happens Every Day* (1962). Biographical information on Graham can be found in "Girl Who Beat Paralysis Publishes Volume of Verse," *Pittsburgh Post Gazette,* September 20, 1939, and "Class A Contributor," *Bulletin Index,* September 14, 1939.

27. Eleanor Graham, "Pittsburgh 1932" in "Pittsburgh, Poems about Pittsburgh."

28. Lewis Mumford, *Technics and Civilization,* 1963 ed. (San Diego: Harcourt, Brace Jovanovich, 1934).

29. Lewis Mumford, *Technics and Civilization,* 1963 ed. (San Diego: Harcourt, Brace Jovanovich, 1934).

30. This is evident also in the fading of the idea of the "natural fuel" for a region from smoke-abatement rhetoric and in the introduction of research focused on the competing type of coal at Mellon Institute, under the auspices of the Anthracite Institute.

31. "Garland Makes Move to Bring Smokeless Era—Resolution Asks Mayor for Inquiry on Railroad Plans for Electrification—Councilmen in Accord," *Pittsburgh*

Sun, February 24, 1926; "Pittsburgh's Fight on Smoke," *Greater Pittsburgh,* March 23, 1929.

32. Aluminum was developed over the same period as central power plants.

33. John W. Servos, "Changing Partners: The Mellon Institute, Private Industry and the Federal Patron," *Technology and Culture* 35, no. 2 (1994).

34. John W. Servos, "Changing Partners: The Mellon Institute, Private Industry and the Federal Patron," *Technology and Culture* 35, no. 2 (1994).

35. *A Description of the Symbolism in Mellon Institute* (Pittsburgh: Mellon Institute, 1957).

36. *A Description of the Symbolism in Mellon Institute* (Pittsburgh: Mellon Institute, 1957).

37. *Addresses at the Exercises and Science Symposium during the Dedication of the New Building of Mellon Institute* (Pittsburgh, 1937).

38. H. B. Meller, "Smoke Abatement, Its Effects and Its Limitations," *Mechanical Engineering* (mid-November 1926).

39. "City Bureau Begins Drive against Many Violators of Smoke Laws—Railroad Firemen Held Chief Offenders—Ordinance to Be Enforced," *Pittsburgh Post,* July 11, 1929.

40. H. B. Meller, "What Smoke Does and What to Do about It," *American City* (April 1931).

41. H. B. Meller, "Practical Procedures and Limitations in Present-Day Smoke Abatement," *American Journal of Public Health* 29 (1939): 645–50.

42. H. B. Meller, "Practical Procedures and Limitations in Present-Day Smoke Abatement," *American Journal of Public Health* 29 (1939): 645–50; Joel Tarr, "Changing Fuel Use Behavior and Energy Transitions: The Pittsburgh Smoke Control Movement, 1940–1950—A Study in Historical Analogy," *Journal of Social History* 14 (1982): 561–88.

43. "District Has Best Chance Now to Clear the Atmosphere," *Pittsburgh Press,* November 5, 1945; "Mine Leaders Fight Pennsy Diesel Plan," *Pittsburgh Sun Telegraph,* January 23, 1947; "Super-Salesman," *Pittsburgh Press,* December 11, 1947; "Oil vs. Coal," *Pittsburgh Post Gazette,* December 11, 1947; "Dealers Say Lewis Undermines Coal," *Pittsburgh Press,* October 4, 1949; "John L.'s Heavy Hand," *Pittsburgh Press,* January 3, 1950. Joel Tarr, "Changing Fuel Use Behavior and Energy Transitions: The Pittsburgh Smoke Control Movement, 1940–1950—A Study in Historical Analogy," *Journal of Social History* 14 (1981): 561–88. I am indebted to Joel Tarr for calling to my attention these and the following articles from 1940s and 1950s Pittsburgh newspapers.

44. *Pittsburgh* (1942), Universal Pictures.

45. Joel Tarr, "Changing Fuel Use Behavior and Energy Transitions: The Pittsburgh Smoke Control Movement, 1940–1950—A Study in Historical Analogy," *Journal of Social History* 14 (1981): 561–88; Gilbert Love, "Writer Gives Answers to

Smog Quiz," *Pittsburgh Press*, November 9, 1945; "Coal Official Raps Gas Companies," *Pittsburgh Sun Telegraph*, February 6, 1947; "Biggest Story in the History of Coal: $120,000,000 Plant to Turn Coal into Gas and Oil Here," *Pittsburgh Press*, March 25, 1947; "By-Products Plant Slated for District, *Pittsburgh Post Gazette*, March 26, 1947; Stefano Luconi, "The Enforcement of the 1941 Smoke-Contral Ordinance and Italian Americans in Pittsburgh," *Pennsylvania History* 66 (1999): 580–94.

46. "Newspaper Articles Pertaining to Smoke Control, 1941–1950," notes by Joel Tarr, personal files.

47. By 1945, coal had fallen on hard times due to the replacement of steam locomotives with diesel-electric power. As miners complained about these developments, coal merchants expressed their fears of competition from natural gas to be piped through the Big and Little Inch pipelines, originally built to transport oil for war production. "Super-Salesman," *Pittsburgh Press*, December 11, 1947; "Oil vs. Coal," *Pittsburgh Post Gazette*, December 11, 1947; "Dealers Say Lewis Undermines Coal," *Pittsburgh Press*, October 4, 1949; "Coal Official Raps Gas Companies," *Pittsburgh Sun Telegraph*, February 6, 1947; "Biggest Story in the History of Coal: $120,000,000 Plant to Turn Coal into Gas and Oil Here," *Pittsburgh Press*, March 25, 1947; "By-Products Plant Slated for District," *Pittsburgh Post Gazette*, March 26, 1947; "John L.'s Heavy Hand," *Pittsburgh Press*, January 3, 1950; "Big Coal Firm May Market Other Fuels," *Pittsburgh Press*, March 22, 1950.

48. Henry W. Castner, "Sootfall in Pittsburgh: An Evaluation of the Sootfall at Selected Stations before and after Smoke Control" (masters thesis, University of Pittsburgh, 1960).

6

The Merits of the Precautionary Principle

Controlling Automobile Exhausts in Germany
and the United States before 1945

Frank Uekoetter

This chapter seeks to explain why the control of automobile exhaust failed miserably in Germany and the United States of America before 1945. Following the contemporary definition of the exhaust problem, the essay concentrates on three issues: (1) the visible and malodorous components of the exhausts, (2) the carbon monoxide problem, and (3) the lead emissions that resulted from the use of tetraethyl lead as an antiknock fuel additive. In all three cases, contemporary knowledge gave reason for concern, but abatement never moved beyond the first stages. The key problem was the deficient communication between the parties involved. The public at large usually emphasized the visible and malodorous components of the exhausts, while scientific experts were more interested in carbon monoxide and lead emissions; as a result, the bureaucracy was faced with an incongruous agenda. The interaction between scientific and administrative experts—the Achilles' heel of the science-based regulatory state—was particularly insufficient. Scientists and bureaucrats inadvertently turned into "partners in lethargy": while scientists were hesitant to attest a clear and imminent threat to public health, bureaucrats were hesitant to push scientists into the systematic investigation of automobile exhaust problems. It was only after 1945 that an alternative rationale of action emerged. The key innovation was the rise of the precautionary principle, which allowed basing control measures on circumstantial evidence alone, rather than on a definite medical proof of harm. In this perspective, the hapless control of automobile exhausts before 1945 demonstrates the merits of the precautionary principle.

It is only in the last few years that environmental historians and historians of technology have discovered the contested nature of the rise of automobilism. As recently as 1989, the German historian of technology Joachim Radkau had commented on the deplorable state of research: "Unlike the rise of the railroad in the nineteenth century, the rise of automobilism in the twentieth century appears as if it were a natural process. As the narrative stands, there are no key actors, no decisions, no periodizations."[1] In the meantime, a number of publications have helped to correct this impression, showing that the early automobiles met with stiff resistance in both Germany and the United States, and that this resistance was by no means a stubborn opposition of modernity but rather a very understandable reaction to the early excesses of automobile users.[2] However, automobile exhausts have heretofore been a minor issue in this burgeoning field of research. On first glance, this may appear a somewhat negligible omission. Contemporary observers were, by and large, unanimous in their opinion that automobile exhausts were indeed an issue of secondary importance compared with other problems of automobilism. Also, the discussions of automobile exhausts before 1945 did not have any significant effect in terms of policy. But it is precisely this lack of consequences that makes the discussions of the automobile exhaust problem before 1945 important, for the failure in this field reveals more fundamental flaws of contemporary air pollution control in general. This chapter argues that the control of automobile exhausts before 1945 provides a showcase of a key deficit of air pollution control in both countries. The argument is that failure was the logical result of a rationale that demanded a clinical proof of a health hazard before effective action could start. In this perspective, the hapless control of automobile exhausts before 1945 also carries an important political message. It provides an explosive demonstration of the merits of the precautionary principle.

In discussing this topic, it is important to realize that the contemporary agenda differed markedly from that of the age of environmentalism. If the reader misses other air pollution problems of automobilism in this chapter, this is exclusively due to the limits of the contemporary agenda. Also, a fourth air pollution problem of early automobilism—the dust nuisance on unpaved roads—is not addressed in the following because it was quickly conceived as an issue of infrastructure policy, rather than regulatory policy.[3]

Automobile Exhausts as a Research Topic

Out of the three problems mentioned at the start of this chapter, researchers usually devoted the least attention to the visible and malodorous components of the exhausts.[4] This was partly a result of this problem being obvious to anyone who had eyes to see and a nose to smell. With the problem being plainly apparent to every city dweller, many researchers felt that a scientific proof of this being a problem was somewhat redundant. "One only needs to walk on a major thoroughfare to detect this evil," one of the first scientific articles on the automobile exhaust problem declared.[5] Also, researchers lacked a clear object for their studies, for the phenomenon popularly referred to as "smell" was actually a mixture of gases and particles, with the composition differing markedly from case to case.[6] However, the most important reason for the lack of scientific interest was that the experts were quickly unanimous on both the technical possibility and the hygienic need for abatement. If a car emitted smoke, it was due either to an incomplete combustion of fuel or an inadvertent burning of the lubricant.[7] This also meant that a solution was desirable not only from the standpoint of public hygiene but also on technological and economic grounds; after all, the smelly exhaust pointed to a waste of fuel and excessive wear of the engine. In the 1920s, the renowned German air pollution researcher Wilhelm Liesegang calculated that the heating value lost in Berlin each year due to the incomplete combustion of automobile fuel equaled about a quarter of the annual gas production of the Berlin gas works.[8] As a result, observers quickly noted "that the public interest and that of the automobilists are completely identical."[9] Similarly, the means of abatement were soon beyond dispute. "There are three main requirements for the hygienic and economical operation of motor vehicles: good carburetion, fuel of a sufficient quality, and proper lubrication with a not too worn-out engine," a much-quoted essay of 1911 read.[10] In other words, the abatement of the car smoke problem required little more than the systematic use of contemporary technological means. In 1909, the public health journal *Blätter für Volksgesundheitspflege* wrote that malodorous omissions existed solely "because Mr. Driver is too lazy to keep his engine clean and in proper shape."[11]

It was commonplace in the contemporary literature to ask for sharp corrective measures by the police to end this kind of laziness. For example, a public health expert wrote in 1914 that it is "good to know that the police have the legal tools to abate the dirt in the sky; alas, one would only wish that these tools were applied more often."[12] Nobody thought of statements of this kind as particularly spectacular; after all, nobody had a positive interest in malodorous automobile exhausts. Not even the automobile industry—nowadays a frequent opponent of environmental policy measures—dared to challenge the rallying cry. Quite the contrary: "Our motor vehicles keep polluting terribly the streets of our cities, and the ensuing nuisance is ever more increasing due to the rapid rise of the numbers of automobiles and taxis. The police currently threaten to impose even stricter rules on this subject, which will surely be met with great sympathy in the public at large," Wilhelm Maybach, a German producer of automobiles and father of the carburetor, wrote in an essay "on the automobile smoke problem" of 1910.[13] The representatives of the automobile industry struck a similar note in a meeting chaired by the German Department of Transportation in 1924: in discussing the problem of automobile exhausts and noise, they were unanimous in their demand for "stricter police surveillance." In fact, one of the lobbyists said that the police "should not rest content with fines but also demand that automobiles creating a public nuisance be put out of service."[14] For contemporary observers, this was anything but surprising; as early as 1908, a German newspaper had declared that it would be "a great service to automobilism itself" if the automobile exhaust problem were solved.[15]

However, this broad consensus in favor of abatement went along with an equally broad skepticism toward end-of-the-pipe devices that sought to clean the exhausts after they left the engine.[16] Inventors were quick to come up with panaceas of this kind. For example the Munich-based Deutsche Saduyn-Gesellschaft tried to sell a special cleaning fluid that the exhaust gases had to pass through before being released into the atmosphere.[17] Other inventors even proposed to add special perfumes to the exhaust to "cover" the awful smell.[18] To be sure, not all the proposals were a fraud. An article of 1928 noted that the catalytic cleaning of the exhausts was the most promising method of cleaning automobile exhausts, and as early as 1913, the German hygienicist Georg Wolff commented on a procedure "to condense the exhausts through the use of platinum and thus induce ignition"—the principle that today's catalytic converters are based upon.[19] Nonetheless, the inventors of automobile exhaust cleaning devices were fighting an uphill battle; inside and outside engineering circles, people were generally of the opinion that a well-adjusted engine was the key to success, making special cleaning devices redundant. And this opinion remained unaltered in spite of the fact that complaints about smelly exhausts did not disappear after several decades. As late as 1928, someone remarked in a session of the scientific committee on automobile fuel, "There can be no doubt that automobiles stink."[20]

Thus, the closer one looks at the seemingly unanimous call for abatement, the more ambivalent it appears. After all, the frequency of calls for abatement contrasted markedly with the fact that the scientific basis for the experts' opinion was somewhat fragile. Many researchers fled into surprisingly vague statements when commenting on the issue. "The odor may be so disagreeable as to disturb sleep," a 1931 resolution of the New York Academy of Medicine read—certainly not a finding that came as a shock to contemporary readers.[21] Some scientists even argued that the malodorous components of the exhausts were not a medical problem at all. For example, a researcher of the Prussian Landesanstalt für Wasser-, Boden- und Lufthygiene declared in 1923 that automobile exhausts—though being "without doubt quite unpleasant"—"do not have a measurable impact on human health in normal ambient air concentrations to the best of our current knowledge."[22] The industrial hygiene experts Ferdinand Flury and Franz Zernik were somewhat more cautious in their 1931 book on "deleterious gases": "As of now, we must admit that the question whether automobile exhausts have a chronic effect is still open."[23] However, solving the mysteries of this question was anything but attractive from a researcher's standpoint. Of course, one could point to indirect health effects such as the reduced depth of breathing.[24] However, those who asked for further evidence inadvertently ended up in the realm of shades that was the world of chronic health hazards at that time, with a lot of vague indications and little hope for a definite proof. To be sure, there were a number of potentially unsettling findings. A series of experiments under the auspices of the German public health service and the chemical giant I. G. Farben found laboratory animals to have severe lung damage after inhaling a condensate of automobile exhausts—however, the experiments were conducted with concentrations far above normal ambient air concentrations.[25] A pathologist from Stuttgart exposed rabbits to the smoke particles of a diesel engine, finding a whole series of lung diseases, but his conclusion was lukewarm: he wrote that it would be "desirable if one could avoid the production of large clouds of smoke."[26] Yet another author noted that there were "some statements from physicians which attribute the recent rise of lung cancer to the pollution of the city air by automobiles" and declared at the same time that this was "a priori unlikely."[27] Thus, there were a number of worrisome findings and a subliminal suspicion in the scientific literature that there was indeed a hidden health hazard.[28] But at the same time, researchers were hesitant to go deeper into this issue, obviously waiting for someone else to take the initiative. Since the state never asked for a systematic investigation, researchers generally remained in their state of lethargy. As a result, the scientific literature tended to see the visible and malodorous automobile exhausts as "quite a nuisance" but not as a clear health hazard.[29]

The carbon monoxide problem received somewhat more attention among researchers. In contrast to their vague descriptions of the perils of automobile smoke and odor, scientists were able to describe the health hazards of carbon monoxide in clear terms. "Carbon monoxide is unmatched as a poison gas in terms of frequency of occurrence, insidiousness, and casualties," the industrial hygiene journal *Zentralblatt für Gewerbehygiene* declared in 1929.[30] From a medical standpoint, carbon monoxide had a number of unsettling characteristics. Enriching in the blood, it strongly inhibited oxygen transport; it was odorless; it resulted in a gradual loss of consciousness, making it difficult for victims to escape; and it was poisonous even in low concentrations—scientists generally agreed that the threshold poison level was between fifty and two hundred parts per million.[31] Even more, carbon monoxide was the typical product of an imperfect combustion of carbon-based fuels, which meant that automobile exhausts were by no means the only source of carbon monoxide. "Carbon monoxide is the most frequent poisonous substance in daily life," Wilhelm Liesegang wrote in 1934, while Flury and Zernik called carbon monoxide "the most important industrial poison."[32] The household hazard of carbon monoxide was the most conspicuous one: between 1926 and 1930, the annual number of deadly household incidents in Germany was between 490 and 665—not counting suicides, which varied in number between 1,986 and 2,918.[33]

As a result, researchers were quickly alert to the health hazard of carbon monoxide in automobile exhausts. As early as 1911, the German hygienicist A. Korff-Petersen warned that "there could be an alarming accumulation of carbon monoxides at busy intersections and taxi stands."[34] However, it was not until the construction of long automobile tunnels in New York and Pittsburgh that a more enduring discussion of the carbon monoxide problem of automobiles took place.[35] Also, there was an intensive discussion of the accumulation of the gas in parking garages and repair shops.[36] At the same time, however, scientists generally agreed that these were special situations "without significance to the problem of atmospheric pollution as a whole."[37] After all, it was clear that there was an easy solution to the carbon monoxide problem in tunnels and garages: proper ventilation.[38] Reducing carbon monoxide in the ambient air was much more of a challenge in relation to abatement technology, which gave a special degree of drama to pending discussions of the automobile's carbon monoxide emissions. If scientists had found that there were dangerous concentrations of carbon monoxide in the ambient air, this would have required either less-polluting cars or restrictions on automobile traffic—two horror scenarios from the point of view of regulatory policy. To be sure, it was possible to reduce the carbon monoxide content of the exhaust gases through proper adjustments in the engine and the carburetor; measurements showed that carbon monoxide concentrations could vary by several percentage points.[39] However, it was one thing to make these adjustments in the laboratory but quite another to systematically control these adjustments in all cars in use. As an alternative, some researchers proposed special devices to dilute the exhausts;[40] a smokestack-like design put forward by Yandell Henderson and Howard Haggard in the United States was perhaps the device that attracted the most attention.[41] However, devices of this kind were generally seen as make-shift. In 1925, a researcher commented on similar ideas, "It is to be hoped that something better than any of these solutions may be brought forward."[42]

There is no indication in surviving documents that scientists were under direct pressure to play down the health hazard of carbon monoxide from automobiles. However, the indirect pressure would have been immense; after all, researchers must have been aware of the far-reaching implications that attesting to a clear and imminent health hazard would have had. Therefore, it seems reasonable to assume that simply knowing of these far-reaching implications made researchers particularly cautious. This general orientation is of special importance because the researchers' findings themselves were ambiguous. The majority of measurements found concentrations to be below the critical standard, but in some cases concentrations reached 200 ppm and more—in one case, even 700 ppm.[43] Of course, one could (and did) argue that while these concentrations were indeed a health hazard, almost no one had to spend an extended period of time breathing heavily polluted street air.[44] But saying so implied that one accepted a special health hazard for all those people who, like policemen, were working in the streets. In 1926, the *Journal of the American Medical Association* published a much-quoted study showing that Philadelphia policemen had a carbon monoxide saturation level of up to 30 percent in their blood at the end of their shifts.[45] This level not only resulted in headaches and dizziness (which the policemen were indeed complaining about),[46] but it also lay dangerously close to the level where life was in imminent danger; scientists generally agreed that "self-rescue was in doubt" beyond a saturation level of 40 percent.[47] However, contemporary scientists shied away from sounding the alarm as a result of these findings. "So far, measurements have not found a detrimental concentration of carbon monoxide in street air in Germany," a statement of 1936 read.[48] To be sure, there was always a tacit suspicion of a chronic health hazard, which was quite similar to the worries about the long-term effects of automobile smoke. "We do not know enough about the effect of low-level concentrations of carbon monoxide," a 1931 Ph.D. of the Dresden Institute of Technology noted.[49] However, as with the smoke and odor problem, the state refrained from forcing researchers into a closer study of the issue.

So, with regard to smoke and carbon monoxide, the researchers' discussion can generally be described as lukewarm, with researchers taking an unclear position, speaking of more than a nuisance but less than a health hazard. In contrast, the researchers' discussion of tetraethyl lead commenced quickly after its introduction in 1923 as an antiknock fuel additive.[50] In some scientists, it instilled a reaction that neither smoke nor carbon monoxide had ever evoked: panic. After all, lead was a well-known poison, which many professionals in the field of industrial hygiene had spent years to curb.[51] Faced with the prospect of a large-scale distribution of this poison through the use of leaded gasoline, researchers reacted with urgency. "It would be an unbearable aberration [unerträgliche Verirrung] to 'poison' our traffic life in the most literal sense, especially with a gaseous lead compound which, if put out in large quantities, will jeopardize the population to an incalculable extent," Georg Wolff declared in 1925, adding that it was "already extremely difficult in itself to curb lead emissions from industrial sources."[52] Similarly, Yandell Henderson warned that lead is "the most perfect example of a substance which may cumulate little by little over long periods of time until a toxic amount is reached"; Henderson developed a horror scenario of a widespread contamination of drivers and city dwellers.[53] Even a high-ranking official of the Prussian Department of Public Welfare—habitually trained to be cautious in sounding the whistle—was alarmed: the substances in question "are medically known to be strong nerve poisons," and he "feared that many and severe cases of poisoning will occur in the urban population at large."[54] If the question had been decided on the basis of the intuitive reaction of the medical experts, leaded gasoline would never have had a chance.

However, physicians had a hard time supporting their intuitive reaction with hard medical facts. To be sure, this was due not only to deficient scientific instruments but also to the characteristics of the matter itself. In 1925, the Swiss hygienicist H. Zangger justly pointed out that the impending chronic lead poisoning would not result in a clear medical picture; therefore, physicians "would have to concede that even if we join forces with chemistry, we will not be able to make a causal connection between the poison and the effect even in the case of mass poisoning."[55] The ensuing medical debate quickly focused on those situations where the hazard was particularly imminent—not out of an ill sense of priorities but mostly because these kinds of situations offered the best prospects for a clinical proof of the physicians' fears. Therefore, the production and distribution of tetraethyl lead, together with repair shops for automobiles, became the key issues of the debate. And since there was soon general agreement that there was no imminent health hazard in these areas if employees observed a number of security precautions, there was no basis for a continuing discussion of the hazard for the population at large.[56] A key figure in this story was Robert Arthur Kehoe, director of the Kettering Laboratory of the University of Cincinnati, who argued that there would never be a case of poisoning from tetraethyl lead if the substance was handled properly. Kehoe made that point not only in a number of articles but also as an expert witness for tetraethyl lead producers, and Christopher Sellers has argued with some justification that, in doing so, Kehoe felt in perfect accord with his scientific ethos.[57]

It is surprising how quickly the issue disappeared from the radar screen of the scientific community. The Bureau of Mines canceled its research efforts after only two years: "As far as can be determined from experiments with animals there is no apparent danger from the normal use of ethyl gasoline," the bureau concluded.[58] A committee of the Public Health Service called for some long-term studies, but nobody cared to follow up on them—and it would take more than three decades until someone would regret it.[59] It was not until the petroleum industry sought to increase the maximum lead content of gasoline by a third in the late 1950s that the health effects of tetraethyl lead again received attention from the medical community. With independent research essentially suspended in the meantime, researchers had to grapple with massive uncertainties.[60] Characteristically, the report of the Surgeon General's Ad Hoc Committee on

Tetraethyl Lead of January 1959, began by declaring, "The Committee wishes to point out that a conclusive answer is impossible at the present time because of the lack of medical data."[61]

While research was sporadic in the United States, it was virtually nonexistent in Germany. The reason was simple: tetraethyl lead was not in use in Germany in the 1920s.[62] Therefore, the German Bureau of Public Health found in 1927 that "for the time being, there is no reason to take a closer look at tetraethyl lead"; rather, the department confined itself to a review of the literature "so as to not lose the issue entirely out of sight."[63] In a similar vein, the German Department of Transportation declared in 1928 that there was no need for further research; however, the department proposed, without a trace of irony, "to keep track of the large-scale experiment currently underway in the United States."[64]

It should come as no surprise that silence prevailed on this issue after these statements. Even when tetraethyl lead was finally allowed by ministerial decree for automobiles in Germany, in 1939, nobody cared to conduct an independent scientific investigation. The essay accompanying the decree simply quoted Robert Kehoe's publications at length, referred to investigation in other countries, and finally concluded that these studies "had generally resulted in similar findings, leading to the desired clarification in the positive sense."[65] As in the United States, the alarmist mood of the early years had disappeared without a trace.

The Public's View on Automobile Exhausts

"Concerning these automobiles, I might say that in the entire country, and especially in rural areas, there is a profound bitterness concerning certain proprietors of these cars," a speaker in the parliament of the state of Bavaria declared in October 1905; the ensuing comment of the other representatives—"oh yes"—showed that this was by no means a singular opinion.[66] In fact, a giant wave of public outrage confronted the early automobilists, and the motives had little to do with envy or a fundamentalist opposition to technological progress but much to do with the social costs of early automobilism.[67] The key criticisms were the excessive speed of car drivers, reckless driving habits, and the ensuing accidents; but some complaints also focused on automobile exhaust. For example, a citizen of the German city of Wiesbaden complained that cities were growing into "first-rate stench centers" and that "respect and love of human beings are incompatible with a driver who exposes his entire surroundings to dust and odor."[68] As a rule, angry complaints went along with calls for severe punitive measures. For example, a resident of New York who was especially angered by "smoking taxicabs" proposed, "If the Presidents of the various taxicab companies could be given about thirty days each in jail, there would be no more smoking taxis and 75 per cent of the smoke nuisance would be abated."[69] The anonymous author of a German treatise on the subject called for "the formation of automobile inspectorates providing for a sufficient protection against the automobilists' excesses."[70] Still other observers took refuge in gloomy predictions: if the automobile actually became the transportation device of the future, "Berlin would probably be the smelliest city in the world," a Prussian member of parliament declared.[71] A Berlin-based Society of Residents of the Lower Friedrichstadt came up with similar ideas: if the "oxygen robbery" of gasoline-powered automobiles were allowed to continue, "tuberculosis, scrofula, rickets, metabolic diseases, eye injuries etc. would destroy the health of children as well as adults."[72] An anonymous judge of southern Germany wrote that people were routinely and rightly referring to cars as "stench vehicles [*Stinkkarren*]"; after all, automobiles were "routinely producing a smell which everyone with a proper sense of smell will find to be a nuisance."[73] The anger did not stop at class barriers. When a rightist member of parliament denounced the "clouds of gasoline" and "steam" in public parks in a session of the German Reichstag, adding the rhetorical question of where "working people were to go for relaxation on a Sunday," he could rejoice over a sympathetic comment of socialist member of parliament, August Bebel.[74]

However, protest rarely moved beyond proclamations of this kind. There were few people complaining about specific cars producing excessive air pollution; when they did, the cases were frequently of an anecdotal nature. For example, a citizen of Bremen named Fritz Vielhaben filed a number of formal complaints in 1926, launching something like a private crusade against smoking automobiles.[75] The city council of Wiesbaden voted in 1907 "to urge the local police that in the future, only non-odorous taxis will be granted a concession," but concrete steps of this kind were clearly the exception.[76] After all, it was not for nothing that the Berlin hygienicist Julius Hirsch complained of the "inexplicable tolerance" for automobile exhaust from the public at large in 1928.[77] Nor was there a permanent movement against malodorous cars in the United States. In New York, influential civic organizations such as the Fifth Avenue Association and the Woman's Municipal League at one time or another started to look into the issue, but only to turn to other causes soon afterward.[78] At a time when participation of civic organizations was rather strong, particularly on urban issues, the weakness of civic activity concerning automobile exhausts is peculiarly apparent.[79]

While civic activism was weak on the visible and malodorous components of the automobile exhausts, it was almost nonexistent when it came to carbon monoxide.[80] If there was a role for the public on this issue, it was clearly a passive one: instead of urging researchers and officials to take care of the problem, the public was the recipient of numerous calls for caution. "Of course, a layperson only knows of those exhaust components which offend the nose and the eye," an expert wrote in 1928, complaining that "most people never come to realize" the hazards of carbon monoxide.[81] The inevitable result of this state of affairs was a horrendous number of carbon monoxide deaths in closed spaces. As Flury and Zernik gloomily noted, "Death in the garage is anything but rare nowadays."[82] An American researcher even asserted that during the wintertime, one could barely open a newspaper without reading of some poor person having died due to carbon monoxide from an running engine.[83] Time and again, scientists stressed the need for ventilation of garages and repair shops.[84] However, the success of these admonitions remains an open question. On the one hand, Wilhelm Liesegang wrote of a significant decline of cases of carbon monoxide poisoning "due to special rules and regulations and a corresponding campaign in the media" in an article of 1932.[85] On the other hand, there was a comment in a public hygiene journal as late as 1939 that casualties due to automobile exhausts were totaling "200 to 300 per year in Germany."[86]

In any case, there was obviously no civic lobby urging a solution to the carbon monoxide problem. And neither was there such a lobby on the issue of tetraethyl lead. Quite the contrary: if scientific studies indicated that there was no health hazard, the public was apparently willing to calm down. In typical fashion, the New York Times commented on a number of scientific studies that they presented "the scientific view of the matter, as opposed to the sentimental."[87] To be sure, a vague skepticism on the merits of leaded gasoline seems to have persisted for some time; as late as the 1930s, Sun Oil was marketing its unleaded gasoline as "poison-free."[88] However, this skepticism never led to anything; after all, leaded gasoline obviously found its customers. As a result, there was an incongruous agenda on automobile exhausts: public protest was weak on the issues that researchers deemed the most important, and vice versa—not an ideal situation for politicians and officials who had to make up their minds on what to do about it.

The Governments' Reaction

Contemporary observers mostly agreed that controlling automobile exhausts was a task for the government. However, this was not as self-evident as it might appear on first glance. Theoretically, there was also a chance for a solution based on self-regulation, since in the fight against reckless driving, automobile clubs had shown to be of some help in the early 1900s, at least in Germany.[89] Some proposed a similar approach on automobile pollution; for example, Georg Wolff wrote in 1911 "that it would be a clever move on the side of the car users to appease the public at large by quickly and effectively controlling the automobile's negative side effects."[90] However, the vast majority of the observers put their trust in the regulatory power of the government—without becoming too specific in most cases. German researchers in particular were displaying a tendency to leave it to the government to decide on policy issues.[91]

German and American approaches to solving the automobile exhaust problem were somewhat different, though the ultimate result was basically the same. In the United States, governmental activities (if they existed at all) usually took the form of a campaign. On the issue of smoking automobiles, such a campaign usually started with the passage of a special ordinance. One of the first of these ordinances went into effect in New York in 1908, restricting smoking automobiles' access to Central Park.[92] In 1910, the prohibition was extended to the entire city, with enforcement being somewhat active initially: during the first year, more than two thousand offenses were dealt with in court.[93] However, two years later, the *New York Times* complained about the administration's declining attention: "The emission of dense clouds of smoke from the exhaust pipes of automobiles [. . .] is becoming again an offense to the eyes and nostrils of the city."[94] Officials reacted quickly, fining a number of automobiles on Fifth Avenue for excessive smoke; however, the long-term effect of this kind of activity seems to have been somewhat limited, especially considering that drivers usually received a fine of between two and five dollars.[95] So, after several years, the provisions on smoking automobiles were nothing more than dead letters. As a New Yorker noted in 1924, "Despite the ordinances against it in many cities, the [automobile] smoke nuisance continues to prevail all too frequently."[96]

There was a similar scheme in the American approach to tetraethyl lead. Interestingly, it was not the medical experts' fears concerning the public at large that instilled a political reaction but an accident in a factory producing tetraethyl lead. On October 26, 1924, forty workers suffered severe cases of lead poisoning in a Standard Oil plant in New Jersey, with five of them dying from it during the next few days. Due to intensive press coverage, with the *New York Times* as the vanguard, a number of cities, including New York and Philadelphia, as well as numerous states quickly moved to ban the sale of leaded gasoline.[97] In fact, the situation became so tense that the production of tetraethyl lead virtually ceased for nine months in 1925. However, people ultimately found that a workplace accident did not provide a sufficient basis for a total ban of tetraethyl lead. With scientific studies painting a rather soothing picture, restrictions on the sale of leaded gasoline were suspended almost as quickly as they had been passed. The New York ordinance, which was suspended after about three years, seems to have been one of the last of its kind.[98] "Your committee begs to report that in their opinion there are at present no good grounds for prohibiting the use of ethyl gasoline [. . .] as motor fuel, provided that its distribution and use are controlled by proper regulations," a federal public health committee declared in January 1926.[99] As a result, tetraethyl lead was a common component of American gasoline until the federal government gradually banned its use in the 1970s.[100]

The German policy on automobile exhausts differed to a certain extent from the campaign-style U.S. regulatory approach. In essence, the German approach was a curious mixture of a quick imposition of rules and regulations and an extremely lax enforcement policy. From a juridical standpoint, the matter was crystal clear after a brief period of time. "It is unlawful for automobiles to produce offensive smoke, steam, or odors," a provincial law of 1901 for the Rhineland area declared.[101] Similarly, regulations of the Bavarian Department of the Interior of 1902 read, "Motor vehicles must be built and equipped in such a way that the possibility of fire, explosions, or a noise or odor nuisance to people and horse-drawn carriages is excluded as much as possible."[102] Provisions of this kind quickly became a standard part of the German automotive law.[103] The legal implications for automobile owners were far-reaching indeed, as a Berlin court ruling of 1908 showed. The court dismissed the driver's apology that the smoke problem had developed during the trip, arguing that a car driver had the obligation to abate smoke even in the course of travel.[104] German officials were also allowed "to mandate an inspection of the vehicle at the owner's expense at any time to see whether it complied with all rules and regulations"—with the intention being, as the German Department of Transportation wrote in a memo of 1924, "that this inspection implies considerable discomfort and costs" for car drivers.[105] Unlike in the United States, where nothing happened before a group of reformers put the issue on the agenda, German bureaucrats eagerly developed rules on automobile smoke all by themselves, and as a result, they quickly had (as the Prussian government once wrote) "the working tools to eliminate automobiles producing noise and awful smell from our public streets."[106]

However, enforcement was quite a different story. Complaints were processed only slowly and with obvious distaste. In 1910, a member of the Prussian parliament reported his ill-fated attempts to push the Berlin police into prosecuting smoke offenders. The usual response of a policeman, the politician told, was simply a shrug of the shoulders and a lethargic comment of the "Well, if you want to file a complaint, you have the right to do that" kind.[107] Fritz Vielhaben was not more successful when he filed numerous complaints against smoking cars in the city of Bremen. Obviously thinking that it was not their job to combat automobile exhausts, the police were apathetic from the outset. Characteristically, an addition to the first police report (written immediately after Vielhaben visited them and before the police went out to check the authenticity of his complaints) noted, "Vielhaben gives the impression that he is very nervous."[108] After controlling a number of automobiles, the officials found their suspicions confirmed: "Vielhaben is a complete layman in this field, and he does not know what normal smoke emissions are," the report read; the police decided to "use great caution" in case Vielhaben would file further complaints.[109] When the exhausts of so-called Bulldog tractors were the target of frequent complaints in the mid-1920s, the Prussian Department of Commerce simply issued a decree saying that these engines had to use "a kind of fuel which will preclude the formation of smoke and odor."[110] However, even disregarding the fact that the decree applied only to Bulldog tractors within city limits—since there had been no complaints from rural areas, the department sharply concluded that Bulldog tractors could just as well pollute the countryside[111]—enforcement was once again next to nonexistent. For example, the police in Hannover simply confined their efforts to a one-time admonition to the policemen and the publication of a brief note in the local newspapers.[112] In Berlin, the police maintained special "smoke patrols" for some time; at least, that is what a government representative recounted in parliament, to respond to repeated complaints of the administration's do-nothing stance on the issue.[113] However, it remains in doubt whether the measures actually "had success," as the administration claimed.[114] When the city of Augsburg took similar measures in 1929, the noise problem quickly received most of the attention. In the end, the number of reports on smoking vehicles was four.[115]

Time and again, government records demonstrate the administration's lethargy above anything else. For example, when the German Bureau of Public Health received a complaint in 1910, it responded simply that the exhaust problem was "well known" and that it was ultimately "a technical question" beyond the purview of the bureau.[116] Similarly, the president of the Landesanstalt für Wasser-, Boden- und Lufthygiene wrote in 1928 that policemen were checking for smoke "more than before," adding in an inexplicable twist of the argument that one should refrain from "further measures" for the time being "because improvements should come of themselves to a certain extent."[117] When the Prussian Department of Public Welfare asked for "sharper steps" in 1927, the Department of the Interior refused to become active: "I have called upon the police of Berlin repeatedly to keep an eye on the automobile smoke nuisance," calling this "sufficient reason to refrain from yet another admonition."[118] Obviously, the existing rules and regulations provided a perfect alibi to lethargic public officials, even while the regulations were barely ever used.

Perhaps the most drastic evidence of the deficient sense of direction of the German administration was that there was not even a clear policy in dealing with the aforementioned special cleaning devices. The German Chancellor's Office accepted an offer of the Deutsche Saduyn-Gesellschaft to demonstrate the use of its device, a rather unusual step given the fact that other offices usually took care of technology issues. However, the results were not terribly convincing: "The device does not do away with odor altogether. It only eliminates gasoline vapor, but the exhausts smell strongly of bitter almonds," an official noted, calling it "not advisable to prescribe its use for all automobiles."[119] At the same time, the official was somewhat optimistic: "We may talk about the use of the device after some improvements are made."[120] However, when the Saduyn-Gesellschaft notified the Chancellor's Office of its new model one year later, nobody wanted to be reminded of the previous interest. Officials simply sent the material to the Emperor's Patent Office "for them to take notice" and filed the documents after they returned.[121] With officials failing to pursue a clear policy in this field, where there was general agreement as to the limited usefulness of special cleaning devices, one might guess at the amount of bureaucratic incompetence on the issue as a whole.

The administrative record was not much better on the carbon monoxide issue. The only exception was the carbon monoxide hazard in garages and the need for proper ventilation in these places.[122] Regarding carbon monoxide in the ambient air, officials basically refrained from taking any steps. In fact, the German Department of Transportation found as early as 1924 (when research was just starting on this topic) that there was no need for corrective steps: "So far, I do not know of one case of carbon monoxide poisoning in street traffic," the department declared, speaking of the "great dilution" of carbon monoxide in the ambient air.[123] And with research slowly moving forward to a similar conclusion, a debate on controlling carbon monoxide from automotive sources never got off the ground. Ultimately, scientists and bureaucrats were turning into "partners in lethargy": while scientists were hesitant to emphasize the health hazards of carbon monoxide, bureaucrats were hesitant to ask the critical questions. Scientists refrained from a closer look at the issue—and bureaucrats did not push them to. As a result, the solution of automobilism's carbon monoxide problem was postponed until the age of environmentalism.

The German policy on tetraethyl lead was somewhat different from that on carbon monoxide and automobile smoke, at least at first glance. The administration quickly acknowledged that tetraethyl lead was an important issue, and officials monitored closely the contemporary debate in the United States. In fact, the German Bureau of Public Health declared as early as 1925 "that a substance as poisonous as tetraethyl lead should not have a place in traffic";[124] it is likely that the German administration would have passed a law banning leaded gasoline if tetraethyl lead had been sold in Germany (a preemptive prohibition was deemed unwise out of foreign trade policy concerns).[125] This alert reaction was all the more remarkable because experts did not offer more than an intuitive reasoning on the subject. "For chemists like me, lead is a substance that we confront with great distrust," Oskar Spitta, an expert official of the German Bureau of Public Health, declared in an internal meeting in 1928, urging "great caution in dealing with this substance."[126] In fact, Spitta used the opportunity to make a statement on the professional ethos of the medical official: "Taking into account the development that automobile traffic is currently taking, it would be irresponsible to wait until something has happened; rather, we should take precautionary measures to preclude any hazard."[127]

However, in evaluating Spitta's bragging about his professional ethos, it is important to keep one thing in mind: there was no risk involved. "We are currently not distributing tetraethyl lead in Germany," a representative of the German Petroleum Association [Erdöl-Reichsverband] declared at the same meeting, after Spitta's vociferous declaration, "and neither do we plan to in the future."[128] Even more, the technical need for tetraethyl lead was somewhat less urgent in Germany than it was in the United States. For one thing, there were large quantities of benzol available in Germany, and benzol was relatively knock-resistant.[129] Even more, the German chemical company BASF (soon to merge into the giant I. G. Farben) had developed an antiknock fuel additive based on iron rather than lead, which had been distributed since 1926 under the trade name Motalin.[130] It was not until the mid-1930s that I. G. Farben started to build two plants for the production of tetraethyl lead, and the output of these plants was earmarked for use in aviation, where the need for additional fuel power was particularly urgent.[131] It is not completely clear when and how tetraethyl lead came to be used in German automobile traffic as well; it is possible that it was a curious side-effect of the infamous *Anschluss* of Austria, because tetraethyl lead was used to improve low-quality Austrian gasoline.[132] To be sure, it seems that the quantities used were small and stayed that way, since, from the point of view of the Nazi government, the demands of the air force obviously took precedence over the needs of civilian car drivers. Nonetheless, the bottom line was that the German Department of Labor officially sanctioned the use of tetraethyl lead in a decree of June 9, 1939.[133] In doing so, the German administration arrived at the point that U.S. officials had reached about a decade before: there were no good grounds for prohibiting the use of ethyl gasoline as long as there was no definitive proof for an imminent health hazard.

And this, as a matter of fact, was the crucial problem of the entire administrative debate in both Germany and the United States before the advent of World War II. In dealing with the three issues that composed the contemporary automobile exhaust problem, the key issue was dealing with cognitive uncertainty—and in all three cases, cognitive uncertainty did not prompt further research or even preventive measures, but the precise opposite: a legitimation for a do-nothing attitude. The modern state, being, as it is, a science-based regulatory state, requires an intensive consultation between scientific experts and public officials. However, in the case of automobile exhausts, this communication led to a highly problematic tendency to legitimate the lethargy of both partners. While researchers, aware of the difficulties of a clinical proof of harm, were hesitant to emphasize the health effects too strongly, bureaucrats never cared to ask pointed questions or to urge scientists to be more outspoken. The simple idea that cognitive uncertainty could suggest a call for action rather than inaction remained foreign to all parties involved. Therefore, it seems reasonable to assume that the failure of automobile exhaust control before 1945 was the result of a regulatory philosophy that was fundamentally flawed. Contemporary people were obviously lacking a rationale of action that called for a government intervention—be it to abate emissions or to initiate further research—*before* there was a clinical proof of harm. And this is also what one might call the moral lesson of this story.

Conclusion: The Merits of the Precautionary Principle

In November 1970, a hearing of the Air Resources Board of the state of California became the forum for a memorable showdown between two rationales of air pollution control. The issue under debate was a statewide ambient air quality standard for lead, and the administration's proposed standard was so low that drastic measures against lead emissions were imminent. For obvious reasons, the producers of tetraethyl lead decided to oppose this standard. Their expert witness was none other than Robert Arthur Kehoe, now seventy-six years old and for a number of years professor emeritus of occupational medicine at the University of Cincinnati. To no one's surprise, Kehoe's argument followed the lines of his previous work on the subject. Citing his "experimental studies on healthy adults," Kehoe complained "that the proposed lead standard is too low" and asked for a corresponding adjustment.[134] In the 1920s, this argument had remained unchallenged; but now a number of people spoke out against it, voicing an altogether different perspective. One of them was Sumner M. Kalman, M.D., a professor of pharmacology who was "representing [the] Environmental Defense Fund, Sierra Club, Friends of the Earth and the Santa Clara County Medical Society." "Many of the present documented effects are from studies on healthy young males. People with special problems and children require lower levels," Kalman argued, adding that "there are about 3 million people in the United States who are probably at risk right now from body burdens of lead considered within the normal range."[135] Similarly, R. Cree Pillsbury, M.D., president-elect and chairman of the Air Conservation Committee of the Tuberculosis and Respiratory

Disease Association of Santa Clara–San Benito Counties, reported a number of unsettling signs he had observed: "As a physician, I see many patients who have non-specific complaints such as headaches, gastrointestinal upsets, leg cramps, malaise, and anemia. [. . .] These complaints are identical to the symptoms that people with clinical lead poisoning experience, and I suggest to you that many of the everyday nagging complaints of our population may be related to poisoning from air pollution."[136] A third physician finally pointed to the fact that it was beyond dispute that lead was a confirmed poison. Comparing "use of leaded gas to that of certain illegal drugs," he declared, "We are much more certain of the detrimental effects of lead on the body than we are of those of many of these drugs."[137] In addition, "lead has no useful function in the environment and is toxic to many life forms and, therefore, should be eliminated as a potentially dangerous substance."[138]

It is rewarding to take a closer look at these divergent rationales. Kehoe's argument basically followed the aforementioned rationale of action that was dominant in research circles before 1945: key was a clinical proof of harm, and if there was no such proof, there was no sufficient ground for countermeasures. As Kehoe himself pointedly declared during the hearing, "The lead standard should be based on measured effects."[139] In contrast, the dissenters, members of the burgeoning environmental movement, were referring to circumstantial evidence—inexplicable symptoms or the high concentration of lead in the body of ordinary citizens. The basic argument was that while none of these signs, taken in itself, would demonstrate the hazards of leaded gasoline, the combined findings provided sufficient grounds for corrective measures. From this point of view, waiting for a clinical proof of harm—the Kehoe approach—was unnecessary, and even immoral; after all, this would have meant to tolerate potentially harmful conditions for the sake of medical studies. The sheer probability of a health hazard was perceived as a sufficient reason for effective steps, ignoring the objection that as a result of these steps, one would probably never know whether one's suspicions were right.

It was anything but coincidence that this confrontation was taking place in 1970. The environmentalists' arguments mirrored the rise of the precautionary principle in Germany and the United States in the years up to and including 1970.[140] While there is some disagreement as to the precise meaning of the precautionary principle[141]—for example, a recent German reference article declared that it is first and foremost an "ethical principle"[142]—one important line of argument makes a distinction between the precautionary principle and the classic police function of controlling an imminent threat. Instead of focusing only on those cases where there is clear evidence, the precautionary principle allows attack on potential hazards as well.[143] And this was crucial in lowering the threshold for the government to intervene, allowing the control not only of proven but also of suspected risks. This implied a crucial expansion of the administration's argumentative resources, and the environmentalists were obviously eager to use these new resources in the California hearing.

It was perhaps the most obvious expression of this new rationale of action that the environmentalists did not commit themselves to certain standards but rather to the goal of reducing emissions as much as possible. Even if strict standards were met, environmentalists felt a further reduction was desirable, they declared at the California hearing; the ultimate goal was "zero lead emissions from motor vehicles by January 1, 1973."[144] Again, the precautionary principle induced an important change in the administration's powers: in the context of the pre-1945 debates, where discussions centered fruitlessly on a definite proof of harm, the precautionary principle would have implied an almost revolutionary expansion of the government's possibilities to intervene.

The rise of the precautionary principle around 1970 has turned out to be a permanent transformation of regulatory policy, with references to the concept being a common fixture of corresponding debates. To be sure, the *interpretation* of this principle is a matter of ongoing discussion, enough so to keep environmentalists and their opponents busy; as with every ethical principle, the precautionary principle is open to different readings, and a unanimous definition is nowhere in sight. Still, in spite of the heat of current debates, it is worth noting that few people would challenge the precautionary principle *as a matter of principle*: most people assume that it is a self-evident, "natural" principle of the modern regulatory state.[145] However, looking back on the history of automobile air pollution control before 1945, it becomes clear that the precautionary principle is more than a truism: it is actually a first-rate accomplishment of the environmental era. After all, one can barely exaggerate the extent of the administrations' failure before 1945: governments did not set clear goals or meaningful standards, they did not assign clear responsibilities, and they did not even come close to devising proper regulatory strategies. Of course, the incongruous agendas of researchers and the public on automobile exhausts was an important part of the story. However, from a political standpoint, the more alarming feature is the degree of thoughtlessness that contemporary actors displayed: as quoted above, the German Department of Transportation seriously spoke of a "large-scale experiment" with tetraethyl lead in the United States—and nobody gave a thought to what would happen if the experiment came out badly. To be sure, there were also a number of differences between the American and the German approach. But it is probably more surprising that in spite of these differences, there was a common cause of administrative failure in both Germany and the United States: the contemporary logic that control measures presupposed a definite medical proof of harm. From this perspective, the hapless control of automobile exhausts before 1945 provides a fulminant demonstration of the merits of the precautionary principle.

NOTES

1. Joachim Radkau, *Technik in Deutschland. Vom 18. Jahrhundert bis zur Gegenwart* (Frankfurt/Main, 1989), p. 299. [All translations by the author—F.U.]

2. Cf. Christoph Maria Merki, "Den Fortschritt bremsen? Der Widerstand gegen die Motorisierung des Straßenverkehrs in der Schweiz," *Technikgeschichte* 65 (1998), pp. 233–253; Christoph Maria Merki, "Plädoyer für eine Tachostoria," *Historische Anthropologie* 5 (1997), pp. 288–292; Angela Zatsch, *Staatsmacht und Motorisierung am Morgen des Automobilzeitalters* (Konstanz, 1993); Barbara Haubner, *Nervenkitzel und Freizeitvergnügen. Automobilismus in Deutschland 1886–1914* (Göttingen, 1998); Clay McShane, *Down the Asphalt Path. The Automobile and the American City* (New York, 1994); Tom McCarthy, "The Coming Wonder? Foresight and Early Concerns about the Automobile," *Environmental History* 6 (2001), pp. 46–74; Maxwell G. Lay, *Die Geschichte der Straße. Vom Trampelpfad zur Autobahn* (Frankfurt/Main and New York, 1994); Gijs Mom, "Das 'Scheitern' des frühen Elektromobils (1895–1925). Versuch einer Neubewertung," *Technikgeschichte* 64 (1997), pp. 269–285; Dietmar Fack, "Das deutsche Fahrschulwesen und die technisch-rechtliche Konstitution der Fahrausbildung 1899–1943," *Technikgeschichte* 67 (2000), pp. 111–138; Elfi Bendikat, "Umweltbelastung und Stadtverkehr: Fachdiskussionen, Bürgerproteste und Immissionsschutzmaßnahmen, 1900–1935," *Informationen zur modernen Stadtgeschichte* 1 (1997), pp. 14–19; Dietmar Klenke, *Bundesdeutsche Verkehrspolitik und Motorisierung. Konfliktträchtige Weichenstellungen in den Jahren des Wiederaufstiegs* (Stuttgart, 1993). For a review article, see Barbara Schmucki, "Automobilisierung. Neuere Forschungen zur Motorisierung," *Archiv für Sozialgeschichte* 35 (1995), pp. 582–597. The publications of Michael L. Berger (*The Devil Wagon in God's Country. The Automobile and Social Change in Rural America, 1893–1929* [Hamden, 1979]) and Joachim Radkau ("'Ausschreitungen gegen Automobilisten haben Überhand genommen.' Aus der Zeit des wilden

Automobilismus in Ostwestfalen-Lippe," *Lippische Mitteilungen* 56 [1987], pp. 9–23) may be seen as early, pioneering studies.

3. On the dust nuisance, see Louis Edgar Andés, *Die Beseitigung des Staubes auf Straßen und Wegen, in Fabriks- und gewerblichen Betrieben und im Haushalte* (Vienna and Leipzig, 1908), pp. 33–172; Robert Weldert, *Übersicht über das in den Jahren 1911 bis Anfang 1924 erschienene Schrifttum auf dem Gebiet der Lufthygiene, dargestellt vom chemischen, technischen und medizinischen Standpunkt aus* (Munich and Berlin, 1926), pp. 60–69; W. Liesegang, *Die Reinhaltung der Luft* (Ergebnisse der angewandten physikalischen Chemie vol. 3, pp. 1–109) (Leipzig, 1935), pp. 40–44.

4. Cf. A. Korff-Petersen, "Gesundheitsgefährdung durch die Auspuffgase der Automobile," *Zeitschrift für Hygiene und Infektionskrankheiten* 69 (1911), pp. 135–148, p. 136n.; and Hermann Koschmieder, "Die Tätigkeit der Gesundheits-Kommissionen in den Jahren 1906/08 nach den Berichten in der Zeitschrift 'Gesundheit'," *Gesundheit* 34 (1909), cc. 97–109, 129–139, 167–176, c. 176.

5. G. Wolff, "Die Bekämpfung der Automobilauspuffplage," *Die Städtereinigung* 5 (1913), pp. 99–100, 110–111, 122–123, p. 99. Also see J. J. Bloomfield and H. S. Isbell, "The Problem of Automobile Exhaust Gas in Streets and Repair Shops of Large Cities," *Public Health Reports* 43 (1928), pp. 750–765, p. 750.

6. Cf. Georg Wolff, "Straßenhygiene und Automobilauspuff," *Gesundheits-Ingenieur* 44 (1921), pp. 271–274, pp. 272–274; Wolff, "Bekämpfung," pp. 100, 110, 122; Sander, "Die Auspuffgase der Automobilmotoren," *Technische Monatshefte* 3 (1912), p. 248; Wilhelm Liesegang, "Die unvollkommene Verbrennung im Kraftwagenmotor, ihre wirtschaftliche und hygienische Bedeutung," *Zeitschrift für angewandte Chemie* 41 (1928), pp. 712–713, p. 712.

7. Friedrich Barth, *Wahl, Projektierung und Betrieb von Kraftanlagen. Ein Hilfsbuch für Ingenieure, Betriebsleiter, Fabrikbesitzer* (4th ed., Berlin, 1925), p. 408n.; Wolff, "Bekämpfung," p. 99; Julius Hirsch, "Die hygienische Beurteilung der Auspuffgase," *Gewerbefleiß. Zeitschrift des Vereins zur Beförderung des Gewerbfleißes* 107 (1928), pp. 57–62, p. 58; E. Keeser, V. Froboese, R. Turnau, E. Gross, E. Kuss, G. Ritter, and W. Wilke, *Toxikologie und Hygiene des Kraftfahrwesens (Auspuffgase und Benzine)* (Berlin, 1930), p. 94.

8. Wilhelm Liesegang, "Ueber Automobil-Auspuffgase, ihre Zusammensetzung und ihre gesundheitlichen Eigenschaften," *Technisches Gemeindeblatt* 30 (1927/28), pp. 86–91, p. 90. Also see F. Sass, "Die Verbrennung im Kraftwagenmotor, ihre Gefahren und ihre Unwirtschaftlichkeit," *Gewerbefleiß. Zeitschrift des Vereins zur Beförderung des Gewerbfleißes* 107 (1928), pp. 77–87, p. 83; Bundesarchiv (BArch) R 154/9, Verein zur Beförderung des Gewerbfleisses, Entwurf eines Preisausschreibens.

9. Korff-Petersen, "Gesundheitsgefährdung," p. 144. Similarly, Keeser et al., *Toxikologie*, p. 94; Liesegang, "Unvollkommene Verbrennung," p. 713; Friedrich Barth, *Wahl, Projektierung und Betrieb von Kraftanlagen. Ein Hilfsbuch für Ingenieure, Betriebsleiter, Fabrikbesitzer* (Berlin, 1914), p. 402.

10. Korff-Petersen, "Gesundheitsgefährdung," p. 145. Also see Wolff, "Bekämpfung," pp. 99n., 111; Georg Wolff, "Straßenhygiene und Automobilverkehr," *Gesundheits-Ingenieur* 48 (1925), pp. 528–531, p. 528n.; Sander, "Auspuffgase," p. 248.

11. *Blätter für Volksgesundheitspflege* 9 (1909), p. 45. Similar Oskar Spitta, "Gesundheitliche Bedeutung der Luftverunreinigung durch die Auspuffgase der Kraftfahrzeuge," *Die Medizinische Welt* 2 (1928), pp. 1649–1651, p. 1650; Wolff, "Straßenhygiene und Automobilauspuff," p. 274; *New York Times*, Mar. 7, 1910, p. 8 c. 4 and Mar. 12, 1910, p. 16, c. 4.

12. Karl Kisskalt, "Die Gesundheitsschädigung in der Wohnung durch schlechte Luft, Rauch, Lärm usw. und ihre Beurteilung," *Deutsche Vierteljahresschrift für öffentliche Gesundheitspflege* 46 (1914), pp. 545–554, p. 550. Cf. Robert Weldert, "Die Luft in den Städten. Stand und Aussichten der Arbeiten über Lufthygiene," *Wasser und Gas* 13 (1922/23), cc. 643–651, c. 648; Wilhelm Liesegang, "Die Auspuffgase der Kraftwagenmotoren," *Gesundheits-Ingenieur* 52 (1929), pp. 385–391, p. 390; H. Schäffer, "Die Bekämpfung der Staub- und Rauchplage in den Kurorten," *Die Medizinische Welt* 1 (1927), pp. 247–248, p. 247; Korff-Petersen, "Gesundheitsgefährdung," p. 147; Spitta, "Gesundheitliche Bedeutung," p. 1651; Gerhard Buhtz, "Die Beurteilung der durch die Zunahme des Kraftwagenverkehrs bedingten Belästigungen der Bevölkerung und der hiergegen zu ergreifenden Maßnahmen vom Standpunkt der öffentlichen Gesundheitpflege," *Veröffentlichungen aus dem Gebiete der Medizinalverwaltung* 30 (1929), pp. 51–99, p. 89; Friedrich H. Lorentz, "Autoverkehr und Straßenhygiene," *Technisches Gemeindeblatt* 30 (1928), pp. 273–278, 287–290, p. 275; M. Hahn and J. Hirsch, "Studien zur Verkehrshygiene. I. Eine Methode zur Bestimmung kohlenstoffhaltiger Gase in der Luft," *Zeitschrift für Hygiene und Infektionskrankheiten, medizinische Mikrobiologie, Immunologie und Virologie* 105 (1926), pp. 165–180, p. 180; *Blätter für Volksgesundheitspflege* 9 (1909), p. 45; *Rauch und Staub* 15 (1925), p. 54; BArch R 154/64 p. 89.

13. Stadtarchiv Bielefeld GS 12,110, W. Maybach, "Ueber Rauchbelästigung von Automobilen."

14. BArch R 15.01 no. 14144, Minutes of the Meeting on Dec. 16, 1924, p. 5.

15. *Leipziger Tageblatt* no. 48 (Feb. 18, 1908), supplement 4, p. 3. Cf. G. Wolff, "Hygiene und Automobilverkehr," *Gesundheit* 36 (1911), cc. 69–73; c. 73; Wolff, "Straßenhygiene und Automobilverkehr," p. 531; K. Süpfle, "Die Stadtluft als Problem der Städtehygiene," *Medizinische Klinik* (1936), pp. 1288–1290, p. 1290; *Verhandlungen des Reichstags 12. Legislaturperiode*, 1st session, vol. 228 (Berlin, 1907), p. 889.

16. Cf. Korff-Petersen, "Gesundheitsgefährdung," p. 147; Buhtz, "Beurteilung," p. 87n.; H. Görlacher, "Über die Schädlichkeit der Auspuffgase von Explosionsmotoren," *Gesundheits-Ingenieur* 55 (1932), pp. 301–304, p. 303; Robert Meldau, *Der Industriestaub. Wesen und Bekämpfung* (Berlin, 1926), p. 4; BArch R 86 no. 2367 vol. 1, note of Spitta, June 19, 1920, and Commissioner of Police to the Federal Public Health Service, Sept. 15, 1920.

17. Cf. BArch R 15.01 no. 13927/1, Deutsche Saduyn-Gesellschaft to the President of the Federal Public Health Service, Jan. 10, 1909, and R 15.01 no. 13940, Deutsche Saduyn-Gesellschaft to the German Department of the Interior, Apr. 2, 1909.

18. Cf. Korff-Petersen, "Gesundheitsgefährdung," p. 145n.; Hirsch, "Beurteilung," p. 62; Wolff, "Straßenhygiene und Automobilverkehr," p. 529; Georg Wolff, "Straßenteerung, Auspuffbekämpfung und Straßenhygiene," *Die Städtereinigung* 18 (1926), pp. 63–67, p. 67; Liesegang, "Automobil-Auspuffgase," p. 389; Georgius, "Neue Vorrichtungen zum Reinigen und Geruchlosmachen von Motorabgasen," *Rauch und Staub* 3 (1912/13), pp. 220–222, p. 221; BArch R 154/18.

19. M. Hahn, "Zur großstädtischen Verkehrshygiene," *Gesundheits-Ingenieur* 51 (1928), pp. 231–234, p. 233; Wolff, "Bekämpfung," p. 123. Also see Keeser et al., *Toxikologie*, p. 94n.

20. BArch R 154/40, Minutes of the Meeting of the Committee for Studies on Automobile Fuels on Sept. 14, 1928, p. 1. Also see Karl Süpfle, "Hygiene und Kraftverkehr," *Gesundheits-Ingenieur* 62 (1939), pp. 361–364, p. 361; Arthur C. Stern, "Atmospheric Pollution through Odor," *Heating and Ventilating* 41, no. 11 (November 1944), pp. 53–57, p. 57; Philip Drinker, "Atmospheric Pollution," *Industrial and Engineering Chemistry* 31 (1939), pp. 1316–1320, p. 1318; Buhtz, "Beurteilung," p. 88n.

21. Milwaukee County Historical Society, Daniel Webster Hoan Collection Box 1, File 2, Air Pollution, "Effect of Air Pollution on Health. Report of the Committee on Public Health Relations of the New York Academy of Medicine," p. 2.

22. Weldert, "Luft in den Städten," c. 647. Also see Kisskalt, "Gesundheitsschädigung," p. 550; Sass, "Verbrennung," p. 80; *New York Times*, Mar. 3, 1924, p. 16, c. 7. The Landesanstalt für Wasser-, Boden- und Lufthygiene was a scientific institution that provided the most highly regarded expert opinion on issues of environmental pollution in the state of Prussia.

23. Ferdinand Flury and Franz Zernik, *Schädliche Gase. Dämpfe, Nebel, Rauch- und Staubarten* (Berlin, 1931), p. 487. Similarly, Hans Lehmann, "Die Wirkung des Kohlenoxyds auf den menschlichen Organismus und ihre Bedeutung für die öffentliche Gesundheitspflege," *Kleine Mitteilungen für die Mitglieder des Vereins für Wasser-, Boden- und Lufthygiene* 6 (1930), pp. 199–215, p. 213.

24. Cf. Korff-Petersen, "Gesundheitsgefährdung," pp. 136, 142; Hahn and Hirsch, "Studien zur Verkehrshygiene I," p. 167; Hirsch, "Beurteilung," p. 62; Lehmann, "Wirkung des Kohlenoxyds," p. 214; Buhtz, "Beurteilung," p. 86.

25. Keeser et al., *Toxikologie*, p. 94.

26. M. Schmidtmann, "Über chronische Autoabgasschäden. Untersuchungen am Dieselmotor," *Archiv für Gewerbepathologie und Gewerbehygiene* 8 (1937/38), pp. 1–13, pp. 5, 13.

27. Spitta, "Gesundheitliche Bedeutung," p. 1651. Also see BArch R 86 no. 2367, vol. 4, Minutes of the Meeting on Nov. 22, 1929, p. 5n.

28. Cf. BArch R 154/64 p. 89; Liesegang, *Reinhaltung*, p. 47; Hahn, "Zur großstädtischen Verkehrshygiene," p. 233; Korff-Petersen, "Gesundheitsge-

fährdung," p. 139; Weldert, "Luft in den Städten," c. 648; Görlacher, "Schädlichkeit," pp. 302, 304; Friedrich H. Lorentz, "Automobilverkehr und Städtehygiene," *Technisches Gemeindeblatt* 26 (1923), pp. 127–130, p. 128; Hahn and Hirsch, "Studien zur Verkehrshygiene I," p. 166; Paul Schmitt, "Straßenhygiene," *Gesundheits-Ingenieur* 51 (1928), pp. 701–704, p. 702.

29. BArch R 154/9, President of the Prussian Institute for Water, Soil, and Air Conservation to the Prussian Minister of Public Welfare, May 13, 1927.

30. F. Wirth and O. Küster, "Das Kohlenoxyd, seine Gefahren und seine Bestimmung," *Zentralblatt für Gewerbehygiene* 16 (1929), pp. 149–153, p. 149.

31. Carl Flügge, *Grundriss der Hygiene für Studirende und praktische Ärzte, Medicinal- und Verwaltungsbeamte* (5th ed., Leipzig, 1902), p. 531; Fritz Wirth and Otto Muntsch, *Die Gefahren der Luft und ihre Bekämpfung im täglichen Leben, in der Technik und im Krieg* (Berlin, 1933), p. 54; Lehmann, "Wirkung des Kohlenoxyds," pp. 201, 203; Hans Lehmann, "Entwicklung, Zweck und Ziel der Lufthygiene im Hinblick auf die menschliche Gesundheit und öffentliche Gesundheitspflege," *Kleine Mitteilungen für die Mitglieder des Vereins für Wasser-, Boden- und Lufthygiene* 8 (1932), pp. 308–334, p. 317n.; Wirth and Küster, "Kohlenoxyd," p. 149; Spitta, "Gesundheitliche Bedeutung," p. 1651; J. Goldmerstein and K. Stodieck, *Wie atmet die Stadt? Neue Feststellungen über die Bedeutung der Parkanlagen für die Lufterneuerung in den Großstädten* (Berlin, 1931), p. 12; Sass, "Verbrennung," p. 80; Hirsch, "Beurteilung," p. 61; Leo G. Meyer, "Über Luftverunreinigung durch Kohlenoxyd, mit besonderer Berücksichtigung einiger weniger bekannter Quellen derselben," *Archiv für Hygiene* 84 (1915), pp. 79–120, p. 80; Liesegang, "Automobil-Auspuffgase," p. 90; Georg Bartsch, "Untersuchungen über den Gehalt an Kohlenoxyd, Kohlenwasserstoffen und Kohlensäure in der Luft von Straßen, Autobussen, Garagen und Betrieben Dresdens" (diss., TH Dresden, 1931), p. 33; Yandell Henderson, Howard W. Haggard, Merwyn C. Teague, Alexander L. Prince, and Ruth M. Wunderlich, "Physiological Effects of Automobile Exhaust Gas and Standards of Ventilation for Brief Exposures," *Journal of Industrial Hygiene* 3 (1921), pp. 79–92, 137–146, p. 80; S. H. Katz, "The Hazard of Carbon Monoxide to the Public and to Industry," *Industrial and Engineering Chemistry* 17 (1925), pp. 555–557, p. 555; F. W. Hutchinson, "Atmospheric Sabotage," *Heating and Ventilating* 39, no. 7 (July 1942), pp. 47–49, p. 47; Bloomfield and Isbell, "Problem," p. 750.

32. Liesegang, *Reinhaltung*, p. 79; Flury and Zernik, *Schädliche Gase*, p. 197. Cf. Josef Rambousek, *Lehrbuch der Gewerbe-Hygiene* (Vienna and Leipzig, 1906), p. 38; Alice Hamilton, *Industrial Poisons in the United States* (New York, 1925), p. 371; *New York Times*, July 10, 1925, p. 1, c. 2.

33. Liesegang, *Reinhaltung*, p. 9. Cf. E. R. Hayhurst, "Carbon Monoxide and Automobile Exhaust Gases," *American Journal of Public Health* 16 (1926), pp. 218–223, p. 221.

34. Korff-Petersen, "Gesundheitsgefährdung," p. 139.

35. Cf. Henderson et al., "Physiological Effects"; H. B. Meller, "Clean Air, an

Achievable Asset," *Journal of the Franklin Institute* 217 (1934), pp. 709–728, p. 722; Arnold Marsh, *Smoke. The Problem of Coal and the Atmosphere* (London, 1947), p. 275n.; A. C. Fieldner, W. P. Yant, and L. L. Satler Jr., "Natural Ventilation in the Liberty Tunnels," *Engineering News-Record* 93 (1924), pp. 290–291; A. C. Fieldner, W. P. Yant, and L. L. Satler Jr., "Carbon Monoxide under Traffic in Liberty Tunnels," *Engineering News-Record* 93 (1924), pp. 1022–1024; A. C. Fieldner, S. H. Katz, and E. G. Meiter, "Continuous CO Recorder in the Liberty Tunnels," *Engineering News-Record* 95 (1925), pp. 423–424; C. B. Maits et al., "Carbon Monoxide Survey in Liberty Tubes, Pittsburgh," *Journal of Industrial Hygiene* 14 (1932), pp. 295–300; George A. Soper, "The Atmosphere and Its Relation to Human Health and Comfort," *Proceedings of the American Society of Civil Engineers* 51 (1925), pp. 1160–1165, p. 1162; Katz, "Hazard," p. 557. On the reception in Germany, see Liesegang, *Reinhaltung*, p. 44; Wirth and Küster, "Kohlenoxyd," p. 151; Görlacher, "Schädlichkeit," p. 302.

36. Flury and Zernik, *Schädliche Gase*, pp. 197, 486; Wirth and Küster, "Kohlenoxyd," p. 153; Meyer, "Luftverunreinigung," pp. 116–119; Wirth and Muntsch, *Gefahren der Luft*, p. 59; A. Lion, "Wirken unsere Kraftfahrzeugbetriebsstoffe giftig?" *Zentralblatt für Gewerbehygiene* 16 (1929), pp. 212–213, p. 212; Liesegang, "Unvollkommene Verbrennung," p. 713; Liesegang, "Automobil-Auspuffgase," p. 386n.; Rumpf, "Die Kohlenoxydgefahr in Autogaragen," *Der Motorwagen* 31 (1928), pp. 346–347, p. 346; Yandell Henderson and Howard W. Haggard, "Health Hazard from Automobile Exhaust Gas in City Streets, Garages and Repair Shops," *Journal of the American Medical Association* 81 (1923), pp. 385–391, p. 390; Hamilton, *Industrial Poisons*, p. 393n.; Ettore Ciampolini, "Carbon Monoxide Hazard in Public Garages," *Journal of Industrial Hygiene* 6 (1924), pp. 102–109, p. 102; Bloomfield and Isbell, "Problem," p. 763; C.-E. A. Winslow, "The Atmosphere and Its Relation to Human Health and Comfort," *Proceedings of the American Society of Civil Engineers* 51 (1925), pp. 794–810, p. 806; Meller, "Clean Air," p. 722.

37. Lehmann, "Wirkung des Kohlenoxyds," p. 208.

38. Cf. P. Mensing, "Lüftungsfragen in Einstellräumen und Instandsetzungswerkstätten für Kraftfahrzeuge," *Gesundheits-Ingenieur* 60 (1937), pp. 39–40; H. Kämper, M. Hottinger, and W. von Gonzenbach, *Die Heiz- und Lüftungsanlagen in den verschiedenen Gebäudearten* (2d ed., Berlin, 1940), pp. 311–313; Meyer, "Luftverunreinigung," p. 120; Wirth and Muntsch, *Gefahren der Luft*, p. 59; Meldau, *Industriestaub*, p. 16; Fieldner et al., "Natural Ventilation"; Fieldner et al., "Carbon Monoxide"; Fieldner et al., "CO Recorder," p. 423; Maits et al., "Carbon Monoxide Survey," p. 300; Carroll M. Salls, "The Ozone Fallacy in Garage Ventilation," *Journal of Industrial Hygiene* 9 (1927), pp. 503–511, p. 510; Ciampolini, "Carbon Monoxide Hazard," p. 108; Bloomfield and Isbell, "Problem," p. 763n.; Katz, "Hazard," p. 557; *S.A.E. Journal* 22 (1928), p. 573.

39. Bartsch, "Untersuchungen," p. 2; Wilhelm Liesegang, "Die Bekämpfung von Rauch, Staub und Abgasen als hygienische Aufgabe," *Zeitschrift für Desinfektions-*

und Gesundheitswesen 22 (1930), cc. 331–338; c. 338; Liesegang, "Automobil-Auspuffgase," pp. 385, 389; Wirth and Küster, "Kohlenoxyd," p. 150n.; Görlacher, "Schädlichkeit," p. 301n.; O. Ulsamer, "Großstadtluft und ihre Bedeutung für die menschliche Gesundheit," *Kleine Mitteilungen für die Mitglieder des Vereins für Wasser-, Boden- und Lufthygiene* 6 (1930), pp. 169–191, p. 173; A. C. Fieldner, A. A. Straub, and G. W. Jones, "Gasoline Losses due to Incomplete Combustion in Motor Vehicles," *Journal of Industrial and Engineering Chemistry* 13 (1921), pp. 51–57, p. 55; Norman Fuchsloch, *Sehen, riechen, schmecken und messen als Bestandteile der gutachterlichen und wissenschaftlichen Tätigkeit der Preußischen Landesanstalt für Wasser-, Boden- und Lufthygiene im Bereich der Luftreinhaltung zwischen 1920 und 1960* (Freiberg, 1999), p. 357.

40. H. Wislicenus, "Ueber die hygienische Aufgabe und Zweckgestaltung der Abgasschlote, Industrieschornsteine und anderer technischer Abgasquellen," *Rauch und Staub* 1 (1910/11), pp. 2–7, p. 7; Julius Hirsch, "Studien zur Verkehrshygiene. II. Die Anwendung der titrimetrischen Bestimmung kohlenstoffhaltiger Gase in der Praxis der Autoabgas-Analyse," *Zeitschrift für Hygiene* 109 (1928), pp. 266–271, p. 267; Liesegang, "Automobil-Auspuffgase," p. 389; Hahn, "Zur großstädtischen Verkehrshygiene," p. 233; *New York Times*, May 23, 1925, p. 17, c. 2.

41. Henderson and Haggard, "Health Hazard," p. 385. On the reception, see Winslow, "Atmosphere," p. 806; Drinker, "Atmospheric Pollution," p. 1318; Flury and Zernik, *Schädliche Gase*, p. 486; *New York Times*, May 20, 1923, part 8, p. 6, c. 4n.

42. Soper, "Atmosphere," p. 1165. Cf. Keeser et al., *Toxikologie*, p. 70; *New York Times*, Sept. 21, 1924, part 8, p. 11, c. 2n.

43. Keeser et al., *Toxikologie*, pp. 73, 75; Spitta, "Gesundheitliche Bedeutung," p. 1651; Görlacher, "Schädlichkeit," p. 302; Bloomfield and Isbell, "Problem," p. 757; Henderson and Haggard, "Health Hazard," p. 386n.; Liesegang, "Automobil-Auspuffgase," p. 386; Liesegang, *Reinhaltung*, p. 46; K. B. Lehmann, *Kurzes Lehrbuch der Arbeits- und Gewerbehygiene* (Leipzig, 1919), p. 183; Hirsch, "Beurteilung," p. 62.

44. See, for example, Keeser et al., *Toxikologie*, p. 93.

45. Elizabeth D. Wilson, Irene Gates, Hubley R. Owen, and Wilfred T. Dawson, "Street Risk of Carbon Monoxide Poisoning," *Journal of the American Medical Association* 87 (1926), pp. 319–320. For the reception see Bloomfield and Isbell, "Problem," p. 752; Spitta, "Gesundheitliche Bedeutung," p. 1651; Liesegang, "Unvollkommene Verbrennung," p. 713; Lehmann, "Wirkung des Kohlenoxyds," p. 211; Lehmann, "Entwicklung," p. 318; Goldmerstein and Stodieck, *Wie atmet*, p. 12; Wirth and Küster, "Kohlenoxyd," p. 151.

46. Wilson et al., "Street Risk," p. 319.

47. Liesegang, *Reinhaltung*, p. 47.

48. Süpfle, "Stadtluft," p. 1289. Similarly, Süpfle, "Hygiene," p. 361n; Spitta, "Gesundheitliche Bedeutung," p. 1651; Lehmann, "Wirkung des Kohlenoxyds," p.

209; Flury and Zernik, *Schädliche Gase,* p. 487; Liesegang, "Automobil-Auspuffgase," p. 386; L. H. Kramer, "Vergiftet das Auto die Luft?" *Rauch und Staub* 22 (1932), pp. 76–77, p. 77; Wirth and Muntsch, *Gefahren der Luft,* p. 59; Hirsch, "Beurteilung," p. 61; Lorentz, "Automobilverkehr," p. 129; Bloomfield and Isbell, "Problem," p. 762; Meller, "Clean Air," p. 722; Joel I. Connolly, Mathew J. Martinek, and John J. Aeberly, "The Carbon Monoxide Hazard in City Streets," *American Journal of Public Health and the Nation's Health* 18 (1928), pp. 1375–1383, p. 1383; *New York Times,* Oct. 26, 1924, part 9, p. 18, c. 1; Nov. 3, 1925, p. 27, c. 7; *Baltimore Sun,* May 6, 1928, Sports Section, p. 15, c. 1; *Engineering News-Record* 100 (1928), p. 807; *Transit Journal* 80 (1936), p. 441n.

49. Bartsch, "Untersuchungen," p. 33. Cf. Wilhelm Liesegang, "Die Giftigkeit der Motorentreibstoffe und ihrer Verbrennungsprodukte," *Angewandte Chemie* 45 (1932), pp. 329–330, p. 329; Liesegang, *Reinhaltung,* p. 44; Hirsch, "Beurteilung," p. 62; Kramer, "Vergiftet," p. 77; Lehmann, "Wirkung des Kohlenoxyds," p. 209; Flury and Zernik, *Schädliche Gase,* p. 209; Hamilton, *Industrial Poisons,* p. 385; Connolly et al., "Carbon Monoxide Hazard," p. 1383; Soper, "Atmosphere," p. 1160; Winslow, "Atmosphere," p. 806; Hutchinson, "Atmospheric Sabotage," p. 47n.

50. David Rosner and Gerald Markowitz, "'A Gift of God'? The Public Health Controversy over Leaded Gasoline during the 1920s," in David Rosner and Gerald Markowitz (eds.), *Dying for Work: Workers' Safety and Health in Twentieth-Century America* (Bloomington and Indianapolis, 1987), pp. 121–139, p. 122.

51. Cf. Christopher C. Sellers, *Hazards of the Job. From Industrial Disease to Environmental Health Science* (Chapel Hill and London, 1997); Peter Brimblecombe, "Themes in the History of Lead," *Environmental History Newsletter* 5 (1993), pp. 39–42, p. 39n.

52. Wolff, "Straßenhygiene und Automobilverkehr," p. 528. Similarly, H. Zangger, "Eine gefährliche Verbesserung des Automobilbenzins," *Schweizerische Medizinische Wochenschrift* 55 (1925), pp. 26–29, p. 26.

53. *New York Times,* Mar. 3, 1924, p. 16, c. 8. Cf. Alice Hamilton, Paul Reznikoff, and Grace M. Burnham, "Tetra-Ethyl Lead," *Journal of the American Medical Association* 84 (1925), pp. 1481–1486, p. 1486.

54. Alfred Beyer, "Gesundheitsschädliche Automobilstoffe," *Zentralblatt für Gewerbehygiene und Unfallverhütung* 3 (1926), pp. 223–225, pp. 223, 224.

55. Zangger, "Gefährliche Verbesserung," p. 28n. Cf. Frederick B. Flinn, "Some of the Potential Public Health Hazards from the Use of Ethyl Gasoline," *Journal of Industrial Hygiene* 8 (1926), pp. 51–66, p. 64.

56. Cf. W. H. Howell, A. J. Chesley, D. L. Edsall, R. Hunt, W. S. Leathers, J. Stieglitz, and C. E. A. Winslow, "Report on Tetraethyl Lead," *Journal of Industrial Hygiene* 8 (1926), pp. 248–256, esp. p. 255; Carroll M. Salls, "Tetraethyl Lead a Menace to Garage Workers," *Nation's Health* 7 (1925), pp. 169–171, esp. p. 169; Hayhurst, "Carbon Monoxide," p. 222n.; *Monthly Labor Review* 20 (1925), p. 174n.; *Industrial and Engineering Chemistry* 18 (1926), p. 432n. It indeed looks like the scientists

succeeded in getting the hazards of producing tetraethyl lead under control. Even William Graebner (whose work is highly critical of both the product and its producers) concedes, "There seems to have been no recurrence of the Bayway disaster until 1960" (William Graebner, "Hegemony through Science: Information Engineering and Lead Toxicology, 1925–1965," in Rosner and Markowitz [eds.], *Dying for Work*, pp. 140–159, p. 140).

57. Sellers, *Hazards*, p. 206. Sellers's argument of a "pax toxicologica," with industry and industrial hygiene entertaining an intensive relationship to their mutual advantage, is a forceful and convincing response to the one-sided presentations of Graebner and Rosner and Markowitz. (Compare Sellers, *Hazards,* esp. chap. 5 with Graebner, "Hegemony," pp. 140–145; and Rosner and Markowitz, "Gift," pp. 129, 135.)

58. National Archives of the United States of America (NA USA) RG 70 A 1 Entry 102, Box 1, "Sixteenth Annual Report of the Director of the Bureau of Mines to the Secretary of Commerce for the Fiscal Year Ended June 30, 1926," p. 14n. Cf. R. R. Sayers, A. C. Fieldner, W. P. Yant, and B. G. H. Thomas, *Experimental Studies on the Effect of Ethyl Gasoline and Its Combustion Products. Report of the United States Bureau of Mines to the General Motors Research Corporation and the Ethyl Gasoline Corporation* (no location, 1927). For criticism, see Hamilton et al., "Tetra-Ethyl Lead," pp. 1484–1486.

59. Rosner and Markowitz, "Gift," p. 135. Cf. Howell et al., "Report," p. 255n.

60. Cf. Graebner, "Hegemony," p. 140.

61. NA USA RG 90 A 1 Entry 36, Box 4, Folder "Lead," Report, Surgeon General's Ad Hoc Committee on Tetraethyl Lead, Jan. 8/9, 1959, p. 2. Cf. ibid., Tabor to MacKenzie, Dec. 24, 1958.

62. BArch R 154/9, Prussian Institute for Water, Soil, and Air Conservation to the Minister for Public Welfare, Feb. 26, 1930, and Sept. 22, 1930.

63. BArch R 86, no. 2367, vol. 3, Federal Public Health Service to the German Minister of the Interior, June 2, 1927.

64. BArch R 86, no. 2368, vol. 1, Federal Department of Traffic to the German Minister of the Interior, July 23, 1928.

65. Szczepanski, "Blei-Tetra-Äthyl als Antiklopfmittel für Motortreibstoffe," *Reichsarbeitsblatt* 19 (1939), part 3, pp. 209–216, p. 215.

66. *Stenographischer Bericht über die Verhandlungen der Bayerischen Kammer der Abgeordneten*, Oct. 26, 1905, p. 378.

67. Merki, "Fortschritt," pp. 237–240. Also see Frank Uekoetter, "Stark im Ton, schwach in der Organisation: Der Protest gegen den frühen Automobilismus," *Geschichte in Wissenschaft und Unterricht* (forthcoming).

68. BArch R 86, no. 2333, vol. 2, Joseph Bittel to Geheimrat Bumm, Feb. 13, 1910.

69. *New York Times*, Oct. 2, 1910, p. 12, c. 6. Cf. ibid., Jan. 23, 1909, p. 8, c. 4.

70. Anonymous, *Autler. Zucht- und Ruchlosigkeiten. Ein Protest gegen die Schreckensherrschaft der Straße. Von einem Rechtsfreund* (Berlin, 1909), p. 11.

71. *Stenographische Berichte über die Verhandlungen des Preußischen Hauses der Abgeordneten 20. Legislaturperiode* 1st session, vol. 7 (Berlin, 1905), c. 9967.

72. BArch R 86, no. 2367, vol. 3, Society of Residents of the Lower Friedrichstadt to the President of the Federal Public Health Service, Mar. 18, 1927.

73. Bayerisches Hauptstaatsarchiv München MJu 16687, Supplement to the *Allgemeinen Zeitung*, Sept. 27, 1905, p. 594.

74. *Verhandlungen des Reichstags 12. Legislaturperiode* 1st session, vol. 230 (Berlin, 1908), p. 3069.

75. Staatsarchiv Bremen 4,14/1 VI.B.16.k, file "Verschiedenes," complaint in police precinct 5, Bremen, July 9, 1926, and notes of July 16, 1926, and July 17, 1926.

76. Stadtarchiv Wiesbaden STVV no. 57, topic no. 8 of the meeting on Oct. 11, 1907.

77. Hirsch, "Beurteilung," p. 58. Similarly, Döllner, "Die öffentliche Pflege der Lufthygiene," *Wasser und Gas* 15 (1924/25), cc. 57–62; c. 62.

78. Cf. *New York Times*, Feb. 4, 1910, p. 5, c. 3, Mar. 10, 1910, p. 8, c. 5.

79. See, for instance, Melvin G. Holli, "Urban Reform in the Progressive Era," in Lewis L. Gould (ed.), *The Progressive Era* (Syracuse, 1974), pp. 133–151, p. 136.

80. Also see McCarthy, "Coming Wonder," p. 57.

81. Spitta, "Gesundheitliche Bedeutung," p. 1650. Similarly, Liesegang, "Automobil-Auspuffgase," p. 390; Wirth and Küster, "Kohlenoxyd," p. 150; Soper, "Atmosphere," p. 1161; Henderson and Haggard, "Health Hazard," p. 385.

82. Flury and Zernik, *Schädliche Gase*, p. 197.

83. Winslow, "Atmosphere," p. 806. Similarly, Liesegang, "Automobil-Auspuffgase," p. 387; Wirth and Küster, "Kohlenoxyd," p. 149; Meldau, *Industriestaub*, p. 16; Hirsch, "Beurteilung," p. 60; Bloomfield and Isbell, "Problem," p. 750.

84. Cf. Max Grünewald, "Ueber die gesundheitsschädigende Wirkung der Auspuffgase in Automobilgaragen," *Rauch und Staub* 22 (1932), pp. 151–152; Flury and Zernik, *Schädliche Gase*, p. 197; Meyer, "Luftverunreinigung," p. 120; Bartsch, "Untersuchungen," p. 34; Ciampolini, "Carbon Monoxide Hazard," p. 108; Rumpf, "Kohlenoxydgefahr," p. 346n.; Rudolf Treu, "Tödliche Kohlenoxyd-Vergiftung durch Automobil-Auspuffgas," *Der Motorwagen* 29 (1926), p. 514; Hamilton, *Industrial Poisons*, p. 393; *New York Times*, Sept. 21, 1924, part 8, p. 11, c. 2.

85. Liesegang, "Giftigkeit," p. 329; Kramer, "Vergiftet," p. 76.

86. Süpfle, "Hygiene," p. 361. Cf. W. Spiegel, "Kraftverkehr und Volksgesundheit," *Städtehygiene* 2 (1951), pp. 165–166, p. 165.

87. *New York Times*, Nov. 28, 1924, p. 14, c. 6.

88. John A. Jakle and Keith A. Sculle, *The Gas Station in America* (Baltimore and London, 1994), p. 58.

89. Cf. Schmucki, "Automobilisierung," p. 590; Haubner, *Nervenkitzel,* pp. 157n., 164; Zatsch, *Staatsmacht,* p. 290.

90. Wolff, "Hygiene," c. 73.

91. Cf. Spitta, "Gesundheitliche Bedeutung," p. 1651; Weldert, "Luft in den Städten," c. 647n; Kisskalt, "Gesundheitsschädigung," p. 550; Liesegang, "Automobil-Auspuffgase," p. 390; Schäffer, "Bekämpfung," p. 247; Korff-Petersen, "Gesundheitsgefährdung," p. 147n.; Hahn and Hirsch, "Studien zur Verkehrshygiene I," p. 180; *Blätter für Volksgesundheitspflege* 9 (1909), p. 45.

92. *New York Times,* Aug. 2, 1908, part 2, p. 2, c. 5; Aug. 3, 1908, p. 5, c. 4; Aug. 5, 1908, p. 12, c. 1; Aug. 6, 1908, p. 5, c. 4; Aug. 28, 1908, p. 2, c. 3; Feb. 4, 1910, p. 5, c. 3. For more on this episode, see McCarthy, "Coming Wonder," p. 59n.

93. *New York Times,* June 12, 1911, p. 10, c. 3. Cf. ibid., April 28, 1910, p. 12, c. 2; June 29, 1910, p. 2, c. 7; July 2, 1910, p. 3, c. 5; Dec. 2, 1910, p. 8, c. 3; Jan. 2, 1911, p. 4, c. 2; May 11, 1911, p. 2, c. 6; June 25, 1911, p. 8, c. 1.

94. *New York Times,* Oct. 30, 1912, p. 12, c. 4.

95. *New York Times,* Nov. 10, 1912, p. 11, c. 1; Nov. 13, 1912, p. 12, c. 3.

96. *New York Times,* Sept. 21, 1924, part 8, p. 11, c. 7.

97. Rosner and Markowitz, "Gift," p. 125n. Alice Hamilton reported in May 1925 that there had been seven accidents in three different factories producing tetraethyl lead. A total of eleven workers had been killed in these accidents. (Hamilton et al., "Tetra-Ethyl Lead," p. 1482.)

98. Rosner and Markowitz, "Gift," p. 121. Cf. Liesegang, "Automobil-Auspuffgase," p. 389; Flury and Zernik, *Schädliche Gase,* p. 248.

99. Howell et al., "Report," p. 255. Cf. BArch R 86, no. 2368, vol. 2, Federal Department of Traffic to the German Minister of the Interior, Dec. 14, 1928.

100. Cf. Samuel P. Hays (in collaboration with Barbara D. Hays), *Beauty, Health, and Permanence. Environmental Politics in the United States, 1955–1985* (Cambridge et al., 1989), p. 196; John Opie, *Nature's Nation. An Environmental History of the United States* (Fort Worth et al., 1998), p. 439.

101. Hauptstaatsarchiv Düsseldorf Regierung Köln no. 7648a, p. 2r.

102. *Amts-Blatt der Königlich Bayerischen Stadt Augsburg* 57 (1902), p. 237. Cf. Geheimes Staatsarchiv Preußischer Kulturbesitz Berlin Rep. 120 BB II b 4, no. 20, vol. 1, pp. 11r–12, 57, 59, 178–178r, 210.

103. Cf. the collection of law in BArch R 15.01, no. 13959; also R 15.01, no. 13927/1, "Aufzeichnungen über die kommissarische Beratung, betreffend die Revision der Grundzüge betreffend den Verkehr mit Kraftfahrzeugen," Feb. 8, 1909; BArch R 15.01, no. 14141, "Entwurf einer neuen Verordnung über den Verkehr mit Kraftfahrzeugen nebst dem Wortlaut der Verordnung über den Verkehr mit Kraftfahrzeugen," Feb. 3, 1910, p. 4n; BArch R 15.01, no. 13976, document enclosed from Kaiserlicher Automobilclub to the German Department of the Interior, June 27, 1907, p. 5; BArch R 15.01, no. 13977, "Convention Internationale Relative à la Circu-

lation des Automobiles," p. 1; BArch R 15.01, no. 14145, "Convention Internationale Relative à la Circulation Automobile," p. 2.

104. BArch R 15.01, no. 13927/1, document enclosed from Minister of Public Works to the Chancellor, Mar. 14, 1909.

105. BArch R 15.01, no. 14143, Federal Department of Traffic to all State Governments, Oct. 8, 1924.

106. BArch R 15.01, no. 13960, Minister of Public Works to the Provincial President, in Sigmaringen, and the Commissioner of Police of Berlin, Feb. 25, 1910.

107. *Stenographische Berichte über die Verhandlungen des Preußischen Hauses der Abgeordneten 21. Legislaturperiode* 3d session, vol. 5 (Berlin, 1910), c. 6735. Similarly, Stadtarchiv Augsburg Polizeidirektion no. 686, Polizeidirektion Augsburg to Ziegelmeier, Sept. 6, 1929; ibid., no. 687, Polizeidirektion Augsburg to Dr. K. Meltzer, June 5, 1935; Hirsch, "Beurteilung," p. 58; *Blätter für Volksgesundheitspflege* 9 (1909), p. 45. Measures taken to curb emissions from repair shops were an exception. (Cf., e.g., Stadtarchiv Essen Rep. 102 Abt. XIV no. 315, police decree of Dec. 12, 1932; Landeshauptarchiv Magdeburg Rep. C 34, no. 146, Regierungspräsident Magdeburg to Hermann Möhle, Sept. 5, 1938.)

108. Staatsarchiv Bremen 4,14/1 VI.B.16.k, file "Verschiedenes," complaint in police precinct 5, Bremen, July 9, 1926.

109. Ibid., note of July 17, 1926.

110. *Ministerial-Blatt für die Preußische innere Verwaltung* 88 (1927), decree of Feb. 10, 1927.

111. Ibid.

112. Stadtarchiv Hannover HR 23, no. 819, Polizeipräsident Hannover to the Magistrat Hannover, May 31, 1930.

113. *Stenographische Berichte über die Verhandlungen des Preußischen Hauses der Abgeordneten 21. Legislaturperiode* 4th session 1911, vol. 3 (Berlin, 1911), p. 3336.

114. Ibid. p. 3337.

115. Stadtarchiv Augsburg Polizeidirektion no. 687.

116. BArch R 86, no. 2333, vol. 2, Federal Public Health Service, Feb. 22, 1910.

117. BArch R 154/9, President of Prussian Institute to the Minister for Public Welfare, Feb. 11, 1928.

118. Ibid., Prussian Minister for Public Welfare to the German Minister of the Interior, July 12, 1927, and response of the Innenminister of Aug. 4, 1927. Similarly, BArch R 154/65, Commissioner of Police in Berlin to the Prussian Institute for Water, Soil, and Air Conservation, Oct. 12, 1932.

119. BArch R 15.01, no. 13939, brochure of the German Saduyn-Society, Munich, note of July 14, 1907.

120. Ibid.

121. Ibid., note of Jan. 18, 1909.

122. E.g., BArch R 15.01, no. 14143, "Entwurf zu einer Polizeiverordnung für den

Bau und die Einrichtung von Einstellhallen für Kraftwagen mit Verbrennungsmotoren," p. 3n.; BArch R 3101, no. 13751, p. 61–62.

123. BArch R 86, no. 2367, vol. 2, Federal Department of Traffic to the German Minister of the Interior, Sept. 22, 1924, p. 3.

124. Ibid., Federal Public Health Service to the German Minister of the Interior, July 15, 1925, p. 5n. On the reception of the American debate, cf. BArch R 86, no. 2367, vols. 2 and 3.

125. Cf. BArch R 86, no. 2367, vol. 2, Federal Public Health Service to the German Minister of the Interior, Mar. 16, 1926; BArch R 86, no. 2367, vol. 3, Federal Public Health Service to the German Minister of the Interior, Mar. 21, 1928, and Prussian Minister for Public Works to the German Minister of the Interior, Feb. 4, 1928; BArch R 86, no. 2368, vol. 1, minutes of the meeting on June 4, 1928, pp. 5–7.

126. BArch R 86, no. 2368, vol. 1, minutes of the meeting on June 4, 1928, p. 6.

127. Ibid.

128. Ibid., p. 9.

129. Buhtz, "Beurteilung," p. 63; Szczepanski, "Blei-Tetra-Äthyl," p. 210.

130. BArch R 86, no. 2368, vol. 1, report on the meeting on Mar. 24, 1927, and "Gutachten des Reichsgesundheitsamts über das synthetische Benzin und das Motalin der I. G. Farbenindustrie Aktiengesellschaft," Jan. 15, 1929; BArch R 86, no. 2367, vol. 3, Federal Public Health Service to the German Minister of the Interior, June 2, 1927, and Prussian Minister for Public Works to the German Minister of the Interior, Feb. 4, 1928.

131. Wolfgang Birkenfeld, *Der synthetische Treibstoff 1933–1945. Ein Beitrag zur nationalsozialistischen Wirtschafts- und Rüstungspolitik* (Göttingen, 1964), pp. 60n., 64–66.

132. Ibid., p. 66.

133. *Reichsarbeitsblatt* N.F. 19 (1939), part 3, p. 208.

134. California State Archives, Sacramento, F 3935, Air Resources Board Records Folder 4, Air Resources Board, "Summary of Testimony Presented at the November 9th and 10th Hearings on Ambient Air Quality Standards," p. 3.

135. Ibid.

136. California State Archives, Sacramento, F 3935, Air Resources Board Records Folder 8, R. Cree Pillsbury, "Statement on the Proposed Changes in the Present Statewide Ambient Air Quality Standards," Nov. 19, 1970, p. 2.

137. Ibid., H. R. Hulett, "Remarks Prepared for Presentation to the Air Resources Board, State of California, at a Public Hearing in Oakland," Nov. 10, 1970, p. 1.

138. California State Archives, Sacramento, F 3935 Air Resources Board Records Folder 4, Air Resources Board, "Summary of Testimony Presented at the November 9th and 10th Hearings on Ambient Air Quality Standards," p. 5.

139. Ibid., p. 4.

140. A declaration of the Council of Europe of 1968 is generally seen as the first

official formulation of this principle. (Cf. Walther Liese, "Umweltschutz—staatliches und gesellschaftliches Ordnungsprinzip," *Gesundheits-Ingenieur* 93 [1972], pp. 66–71, p. 70; Heinrich Stratmann, "Zielsetzung im Bereich des Immissionsschutzes," *Arbeitsgemeinschaft für Rationalisierung des Landes Nordrhein-Westfalen* Heft 133 [1972], pp. 7–29; p. 18.)

141. Cf. Michael Kloepfer, *Umweltrecht* (2d ed., Munich, 1998), p. 167n.

142. Heinrich Freiherr von Lersner, "Vorsorgeprinzip," in Heinrich Freiherr von Lersner, Otto Kimminich, and Peter-Christoph Storm (eds.), *Handwörterbuch des Umweltrechts*, vol. 2 (2d rev. ed., Berlin, 1994), cc. 2703–2710, c. 2709.

143. Hans D. Jarass, *Bundes-Immissionsschutzgesetz (BImSchG). Kommentar* (4th rev. ed., Munich, 1999), p. 160.

144. California State Archives, Sacramento, F 3935, Air Resources Board Records Folder 4, Air Resources Board, "Summary of Testimony Presented at the November 9th and 10th Hearings on Ambient Air Quality Standards," p. 2.

145. Cf., for an exception, Aaron Wildavsky, *But Is It True? A Citizen's Guide to Environmental Health and Safety Issues* (Cambridge and London, 1995), which has a concluding chapter, "Rejecting the Precautionary Principle."

7

Interpreting the London Fog Disaster of 1952

Peter Thorsheim

London has long been synonymous with fog, particularly during the damp and chilly months of November and December. In 1952, however, Londoners experienced an extraordinarily dense and long-lasting period of fog. For five days, over one thousand square miles were blanketed with fog so thick that it was impossible to see more than a few feet. The lack of wind and the temperature inversion that produced this fog trapped pollution from millions of coal fires over the metropolis and caused smoke and sulphur dioxide to rise to critical levels. Half of the devices that measured airborne particulates in London became so full that they could no longer function, and sulphur dioxide reached the highest concentrations recorded since monitoring had begun in 1932.[1] Although newspapers devoted considerable attention to the fog as it was occurring, initial reports said little about its effect on health. Although one article reported that a number of Londoners had sought medical attention for "fog cough," it assured readers that healthy individuals had nothing to fear as long as they breathed through their noses, which were supposed to filter soot particles from the air.[2] Although this story implied that health problems associated with the fog were minor, thousands of Londoners were about to die from it. Soon after it ended, the fog of December 1952 was blamed for killing approximately four thousand people—more than died in the terrorist attacks of September 2001.

To understand the London fog disaster of 1952, one must do more than identify the environmental conditions and toxic chemicals that caused illness and death. Equally important are the attitudes, ideologies, and perceptions that led to the creation of these pollutants and that structured people's understanding of their effects. Building on the anthropologist

Mary Douglas's observation that ideas about pollution are shaped by culture, the historian Bill Luckin has observed that "an environment can never be directly and 'naturally' experienced. Rather, ideological preconception and scientific or proto-scientific theory jointly shape the 'ways of seeing' that enable individuals and social groups to articulate and then to seek to reduce anxiety generated by perceived levels of pollution."[3] The events of 1952 raised a host of questions: How many people became sick or died as a result? Why was this particular fog so fatal? Was exposure to "normal" levels of pollution dangerous? The answers to these and other questions were crucially influenced by an interaction of scientific theory, politics, and statistics, which together acted as mirrors through which people interpreted London's deadliest encounter with fog.

The Nature of Fog

Fog exists at the intersection of nature and culture—it floats freely between country and city, and it reminds people of the connections between the two. During the first half of the nineteenth century, most people believed that fog never originated in urban areas but instead formed in barren and inhospitable "wastelands," from which it carried dangerous vapors into the hearts of cities. Reflecting the idea that fog was the antithesis of civilization, its appearance in cities was typically described as a "visitation." Urban fogs therefore constituted matter out of place—a case of the country polluting the city. As one writer declared in 1853, "Science informs us that the cause of fog is the defective drainage of the lands and marshes, extending for miles on the banks of the Thames, south and east of the city."[4]

As Britain became increasingly urbanized and industrialized, new ideas about fog emerged in the second half of the nineteenth century. In contrast to the earlier belief that fog came exclusively from the natural environment, some observers asserted that it could originate in cities. Fog, they implied, was no longer entirely natural but was a product of both human and environmental processes. As Charles Dickens observed in *Our Mutual Friend* (1864), town fog was of a different character from country fog. In rural areas "fog was grey, whereas in London it was, at about the boundary line, dark yellow, and a little within it brown, and then browner, and then browner, until at the heart of the City . . . it was rusty-black." Ten years later, the *Lancet* commented that although fogs were prevalent throughout Britain, "a real 'London particular' bears no sort of resemblance to an ordinary country fog." The meteorologist Rollo Russell similarly maintained that fogs in rural areas were benign but that those in cities contained soot and acid that were harmful to vegetation and human beings alike.[5]

In the eyes of many, the poor visibility wrought by fog was not only inconvenient but dangerous. Using anthropomorphic language, one observer warned in the 1890s that the "innocent country fogs" with which Britons had long been familiar were giving way to those of an "urban character." Well before Sir Arthur Conan Doyle used fog as an element in his detective stories, observers noted that it provided a highly effective cloak for illegal activity, particularly thefts and assaults. As a popular periodical noted in 1855, "A London fog is a very carnival of petty larceny." Pickpockets, cloaked in the fog, "will contrive to relieve you of any loose cash, pocket-book, or tempting 'ticker,' with a dexterity you cannot but admire, however much you may rue your loss."[6] In addition to associating urban fog with crime, many blamed it as a source of accidents. In it, ships ran aground, pedestrians were struck down by moving vehicles, carriages collided, and people drowned by falling into canals and harbors. According to one report, on the evening of 12 December 1873 fog became so thick in London that no gas-lights could be distinguished in the streets, and the few cabs and omnibuses that ventured out had to be escorted by torch-bearers and could move only step by step. The fog-signals exploding without intermission at the railway stations and the dismal shrieks of the fog-horn served to render the gloom still more melancholy. Many lives were lost; at Wapping, two men walked into the river down the boat-stairs and were drowned. A similar fate befell two respectable artisans, who, on returning from their work to St. John's Wood, walked into the Regent's Canal. Fifteen persons are said to have perished in the docks on the north side of the river alone.[7]

Murders and mishaps accounted for only a tiny proportion of fog deaths, however. Acute respiratory problems killed far more. The dense fog that paralyzed London in 1873 caused numerous animals at the Smithfield Cattle Show to die of respiratory failure, and the human death rate rose 40 percent above that of the previous week. Declaring this fog to be the most persistent in living memory, the *Lancet* reported that London's air had been nothing short of "abominable, so laden was it with smoke and dirt." In response, the *Times* recommended a short-sighted solution:

the creation of a corps of uniformed guides to assist the police in directing pedestrians and carriages through the streets during times of fog.[8]

Although some people maintained that coal smoke had little to do with the onset, persistence, or character of fogs, many thought otherwise. Emphasizing that the fog problem was almost entirely the result of bituminous coal, Rollo Russell claimed that "cities which use wood as a fuel, or anthracite, or gas, or oil, are no more visited by fogs than the surrounding country." In contrast to this, he asserted that "all large towns which burn smoky coal have an excess of fogs and darkness."[9] John Aitken's research in the early 1880s showed that smoke and sulphur dioxide acted as highly effective condensation nuclei for water vapor, thereby increasing the likelihood that fog would form.[10] Aitken's findings were supplemented by those of the chemist Edward Frankland, who suggested that tarry compounds in smoke made fogs more persistent by coating each droplet of water with an oily layer that prevented evaporation. Drawing on these discoveries, the physician Louis Parkes declared that it was a mistake to assume that London's fogs were a natural phenomenon, the result of the geography and meteorology of the metropolis. "Yellow fogs," he told members of the Sanitary Institute in 1892, "are the products of coal combustion mixed up with nature's white mists, the latter being of a comparatively harmless kind."[11] The close association between fog and smoke led many to conflate them as "London fog." This practice had the effect of naturalizing pollution, for it implied that smoke, like the weather, was beyond human control.[12] In addition, it suggested that air pollution constituted a problem only when fog was present. Yet not all fogs were associated with high concentrations of smoke, and elevated levels of pollution sometimes occurred in the absence of fog. In an attempt to make people recognize that smoke-filled fogs were neither natural nor inevitable, the physician (and member of the Coal Smoke Abatement Society) H. A. Des Voeux coined the word *smog* in 1905.[13] Although some people adopted this term, most continued to use the word *fog* to describe the mixture of moisture and coal smoke that often filled the air of London, particularly during autumn and winter.

Fog and Politics

Newspaper reports during the 1952 fog said virtually nothing about its possible health effects. Most articles focused instead on the visual aspect of fog. Some newspapers, celebrating the ability of dense fog to transform the appearance of London, published ghostlike photographs that depicted the fog-enveloped city as mysterious and sublime. In doing so, they were following a long tradition. Ninety-nine years earlier, in 1853, the *Leisure Hour* had similarly noted the ability of fog to change London into a strange and mythical landscape, with "visions—looming rapidly into view, and as rapidly disappearing—of monstrous moving mountains, drawn by mammoths and megatheriums [prehistoric sloths], and driven each one by a shadowy colossus of Rhodes, and crowned with other colossi, sprawling in attitudes absurdly familiar, considering their immensities, on the top. These we know well enough to be the omnibuses, magnified in the gloom. Every man we meet, indeed, is magnified to ten times his proper size at a distance, and only dwindles down to human dimensions as he rubs shoulders with us, and is gone."[14]

Although a small number of articles portrayed fog as an interesting visual display, most suggested that its occurrence was unwelcome. Yet even the most negative coverage of the fog tended to consider it an exclusively visual phenomenon. Reflecting this understanding, the first article to appear in the *Times* about the 1952 fog carried the headline "Fog Delays Air Services." In addition to grounding nearly all flights in and out of London (Heathrow) Airport, poor visibility caused the suspension of bus and trolley routes, forced boat traffic on the Thames to a standstill, and prompted the Automobile Association to warn motorists against driving until conditions improved. After three days of fog, the *Times* reported that "those who ventured on to the roads in the gloom of what should have been daylight made little progress, and many had to abandon their cars and walk." Echoing nineteenth-century reportage of fogs, newspapers in 1952 reported that criminals were deftly exploiting the fog to conceal a rash of "burglaries, attacks, and robberies." All five of the Football League games scheduled to be played in London on 6 December were canceled due "a complete black-out," and Wembley Stadium was forced to remain closed for the first time since it had opened in 1923. Organizers of a cross-country running match in south London went ahead with their race, but fog restricted visibility for spectators and competitors alike to only ten yards, and runners quickly became "lost in the gloom." Even the BBC was affected, for a number of people who were scheduled to go on the air found it impossible to reach its studios. The fog did not remain confined to the outdoors but also seeped into houses, offices, and concert halls. A music critic, reporting on a concert held on 5 December near Oxford Circus, complained of difficulty in seeing the performance through the fog in the auditorium. Noting that the vocalist had struggled to reach high notes, the critic remarked that "perhaps the weather was to blame." On 8 December the fog inside Sadler's Wells Theatre became so intense that a performance of *La Traviata* was halted after its first act. The manager, who issued refunds to everyone in the audience, noted that such a closure was unprecedented in the history of that theatre.[15]

For many Londoners, the fog of December 1952 caused little more than irritated throats and transportation difficulties. For thousands of others, however, it made breathing impossible. The Emergency Bed Service, an agency that coordinated hospital admissions, experienced an unprecedented demand for hospital care during the fog. During the week ending 13 December, it facilitated the hospitalization of 2,019 individuals, 73 percent more than the existing weekly record and more than twice as many as had been admitted under its auspices during the corresponding week of 1951. During the last day of intense fog, 492 individuals applied for emergency admission, 102 of whom were turned away because hospitals were already filled to capacity.[16]

Although medical personnel noticed a sharp rise in health problems during the fog, public recognition of the disastrous effects of the fog was slow to emerge.[17] Delayed reaction to the fog can be attributed in part to the time needed to assemble and analyze mortality statistics, but it also resulted from the ruling Conservative Party's attempt to escape blame for the tragedy and to avoid being pressured into stricter controls on air pollution. On 16 December, a member of Parliament from the Labour Party asked the minister of health to reveal "how many persons died of bronchial or other ailments in the Greater London area as a result of the recent severe fog." The minister, Iain Macleod, initially sidestepped the question by answering that data were not yet available for any dates past 6 December. The next day, the same M.P. called for the creation of a committee to study "the causes and cure of London fog." A representative of the Ministry of Works rebuffed this proposal and asserted that "a committee, the Atmospheric Pollution Research Committee, already exists under the Fuel Research Board and includes representatives of all the interested Departments." On 18 December, in response to further questions, this time from fellow Conservatives, the minister of health issued a shocking statement: "The number of deaths from all causes in Greater London during the week ending 13th December was 4,703 compared with 1,852 in the corresponding week of the 1951." Newspaper headlines screamed, "Fog Week

Deaths Rose by 2,800," and the *British Medical Journal,* not known for sen-sationalism, referred to this rise in the death rate as nothing less than "spectacular."[18]

In the weeks and months that followed the fog, the government at-tempted to minimize the magnitude and significance of the deaths that the phenomenon had caused. In spite of this, public interest and concern remained high. Six weeks after the fog lifted, a member of the House of Commons asked the minister of health to describe how his department was represented on the Atmospheric Pollution Research Committee. In contrast to the government's earlier claim that this committee included "all the interested Departments," Macleod admitted that the Ministry of Health was not, in fact, represented on it. Criticism of the government's handling of the fog continued to rise, and members of the Labour Party sought to portray the Conservative administration as inattentive and cal-lous. This impression was reinforced two days later when the minister of health publicly complained that he "seemed to get nothing except ques-tions about fog and its effect on people's health. 'Really, you know,' he said, 'anyone would think fog had only started in London since I became Min-ister.'"[19]

The future prime minister Harold Macmillan, then minister of housing and local government, also endured harsh criticism in Parliament. In late January 1953, one Labour M.P. asked him, "Does the Minister not appreci-ate that last month, in Greater London alone, there were literally more people choked to death by air pollution than were killed on the roads in the whole country in 1952? Why is a public inquiry not being held, seeing that inquiries are held into air and rail disasters which do not affect so many people?" Joining in, another M.P. asked, "Is the Minister aware that his complacency in dealing with this problem is creating a lot of dismay ...?" Two months after the fog lifted, the government continued to deflect calls for an investigation by claiming that it would needlessly duplicate the work of the Atmospheric Pollution Research Committee. On 12 February, however, this tactic was exposed as a diversion. Asked what actions that committee was taking in response to the December fog, a government spokesperson replied, incredibly, "None. The Committee is essentially an advisory body concerned with the collection of data on atmospheric pol-lution and with the researches into its measurement and prevention." In response to further questioning, he stated that the committee had met only two times in the previous year. Shortly after this embarrassing revela-tion, the minister of health announced that his department had begun an inquiry into fog deaths—the results of which were not made public until 1954.[20] Although this move suggested that the government had begun to take the pollution issue more seriously, it failed to satisfy many critics. Addressing the Commons five months after the fog episode, Labour M.P. Norman Dodds declared,

> There is still an amazing amount of alarm on the part of the public about the heavy death roll [*sic*] and the widespread sickness following the December fogs. This alarm has been greatly increased by the amazing, at least outward, apathy of the Government. Most people who have deep feelings about this just cannot understand why there has not been a public inquiry after thousands of people were choked to death.

Predicting that a future fog could kill even more, Dodds warned that London might again be filled with the plague cry "Bring out your dead." Responding to Dodds's speech, the deputy minister of housing and local government announced that the government would create a committee "to undertake a comprehensive review of the causes and effects of air pollution."[21] In July 1953, seven months after the fog cleared, the government finally appointed this committee, which was led by the engineer and industrialist Sir Hugh Beaver. The Beaver Committee, as it soon became known, would issue its final report just one month short of the second anniversary of the 1952 fog.[22]

Counting the Dead

The ability to "see" the fog of 1952 as a disaster depended crucially on the collection and interpretation of statistical data. In contrast to the generally straightforward matter of determining the number of injuries and deaths from disasters such as fires, floods, and train wrecks, determining how many people died from the fog of 1952 was a complex and imprecise task. Detailed records existed about the number of deaths that occurred in and around London each day and week, but which times and places were relevant was open to interpretation. Decisions had to be made about the geographical scope of the inquiry: some looked at the Administrative County of London, home to 3.4 million people, which was ruled by the London County Council. Others considered Greater London, population 8.4 million, which included parts of the counties of Middlesex, Surrey, Kent,

Hertfordshire, and Essex. Another important issue was the chronological scope of the inquiry: should it encompass only the immediate period of the fog, or subsequent weeks as well? Only after these decisions had been made was it possible to determine how many people had died during the fog. Such a procedure did not, of course, distinguish between people who died because of the fog and those who would have died anyway, from other causes. Although it would have been possible to analyze the health records of everyone who died in an effort to determine whether fog had caused their deaths, such an approach would have been massive and time-consuming. In addition, such an exercise would have produced doubtful results, for concluding whether fog was the decisive cause of death in a person with a chronic illness would have been a choice fraught with ambiguity. Instead of examining each case individually, experts compared the total number of deaths during the fog with an estimate of the number who would have died in the absence of fog. Although such a procedure may sound simple, there was no clear way to accomplish it. Some statisticians used the week preceding the fog as their reference point, while others used data from the corresponding week of the previous year. A third option, designed to control for the possibility that the previous week or year was atypical, compared the number of deaths that occurred during and after the 1952 fog with an average based on the same period over the preceding five years.[23]

Two months after the fog episode, the *British Medical Journal* reported that the overall death rate in London during the week ending 13 December 1952 had been nearly as high as that experienced in 1866 during one of the country's worst outbreaks of cholera. If one viewed these data against the prevailing mortality rates for each period, it became evident that Londoners had experienced a greater risk of dying from fog in early December 1952 than from cholera in the epidemic of 1866. During the week of 7–13 December, the death rate in the Administrative County of London jumped to 2.6 times what it had been during the previous week. In Greater London, the death rate also rose sharply, increasing by a factor of 2.3. Two particularly hard-hit boroughs of London, East Ham and Stepney, saw a fourfold increase in their weekly death rates.[24]

Several weeks after his bombshell that 2,851 people had died as a result of the fog, the minister of health announced a new estimate that placed the death toll from the fog at approximately 6,000. This number was reached by comparing the number of deaths in Greater London during a five-week period that encompassed the fog of 1952 with the same period of the previous year.[25] Shortly after Macleod raised the official death toll, W. P. D. Logan, the government's chief medical statistician, argued for a smaller figure. Although he noted that the 1952 fog "was a catastrophe of the first magnitude in which, for a few days, death-rates attained a level that has been exceeded only rarely during the past hundred years—for example, at the height of the cholera epidemic of 1854 and of the influenza epidemic of 1918–19," he made the assumption that the effects of the fog were confined to a two-week period and focused his attention on the Administrative County of London, which contained five million fewer residents than Greater London. Logan admitted that it was "not possible to be sure . . . that all the deaths brought about by the fog had been registered within the two weeks ended Dec. 13 and 20. *Assuming that they were,* the number of deaths so caused can be estimated to lie between 3717 (the excess in the weeks ended Dec. 13 and 20 over the week ended Dec. 6, 1952) and 4075 (the excess in the weeks ended Dec. 13 and 20, 1952, over the corresponding average for 1947–51)."[26] Inexplicably, he failed to consider whether any of the deaths registered during the week ending 6 December were fog-related, even though the fog began on the morning of 5 December and the data he used showed that deaths that week exceeded the five-year average for that week by 257. Even more significant is Logan's assumption, inherent in his calculations, that no deaths after 20 December should be attributed to fog exposure. Yet death rates remained high well after the end point of Logan's study. Between mid-December and mid-February, approximately eight thousand more people died in London than during the same period one year earlier. The government's top air pollution scientist, E. T. Wilkins, pointed out that these deaths also coincided with substantially higher than usual concentrations of air pollution. In his words, this constituted "a second pollution shock to Londoners whose powers of resistance may have been reduced by the earlier smog incident."[27] Rejecting Wilkins's arguments, others maintained that influenza solely was responsible for the elevated mortality in early 1953, a view that was shared by the Ministry of Health. In light of the government's attempts to minimize the extent of the disaster, it comes as little surprise that it endorsed Logan's calculation of four thousand deaths as "the best estimate that can be made." A recent study, however, supports Wilkins's much higher estimate. Its authors, Michelle L. Bell and Devra Lee Davis, note that even if influenza deaths are excluded, approximately seventy-seven hundred more deaths than usual occurred in London during and soon after the fog disaster of 1952.[28]

Air Pollution and Health

In the aftermath of the 1952 fog, expert opinion was divided about the relative risk that polluted air posed to the "general public." The minister of health, in effect blaming the victims, asserted that "the real problem of the 'smog' is that of persons—and particularly old persons—suffering from weaknesses of the lungs or heart."[29] In contrast to this, a report issued by the health committee of the London County Council emphasized that the increase in the death rate during the second week of December 1952, "although more pronounced among babies and the elderly, was not confined to persons of any particular age."[30] Echoing this perspective, the *British Medical Journal* noted that fog had nearly killed "a stalwart London policeman of 35 who collapsed and was admitted to hospital only just in time to save his life by means of oxygen and treatment for shock." In its view, "[t]here is a danger that the obvious effects of the fog on babies and the elderly may divert attention from the damage possibly done to people in the middle years of life."[31] More stridently, the journal *Planning* insisted that "it was not, as has been occasionally suggested, merely a matter of old people, who were due to die soon in any case, being killed. Many of those affected might have had years of useful life ahead of them."[32]

Related to the idea that "normal" people, that is, healthy individuals in the prime of life, had emerged unscathed from the 1952 fog episode was the view that everyday levels of air pollution were acceptable. Attempting to reassure the public as the 1953 fog season approached, the minister of health declared that prolonged intense fog was "an extremely rare occurrence" and that it was "important not to confuse it with the more normal fogs with which we have long been familiar nor to exaggerate its effect on normal healthy people."[33] In contrast to this view, the *Times* asserted that although the 1952 fog "was admittedly an exceptional occurrence, it is obvious that even under less abnormal conditions the noxious matter in polluted air must have a detrimental effect on human and animal health and comfort; no doubt the effect is less violent, but all the more persistent."[34] Statistical data lent credence to such concerns, as deaths from respiratory diseases associated with air pollution were many times higher in Britain than in much of the rest of Europe. In 1952, the bronchitis death rate in England and Wales was 62.1 per 100,000 people, compared to 18.3 in Belgium, 4.5 in France, and 3.4 in Denmark.[35] In addition to comparing Britain with other countries, the Beaver Committee noted that large cities in Britain experienced much higher death rates from bronchitis than did less-polluted rural areas.[36] In his frequent public statements, Beaver also made historical comparisons in an effort to build support for clean air. He noted, for example, that respiratory diseases attributable to air pollution were killing a larger proportion of the British population in the 1950s than typhoid had killed in the 1870s.[37]

After the 1952 disaster, many experts believed that the public needed to distinguish between natural and unnatural fogs. Seeking to educate its readers in this matter, the *Times* noted, "Fog is a natural phenomenon and is intractable by human agencies. Except for reducing visibility on sea and land, nature-made fogs are comparatively innocuous in themselves. It is when they get contaminated by man-produced impurities in cities and industrial areas that they become dangerous."[38] Beaver similarly emphasized the distinction between natural and artificial fogs. Speaking at the University of London in 1955, he noted, "Although it is nature that produces the fog, it is we who produce the smoke. And this we have been doing for generations, to such an extent that we had almost come to accept it as natural and inescapable."[39]

Beaver's perspective echoed that of E. T. Wilkins. In a 1953 address to the Royal Sanitary Institute, which had long played an important role in efforts to reduce air pollution, Wilkins noted, "The bad effects of air pollution are, of course, not confined to periods of smog, for there is evidence that even the lower concentrations normal to many densely populated areas have persistent and insidious effects on public health, vegetation and on materials of all kinds. Thus the problem of smog is, in some respects, a short-term magnification of the general problem of atmospheric pollution." He added that "because the effects of normal pollution are ever present they undoubtedly represent, in the long run, a greater damage and loss to individuals and to the nation than does an occasional smog incident."[40] After his committee had concluded its work, Beaver recalled, "We expressly avoided basing our arguments on the danger to health of particular incidents, such as the London Smog of 1952. Not that we minimised that catastrophe in any way, but we felt that undue emphasis on it, would distract attention from the fact that damage to health and danger to life were going on all over the country, all the time, year in and year out." All of Britain, as he put it, constituted a "single permanently polluted area."[41]

Conclusion

Initial reactions to the London fog of 1952 portrayed it as a natural disaster that was impossible to foresee or prevent. Fatalism and myopia may provide comfort in the face of tragedy, but they do so at the cost of concealing historical connections. Serious fogs *had* happened before in London, and their effects were in many ways similar between the mid–nineteenth and mid–twentieth centuries. Throughout that period, the air of London was polluted with smoke, soot, and sulphur dioxide from millions of coal fires. Unusually still air and cool surface temperatures—the same conditions that made fog likely—caused pollution concentrations to rise to levels that interfered with breathing and proved deadly to thousands who suffered from bronchitis, asthma, and other diseases of the respiratory and circulatory systems.

As Mary Douglas and Bill Luckin have shown, pollution affects not only health and the environment but also culture. In other words, the ways in which a particular society perceives pollution and gives it meaning provide an important lens through which that culture projects its values and beliefs. Longstanding ways of seeing fog—particularly, a tendency to view its effects as primarily visual—re-emerged with the onset of fog in 1952. Yet public reaction to severe fog was markedly greater in 1952 than in the nineteenth century. Instead of viewing it with a sense of complacency, many believed that it could be prevented, and that government had a responsibility to see that it was. If deaths increased during foggy weather not because of cold air or high humidity but because of the intense air pollution that often accompanied the fog, this suggested that air pollution was unhealthy even in the absence of fog. Determining what had happened in December 1952 was a complicated and highly contested process, but one that ultimately led to the emergence of new ideas about air pollution and new policies to clear the air. What was initially viewed as a natural disaster eventually came to be seen as a catastrophe that human beings had helped to create—and something that they ought to prevent from recurring.

NOTES

1. C. K. M. Douglas, "London Fog of December 5–8, 1952," *Meteorological Magazine* 82 (1953): 67–71; E. T. Wilkins, "Air Pollution and the London Fog of Decem-

ber, 1952," *Journal of the Royal Sanitary Institute* 74 (Jan. 1954): 1–21; Ministry of Health, *Mortality and Morbidity during the London Fog of December 1952* (London: HMSO, 1954), table 3.

2. *Daily Mirror*, 8 Dec. 1952.

3. Mary Douglas, *Purity and Danger: An Analysis of Concepts of Pollution and Taboo* (1966; reprint, London: Routledge, 1992), esp. 1–6, 159–79; Bill Luckin, *Pollution and Control: A Social History of the Thames in the Nineteenth Century* (Bristol: Adam Hilger, 1986), 52.

4. "A London Fog," *Leisure Hour*, 1 Dec. 1853, 772–74, quotation on 774.

5. Charles Dickens, *Our Mutual Friend*, ed. Michael Cotsell (Oxford: Oxford University Press, 1989), 420; "The Fog in London," *Lancet*, 3 Jan. 1874, 27–28, quotation on 27; Francis Albert Rollo Russell, *The Atmosphere in Relation to Human Life and Health* (Washington, D.C.: Smithsonian Institution, 1896), 32–35.

6. Robert H. Scott, "Fifteen Years' Fogs in the British Islands, 1876–1890," *Quarterly Journal of the Royal Meteorological Society* 19 (1893): 229–38, quotations on 232; "Observations in a London Fog," *Hogg's Instructor* 5 (1855): 53–55, quotation on 55.

7. G. Hartwig, *The Aerial World: A Popular Account of the Phenomena and Life of the Atmosphere* (New York: D. Appleton, 1875), 138–39.

8. "The Fog in London," *Lancet*, 3 Jan. 1874, 27–28, quotation on 27; *Times* (London), 12 Dec. 1873, 7.

9. Russell, *Atmosphere*, 34; idem, "Haze, Fog, and Visibility," *Quarterly Journal of the Royal Meteorological Society* 23 (1897): 10–24, quotation on 19.

10. John Aitken, "On Dust, Fogs, and Clouds," *Nature* 23 (30 Dec. 1880): 195–97; idem, "Dust and Fogs," *Nature* 23 (3 Feb. 1881): 311–12. For contemporary discussions of Aitken's theories, see Douglas Galton, "Inaugural Address," *Transactions of the Sanitary Institute of Great Britain* 4 (1882–83): 21–54, esp. 33; "The Etiology of Fogs," *Lancet*, 26 Feb. 1887, 443.

11. Louis C. Parkes, "The Air and Water of London: Are They Deteriorating?" *Transactions of the Sanitary Institute* 13 (1892): 59–69, quotation on 62.

12. Attempts to deny human culpability when disaster strikes are by no means limited to Britain. See Theodore Steinberg, *Acts of God: An Unnatural History of Natural Disaster in America* (New York: Oxford University Press, 2000), esp. xvii–xx, 151–52.

13. *Encyclopaedia Britannica*, s.v. "smog." For more on the Coal Smoke Abatement Society and other groups that sought to reduce coal smoke before the First World War, see David Stradling and Peter Thorsheim, "The Smoke of Great Cities: British and American Efforts to Control Air Pollution, 1860–1914," *Environmental History* 4 (Jan. 1999): 6–31.

14. "A London Fog," *Leisure Hour*, 1 Dec. 1853, 772–74, quotation on 773.

15. *Times* (London), 6 Dec. 1952, 6; ibid., 8 Dec. 1952, 3, 8; ibid., 9 Dec. 1952, 8.

16. G. F. Abercrombie, "December Fog in London and the Emergency Bed Service," *Lancet*, 31 Jan. 1953, 234–35.

17. John Fry, "Effects of a Severe Fog on a General Practice," *Lancet*, 31 Jan. 1953, 235–36.

18. *Parliamentary Debates*, Commons, 5th ser., vol. 509 (1952), cols. 188, 221, 237; *Daily Telegraph*, 19 Dec. 1952; "Deaths in the Fog," *British Medical Journal*, 3 Jan. 1953, 50.

19. *Parliamentary Debates*, Commons, 5th ser., vol. 510 (1953), col. 382; *Evening Standard*, 24 Jan. 1953, quoted in *Parliamentary Debates*, Commons, 5th ser., vol. 515 (1953), cols. 842–43.

20. *Parliamentary Debates*, Commons, 5th ser., vol. 510 (1953), cols. 828–30; ibid., vol. 511 (1953), col. 75; ibid., vol. 513 (1953), col. 189.

21. *Parliamentary Debates*, Commons, 5th ser., vol. 515 (1953), cols. 841–50.

22. Committee on Air Pollution, *Report*, Cmd. 9322 (1954).

23. Ministry of Health, *Mortality and Morbidity*, table 1.

24. *Times* (London), 31 Jan. 1953, 3; "The Toll of Fog," *British Medical Journal*, 7 Feb. 1953, 321; Ministry of Health, *Mortality and Morbidity*, 2; W. P. D. Logan, "Mortality in the London Fog Incident, 1952," *Lancet*, 14 Feb. 1953, 336–38, quotation on 337.

25. *Parliamentary Debates*, Commons, 5th ser., vol. 510 (1953), col. 42.

26. Logan, "Mortality," 336. Emphasis added.

27. Wilkins, "Air Pollution," 11.

28. Ministry of Health, *Mortality and Morbidity*, 14; Michelle L. Bell and Devra Lee Davis, "Reassessment of the Lethal London Fog of 1952: Novel Indicators of Acute and Chronic Consequences of Acute Exposure to Air Pollution," *Environmental Health Perspectives* 109, supp. 3 (June 2001): 389–94. See also Devra Lee Davis, *When Smoke Ran like Water: Tales of Environmental Deception and the Battle against Pollution* (New York: Basic Books, 2002), 42–54.

29. *Parliamentary Debates*, Commons, 5th ser., vol. 518 (1953), col. 407.

30. Quoted in *Times* (London), 31 Jan. 1953, 3.

31. "The Toll of Fog," *British Medical Journal*, 7 Feb. 1953, 321.

32. "The Menace of Air Pollution," *Planning* 20 (16 Aug. 1954): 189–216, quotation on 193–94. Similar debates about the "reality" of deaths attributed to public health disasters have occurred in other contexts. See Eric Klinenberg, *Heat Wave: A Social Autopsy of Disaster in Chicago* (Chicago: University of Chicago Press, 2002), esp. 24–31.

33. *Parliamentary Debates*, Commons, 5th ser., vol. 520 (1953), col. 105.

34. *Times* (London), 20 Apr. 1953, 7.

35. Committee on Air Pollution, *Report*, Cmd. 9322 (1954), 8. The committee's attention to the high rate of bronchitis in Britain relative to other countries was likely influenced by Neville C. Oswald et al., "Clinical Pattern of Chronic Bronchi-

tis," *Lancet,* 26 Sept. 1953, 639–43; United Nations, *Demographic Yearbook, 1954* (New York: United Nations, 1954).

36. Committee on Air Pollution, *Report,* Cmd. 9322 (1954), 9.

37. Hugh Beaver, typescript of a speech to the Engineering Institute of Canada, 17 March 1955, Beaver Papers, British Library of Political and Economic Science, London.

38. *Times* (London), 20 Apr. 1953, 7.

39. Hugh Beaver, typescript of a speech delivered at London University, 1 Dec. 1955, 4, Beaver Papers, British Library of Political and Economic Science, London.

40. Wilkins, "Air Pollution," 14.

41. Committee on Air Pollution, *Report,* Cmd. 9322 (1954), 5; Hugh Beaver, typescript of a speech delivered in New York, 2 March 1955, 11–12, Beaver Papers, British Library of Political and Economic Science, London.

8

Localizing Smog
Transgressions in the Therapeutic Landscape

Joshua Dunsby

In May 1946, the office of the mayor of Los Angeles hosted a conference to address the mounting problem of smog. Anson Ford, a member of the Los Angeles County Board of Supervisors, began the conference by reading a letter from what he called a "typical citizen." The letter described a family that came to Sierra Madre—a town in the foothills of the San Gabriel Mountains, adjacent to Pasadena—from their home in Seattle "to establish a part-time residence, in order to enjoy the sunshine, wonderful, clear mountain air and health-giving qualities of this area, as publicized so widely by the State of California." The letter writer, who had asthma, was assured that Sierra Madre was the "third most healthful spot in the world for asthmatics." Yet in April he had five severe asthma attacks, and during heavy smogs he reported his "eyes would smart, and burn, the throat burned and felt swollen and the head ached with a dull, intermittent ache all day." The homeowner concluded, "We want to like and live in Southern California. We have paid a high price for a scrap of land in this wonderful state, with a mountain view which is obscured by smog, and with dry, healthful air which is polluted by smog. We have spent quite a sum of money constructing a house on this land. How do you think we, and many other newcomers with whom we've talked, feel about [it] now?"[1]

Perceptions of smog and the social process of interpreting its meaning—that is, the social cognition of smog—shaped a collective response. Smog materialized during the early 1940s and fueled what would be, at times, a major political controversy for the City and County of Los Angeles. Although the primarily white middle-class settlers of places like Sierra

Madre often had exceedingly high expectations for a salubrious environment, residents of the entire Los Angeles area were becoming aware of deteriorating visibility and irritating hazes. Smog grabbed attention with its direct and sometimes intense effect on the senses, and through the media's ability to dramatize it with graphic photographs, frightening headlines, and personal stories. Collective feelings of duress and anxiety and perceptions of community and environmental degeneration accompanied the physical changes brought by smog. By the time of the mayor's 1946 conference, smog had been a source of public concern for several years. Common sense first directed attention to visible emissions from industrial factories. Moreover, the conventional wisdom that industry was primarily or exclusively to blame for smog was highly durable among lay smog reformers (Brienes 1976). Initially, lay reformers were not alone in this assumption; many experts experienced with smoke and fume problems in other cities drew similar conclusions. From the end of World War II through the mid-1950s, many citizens of Los Angeles not only blamed industry but also perceived little progress in controlling smog. Consequently, individuals grew frustrated and increasingly vocalized their malcontent for local government.

This chapter examines the early history of the Southern California smog reform movement and seeks to explain its incipient character by reference to the resources and traditions through which this new phenomenon was understood and defined. The 1940s are characterized by the lack of an authoritative explanation and control policy, and therefore are themselves insufficient explanations of smog politics. Retrospectively, the period can be thought of as a prelude to the contemporary understanding of smog—the belief that what is called smog is created by a photochemical reaction of car exhaust with oxygen to produce ozone, which is then trapped by a temperature inversion in the atmosphere. Not until the mid-1950s would the validity of the photochemical theory of smog go unquestioned and the significance of the automobile as the major source of smog be fully established. In short, beliefs until then were speculative, less rationalized, and less dominated by expert authority; moreover, in the early years of smog, distinctions between moral and technical conceptions of the problem were less pronounced. With basic knowledge of smog almost non-existent, interested lay and expert communities expressed the meaning of smog through speculations and hypotheses that relied on assumptions, past experiences, and skills—in other words, inherited cultures of understanding and problem solving. These hypotheses helped frame smog as a social problem as well, suggesting who was responsible and implying a range of legitimate solutions.

I argue that the intensity and tenor of the response by citizens, as well as by local and distant expert communities, stemmed from the ways in which smog permeated Southern California life and challenged its order on many levels. Smog was an institutional crisis (What was to be done about it? Whose responsibility was it?), a moral crisis (Who was to blame? Where did it come from? Why us?), and a crisis of meaning (What kind of thing is smog—natural or man-made? What kind of place or society do we live in to have encountered such a thing?). The theoretical framework for this analysis is discussed in more detail in the first section. Reasons for the particular response to smog are found in the "cultural environmental" history of Southern California. I identify two traditions that mediated the relations between Los Angeles society and its pollution: the urban environmental reform movements (including smoke abatement) and the "health-seeker" movement.[2] These two traditions can be categorized as public health movements, and both represent a mixture of lay and expert communities. The health-seeker movement, however, which brought many ill persons to the southwest United States in the hopes of improving their well-being, had its most direct influence on the actions and beliefs of local residents and physicians. The irony is immediately apparent. Smog corrupted one of Southern California's most valued qualities: its healthful atmosphere. It physically affected the health of individuals, but at least as important to smog reform, it undercut a collective identity that held that Southern California was a health paradise—it was believed to be place apart (that, by implication, was inhabited by a special, fortunate, or knowing population).[3] After addressing the specific politics of smog in Los Angeles in the 1940s, the chapter discusses the relationship between the "cultural transgressions" of smog and its politics.

Social Disorder and Therapeutic Landscapes

The public health movements upon which the Los Angeles smog debates unfolded illuminate the relationship between identity, pollution, and health and its implications for understanding environmental health politics. Attributing the problem, and even knowledge of the phenomenon, to some objective danger often cannot explain the variation in social responses and beliefs. Beyond the narrow material effects of certain contaminants, a more adequate account of smog and other environmental health problems must not ignore the threat pollution poses to a way of life, to a historically specific social order. Hence, societies solve their pollution problems not only by physically restoring the environment but also by restoring social order—solidarity, trust, legitimacy. Part of what was troubling about smog, among other things, was that it was internally generated—the problem was not just man-made but locally made as well, and thus it was the occasion for dissent and social strife. Expressed in the terms of social theory, the occurrence of this social conflict can be analyzed as a problem of cultural boundaries. I discuss this theoretical issue briefly in this section and also aim to further the cultural analysis of environmental health by incorporating notions of material culture not found in classic statements on the matter. In this way I can better theorize the social significance of place—of specific locales—and produce an account of smog that reduces to neither an unsatisfactory materialism nor idealism.

Perception and explanation of a new phenomenon are necessarily social processes. They are activities that are possible through the engagement with specific communities that have particular histories and cultures.[4] Thus, collective perception, which comprises common concepts and categories for apprehending the world, precedes a collective response. The classic sociological statement on this topic is Emile Durkheim's (1915) analysis of religious classification, the sacred and the profane; however, it is Mary Douglas's adaptation of his theory that is the most relevant entrance into the relationship between cultural classification and environmental problems. In her various works (Douglas 1966, 1982; Douglas and Wildavsky 1982), Douglas applies cultural analysis to beliefs about pollution. In her view, pollution is fundamentally disorder, something that does not fit within a "systematic ordering of ideas," that, is a cultural classification scheme (Douglas 1966: 41).

In her later work, *Risk and Culture,* Douglas elaborates on the topic of social cognition and asks a related question about why some risks are perceived and others are ignored. Douglas and Wildavsky summarize their approach with the claim that risk is a "collective construct" (Douglas and Wildavsky 1982: 192). Thus, just as categories of social kinds are not given but are constructed, so are natural kinds socially constructed. The approach relativizes the assessment of risks in the sense that evaluation becomes contingent on, or relative to, a specific form of social organization.

Risk is not something that can be assessed by an individual through rational contemplation alone (Douglas and Wildavsky 1982: 8). Thus, a choice about risks is also a choice about a kind of society.

Following these arguments, we cannot expect to explain the perceived danger of air pollution based on its physical effects alone. There were not clear cause-and-effect relationships; and effects, such as eye irritation, that were clearly attributable to smog did not necessarily demand immediate attention.[5] Furthermore, in the context of smog, to ask about causation was to ask about blame. Not every kind of pollution source was going to mobilize expert and lay reformers. To understand the specific response to smog that did occur, we need to consider the physical and cultural boundaries that it transgressed; therefore, it is important to locate smog within specific material and symbolic environments. Nevertheless, Douglas's approach has some limitations for theorizing the relationship between health and place because it is largely oriented toward analyzing abstract cultural categories. To more fully grasp the cultural dimensions of air pollution, a concept of culture that emphasizes its locationally and temporally specific qualities is beneficial—in other words, one that foregrounds the interaction of historical forces that materially and symbolically shape a particular place.

Therapeutic landscape is a term suggested by the geographer Wilbert M. Gesler to unite the diverse literatures concerned with explicating "therapeutic processes in various settings" (Gesler 1992: 735). In particular, he wants to expand analyses beyond a focus on specific healing powers of nature. He draws inspiration from the "new cultural geography," which holds that "landscapes, as well as being influenced by physical and built environments, are a product of the human mind and of material circumstances, that landscapes reflect both human intentions and actions and the constraints and structures imposed by society" (Gesler 1992: 743).[6]

The work of Gesler and others suggests a cultural analysis of the problem of smog. The Los Angeles environment itself must be thought of as a kind of material artifact, a product of human labor and culture in interaction with the natural world. Smog is one outcome of this hybridization of culture and nature. In Douglas's formulation, smog would be considered pollution, and a social problem, because it creates cognitive disorder; however, smog also creates material disorder. In other words, societies label something as pollution within a cultural classification system but also generate particular kinds of waste during specific moments in history. The suggestion is that smog should be considered part of the built environment, as material culture; however, it has a negative quality. It is the product of "human unintentions" and lack of knowledge. The idea of the therapeutic landscape signals these complex cultural relationships and histories that relate health and place.

This theoretical framework provides a way to more adequately conceptualize the complex social and physical problem of air pollution. Environmental problems are man-made problems in two ways: they are produced both physically and symbolically. Smoke and other wastes are the products of human activity, but without a cultural frame, there is no meaning to the actions, and there is no problem per se. I adapted the concept of the therapeutic landscape to capture some of this interplay as well as the integrity of the actor's conception of the problem. Human activity infuses landscapes with history, with material culture, and with symbolic meaning.[7] As cultural geographers and others have recommended, landscapes can be considered to be human artifacts: the meaning of the artifact can change, but so can its use. Therefore, the cultural ladenness of landscapes is not exhausted by its interpretative variability (e.g., the perception of smoke, good or bad) but also incorporates the physical possibilities and impossibilities that are built into it. More specifically, beauty and health are not necessarily mutually exclusive—the beautiful city is the healthful city. Only by locating air pollution reform in particular places can the analyst fully understand the relationship between these abstract social values and cultural beliefs, because it is here that they are instantiated in everyday life. This approach is especially of value when seeking to understand the perspective of laypersons, for whom the relationship to the environment, and pollution of the environment, is typically direct, immediate, and localized—as evidenced the in remarks of the man from Sierra Madre.

Earlier Pollution Reform Movements

The relationship between health beliefs, morality, and environment, discussed above in theoretical terms, can be understood more concretely through the history of public health reform in the late-nineteenth-century and early-twentieth-century United States. The first response to smog in Los Angeles is better understood in this broader historical context for two reasons. First, such a history identifies the urban environment, the kind of (anti-)therapeutic landscape, that many health-seekers were abandoning; second, it describes the elements of the smoke-abatement movement that shaped the expert understanding of air pollution. The perception of smog in Southern California was filtered through these earlier experiences and reform efforts, which express a recognizable moral vision.

The Unhealthy City: Moral Reform of the Urban Environment

Environmental pollutions arose primarily in conjunction with the processes of industrialization and urbanization: the types of wastes and pollutants, the population density of urban areas, and the geography of Americans and their pollutants all began to take on their contemporary character in the second half of the nineteenth century.[8] Housing was often unventilated, streets were places of refuse, the water supply was poor, and there was the stench of open sewers (Leavitt 1982: 22). These environmental conditions were the norm for mid-nineteenth-century American cities, but in the last decades of the century, calls for reform were coming from technical elites, middle-class associations, and civic organizations.[9] Medical theory provided one of the most authoritative tools for making sense of pollution and thus shaped the beliefs of the sanitarians and the civic reformers. Beginning in the 1840s, throughout Europe and the United States, the theory of miasmas—that dirt and decaying material generated sick air—dominated beliefs about sanitation (Fee and Porter 1992: 253), and only slowly, in the last quarter of the century, did the germ theory of disease take hold.

Reformers came in several forms. The leading reformers were frequently women's organizations that took up the cause of "municipal housekeeping," as urban sanitation was sometimes called. For the middle-class women who became involved, working toward sanitation reform seemed a natural extension of their domestic responsibilities, an expansion of the boundary of the home (Hoy 1995: 72–75; Leavitt 1982: 191; Melosi 1981: 118–124; Grinder 1980: 86). This "moral environmentalism" of the civic organizations, as the historian Stanley Schultz has called it, "carried the conviction that if one altered the physical environment, the moral seasons were certain to change as well" (Schultz 1989: 113). In contrast, according to Melosi (1981: 32), the elite sanitary engineers who advocated engineering solutions never united with these civic reformers[10]—a pattern echoed in smoke and smog reform movements.[11] Not until just after World War II did reformers in places like St. Louis, Pittsburgh, and Chicago achieve their goals for coal-smoke control. In short, during the early twentieth century the dominant premise for smoke control shifted from health and aesthetics to economics and efficiency, and the locus of the reform movement shifted from women and physicians to engineers and economists (Stradling 1999: 136).[12]

This organizational change involved a shift in social perception as well. The billowing smokestack does not have a fixed visual meaning: what is now one of the most negative iconic images of modern environmentalism once had positive connotations.[13] Much like Melosi's garbage reformers, the middle-class smoke-abatement reformers had to change the perception of smoke. As late as the 1940s in Pittsburgh, a city heavily dependent on the coal-mining industry, city politicians and working-class people saw smoke as an annoying but beneficial sign (Tarr 1996: 232). Employing a moral tone similar to that of the sanitary reformers, the smoke control reformers began various educational and publicity campaigns to convey their sense of the dangers of smoke.

Moral beliefs about air pollution are also evident in the reform language, which the environmental historian Adam W. Rome has carefully documented. *Smog* was part of the modern environmentalist vocabulary that had been growing since the late nineteenth century in conjunction with the industrial city. A contraction of *smoke* and *fog, smog* was first coined by a nineteenth-century London physician active in the smoke-abatement movement, to describe the mixture of smoke and fog that ailed Londoners (Brienes 1975: 10). Not until the 1930s, Rome observes, was the term *air pollution* used in its modern sense, that is, meaning chemical emissions and combustion by-products.[14] The more general term, *pollution,* also took on new meaning during this time. According to Rome, the middle-class urban activists who fought for environmental reforms typically used the term *pollution* in its religious sense, to mean moral corruption, defilement, or profanity, and only infrequently referred to the "environment" (Rome 1996: 7). Echoing Mary Douglas's perspective, Rome remarks that for some reformers "to pollute the air was to transgress, to threaten the foundations of society" (1996: 9).[15]

"Health-Seekers" and "Climatic Therapy"

The man from Sierra Madre described at the 1946 Los Angeles mayor's conference was not the first person to bring his family to Southern California in the hopes of a better life. His family's move coincided with the late stage of a migration of individuals and families to the southwest United States—collectively known as "health-seekers"—that began in the mid–nineteenth century and peaked in its last decade. The belief that a different climate or place might improve their well-being was a strong motivation.

Health and environment are linked concepts, and common sense in the nineteenth century held that one's environment influenced one's health: bad environments, social and physical, produced poor health (Schultz 1989; Rosenberg 1992a: chap. 12; Valencius 2000a). Therefore, changing one's environment was seen sometimes as the only therapy for diseases with no other effective treatments. Medical professionals, especially those identifying with a specialized field called medical climatology, encouraged this belief among laypeople. One irony of the onset of smog was that the very aesthetic and therapeutic qualities of the climate that were drawing sickly individuals to the area, particularly the healthful air, were precisely the ones it tainted. The response to smog in the 1940s was built on an earlier history that mapped out complex and dynamic relationships between health, environment, and quality of life. Central to understanding this unfolding of events is the way that residents constructed regional identities around beliefs about health, illness, and pollution, and the way in which smog violated these material and symbolic boundaries.

Health-seekers are a significant but often overlooked part of the nineteenth-century western migration, according to the historians of the southwest United States John E. Baur (1959) and Billy M. Jones (1967). During the second half of the nineteenth century, states and territories such as Arizona, New Mexico, Colorado, and California received an influx of individuals, the earliest of whom were looking to escape the diseased conditions of the Mississippi Valley.[16] They were known most frequently as health-seekers but also sometimes "lungers, consumptives, phthistics, coughers, hackers, invalids, valetudinarians, sanitarians, asthmatics, white plaguers, pukers, and walking death" (Jones 1967: 44–45). These migrants often suffered from serious diseases, particularly tuberculosis, that medicine had been unable to treat, leading to great desperation and hope. A change in location was often the choice of last resort (Jones 1967: vii). "Climatic therapy," as it was called, was viewed as "a godsend to consumptives and a boon to the medical profession," according to Jones: it provided some relief to patients and increased the prestige of an otherwise loosely ordered profession of physicians. For a time, "many doctors confidently dispatched their patients (sometimes quite indiscriminately) to a region they regarded as having been providentially created 'for the betterment of the human race' [in the words of George M. Kellog]" (Jones 1967: 147). Following this reasoning, land was not an abstract space but an integral part of a civilized, and healthy, society; almost no place exemplified these ideas more than Southern California.

Beginning in the middle of the nineteenth century, commentators recognized the appeal of Southern California's climate, especially its purported healthful qualities. The quality of the air was the source of frequent remarks, and nineteenth-century commentators typically described the air as "pure" and pointed—as people still do—to the sunshine, moderate temperatures, and low humidity (Thompson 1972: 203). The legend of the region's salubrious environment, promoted extensively by boosters and fostered by an accumulation of health resorts, drew a large number of therapeutic travelers and migrants, especially those suffering from respiratory ailments (Baur 1959: 48). Adding to the attraction was the lack of smoke relative to other parts of the country, because coal was a much less common fuel in Los Angeles—advertised as the "smokeless city" by some boosters. According to Jones, by 1873, towns in Southern California were receiving national publicity for the beneficial effects for consumptives, and after 1880, Los Angeles,

> until then a struggling town with only a few score of invalids, began [its] mercurial growth and in time became the "Capital of the Sanitarium Belt," the queen city of southern California invalidism.

It was, however, the "hundreds" and "thousands" of vaguely identified valetudinarians who helped to triple the state's population between 1870 and 1900 (Jones 1967: 102).

No exact figures are available, but at least 10 to 25 percent of the migrants to California during the 1870s to 1890s were believed to be in search of health (Baur 1959: ix, 176). According to Baur, the health-seeker movement also dovetailed with the "city beautiful" movement in the late nineteenth century, although this movement did not really blossom until the twentieth century (Baur 1959: 38–42). In the early twentieth century, it was also adapted to the "back-to-nature" movement, associated with Dr. J. H. Kellogg and Seventh-Day Adventism, and its emphasis on health food (Baur 1959: 48–50).

Already by the 1870s, the feeling among leaders of the health-seeker movement was that the urbanizing center of Los Angeles had become less than ideal for invalids. The leaders targeted nearby areas for development, and no area reflected the instantiation of the ideal of the therapeutic paradise more than Pasadena. A group of families from Indiana settled the area in 1874. The settlers all had an interest in the health benefits of Southern California, and a particularly severe winter in Indiana the year before had prompted the move (Baur 1959: 54–55). The exact location for the settlement was chosen for reasons of health by D. M. Berry, one the founding fathers of Pasadena. Baur describes the inspired decision to relocate the community to the foothills of the San Gabriel Mountains:

> In 1873 D. M. Berry had been sent by the colony planners to find a well-watered and timbered tract for the proposed settlement. Exhausted more by long-standing asthma than from his lengthy trip, Berry spent a night at the Fair Oaks Ranch of Judge Benjamin S. Eaton, an estate just northeast of modern Pasadena. For Brigham Young revelation had decided the place for his valley city, but for Pasadena's founders asthma chose the spot! Next morning Berry arose, struck his chest, and exclaimed, "Do you know, sir, that last night is the first night in three years that I have remained in bed all night?" He usually had to sit up in a chair to breathe. (Baur 1959: 55)

Berry immediately wrote back to Indiana with the recommendation to build a sanitarium next to the mountains. Over the next decade Pasadena grew slowly, the majority of the newcomers still invalids, particularly from the wealthy farm state of Iowa. By the 1880s there was a local saying that "widows owned Pasadena, since their invalid husbands had died there," and its main thoroughfare, Colorado Street, was often referred to as "Doctor's Row" (Baur 1959: 57).[17] The discovery of oil and the industrialization of Los Angeles County brought major changes to the region, which were followed by an economic depression and then World War II. Pasadena, however, remained relatively immune to industrial growth, and its residents actively cultivated the place they considered to be where the best people enjoyed the best environment (Brienes 1975: 3).

Nearby Sierra Madre had similar therapeutic origins and became Southern California's most famous health retreat. In 1880, the California state health board designated Sierra Madre as the perfect site for a state sanitarium, making the town almost immediately famous. Health-seekers were the majority of permanent residents by the 1890s, and tubercular migrants continued to arrive through the early twentieth century. Monrovia was another destination for tuberculars.[18] The area was promoted by doctors who themselves had migrated there. In particular, Dr. Francis M. Pottenger came in 1895, for his wife's health, and opened the Pottenger Sanatorium in 1903. It was the first and most successful sanitarium in Southern California and received much attention because of its advanced methods and high recovery rates (Baur 1959: 60). Notably, Pottenger later served as the chairman of the Smog Committee of the Los Angeles County Medical Association in the 1940s.

Doctors were not just recommending that their patients move to the Southwest; many were relocating themselves, further fostering a culture of health awareness. Pottenger and other physicians were part of a "grassroots" effort to promote Southern California for invalids (Jones 1969: 153). In 1900, California had more doctors per capita than any other state (one doctor for every 416 persons, compared to a national average of one to 655; in the city of Los Angeles it was one to 273) (Baur 1959: 80). A rapidly growing Southern California was also becoming a major medical research center. According to Baur, "by the [nineteen-]nineties southern California's medical men were at least as far advanced in the study of lung diseases as their eastern colleagues," with "[f]ew individuals [having] written more words on tuberculosis than Francis M. Pottenger" or matching the philanthropy of Walter Jarvis Barlow (Baur 1959: 86).

The health-seeker movement also expanded via a new medical specialty: medical climatology. A group of physicians who themselves were afflicted with tuberculosis had migrated to the Southwest, especially Colorado, and were instrumental in founding and developing this new field. An association was first suggested in 1873 but only formed eleven years later. The practitioners were aware of the patient's distrust of doctors and of their ineffective drug treatments, and they sought to systematize knowledge of invalids and the beneficial effects they received from the climate (Jones 1967: 129). According to Jones, "the most important factor in the study of climatology was the air. If it was pure—that is, free of moisture, dust, pollen, and the like—medical climatologists believed it was also free of the infectious miasmata so prevalent in the atmosphere of the Mississippi Valley and eastern United States. Elevation and sunshine were regarded as important sterilizing agents and life in the out-of-doors as the best method of obtaining a maximum of hygienic values from atmospheric elements" (Jones 1967: 133). Medical climatologists debated about which climate was ideal for a particular ailment, but there was general agreement that the climate of the foothill communities was favorable to consumptives; the climate of the coastal communities, due to its moisture, less so (Jones 1967: 141).[19] Although medical climatology came relatively late to California, it persisted and prompted many studies and reports. Much of the information was probably communicated through word of mouth and through non-scientific print outlets (Thompson 1971: 120).

Even with all the purported success of climatic therapy and the booming health resort industry, the fortunes of health-seekers and their boosters shifted with the rise of germ theory.[20] During the "white scare" period of the 1890s, public reaction to tuberculosis became increasingly negative. As a result, tuberculars, instead of being courted by the California health resort industry, were increasingly stigmatized because of the fear of contagion (Baur 1959: 161–173). Furthermore, medical climatology declined in significance because, in light of the germ theory, the medical establishment viewed it as lacking in causal explanations. Consequently, the health-seeker movement waned, and as the economy of the Southwest diversified, the movement was a less visible part of life in Southern California (Baur 1959: 174–176). According to Baur, by 1900, the health-seeker movement in Southern California had reached is climax, but it never disappeared entirely: "Apparently, it is unending. The movement has lived on as a minor factor of western life" (Baur 1959: 178). Southern California's famous temperate climate continued to draw many to the region, some still for general reasons of health.

Strong believers in climatic therapy persisted into the twentieth century.[21] One adherent's views are notable because he later acted as a medical expert on air pollution: in the years just before smog struck Los Angeles, Clarence A. Mills, professor of Experimental Medicine at the University of Cincinnati, published a monograph titled *Medical Climatology: Climatic and Weather Influences in Health and Disease* (Mills 1939). He states his central medical belief that climate affects the basic physiology of the body by "altering combustion rate, energy level, rate of growth and development, resistance to infection and many other vital characteristics" (Mills 1939: v). In this view, man varies from place to place because his body varies from place to place. Mills lays particular importance on the loss of body heat, which, he states, dominates human existence. At one point in his survey he comments specifically on the variations in Los Angeles's climate:

> At Los Angeles, in the south, the climate is mildly relaxing during the summer months when the mean temperature remains slightly above the human optimum. However, low humidity during these months robs the mild de-

gree of heat of any deleterious action. The final effect on man is one of mild relaxation, with just enough variability throughout the year to avoid monotony. It therefore justly deserves its popularity as a health resort, particularly for persons in the later decades of life. (Mills 1939: 67–68)

In his review, Mills maintains the once more common belief that climatic therapy is of value for "a considerable number of disease conditions and instances of disturbed metabolism," especially respiratory diseases; moreover, "fortunately for the medical profession, climatic therapy offers greatest benefit for those very diseases in which other forms of treatment have been least helpful" (Mills 1939: 220). He thus made the familiar recommendation that individuals with respiratory problems should consider relocating to the Southwest. Moreover, he went so far as to suggest the development of a federal program for "colonization for climatically handicapped individuals" who were unable to afford the expense: "The suggestion, then, is that the Federal government, through its Public Health Service, initiate the establishment of camps or colonies for the treatment of patients handicapped by climatically conditioned diseases" (Mills 1939: 237). This, of course, did not come to pass. Indeed, not more than a decade later, Los Angeles–area physicians were offering just the opposite advice: those with respiratory conditions should consider leaving behind the smoggy, unhealthful atmosphere of the Los Angeles Basin.

Besmirching Los Angeles: Reformers and the Politics of Pollution

The legend of the purity of Southern California air collapsed in the 1940s, giving way to entirely new, and infamous, legends. Around 1940, workers in the downtown Civic Center area of Los Angeles were the first to complain of eye- and throat-irritating fumes occurring during isolated episodes lasting a few hours (Brienes 1976: 516). In later years, complaints of stinging eyes, coughing, sore throats, and acrid or bleach-like odors came from areas ever more distant to downtown, particularly Burbank and Pasadena. At times, motorists reported difficulty driving because of watery eyes. Farmers in neighboring areas complained of a new type of damage to their crops from the discoloration of leaves. Tire manufacturers noticed that rubber deteriorated more quickly in Los Angeles than in other parts of the country. And all over citizens complained of the poor visibility from low-lying smoke and fumes and "daylight dimout" conditions, which occurred during particularly bad times. By 1949, California commentator Carey McWilliams wrote: "No problem of the post-war period has occasioned more agitation and discussion in Los Angeles than the problem of 'smog,' which is far from being solved today" (McWilliams 1999: 245).

The phenomenon was an unknown for lay citizens as well as for those with some expert knowledge of pollution and health. The diverse experiences of smog and the widespread speculation about its causes were richly characterized by I. A. Deutch, who was assistant director at the Los Angeles County Office of Air Pollution Control—the first government agency in the region to deal exclusively with air pollution. He is worth quoting at some length. Deutch began the agency's 1946–1947 annual report with a cautionary tale for those "who profess to be air pollution experts or who are desirous of securing a hurried partial picture which will limit the air pollution attack." He recounted the tale familiar to many readers about the six blind men asked to describe the elephant, his point being that "each worried citizen is likely to judge the whole of the local air pollution problem by the small part that he comes in contact with" (LACAPCD 1947: i). Smog thus had many meanings to individuals:

> The citizen whose house turns black over night believes "smog" to be the fumes which react with lead paints; the aviator who has difficulty landing in the blinding, murky pall that so frequently hangs over the Los Angeles basin cusses the visibility reducing man-made components of "smog." The resident of the foothill cities who is awakened at three in the morning by offensive garlic-like odors condemns the refinery which spews mercaptans into the atmosphere. The downtown shopper whose eyes burn and tear is bitter against any sources which produce lachrimating substances. The homeowner whose property is located close to a burning dump, pictures smog as the offensive smoke, sleep-disturbing odors and filth-producing charred embers and grime resulting from the thoughtless and irresponsible operation of dumps in crowded metropolitan areas. And the driver on the highway who is blinded by smoke and fumes from the exhaust of vehicles blames the lack of pure air upon the type of vehicle which he has been forced to follow. (LACAPCD 1947: i)

Deutch's description of the state of common smog knowledge underscores the fundamental uncertainties present, the tendency of individuals to blame the most immediately apprehended source, and the set of back-ground assumptions—represented in the multitude of hypotheses—that conceptually framed the problem.

In further describing the initial response to smog during the 1940s, I focus on a series of episodes that exemplify the assumptions that layper-sons and air pollution control experts brought to the smog problem, prior to—but in the case of activist citizens, also after—the rationalization of control policy in accordance with the discovery of the photochemical re-action. I do not suggest that I am providing a comprehensive explanation of air pollution politics, but rather that I am continuing an analysis of the cultural resources that shaped social action on the part of city and county politicians, outspoken residents, and public health experts. The first inci-dent that I discuss is the initial focus on controlling the activities of an in-dividual manufacturing plant near downtown Los Angeles,[22] and the sec-ond is the emphasis on smoke and other visible emissions by many air pollution control experts (and laypersons as well). The former illustrates a highly durable perspective on the part of civic reformers, that industry was to blame; whereas the latter, the engineering culture that shaped ex-pert opinion. The remainder of the discussion follows the history into the 1950s to examine the political turmoil over a historically severe smog episode in October 1954 and controversial attempts by local officials to control backyard incinerators.

Public Fumes: The Rubber Plant Controversy

In July 1943, an irritating smog lasting several days in downtown Los An-geles caught the attention of residents and local government. Although the episode marked the start of a historic battle with air pollution, the phe-nomenon was not entirely new to public health officers. The City Health Department's Industrial Hygiene Division had been investigating com-plaints of eye and throat irritation in downtown Los Angeles as early as July 1940. An episode of what local health officials were calling the "abnor-mal atmospheric condition" occurred again on September 21, 1942. By this time it was clear that the problem was not confined to the downtown Civic Center area. Taking the tools of industrial hygiene into residential areas, city officials began to inventory, as best they could, the Los Angeles atmosphere.[23] It was a landscape that had been greatly changed by wartime production—with city boosters proudly acknowledging "the new skyline of smoking industrial stacks" (Brienes 1976: 517–518).[24]

After the July 1943 "gas attack" persisted for several days, public complaints rolled in, and the Los Angeles City Council ordered the city health officer to investigate the "peculiar atmospheric condition." That this particular episode began during a streetcar strike did not go unnoticed; however, the fact that smoggy conditions continued after the strike led all to agree that automobiles were an unlikely source (Brienes 1976: 515). As Brienes describes it:

> Health officials wisely concluded that the problem had been in incubation for some years, and that no magic, painless formula existed to end it. But this was subtle thinking for the times. The public, and officials, had identified one notorious contributor to the general pollution. In the downtown area where, so it appeared, the menace had come to life first, stood the smoky, smelly butadiene plant on Aliso Street. It was here the fight against smog began. (Brienes 1976: 518)

For a time, public attention turned primarily to this single factory, which had recently been converted to the production of a component of synthetic rubber (butadiene) as part of the war effort. The odor and irritation from the fumes were a source of frequent complaint, but residents were told to endure because wartime production necessitated it. Complaints came in about paint blistering on cars parked near the factory. Workers in the vicinity were reported to be leaving their jobs because of the fumes, and the irritation was particularly difficult to handle in the nearby tuberculosis ward of the County General Hospital. Home-owners in Altadena and Pasadena, in the foothills of the San Gabriel Mountains, were especially vocal and expressed their fears about the health problems the fumes seemed to cause. Health experts concurred with the residents, calling the plant a "definite health menace," although the plant was not their own focus (Brienes 1976: 518–521).

Over the next several months, installation of control technologies, attempts to reduce production, and temporary shutdowns did not reduce complaints. The gas company that owned the plant continued to argue that operations were necessary for the war effort and that the fumes were not harmful; nonetheless, the mayor and City Council moved to bring suit against the company. The opposing sides reached a compromise, and eventually a long-term shutdown was ordered and more extensive control devices were installed. When production resumed in December, no immediate complaints were heard, and some residents of Pasadena felt that "a second Pittsburgh" had been avoided. Public health officials were less certain, believing that the butadiene plant was only part of the "general smoke and fumes condition." Their investigations had found that eye irritation could be found upwind from the factory and sometimes was reported simultaneously in areas ten miles apart (Brienes 1976: 521–527). Still, for the moment the controversy was over.

Brienes observes that the response reinforced well-established patterns. A single villain was identified, making the new air pollution problem more comprehensible and manageable. In addition, abatement followed straightforward, commonsense methods. But, Brienes notes, the immediate availability of control technologies was "pure coincidence" and served to reinforce the view that pollution control did not require new developments. Finally, not to be overlooked is the capacity of the community to blame and punish. The butadiene plant stood out because it stood outside the community, and Washington's war effort could be held responsible (Brienes 1976: 526–529).

Controlling Visible Sources

The butadiene plant controversy did not lead to a direct collective response, but when smog returned the following year, the dormant Altadena Property Owners' League became involved and instigated the first organized actions. They enlisted as many allies as possible in an attempt to get rules enforced and actions taken against the Standard Oil refinery and the General Chemical plant in El Segundo. Working through petitions and pushing legal actions, they got the attention of County Board of Supervisors. In September 1944, they successfully lobbied the legislators to pass a county ordinance, although the association played no role in writing the policy. One outcome of their actions was the formation of the Smoke and Fumes Commission, which, according to Brienes, was a relatively weak agency: "From the lack of support given to it by the county, the technical inward-looking orientation of its scientific members, and the inappropriately controversial nature of its chairman, the [Smoke and Fumes Commission] became the prototype for ten years of failures" (Brienes 1975: 79). The commission took a slow and gradual approach, emphasizing research and voluntary cooperation. The Altadena Property Owners' League, however, maintained that smog was a public nuisance and did not need to be researched. They advocated immediate action directed at industrial polluters with unsightly emissions (Brienes 1975: 83).

After a brief period, smog problems returned, and the public again demanded action. In 1946, upon prompting from his wife,[25] the editor of the *Los Angeles Times* invited a nationally recognized air pollution expert to help the citizens of Los Angeles. Raymond Tucker was a professor of engineering from St. Louis and was considered instrumental in addressing that city's air pollution problems through his ordinances governing the burning of coal. He investigated the problem, and in January 1947, his recommendations were published with great fanfare on the front page of the *Los Angeles Times* and widely reprinted as the "Tucker Report" (Tucker 1947). He took note of the population growth and the 85 percent increase in industry in the previous five years. In slightly oversimplified terms, he inventoried smokestacks and concluded the smog problem was at least partially due to the widespread production of smoke in the area from sources such as backyard incinerators, oil refineries, and other industries, and specifically mentioned that automobiles were unlikely to be the sole cause (Krier and Ursin 1977: 58–59). Many believed that proper smoke control ordinances and pollution control devices would promptly solve the problem. In sum, although the Tucker Report broadened the range of implicated sources, it continued to focus attention on industrial sources and sources with the most visible smoke emissions.

The dominant position guiding political decision-making at the time was that smoke and other visible emissions from industry were the source of smog and the most politically acceptable targets for control. The first director of the Los Angeles County Air Pollution Control District further institutionalized the position represented in the Tucker Report within the local air pollution control agency. In addition, citizen reformers built on these beliefs by forming alliances with local businesses, such as the alliance between Stephen Royce of the Huntington Hotel and Dorothy and Norman Chandler of the *Los Angeles Times* (Dewey 2000: 87).

The tension between simple and complex models of smog is addressed again later (the policy formally came under scrutiny by the California State Assembly in the late 1940s); however, it is worth noting that some public health officials held a more complex view of the problem. The precursor agency to the LACAPCD, the Office of Air Pollution Control, was formed at the start of the 1945–1946 fiscal year, and Roy O. Gilbert, M.D., was appointed as director. In his transmittal letter to the County Board of Supervisors, he noted that the main goals of eliminating eye irritation and reduced visibility would be helped along by the adoption of smoke and fume control ordinances patterned after those of eastern cities. Nevertheless, the "visibility-reducing palls and eye-tearing sieges" were distinct problems (having distinct sources), with the latter being "peculiar" to the Los Angeles Basin. The fact that "John Q. Public" experienced them simultaneously led him to the oversimplified conclusion that they are related, and that eliminating the visible problem will eliminate the eye irritation. Yet, according to Dr. Gilbert, the office believed that "visibility-reducing 'aerial muck'" should be eliminated quickly, "simply because the community does not desire the evil per se." Furthermore, he noted that while there were solutions on hand for the visibility problem, there were none for the eye-irritation problem, and his office would research the problem "despite the many handicaps that hinder pure research by a public agency of the type of the Office of Air Pollution Control" (LACAPCD 1947: n.p.).

Local Politics Comes to a Head:
The October 1964 Los Angeles Smog Attack

The period from 1950 to 1955 was the most tumultuous time in Los Angeles air pollution politics (Brienes 1975). The uncertainties of smog, particularly the lack of knowledge about the health effects, caused a great deal of anxiety among the residents of Los Angeles. This anxiety was most pronounced among the middle-class citizens of the foothill communities, who had high expectations for the quality of their environment. When combined with a severe smog episode lasting more than a week, and a political election, public outrage reached a historic level.

In mid-October 1954, a smog settled into the Los Angeles Basin that lasted longer than usual. By the ninth day the *New York Times* was reporting on the "choking eye-searing smog," adding, "Hospitals were deluged with calls for advice on the treatment of the eye-searing ef[f]ect. In adjacent Pasadena, Mayor Clarence Winder called for public prayer 'to deliver us from this scourge,' while the Los Angeles City Council donned gas masks to demonstrate that the fumes were even entering the Council chambers" (*New York Times*, October 16, 1954). Although the smog was severe, its occurrence just before the November gubernatorial election brought additional attention. What made it national news was that local news was reporting that smog might be to blame for the death of a ten-year-old girl who choked to death. California governor Goodwin Knight was forced to interrupt his re-election campaign to deal with the growing unrest in Los Angeles County—a problem that he previously treated as a local matter, outside his authority.

Citizens of Pasadena were enraged at county officials who, they believed, were not properly enforcing laws to regulate pollution from industry, and they demanded that the governor use his emergency powers to take control of the situation. The smog and the protests continued, culminating in an organized demonstration of forty-five hundred residents at the Pasadena Civic Auditorium. The co-chairman of the Citizens' Anti-Smog Action Committee threatened the jobs of local authorities. When criticizing Gordon Larson, director of the LACAPCD, the crowd unrolled a banner saying "RESIGN." The group wanted immediate action and did not want to be "guinea pigs" and "sitting ducks" to the health effects of smog. Dramatic protests continued that day when "a group of Pasadena housewives calling themselves the 'Smog-A-Tears' (in a spoof of Walt Disney's Mouseketeers) paraded through downtown Pasadena wearing gas masks and carrying signs" (Dewey 2000: 93–94; Los Angeles Times, October 21, 1954). A few days earlier, the Highland Park Optimists Club had all donned gas masks at their meeting and displayed a sign reading "Why Wait Till 1955. We Might Not Even Be Alive" (Los Angeles Times, October 15, 1954: 1, 3).

The Los Angeles Times also carried various stories about the disruptive effects of smog. One was about how teachers were having difficulty keeping order in the classroom because the "youngsters were made irritable by the atmospheric conditions" (Los Angeles Times, October 16, 1954). In another story, they reported on a thirteen-year-old boy whose eye swelled shut—due to the smog, according to his doctor (Los Angeles Times, October 17, 1954). The smog continued into the next week, as did the political pressure. In response to the demands of angry Pasadenans, Governor Knight tried to get a temporary shutdown of the oil refineries to "test" how responsible the industry was for the problem, but the refineries refused the request (Los Angeles Times, October 23, 1954).[26] By this point the Los Angeles Times had written its second editorial asking for a less "hysterical" response from the public (Los Angeles Times, October 23, 1954). In the midst of the political turmoil, the Los Angeles Times, like Governor Knight, was trying to frame the problem as a "scientific and technological one," not a legal one.

The uprising had some important consequences for air pollution politics. Although the governor did not call a state of emergency—and health experts supported him by calming the public with the message that there was no immediate danger to health—he was forced to acknowledge that smog was a "statewide" problem. A grand jury investigation of the activities of the LACAPCD began—specifically focusing on the lack of an emergency warning system—and resulted in the demotion of Gordon Larson (*Los Angeles Times,* October 27, 1954). In 1955, the first air pollution emergency warning system was put into place by the LACAPCD. A further consequence was that attention was given to backyard incineration. At the time, there was no mandatory garbage collection in the county, and many residents used incinerators to rid themselves of the waste. The LACAPCD had been working to ban incinerators; however, the agency ran into political obstacles because some individuals felt the policy encroached on their freedom.[27] By 1957, incinerators had been effectively banned from the county.

Furthermore, the episode changed the tenor of the leadership of the LACAPCD and led to a full-scale reorganization of the agency: "To execute the expressed will of the community that atmospheric pollution of the Los Angeles Basin be curbed, the new administration completely reorganized the District" (LACAPCD 1955: [6]). The new director, S. Smith Griswold, gave the task of public relations much more weight in the district. He understood that without public support there could be no air pollution control program, and he therefore invested substantial resources in a public education campaign, which ran through the second half of the 1950s, and in a more visible inspection and enforcement program. The LACAPCD produced an especially readable and visually striking 1954–1955 annual report that announced major changes at the agency. For example, it proudly displayed the new inspection vehicles, which resembled police cars in their design, and pictured one of the vehicles at night next to an ominous industrial plant "as part of the regular duty of the 24–hour watch kept by the Enforcement Division." Graphs also showed the dramatic rise in personnel (from 196 in 1954 to 356 in 1955), in citations issued (from around three hundred in 1954 to over twelve hundred in 1955), as well as in the number of inspections, expenditures, and applications for permits (LACAPCD 1955: [6–7]). Much of the public protest died down in the late 1950s. One of the most active local organizations in Pasadena, the Anti–Air Pollution Committee of the local Chamber of Commerce, had increasingly little involvement, and the issue came before the board of directors only sporadically (Brienes 1975: 264).

Conclusion: "Crossing the Smog Barrier"

In the wake of the political turmoil of the mid-1950s—and the emerging scientific understanding of smog—the LACAPCD began a major public relations campaign. In the second half of 1957, a series of educational articles was published in local newspapers and later reprinted with the title *Crossing the Smog Barrier: A Factual Account of Southern California's Fight against Air Pollution* (LACAPCD 1957). The title reflected the belief that urban growth in Los Angeles and other cities had pushed the atmosphere to the point where "air pollution problems become apparent"—the "smog barrier" or threshold had been crossed (LACAPCD 1957: 1). Although one headline stated straightforwardly that "Weather Explains Smog Attacks," from the discussion in this chapter we can see that more than the dilution capacity of the atmosphere had been crossed: smog transgressed cultural boundaries as well, and disturbed a way of life in the process. Furthermore, smog did not appear full force but grew during the war years, when many disruptions were tolerated and accepted as part of the war effort. Only within specific communities do environmental problems such as smog become "apparent," and thus the perception of smog and its status as a social problem cannot be taken for granted.

Even for those residents who did not suffer directly from medical problems as severe as asthma attacks, smog was perceived to undercut one basis for Southern California community: a healthy environment. The local environment and its ascribed qualities were central to local community, especially the foothill communities of the San Gabriel Mountains. A place with clean air and sunshine was a good place, and it was the kind of place where good people would live. Given the history of health-seekers embedded in the foothill communities, that their reaction should be so strong and organized is not surprising.

To understand the prioritization of smog and the responses to it, we need to see that air pollution can be a disruption to the social order as well as to the natural order. Part of why the public, specifically the residents of places like Pasadena, reacted so strongly to smog, and why they challenged the characterization of smog as temporary annoyance, as a nuisance, as a tolerable cost to either a war effort or economic growth, is that the manifestations of smog were assimilated into a framework that gave them much greater significance. Smog violated the security of residents' lives and negatively transformed the meaning of their highly valued environs.

Furthermore, participants grasped at not only the technical complexity of smog and pollution control but also the moral complexity that the technical problem entailed. How was blame to be assigned? How were causes to be proven? There were not satisfactory answers at the time, and a search began for a language and a conceptual framework with which to describe, understand, and remedy these changes to their home and the dashed expectations of the promise of Southern California.

Expressing the sociological implications of smog another way, environmental problems do not create themselves, and there are two ways in which smog is a "man-made" problem. First, human activity, specifically fuel consumption, produces smog materially—it is an industrial society's garbage. Second, an interpretation of smog is constructed: what is the meaning of smog and what is meaningful knowledge of smog. Thus, smog transformed the landscape, but it also transformed the meaning of the landscape. Arie Haagen-Smit, scientist and discoverer of the photochemical smog reaction, recognized this point when he observed: "The old slogan, 'Prosperity is measured by the number of smoking stacks,' is no longer true. Today, prosperity can be gauged by the number of strange-looking bulges protruding from the roofs of the factories. These bulges are dust- and fume-collectors and indicate that the community and its industry have progressed to a standard of living and social consciousness that does not permit objectionable emissions to spread over other people's property" (1958: 869).

Smog also confounded previous traditions of expert knowledge for controlling air pollution. Smoke was more localized, attributable to specific entities, and seen as coming from somewhere in particular. Initial assumptions that smog was a smoke problem localized around industrial emissions. Yet the black stuff coming out of the smokestacks did not seem to account fully for the phenomenon. The crisis of smog stemmed also from a lack of ability to cope and respond to the problem. The institutions could not eliminate the problem or even unequivocally show signs of success. What was most frightening about smog, most anxiety-provoking, was not what was known about it—the eye irritation, the poor visibility—but what was unknown, all the things it might be doing that hadn't even been observed. Not until the unseen was made visible could the public fear be calmed.

Put another way, another important factor in the response to smog is what we might call the theory of pollution with which the public operated. The reasonably successful attempts to control the smoke problem in cities like London, St. Louis, and Pittsburgh helped structure the public understanding of smog in Southern California. As demonstrated in the Tucker Report, air pollution had several defining traits. It was first and foremost visible to the naked eye, and the denser it was, the more of a problem it was. Air pollution was directly emitted into the atmosphere, and, consequently, the effects could be traced back to specific compounds present in those emissions. Finally, pollution was the product of industrial activity. When things like the backyard incinerator and the automobile were implicated in the problem, some middle-class residents were outraged by the actions of local officials, because to them it was common sense that the problem was dirty industries in need of control or removal from the area entirely. Their own actions were, in their view, in some sense outside the category of pollution.

But even while smog is recognized as the outcome of industry and transportation, blame for the problem can still be placed on nature, on the unfortunate geography of Los Angeles. Alternatively, urbanization and industrialization can be viewed as the cause of smog. In this sense, the material production of smog cannot be separated from its social production (Smith 1989). Particular weather conditions combined with fuel use produce the phenomenon, and there is no inherent way to assign priority to one contributing factor over the other. The contentious politics of smog are explained by the way it confounded conventional categories, becoming a site to express competing visions of society.

NOTES

1. Letter dated May 4, 1946, Ed Ainsworth Collection (UCLA Special Collections, #405). Anson Ford would go on to be one of the elected officials most involved in the smog problem.

2. The smoke-abatement movement is discussed only briefly because it is the subject of a number of other essays in this anthology.

3. A related reason that Southern California inhabitants considered it an exceptional place was that it existed as neither a classic urban nor a rural space—Los Angeles was kind of urban garden. See McWilliams (1973) and Garcia (2001) for a discussion of this identity of California exceptionalism.

4. One of the classic works examining scientific phenomena in this regard is Thomas Kuhn's (1970) The Structure of Scientific Revolutions.

5. Smog in the 1940s was unpredictable and ill defined, and the generalized fear and anxiety provoked by its seeming randomness and uncertainty led to a call

for control. The medical historian Charles Rosenberg notes that this is a general characteristic of epidemics: "Perception implies explanation. Certainly this is the case during epidemics, when fear and anxiety create an imperative need for understanding and thus reassurance" (Rosenberg 1992a: 293–294). Although there was neither contagion nor widespread death, the phenomenon of smog provoked some of the same qualities as an epidemic: it asked to be named and appealed for an explanation.

6. Chandra Mukerji has argued a related point: the coordination of social activity derives not only from a cognitive ordering of the world but also from material practices employed by social actors. The embedding of social relations in physical objects creates a material culture that extends social bonds over time and space, beyond face-to-face interaction (Mukerji 1994: 145).

7. For my own purposes, I want to consider the ways in which the meanings individuals and groups give to places regarding health and illness interact with other historical forces in shaping the landscape of Southern California. Furthermore, the sociologist Douglas McAdam has remarked that spatiality and prior history are two "silences" in the social movements literature (paper presented at the Annual Meeting of the Pacific Sociological Association, San Francisco, April 1998). By covering the history of a particular place over a long period, this case study addresses both of these gaps. The smog reformer movement of the 1940s was built on previous relationships to the landscape and previous health movements. The latter point is seen most directly in the continuity of certain active physicians in both the health-seeker movement and the air pollution reforms that began in the 1940s.

8. See Melosi (1980: 4–14) on industrialization and pollution and Fee and Porter (1992: 254) on social crises engendered by changing urban conditions in the nineteenth century. These circumstances were not unique to the United States, and England, which had industrialized earlier, often served as the model for an American response (Fee and Porter 1992: 274; Melosi 1981: 12–14, 97–98; Tarr 1996: 11).

9. See Melosi (1980: 18) on the growing protest against these "nuisances" by late-nineteenth-century reformers.

10. This is not to say that sanitary engineers did not also have a moral conception of their profession; the term *civil engineer,* in fact implied such a conception. See Melosi (1981: 92).

11. A number of chapters in this volume address this issue, including those by Platt, Gugliotta, and Mosley.

12. Stradling's detailed history of smoke abatement in the United States reveals the dynamic status of health versus engineering perspectives, as is the case with other urban environmental reform movements. He argues that the smoke-abatement movement, in conjunction with the Progressive movement, elevated the status of engineers—who saw smoke as the inefficient use of natural resources—in

American society (Stradling 1999: 88). In contrast, the authority of health-based arguments declined relative to engineering arguments and was further undercut by the rise of germ theory, which downplayed smoke's effect on tuberculosis in particular (Stradling 1999: 108).

13. See Grinder (1980: 85) for examples from Midwestern reform movements.

14. Before this time, the term referred to an atmosphere believed to be contaminated by organic wastes that generated "foul miasmas," "sewer gas," "foetid emanations," "poisonous exhalations," "offensive effluvia," and "stench nuisances." What is now called air pollution was typically referred to as "the smoke nuisance" but also "the smoke problem," "the smoke evil," or sometimes "the smoke plague" or "noxious vapours" (Rome 1996: 6).

15. The first modern usage of *pollution* was not until around the 1870s, when sanitary reformers, such as "public health officials, engineers, and outdoor enthusiasts," used it to refer to water pollution (Rome 1996: 10). The umbrella terms *environmentalism* and *environmental movement*, which are so familiar to the modern ear, did not have much currency or meaning until around 1970.

16. There was a major cholera epidemic in the Mississippi Valley between 1848 and 1849 (Baur 1959: 3). For a history of notions of health and place among American western settlers, see Valencius (2000b).

17. Nonetheless, a hospital was not actually built there until 1895.

18. San Diego was also on the list of popular destinations for health-seekers. Alonzo Horton, Anglo booster and developer of New Town in San Diego, was directed to the region by his doctor (personal communication, May 2000, Jennifer Jordan, assistant professor of sociology, University of Wisconsin, Milwaukee). The famed Hotel Del Coronado also began as a health resort (Baur 1959).

19. Nevertheless, "in spite of these drawbacks, coastal towns in southern California were overrun with wheezing consumptives, a majority of whom seemed always to convalesce satisfactorily" (Jones 1967: 141).

20. It was in 1882 that the German scientist Robert Koch had announced his achievement of isolating the tuberculosis bacillus (Baur 1959: 155).

21. The California historian Kenneth Thompson observed that belief in climatology persisted in the region because it was adaptable and plausible: "It seemed to explain local conditions of public as well as many individual cases of disease and cure" (Thompson 1971: 125).

22. This section in particular draws substantially from the work of Brienes, and his research offers a fuller and more detailed account.

23. Drawing on archival sources of city officials, Brienes writes: "They discovered a brew of 'ammonia, formaldehyde, acrolein, acetic acid, sulfuric acid, sulfur dioxide, hydrogen sulfide, mercaptans, hydrochloric acid, hydroflouric acid, chlorine, nitric acid, phosgene, and certain organic dusts known to be irritants,' for which scores of sources, ranging from fish canneries to oil refineries, could be blamed" (1976: 517).

24. Heavy industries were building more and larger plants to manufacture product such as rubber, nonferrous metals, machinery, and chemicals (Brienes 1976: 517).

25. According to Scott Hamilton Dewey, Dorothy Chandler was particularly appalled by the pollution one day while driving into the Los Angeles area from one of the clearer areas to the east. She immediately went to her husband's office and announced, "Something has to be done." Her husband, Norman Chandler, subsequently gave reporter Ed Ainsworth the task of reporting and coordinating publicity on the smog problem. Ainsworth served as a nexus between concerned citizens and the programs of the city and county (Dewey 2000: 87–88).

26. The request echoed one about a decade earlier from Deutch, who wanted a test ban on automobiles to see if they were part of the problem. He was widely ridiculed for the suggestion, and it contributed to his removal from his post. But as Brienes observes, "The tenacity with which residents, especially in the foothills, maintained their preoccupation with the oil refineries became a central fact with which the control movement had to deal" (Brienes 1975: 226).

27. In the mid-1950s, backyard incinerators were handling the rubbish of 2.5 million residents (about half the county population). Brienes observed: "The incinerator issue reached some Angelenos at a gut level, as though its elimination would destroy a bit of American liberty or was part of a plot to replace simple efficiency with an expensive and self-serving bureaucracy." Incinerators were also big business to a growing city. One opponent to an incinerator ban actually flew Haagen-Smit around in his plane to show him the trails of industrial smoke that he believed were the cause of the smog, but Gordon Larson did not accept this unscientific approach as evidence (Brienes 1975: 229–230). See also Dewey (2000: 96–97), for a discussion of the politics of the incinerator ban.

REFERENCES

Baur, John E. 1959. The Health Seekers of Southern California, 1870–1900. San Marino, Calif.: Huntington Library.

Bottles, Scott L. 1987. Los Angeles and the Automobile: The Making of the Modern City. Berkeley: University of California Press.

Bowler, Catherine, and Peter Brimblecombe. 1992. Archives and Air Pollution History. Journal of the Society of Archivists 13 (2): 136–142.

Brienes, Marvin. 1975. The Fight against Smog in Los Angeles, 1943–1957. A doctoral dissertation prepared for the Department of History, University of California, Davis.

———. 1976. Smog Comes to Los Angeles. Southern California Quarterly: 515–532.

Brimblecombe, Peter. 1987. The Big Smoke: A History of Air Pollution in London since Medieval Times. New York: Methuen.

Brimblecombe, Peter, and Christian Pfsiter, eds. 1990. The Silent Countdown: Essays in European Environmental History. New York: Springer-Verlag.

Clapp, Brian William. 1994. An Environmental History of Britain since the Industrial Revolution. New York: Longman.

Cohn, Morris M., and Dwight F. Metzler. 1973. The Pollution Fighters: A History of Environmental Engineering in New York State. New York: New York State Department of Health.

Corn, Jacqueline Karnell. 1989. Environment and Health in Nineteenth Century America: Two Case Studies. New York: Peter Lang.

Dewey, Scott Hamilton. 2000. Don't Breathe the Air: Air Pollution and U.S. Environmental Politics, 1945–1970. College Station, Tex.: Texas A&M University Press.

Douglas, Mary. 1966. Purity and Danger: An Analysis of the Concepts of Pollution and Taboo. London: Routledge and Kegan Paul.

———. 1982. Environments at Risk. Pp. 260–275 in Science in Context: Readings in the Sociology of Science, edited by Barry Barnes and David Edge. Cambridge, Mass.: MIT Press.

Douglas, Mary, and Aaron Wildavsky. 1982. Risk and Culture: An Essay on the Selection of Technological and Environmental Dangers. Berkeley: University of California Press.

Durkheim, Emile. 1915. The Elementary Forms of Religious Life. Translated by Joseph W. Swain. New York: Free Press.

Epstein, Steven. 1996. Impure Science: AIDS, Activism, and the Politics of Knowledge. Berkeley: University of California Press.

Fee, Elizabeth, and Dorothy Porter. 1992. Public Health, Preventative Medicine and Professionalization: England and America in the Nineteenth Century. Pp. 249–275 in Medicine in Society: Historical Essays, edited by Andrew Wear. New York: Cambridge University Press.

Flick, Carlos. 1980. The Movement for Smoke Abatement in Nineteenth-Century Britain. Technology and Culture 21 (1): 29–50.

Fogelson, Robert. 1993 [1967]. Los Angeles: The Fragmented Metropolis, 1850–1930. Berkeley: University of California Press.

Garcia, Matt. 2001. A World of Its Own: Race, Labor, and Citrus in the Making of Greater Los Angeles, 1900–1970. Chapel Hill: University of North Carolina Press.

Gesler, Wilbert M. 1992. Therapeutic Landscapes: Medical Issues in Light of the New Cultural Geography. Social Science and Medicine 34 (7): 735–746.

Grinder, R. Dale. 1980. The Battle for Clean Air: The Smoke Problem in Post–Civil War America. Pp. 83–103 in Pollution and Reform in American Cities, 1870–1930, edited by Martin V. Melosi. Austin: University of Texas Press.

Haagen-Smit, Arie J. 1958. Air Conservation. Science 128 (3329): 869–878.

Hays, Samuel P. 1987. Beauty, Health and Permanence: Environmental Politics in the United States, 1955–1985. New York: Cambridge University Press.

Heidorn, K. C. 1978. A Chronology of Events in the History of Air Pollution Meteorology to 1970. Bulletin of the American Meteorological Society 59: 1589.

Hoy, Suellen. 1995. Chasing Dirt: The American Pursuit of Cleanliness. New York: Oxford University Press.

Hurley, Andrew. 1994. Creating Ecological Wastelands: Oil Pollution in the New York City, 1870–1900. Journal of Urban History 20 (3): 340–364.

Jones, Billy M. 1967. Health-Seekers in the Southwest, 1817–1900. Norman: University of Oklahoma Press.

Krier, James E., and Edmund Ursin. 1977. Pollution and Policy: A Case Essay on California and Federal Experience with Motor Vehicle Air Pollution, 1940–1975. Berkeley: University of California Press.

Kuhn, Thomas S. 1970 [1962]. The Structure of Scientific Revolutions. 2d ed. Chicago: University of Chicago Press.

Leavitt, Judith Walzer. 1982. The Healthiest City: Milwaukee and the Politics of Health Reform. Princeton, N.J.: Princeton University Press.

Los Angeles County Office of Air Pollution Control (LACAPCD). September 30, 1947. Annual Report of the Office of Air Pollution Control, 1946–1947. Los Angeles County Board of Supervisors.

Los Angeles County Air Pollution Control District. n.d. [1955]. Annual Report, 1954–55. Los Angeles: Los Angeles County Air Pollution Control District.

———. 1957. Crossing the Smog Barrier: a Factual Account of Southern California's Fight Against Air Pollution. Los Angeles: Los Angeles County Air Pollution Control District.

McWilliams, Carey. 1973 [1946]. Southern California: An Island on the Land. Santa Barbara and Salt Lake City: Peregrine Smith, Inc.

———. 1999 [1949]. California, the Great Exception. Berkeley: University of California Press.

Melosi, Martin V. 1980. Environmental Crisis in the City: The Relationship between Industrialization and Urban Pollution. Pp. 3–31 in Pollution and Reform in American Cities, 1870–1930, edited by Martin V. Melosi. Austin: University of Texas Press.

———. 1981. Garbage in the Cities: Refuse, Reform, and the Environment, 1880–1980. College Station, Tex.: Texas A&M University Press.

Mills, Clarence A. 1939. Medical Climatology: Climatic and Weather Influences in Health and Disease. Baltimore: Charles C. Thomas.

Mukerji, Chandra. 1994. Toward a Sociology of Material Culture: Science Studies, Cultural Studies and the Meanings of Things. Pp. 143–162 in The Sociology of Culture: Emerging Theoretical Perspectives, edited by Diana Crane. Cambridge, Mass.: Blackwell.

Rome, Adam W. 1996. Coming to Terms with Pollution: The Language of Environmental Reform, 1865–1915. Environmental History 1 (3): 6–28.

Rosenberg, Charles E. 1987 [1962]. The Cholera Years: The United States in 1832, 1849, and 1866. Chicago: University of Chicago Press.

———. 1992a. Explaining Epidemics and Other Studies in the History of Medicine. New York: Cambridge University Press.

———. 1992b. Framing Disease: Illness, Society, and History. Pp. xii–xxvi in Framing Disease: Studies in Cultural History, edited by Charles E. Rosenberg. New Brunswick, N.J.: Rutgers University Press.

Schultz, Stanley K. 1989. Constructing Urban Culture: American Cities and City Planning, 1800–1920. Philadelphia: Temple University Press.

Smith, Barbara Ellen. 1989 [1981]. Black Lung: The Social Production of Disease. Pp. 122–141 in Perspectives in Medical Sociology, edited by Phil Brown. Prospect Heights, Ill.: Waveland Press.

Snyder, Lynne Page. 1994. "The Death-Dealing Smog over Donora, Pennsylvania": Industrial Air Pollution, Public Health Policy, and the Politics of Expertise, 1948–1949. Environmental History Review 18 (Spring): 117–139.

Stradling, David. 1999. Smokestacks and Progressives: Environmentalists, Engineers, and Air Quality in America, 1881–1951. Baltimore: Johns Hopkins University Press.

Tarr, Joel A. 1996. The Search for the Ultimate Sink: Urban Pollution in Historical Perspective. Akron, Ohio: University of Akron Press.

Thompson, Kenneth. 1971. Climatotherapy in California. California Historical Quarterly 50: 111–130.

———. 1972. The Notion of Air Purity in Early California. Southern California Quarterly 54 (Fall): 203–209.

Tucker, Raymond. 1947. The Los Angeles Smog Report. Los Angeles: Times-Mirror Co. Located in Ainsworth Collection, Special Collection #403, UCLA.

Valencius, Conevery B. 2000a. Histories of Medical Geography. Medical History (SUPP20): 3–28.

———. 2000b. The Geography of Health and the Making of the American West: Arkansas and Missouri, 1800–1860. Medical History (SUPP20): 121–145.

Air Pollution Policy Today

A Fine Balance
Automobile Pollution Control Strategies in California

Sudhir Chella Rajan

When a democratically elected polity is confronted with a severe environmental problem that is caused by the normal and otherwise sanctioned behavior of nearly everyone in its constituency, it generally takes one of two distinct regulatory routes. The state could try to identify a small number of agents as the primary perpetrators and look for justifiable ways to go after them aggressively. Alternatively, it might formulate hedging measures and pool risks among the majority, much as an insurance agency would, to ensure that virtually everyone pays a small but relatively unobtrusive "premium" whose collective impact might mitigate the extent of the problem. But it tends never to choose the more reasonable third option, that of devising regulation to influence large-scale changes in behavior toward sustainable outcomes. That would be "political suicide," in contemporary mediaspeak, given the near certainty in liberal democratic regimes of a mismatch between short-term political priorities and long-term social and environmental needs (cf. Howitt and Altshuler, 1999).

Environmental regulation relating to automobiles and household waste fit this pattern quite nicely. The state acts gingerly when confronting the multitude of individual drivers and waste generators but is generally more assertive toward auto manufacturers and (especially in parts of Europe) purveyors of packaging materials. In neither instance are members of the public required seriously to curtail or even alter consumption patterns *per se*; rather, technological innovations ahead of the individual polluter are generally the primary focus of intervention. In other words, the state prefers to regulate the behavior of a small and identifiable number of actors rather than that of the majority of its citizens.

In this chapter, I explore the implications that this constraint has had on the regulatory modes adopted by the state of California to curb automobile pollution for the past three decades or so. I argue that California's experience provides us with a particularly stark view of the regulatory conundrum because of the dual nature of the stakes: a highly automobilized society having severe air pollution problems. Moreover, by creating for itself the global reputation of being the intrepid pioneer in the field, the state's leading regulatory agency may have become a victim of its own remarkable success, leaving it locked into a particular pattern of regulation. What was initially marveled at as the agility of an independent and environmentally conscious agency has started to become a strenuous circus act that an overgrown organization needs to replay over and over, each new performance having to be an improvement on the previous one. The strain is starting to show even as the agency needs continuously to tread a fine line of legitimacy while devising novel ways to reduce air pollution.

Prelude to the Quandary

California's regulatory problem with respect to cars cannot be understood in isolation, that is to say, without reference to the vast socio-spatial motif that has come to be known as "automobility" (Schneider, 1971; Flink, 1988; Rajan, 1996a; Sheller and Urry, 2000; Paterson, 2002). To drive is not just to exercise a capability but also to realize a human need in the vast "automobilized" spaces of modernity. Under late capitalism, automobility is "a vast self-organizing non-linear system constitutive of social life organized around the juggling of tiny amounts of highly fragmented time spent in movement" (Sheller and Urry, 2000). The experience of driving, identified by the quiet pleasures of the open road, speed, power, and personal control, thus neatly complements the functionality of covering distance, managing time, and maintaining certain forms of individuation. And yet automobility implies not just the proliferation of cars but also the cultivation of an entire physical, social, and regulatory infrastructure to support movement along prescribed routes and modes. It entails vast investments of capital and mammoth social and environmental costs (estimated at roughly $2–3 trillion per year in the United States in current terms; Delucchi, 1998). This is automobility's "enigma": cars serve to reproduce the culture of "socialized individualism" that matters to the economic geography of late modern social order, but driving propagates socially shared effects that could well undermine it (Meyer, 1986; Rajan, 1996a).

Moreover, in one sense at least, automobile pollution defies easy categorization, that is, the naming of agents who could be discerned as primarily responsible for the problem. Its cause and development are complexly woven into atmospheric chemistry, meteorology, car use, and engine design, and all these factors encourage the conception that it has little or no relation to human agency. In the popular imagination, the automobile manufacturer is the most directly liable party but, even so, cannot be held responsible for causing the whole crisis. Automobility is so entrenched in late modern society that several determinants other than a putative conspiracy between the state and auto-industrial oligopoly have to be invoked for analyzing its circumstances. Similarly, one might defend vehicle owners from strict liability for producing automobile pollution. When owners drive, they are part of an obligatory enterprise that is shared by the majority of the populace. And while it is true that certain *types* of vehicles pollute more than others, in a market economy where the relevant goods are all basic needs, it is almost absurd to attribute primary responsibility to owners for possessing such vehicles. The burden of causing air pollution cannot thus be borne solely by the manufacturers, owners, or drivers, any of whom could quite justifiably relate their behavior to the entire milieu they live in of spatiality and mobility.

California's enduring talent for exonerating automobility *per se* in its regulation of pollution from vehicles is therefore almost understandable, yet astonishing in its scale and scope. In Raymond Chandler's Valley of Smokes, choking under hazy layers of aerosols that blanketed the skies in the 1940s, cars remained innocent bystanders. While Angelenos were complaining of breathing problems, headaches, and eye irritation, the conviction that motor vehicles were not culprits was quite widespread—the director of one agency went as far as to refer to such suspicions as "folklore" (Krier and Ursin, 1977: 74). Pockets of resistance continued for a while, even after it was established in 1952 that there was a photochemical basis for the formation of ozone in smog and that the hydrocarbons and oxides of nitrogen from the exhaust gases of automobiles and industrial stacks were the main actors in the process.

But this was also a crucial point in the state's regulatory history, when a clear direction for all future policy was ordained. In 1954, Governor Knight of California asserted that "smog is a scientific and engineering problem and not a political or legal one" (Krier and Ursin, 1977: 95). Already, just as the *means* to regulate automobiles acquired significance, the *need* to regulate them was deflected away from questions involving driving or vehicle use to a focus on the engineering features that could reduce emissions per mile driven. Cars, not drivers or the act of driving, were the problem, so they would have to be cleaned up using the latest technical solutions.

In 1955, the Federal Air Pollution Control Act was enacted; in 1959, California passed its own laws requiring the state Department of Public Health to establish air quality standards and controls for motor vehicle emissions. With this supporting legislation, the California Motor Vehicle State Bureau of Air Sanitation mandated the first automotive emissions control technology in the nation, Positive Crankcase Ventilation (PCV), beginning a decades-long tradition of "technology-forcing" regulation, much to the frustration of neo-liberal policy analysts (Crandall et al., 1986; cf. Leone, 1999).

In subsequent decades, a large number of human clinical and epidemiological studies revealed damaging long-term effects of ozone and other oxidants, adding to the list of acute and chronic health problems caused by smog (Kleinman et al., 1989). But while awareness of the cause and health effects of smog now infused public policy, there was less and less expression in popular culture of any impending possibility of controls on driving behavior to mitigate these risks, indicating the degree to which the policy debates had become professionalized. And although harder to verify, the public discourse of newspaper editorials of the day suggested that popular complaints about air pollution had become significantly muted, even as distinct interest groups of vehicle manufacturers, oil companies, garage owners, and maverick inventors entered the fray.

The Lure of Technology against a Pall of Pollution

In Joan Didion's and Reyner Banham's Los Angeles of the 1970s, notwithstanding the hundreds of harmful ozone days each year, driving was far less likely to be seen as a guilty pleasure than as a rewarding enterprise, perhaps even one with potential for human (and intersubjective) advancement. It is conceivable that passages like the following might have caused Didion's contemporary readers to exult with pride rather than squirm at the irony (as today's more cynical and congestion-wary Angelenos might):

She drove it as a riverman runs a river, every day more attuned to its cur-
rents, its deceptions, and just as a riverman feels the pull of the rapids in the
lull between sleeping and waking. (Didion 1970: 13–14)

Banham's prose suggests an even more spiritual value to driving, attributing democratic promise to the "willing acquiescence in an incredibly
demanding man/machine system":

The private car and the public freeway together provide an ideal—not to say
idealized—version of democratic urban transportation: door-to-door on
demand at high average speeds over a very large area. (Banham, 1971: 217)

But Banham was cautious in his enthusiasm, mindful that it was "hardly
noticed or commented on . . . that the price [of such transport on de-
mand] is the almost total surrender of personal freedom for most of the
journey" (217). Indeed, he was not alone in expressing such reservations.
Several "controversial" accounts (TCRP, 1997) of the interstate highway
system appeared in the early 1970s, by Kenneth Schneider (1971), Helen
Leavitt (1970), and Ronald Buel (1972), not incidentally at the peak of investments in automobile culture concurrent with the destruction of alternative modes of transportation (Flink, 1988). Some of these were quite
blunt:

The social malignancy underlying automobility, *tyrannus mobilitis,* draws
men into inescapable dependence. . . . Automobility gradually permeates the
daily behavior of people, the purpose of institutions, and the structure of
cities and countryside. This tyranny has been promoted under the cunning
popular myth of expanding freedom and affluence. . . . [The] current reality
of auto tyranny is cultural power, social blackmail, physical deprivation, injury, and death. We must not mistake the brutal grip. (Schneider, 1971: 22)

At least in the policy arena, the cultural wars over the automobile were
relegated to the margins of public and regulatory discourse, partly because
technical solutions seemed both imminent and politically attractive (Krier
and Ursin, 1977; Rajan, 1996a). The debate was on the best course available
for setting standards for new vehicles that would be technologically feasible for manufacturers to comply with, and for ensuring that emissions remained within limits for vehicles in use. Initially there were questions as to
whether to add emission control devices to existing vehicles or to require

only that manufacturers install them in new vehicles. But with the reorganization in 1967 of all air pollution regulatory functions under one agency, the California Air Resources Board (CARB), a resolute course was adopted to force manufacturers to use the best available control technology for new vehicles to meet successively higher standards.

The initial improvements were rather modest, including the PCV and the Exhaust Gas Recirculation (EGR) valve, which was meant to control oxides of nitrogen. A few of these controls affected vehicle performance because they reduced engine power, leading to the first set of worries related to in-use controls, namely, consumer "tampering," which I discuss in more detail later. But by the early 1980s, with the introduction of catalytic converters, electronic feedback controls, and computer-controlled engines, the entire underhood architecture had undergone a metamorphosis. Manufacturers subsequently had to adopt on-board diagnostic systems that would monitor all aspects of the engine's performance in real time, storing codes and warning the driver when problems arose. The computer-controlled vehicles were designed to keep emission control systems within their original specifications for a long period and to permit external interrogation of the past performance of the systems.

The result was a cleaner and somewhat more fuel-efficient fleet with little or no loss in power, although people were driving considerably more, wiping out most of the gains in efficiency and emissions.[1] And despite the many encouraging aspects of technological control, the state was burdened with the same set of policy problems during each cycle of technology advancement—having to persuade manufacturers to install the newer systems and consumer-citizens to bear the higher cost of their vehicles and to maintain them properly. The first problem was addressed through a series of delicate maneuvers in which the CARB effectively withheld the pie of automobile sales from manufacturers who refused to meet vehicular standards. In a climate of increasing global competition after the mid-1970s, this strategy worked brilliantly to get all the major domestic and foreign manufacturers in line, even if they had to restructure their production processes globally in order to sell cars built exclusively to meet California's standards.

As I describe further in the next section, the second policy problem, persuading vehicle owners to meet certain obligations, turned out to be far more difficult to overcome. Partly this was because the problem was always regarded as a political issue, if only in the narrowly defined sense of politics as "public acceptability" (Howitt and Altshuler, 1999). Moreover, with each advance of technology, the CARB was already finding itself in the difficult position of having to devise viable strategies for monitoring the performance of increasingly sophisticated systems throughout the life of each vehicle. Still, for a long period during the 1980s and 1990s, the performative competence of technology alone seemed to lend legitimacy to the agency's attempts to introduce new emission controls in vehicles by blending quite nicely with a generalized fetishism over new cars. That is to say, the incentive to buy new vehicles, even if they had surveillance technologies built in, was reinforced by advertising claims boasting the improvements in performance for "fuel-injected, fully computerized" engines (Wernick, 1994; Paterson, 2001).

The federal government, meanwhile, had created one of the most aggressive pieces of environmental legislation ever in the form of 1970 and 1977 revisions to the Clean Air Act. The 1970 amendments directed the Environmental Protection Agency (EPA) to prescribe standards to reduce vehicular emissions of so-called criteria air pollutants (carbon monoxide, hydrocarbons, and nitrogen oxides) by 90 percent within five years. California continued to receive a waiver from federal standards, which it first obtained in 1967, given its "unique situation" with air pollution, as long as its own automobile pollution control regulations remained stricter than those of the federal government.

Congress's extraordinary mandate in 1970, soon after the legendary Apollo mission, was obviously the result of a polity enamored by the power of technology to achieve the impossible, but it was also driven in large part by grassroots social and environmental consciousness and the rise in environmental litigation (DiMento, 1977, Crandall et al., 1986). But political and technological realism prevailed, producing the 1977 amendments, which called for states to employ all "reasonably available control measures" to attain and maintain the standards by 1982, or in some cases by 1987. These included some provisions for transportation control measures, with the stipulation that federal aid for highway construction would be disallowed if there was inadequate progress in air quality improvement programs. It was in this last provision that the federal agencies discovered a lever to influence state-level motor vehicle regulation, but California, which had already won waivers on setting new vehicle standards, was averse to consent to any sort of federal interference on the in-use front. More important, in-use controls involved an area of regulation where citizen participation was critical, and mandating such commitments was an awkward problem.

Recalcitrance over In-Use Controls

Indeed, while the glamour of new technology was effective for getting consumer endorsement of aggressive controls, everyone realized that it was still absolutely crucial to ensure that emissions from "real-world" vehicles in use would remain within acceptable limits. Unfortunately, emissions tended to vary greatly, and to some extent quite independent of use, maintenance, and so on (Rajan, 1996b). This necessitated the creation of a separate mode of regulation, wherein the agency would engage directly driver-citizens. How to create such regulation that would be effective as well as legitimate was a persistent source of worry.

The installation of the first emission control systems in motor vehicles in 1961 was paralleled by a "four-phase public information campaign," whose "most-intensive segment [was] to apprise the public of the problem of exhaust emissions and the inescapable solution through the purchase of exhaust control devices" (Motor Vehicle Pollution Control Board Hearing, 10 March 1961). But by the mid-1970s this was no longer a significant public relations issue, although state legislators and agency officials were already expressing anxiety about enrolling the public in specific programs to control in-use emissions, such as retrofit schemes in the early 1970s and the switch to unleaded fuel around 1975 (Krier and Ursin, 1977). The earliest rumblings for establishing a periodic and state-supervised program in California appeared in 1962, around the same time that legislative approval was solicited for requiring vehicles in use to be retrofitted with crankcase controls. The California Motor Vehicle Pollution Control Act of 1960 had already declared it unlawful to drive an unregistered vehicle, as well as one not equipped with a certified device. But the statute made no provisions for periodic inspections.

By 1963 there was growing clamor from the counties in favor of controls on vehicles in use, which found expression in the California Senate, where an inspection bill was introduced requiring the Department of Motor Vehicles to inspect all vehicles retrofitted with crankcase controls every twelve months after installation. The bill was eventually watered down, in the face of resistance from automobile clubs and rural counties, to require inspection only in those counties that voted for it. But shortly thereafter the requirement that all used vehicles have crankcase devices installed on them generated an outcry of sorts:

Typical public worries were that the devices interfered with vehicle operation and could not be properly maintained. These were legitimate concerns: maintenance was especially troublesome inasmuch as under the inspection program an improperly maintained device could result in failure of inspection and lead to additional expense or even inability to register the vehicle. The basis for the worries might, however, have been illegitimate; much of the concern was generated by claims of the automobile clubs, mechanics and used car dealers that the devices were nuisances. (Krier and Ursin, 1977: 150)

The ensuing regulatory confusion compelled the legislature in 1965 to *abolish* the inspection programs altogether and to restrict crankcase installation for post-1955 vehicles only upon change of ownership. This "rapid enormous setback" in pollution control policy was widely seen as the fallout of a confrontation with the general public and, indeed, seems to have constituted a defining moment for all subsequent in-use motor vehicle policies in the state. The din of protest must have been quite startling to the agency, which up to that point had received every indication of popular support for any kind of decisive regulatory effort to control automobile pollution.

But public opposition to the retrofit and inspection programs appeared to convey a critical loss of confidence in the agency itself, defeating any hope of reviving another inspection program, at least in the short term. By 1966 it was clear that the Motor Vehicle Pollution Control Board had slowly been maneuvered (or had maneuvered itself) into a position where it could do nothing right, where a step in any direction could bring cries of protest from strong interests. The MVPCB's position was to become even more vulnerable to conflicting demands, and almost five years were to pass before any further significant progress was made on exhaust controls for used vehicles (Krier and Ursin, 1977: 160–163).

Attempts to solicit popular support for in-use motor vehicle programs remained few and far between until mounting federal pressure to monitor and control in-use emissions precipitated the state's first Inspection/Maintenance (I/M) Program in 1984. The federal mandate came from the revised Clean Air Act's requirement for periodic State Implementation Plans (SIPs), with the requirement that these provide, "to the extent necessary and practicable, for periodic inspection and testing of motor vehicles to enforce compliance with applicable emission standards" (42 U.S.C. 1857c

5[a][2][G][1976]). The legislation's imposition of deadlines and penalties on states was meant "to allow no escape from a strict standard of compliance for what [Congress] believed to be indolent federal and state air pollution bureaucracies" (Anderson et al., 1984: 142).

But all along, most states seemed recalcitrant toward instituting such programs, and despite its apparent mandate to coerce states to comply, the EPA took little action in that direction for several years (Ostrov, 1984). The delay was attributed to a "variety of shibboleths, misconceptions, and lingering doubts" concerning the effects of emission controls on motor vehicles in terms of their on-road performance, and to the states' reluctance to confront politically the apparent "intrusion of the federal bureaucracy" into the daily lives of motorists (Ostrov, 1984: 141; see also Reitz, 1979). Ora Harris also points to three reasons for the "seemingly widespread aversion to the I/M program. They are (1) an antipathy to federal intrusion in matters considered to be of 'state or local' concern; (2) a concern about the costs attending such programs; and (3) a belief in the existing technological effectiveness and efficacy of most American and foreign made automobiles" (1989: 1317). But, primarily, Congress and the EPA may have themselves "not exhibited the requisite political courage to take stringent actions against those who have adopted a cavalier attitude regarding compliance with I/M requirements" (Harris, 1989: 1321).

The last issue became irrelevant by the 1980s, for by then the EPA was not only actively demonstrating to the states the usefulness and effectiveness of I/M programs for achieving air quality objectives but also threatening them for failing to follow its guidelines (Cackette et al., 1979). The persuasive reason for the failure of implementation in spite of such threats is, of course, the political fact that the gamut of measures of in-use motor vehicle control "directly affected the driving public, sometimes in ways that drivers viewed as extremely restrictive. As a result, these non-technological control alternatives crumbled one by one underneath the political reality of the average American's daily dependence on the automobile" (Andersen et al., 1984: 230). It is odd that most commentators should invoke popular sentiments as steering the course of policy, because there is little evidence that they were ever expressed coherently. Rather, local politicians and policy makers seem to have projected onto to an imaginary public their own sense of stricture in the face of having to address the "political reality" of "dependence on the automobile."

But by the time the I/M Program was instituted, California's overall regulatory process had developed into a fairly robust system of risk management, intended to maintain a sustained level of oversight on emissions throughout the life of a vehicle while striving to reduce overall fleet emissions. The primary strategy involved certification standards made progressively stringent through technology-forcing regulation directed at manufacturers. As a secondary layer of protection, warranty requirements assured that systems would remain effective throughout a fixed "useful life" of the vehicles. The tertiary level of coverage, in effect throughout the actual life of the vehicle, was expected to be obtained by the I/M Program. The strategy turned out to be a huge success. By 1995, cumulative California auto emissions for nitrogen oxides and hydrocarbons were about one-third lower than 1970 levels, even though total vehicle miles traveled had more than doubled. At the same time, there were still several "non-attainment" areas that the federal government was watching over, and the state had to continue along its path of aggressive regulation.

At the end of 1987, California missed the Clean Air Act's deadline to meet National Ambient Air Quality Standards and had to produce a new state implementation plan, announcing actions to ensure "reasonable progress" in air quality. Sadly, the vitality and optimism engendered by the agency's technology-forcing measures for new vehicles had no counterparts in the area of in-use vehicle policy. And yet, time was running out: Congress enacted further amendments to the Clean Air Act in 1990 that required the EPA to implement an "enhanced" I/M program by 1994. If states refused to comply, federal highway funds could be withdrawn, a threat that had to be taken seriously in the relatively gloomy economic climate of the period.

The EPA developed new regulations in 1992, requiring non-attainment regions to have an annual centralized enhanced I/M program. The states that elected to implement decentralized programs or a program consisting of centralized and decentralized inspection facilities were to have their emission reduction credits discounted by approximately 50 percent for the decentralized portion of their programs, unless they could demonstrate that their programs were as effective as a centralized program. There was considerable opposition to this approach, not only since the new inspection procedures would be time-consuming and costly compared to the so-called no-load tailpipe tests and underhood inspections carried out at licensed garages but also because independent station owners would lose their business to contractors setting up centralized facilities. The EPA contended that there was considerable evidence of "tampering" by vehicle owners and "fraud" by independent garages, and that

214 S U D H I R C H E L L A R A J A N

the no-load tests were inadequate measures of actual emissions from vehicles.

Meanwhile, a strong lobby primarily composed of research scientists and technologists was developing its own opinion of how in-use emissions ought to be controlled. Based on roadside measurements by an infrared remote-sensing device, they argued that only a small number of vehicles on the road, known as "gross emitters," had emissions that were inexplicably much higher than those of the average vehicle, and that it would be far more cost effective to selectively test and repair them than to subject the entire fleet to such inspections and repairs (Bishop et al., 1993; cf. Rajan, 1996b). For many of the reasons described earlier, the California Air Resources Board (CARB) was for several months understandably reluctant to shift its regulatory focus to any single group of vehicles, no matter how stark the contrast was between the average vehicle and the gross emitter.

In the aftermath of a three-way struggle involving the EPA, the CARB, and some scientists who were adamant about the need for selective testing and repair of gross emitters, the state legislature decided to revise the I/M Program toward a hybrid solution. The majority of vehicles would go through a routine biennial inspection, but those identified as gross polluters by roadside emission sensors would be subject to special tests at centralized facilities, with no cost limits on repair. But even this solution was tenuous, given the new intrusiveness of the roadside sensors, and a carefully orchestrated public outreach program was developed describing the need for such surveillance to weed out the worst offenders.[2]

Indeed, the enhanced program has had many of the same problems as its forerunners. As an official review recently concluded:

> As the previous chapters show, the Smog Check II program is not achieving the SIP-required emission reductions. [Overall, the program achieved 36 percent of the expected emission reductions for 1999.] It does not meet the SIP emission reduction targets because we have not implemented final cut points, some stations are not fully or properly repairing vehicles that fail inspection, the anticipated evaporative emission test cannot be used because it is not reliable, the program exempts older vehicles that would benefit from repair, and some aspects of the program we assumed in the SIP are not being executed in practice. (CARB, 2000)

Technology at the End of Its Tether

The CARB's approach appears to have developed elements of the two main regulatory options mentioned at the beginning of this chapter, although they have remained somewhat bifurcated depending on whether they have been applied to manufacturers or car owners. A relatively small, though powerful, group of actors, vehicle manufacturers, has been identified as the primary target of regulation. To the multitude of car users, the CARB has proposed a relatively painless procedure, the biennial vehicle inspections at decentralized garages, thereby pooling their risks collectively so that each had to "pay" a small premium roughly corresponding to the deviation of their vehicle's emissions from the standard for which it was certified (Rajan 1992). A variation on this mode, culling out the gross emitters and subjecting them to special penalties, was reluctantly adopted in the mid-1990s with pressure from some scientists and policy makers. But the CARB has assiduously avoided making any attempt to include land-use and transportation planning controls in its regulatory program, occasionally providing the explanation that these were beyond its mandate. Indeed, they were.

Still, it is difficult to understand precisely how the CARB could propose—and why automobile manufacturers would eventually comply with, though not without protest—the decades-long regimen of tough emissions standards for new vehicles that were sold exclusively in California. Surely, automobile lobbies must have been all-powerful and could have managed to tame the regulatory juggernaut toward setting far more lenient standards than the fairly draconian ones that came out year after year. A close, and as yet unwritten, analysis of the political economy of air pollution regulation in the state is needed to unravel this mystery, but a few candidate factors are worth mentioning.[3]

First, and perhaps most important, as I have argued, the CARB would have preferred to regulate manufacturers rather than vehicle owners in any case, given the complexity of having to deal with transportation and land-use policies influencing the total miles driven. And since even the gains it was making in the early years of regulating new vehicles were being eroded by the increases in miles driven, it chose to go in the former direction even more aggressively than it heretofore had done. Second, California represented a huge market comprising roughly a million new vehicles per year in its peak, and if the CARB was going to dig in its heels and propose tough new standards, no manufacturer wanted to lose its chance to participate in it. As mentioned earlier, this dynamic was made more complex by competition among manufacturers, the Japanese and Europeans routinely being more willing than the Americans to comply with new standards to gain market share. And finally, between the late 1970s and the mid-1990s, many of the technology fixes proposed by the CARB were generated in consultation with automotive industry experts, which provided substantial room for manufacturers to influence modest changes that helped them streamline emissions control technology into their normal vehicle design development.

But in the early 1990s, California literally came to the end of the tether in its approach to limiting vehicular emissions. For both new and existing vehicles, emissions control had become a matter of considerably high stakes, for which the possibility of direct closure had all but expired. New vehicle standards for carbon monoxide, hydrocarbons, and oxides of nitrogen were ten- to twenty-fold tighter than they were before the controls were initiated, and the emphasis had shifted dangerously to in-use emissions.

In September 1990, in an announcement that shook the industry and the environmental movement, the CARB adopted a Low-Emission Vehicle and Clean Fuels Program, requiring that by 1998 a minimum of 2 percent of the vehicles offered for sale by major automakers in California be Zero-Emitting Vehicles (ZEVs) and that this be extended to 5 and 10 percent, respectively, by 2001 and 2003. The regulations, which were designed with biennial reviews to monitor the development of technology, were modified substantially over the years, the most dramatic revision being the one in 1996, which essentially rescinded the 1998 and 2001 mandates but kept the 10 percent requirement for 2003. The reasons for the *volte face* were multiple, including intense political lobbying by the oil and automotive industries and uncertainties in battery technology. But as Mark Brown argues, the CARB ignored the tremendous public support for electric vehicles and imputed to them instead the "unacceptability" of having vehicles with relatively short ranges:

> [D]espite enormous public opposition to changing the mandate, CARB determined that very few consumers would want to buy the currently available [electric vehicles]. . . . CARB's conception of citizenship was closely bound up with its understanding of technology and expertise. . . . The Board appealed to experts as the voice of the public good, discounting the

very statements it had solicited from the public itself. While CARB faced intense political pressure to postpone the program, its appeals to expertise were not simply ways of rationalizing a decision caused by interest group lobbying. (Brown, 2001)

Subsequent reviews completely modified the 2003 mandate, without actually removing the 10 percent requirement but allowing manufacturers partial credits for selling low-emission vehicles rather than "pure ZEVs" (CARB, 2001). Even as these policies were being shaped into increasingly tangled forms, discussion elsewhere in the state had commenced to develop a strategy to reduce petroleum dependence in California. This was necessitated by the realization that a combination of extremely stringent local air pollution regulations governing the siting of refineries, complex refining requirements related to the CARB's low-emissions mandate, and falling oil reserves in California would lead to a growing shortage of transportation fuels in the state.[4] This placed the CARB in an awkward position: a strong ZEV mandate and incentives to reduce driving would have gone a long way toward mitigating the problem, but the agency had somehow locked itself out of both options.

The most recent drama in the state's air pollution regulatory history involves the passage of Assembly Bill 1493 in 2002, which would require the CARB to develop carbon pollution, or greenhouse gas, standards for vehicles in model years 2009 and beyond. It is likely that the bill's success was itself predicated on a number of important political considerations at the time: a strong environmentalist lobby, a growing sense of despair over the issue of petroleum dependence (which would have been alleviated considerably by introducing more energy efficient, and therefore "greenhouse gas–friendly" vehicles), and a Democratic governor who wanted to push strong energy legislation in the wake of the electricity debacle in the state. At the same time, some of the provisions in the bill clearly reflect the compromises that were made to various political lobbies. These include bans on mandatory trip-reduction measures or land-use restrictions; on additional taxes on fuels, vehicles, or vehicle miles traveled; on reductions in vehicle weights or speed-limit reductions or limitations; and on restrictions on vehicle miles traveled (California Legislature, 2002). In other words, the language of the bill was simply a continuation of the philosophy adopted by Governor Knight a half century earlier, that "automobile pollution is a technical" rather than a political problem.

It is, of course, somewhat absurd to make the case that the CARB played any strong role in supporting the language of the final bill, especially given its own discomfort over its ability to implement the ZEV mandate. At the same time, it is arguable that this provided yet another opportunity for the agency to engage itself in a form of political deflection and gain more widespread support for promoting fuel-celled vehicles, the latest technological promise that its staff were becoming fascinated with (see various board documents available at http://www.arb.ca.gov).

At any rate, despite growing public awareness of the links among land-use, transportation, life-style choices, and climate change (e.g., http://www.transact.org), the CARB's discourse is more than likely to remain focused on emissions control technology from new vehicles (see, for instance, CARB, 2002a).[5] In the past, such a strategy led only to ever more convoluted forms of regulation, with narrowly defined technology categories and increasingly costly implications for administration (Rajan, 1996a). But the CARB's fascination with technology and actuarial practice appears in no way to be diminishing, as evident in the most recent changes it has proposed to the ZEV mandate (CARB, 2002b). Meanwhile, matters have been complicated by a legal challenge by General Motors, Daimler-Chrysler, and several California car dealers, alleging the new ZEV rules violate a federal law barring states from regulating fuel economy in any way. The final insult came when the federal government itself intervened in the lawsuit by filing an amicus brief on behalf of the plaintiff automakers.

By both chance and circumstance, the control of automobile pollution in California has been represented, acted upon, and thereby constrained as a technocratic problem that leaves the polity with few choices. This predicament has paralyzed the state's capacity to respond to what it perceives to be a double gesture from its citizens: they demand clean air but are unwilling to take responsibility for achieving it, especially when it involves setting limits on automobile use. But as Mark Brown and I have argued separately, the official reading is specious because it is founded on an individualist metaphor that, in turn, contracts the space of politics and fosters a security mode of governance. By relying on elaborate techniques of risk management and technological controls, policy tends to move away from a shared public effort to generate normative discourse. At most, under a narrow utilitarian logic, "willingness to pay" forms the principal component of the consumptive aspects of the problem, and the task of (state-organized) production to meet this demand is simply to select the most cost-effective administrative program for implementation.

To the extent that automobility is itself entrenched as a set of routine practices, there has been little hope for citizens themselves to articulate any long-term common interests that could lead to meaningful policy solutions. This apparent public disengagement from political affairs has had further vitiating consequences: the domination of policy making by interest groups representing industry, academia, and the state bureaucracy itself, whose only common theme has been the development of new technology, rather than the realization of social policy ideals. The vast majority of drivers have thereby become more alienated than ever from the conditions of their daily life, at the same time that their ability to speak as responsible citizens has been clouded by the lure of advertising.

In its insurance-oriented view of social behavior, state administration degenerates toward limited solutions that are concerned with optimizing ownership of cars and providing incentives to buy newer cars, instead of addressing the political demands for a common future of transportation and clean air. The contradictions in this model have become increasingly apparent, but it is by no means obvious that these will yet take root in a new form of democratic and pluralist politics around automobile pollution, given the institutional embeddedness of automobility in daily life. The car remains, as it were, "king" in California (Zizek, 1991).

NOTES

Portions of this chapter are drawn on material in relevant chapters in my book (Rajan, 1996a).

1. The growth in vehicle miles traveled was in fact quite a serious concern for air pollution regulators. In California, between 1960 and 1970 there was a 55 percent increase in total miles traveled; in the 1970s, this grew by a further 41 percent (CARB Web site, http://www.arb.ca.gov).

2. The auto club was recruited to play a strong role in this effort. See, for instance, "What Is Smog Check II" (http://www.aaa-calif.com/auto-own/maintain/smog.asp).

3. Unfortunately, the few political studies of automobile pollution regulation do not quite tell this part of the story well; Krier and Ursin, 1977; Lowry, 1992; Hempel, 1995; Grant, 1995; Rajan 1996a; Gómez-Ibáñez and Tye, 1999; Brown, 2001).

4. Under the mandate of state legislation, a number of studies were conducted by the California Energy Commission to study the problem (http://www.energy .ca.gov/fuels/petroleum_dependence/), many of which recommended that more energy efficient vehicles be introduced for sale in the state, which would provide the dual benefit of reducing criteria air pollutant emissions and gasoline consumption. Environmentalists were making similar arguments; see, for instance, NRDC (2002).

5. Notably, perhaps as a way to counter strong opposition from automakers to the bill, environmentalists expressed warm support for it.

REFERENCES

Anderson, Frederick R., Daniel R. Mandelker, and A. Dan Tarlock. 1984. *Environmental Protection: Law and Policy.* Boston: Little, Brown.

Banham, Reyner. 1971. *Los Angeles: The Architecture of Four Ecologies.* London: Allen.

Bishop, G. G., D. H. Steadman, J. E. Peterson, and T. J. Hosick. 1993. "A Cost-Effectiveness Study of Carbon Monoxide Emissions Reduction Utilizing Remote Sensing." *Journal of Air and Waste Management Association* 43 (7): 978–88.

Brown, Mark B. 2001. "The Civic Shaping of Technology: California's Electric Vehicle Program." *Science, Technology, and Human Values* 26 (1) (Winter): 56–81.

Buel, Ronald. 1972. *Dead-End: The Automobile in Mass Transportation.* New York: Prentice-Hall.

Cackette, Thomas, Philip Lorang, and David Hughes. 1979. "The Need for Inspection and Maintenance for Current and Future Vehicles." SAE Technical Paper 790782. Warrendale, Pa.: Society for Automotive Engineers.

California Air Resources Board (CARB). 1996. "Initial Statement of Rulemaking: Proposed Amendments to the Zero-Emission Vehicle Requirements for Passenger Cars and Light-Duty Trucks." Staff report, Sacramento, February 9.

———. 2000. *Evaluation of California's Enhanced Vehicle Inspection and Maintenance Program (Smog Check II),* El Monte.

———. 2001. "Zero Emission Vehicle Program Changes," El Monte.

———. 2002a. Board hearing, Sacramento, September 26.

———. 2002b. "Possible Amendments to the California ZEV Program." Board workshop, Sacramento, December 5–6.

California Legislature. 2002. Bill Analysis of AB 1493. Sacramento, July 1.

Crandall, Robert W., Howard K. Gruenspecht, Theodore E. Keener, and Lester B. Lave. 1986. *Regulating the Automobile.* Washington, D.C.: Brookings Institution.

Delucchi, Mark. 1998. *The National Social Cost of Motor Vehicle Use.* Metropolitan Planning Technical Report no. 10, FHWA-PD-99-001, June.

Didion, Joan. 1970. *Play It as It Lays.* New York: Pocket Books.

DiMento, Joseph F. 1977. "Citizen Environmental Litigation and the Administrative Process: Empirical Findings, Remaining Issues and a Direction for Future Research." *Duke Law Journal* (22): 409–48.

Flink, James J. 1988. *The Automobile Age.* Cambridge: MIT Press.

Gómez-Ibáñez, José A., William B. Tye, and Clifford Winston, eds., 1999. *Essays in Transportation Economics and Policy: A Handbook in Honor of John R. Meyer.* Washington, D.C.: Brookings Institution.

Grant, Wynn. 1995. *Autos, Smog, and Pollution Control: The Politics of Air Quality Management in California.* Aldershot, U.K.: Edward Elgar.

Harris, Ora Fred, Jr. 1989. "The Automobile Emissions Control Inspection and Maintenance Program: Making It More Palatable to 'Coerced' Participants." *Louisiana Law Review* 49 (6): 1315–49.

Hempel, Lamont C. 1995. "Environmental Technology and the Green Car: Towards a Sustainable Transportation Policy." In *Greening Environmental Policy: The Politics of a Sustainable Future,* ed. Frank Fischer and Michael Black, pp. 66–86. New York: St Martin's Press.

Howitt, Arnold, and Alan Altshuler. 1999. "The Politics of Controlling Auto Air Pollution." In *Essays in Transportation Economics and Policy,* ed. Gómez-Ibáñez and Tye, pp. 223–55. Washington, D.C.: Brookings Institution.

Kleinman, M. T., S. D. Colome, D. E. Foliart, and D. F. Shearer. 1989. "Effects on Human Health of Pollution in the South Coast Basin." Final Report to South Coast Air Quality Management District. University of California, Irvine.

Krier, J. E., and E. Ursin. 1977. *Pollution and Policy: A Case Essay on California and Federal Experience with Motor Vehicle Air Pollution, 1940–1975.* Berkeley: University of California Press.

Leavitt, Helen. 1970. *Superhighway-Superhoax.* New York: Doubleday.

Leone, Robert A. 1999. "Technology-Forcing Public Policies and the Automobile." In *Essays in Transportation Economics and Policy: A Handbook in Honor of John R. Meyer,* ed. José Gómez-Ibáñez, William E. Tye, and Clifford Winston, pp. 291–323. Washington, D.C.: Brookings Institution.

Lowry, William R. 1992. *The Dimensions of Federalism: State Governments and Pollution Control Policies.* Durham: Duke University Press.

Meyer, John W. 1986. "Myths of Socialization and Personality." In *Reconstructing Individualism: Autonomy, Individuality, and the Self in Western Thought,* ed. Thomas C. Heller, Morton Sosna, and David Wellbery, pp. 208–21. Stanford, Calif.: Stanford University Press.

Natural Resources Defense Council. 2002. *Fueling the Future: A Plan to Reduce California's Oil Dependence.* San Francisco: NRDC.

Ostrov, Jeremy. 1984. "Inspection and Maintenance for Automobile Pollution Controls: A Decade-Long Struggle among Congress, EPA, and the States." *Harvard Environmental Law Review* (8): 139–72.

Paterson, Matthew. 2001. *Understanding Global Environmental Politics: Domination, Accumulation, Resistance.* London: Palgrave.

———. 2002. "Climate Change and the Politics of Global Risk Society." Paper presented at the International Studies Association Annual Convention, New Orleans, March 24–27.

Rajan, Sudhir Chella. 1992. "Legitimacy in Environmental Policy: The Regulation of Automobile Pollution in California." *International Journal of Environmental Studies* (42): 243–58.

———. 1996a. *The Enigma of Automobility: Democratic Politics and Pollution Control.* Pittsburgh: University of Pittsburgh Press.

———. 1996b. "Diagnosis and Repair of Excessively Emitting Vehicles." *Journal of the Air and Waste Management Association* (46): 940–52.

Reitz, David. 1979. "Controlling Automotive Air Pollution through Inspection and Maintenance Programs." *George Washington Law Review* (47): 705–20.

Schneider, Kenneth R. 1971. *Autokind vs. Mankind.* New York: Norton.

Sheller, M., and J. Urry. 2000. "The City and the Car." *International Journal of Urban and Regional Research* 24 (4): 737–57.

Transit Cooperative Research Program (TCRP). 1997. "Consequences of the Development of the Interstate Highway System for Transit." *TCRP Research Results Digest* (21) (August).

Wernick, Andrew. 1994. "Vehicles for Myth: The Shifting Image of the Modern Car." In *Signs of Life in the U.S.A.: Readings on Popular Culture for Writers,* ed. Sonia Maasik and Jack Solomon, pp. 78–94. Boston: Bedford Books.

Zizek, Slavoj. 1991. "'The King Is a Thing': The King's Two Bodies." In *For They Know Not What They Do: Enjoyment as a Political Factor,* pp. 254–77. London: Verso.

Who Owns the Air?

Clean Air Act Implementation as a Negotiation of Common Property Rights

E. Melanie DuPuis

"Who owns the air?" Because our everyday breathing appears to put us under no financial obligation, people seldom think of air as property. Economists tend to agree, defining air as a "public good," a resource that is indivisible and therefore non-appropriable by any private party or group. This "non-appropriability" aspect of air tends to make it uninteresting to those concerned with the politics of resource use. The idea of "air use struggles" simply doesn't have the same resonance as more clearly definable and visible struggles over water, land, or trees. Yet, as other chapters in this book have shown, the invisibility of air use does not mean that politics is absent. Even if air is not entirely appropriable, there are struggles over air use, in particular, its use as a "sink" for polluting emissions (Tarr, 1996). As this chapter will show, U.S. air pollution control policies, culminating with the Clean Air Act Amendments of 1990 (CAAA), have made air into an increasingly "property-like" thing. Concurrently, the politics of air pollution control policies for implementing the CAAA can be seen as property-like struggles over the right to use the air. This chapter looks at one case of CAAA policy implementation, the Emission Reduction Credits (ERC) Program under New Source Review in New York State, to show how state officials, polluting industrialists, and environmentalists have struggled over the rights of air use in that state.

To investigate this case, the analysis draws on two current perspectives on resource struggles and property rights. The first is political ecology. Political ecologists look at the struggles over access to resources within local institutional contexts and power relationships. Second, in their analysis of claims over resources, political ecologists share certain perspectives with those who study common-property institutions (Ostrom, 1990; Rose, 1994). However, common-property scholars tend to look at the ways in which rights to use resources are struggled over and, sometimes, stabilized in particular institutional regimes. This study looks at the history of air use regulation in the United States as one in which air has been increasingly treated as a bounded property held in common. The property "regime" of air use under the CAAA, this analysis will show, is a struggle over common-property rights. In particular, the case study shows that these rights are legally ambiguous. It is this ambiguity that sets the stage for air rights struggles.

The questions surrounding air use mirror those of other common-property issues, namely, how is this resource held (managed) and by whom? This chapter looks at how the Clean Air Act, particularly the Clean Air Act Amendments of 1990, attempts to create boundaries around air use and to treat and manage the air increasingly as a common good. In this attempt to bound air use, the U.S. government—along with the subnational states that implement clean air regulations within the U.S. federal system—has been assisted by certain legal institutions, namely, parts of the Constitution (the Fourteenth Amendment, the Commerce Clause), "nuisance law" in common law, as well as the tradition of Roman Justinian law, which is part of many state constitutions. Yet, despite this institutional support, the attempt to make air into common property in the United State has been frustrated somewhat by the existence other American legal institutions, namely, the Fifth Amendment (read as the Takings Clause defense of private property), as well as other aspects of the U.S. reliance on English common law. It is this ambiguity in property law that creates the "arena of ambiguity" in which interested parties struggle over the rights to air use. This study looks specifically at one case to show how the struggles over the rights to air use can be embedded in, and can strategically exploit, these institutional ambiguities. In this case, potential users of air property have negotiated rights of use through processes set up by the CAAA. Different user interests have made property rights "claims" in the political arena, and state institutions have had to respond to those claims through the restructuring of property rights regimes.

Therefore, the state implementation of the Clean Air Act Amendments of 1990 can be understood as a creation of common-property boundaries and the negotiation of use "rights" by various user groups within these boundaries. The second is the study of common property institutions. The discourse over rights takes place amid the institutional ambiguities and contradictions of U.S. legal institutions dealing with environmental resources. Looking closely at the negotiation of air use as a struggle over property rights—and air use "management" as an institutional attempt to resolve those struggles—can therefore shed new light on the politics of air pollution control policy.

Perspectives on Use Rights: Political Ecology and Common Property

Both political ecologists and common-property scholars examine the issue of "use rights" over resources. However, political ecologists tend to focus on struggles over use rights, while common-property scholars focus on their stabilization within common-property regimes. The similarities between the terms *political ecology* and *political economy* is not accidental. While shunning the meta-theories of Marxist ecology, political ecologists attempt to incorporate attention to social inequalities and political conflict within a materialist (read, economy and nature) perspective. In varying measures, political ecologists share the perspectives of subaltern environmental thought (sharing Ramachandra Guha's post-colonial critique of Eurocentric notions of wilderness, for example) and cultural studies' emphasis on discourse as a way to understand political struggles. Discourse analysis in political ecology most often involves a look at "talking claims" (Fortmann, 1995), that is, at discursive struggles involving "claims" of rights over access to resources. In particular, political ecologists examine the embeddedness of these claims in networks of power (Peet and Watts, 1996; Peluso and Watts, 2001; Vandergeest and DuPuis, 1996). In other words, political ecologists tend to see resource struggles in the context of power, domination, and politics, as well as in the subtler hegemonic struggles over legitimacy and knowledge.

Common-property scholars focus on one particular kind of property right: the common use of a bounded set of resources. In common-property regimes, rights to resource use are restricted to a certain group, and this resource use is managed by particular formal and informal institutions, from national constitutions to local kinship networks. Of particular interest, from this perspective, are the ways in which common-property institutions can be stabilized so as to avoid the "tragedy of the commons" (Hardin, 1968), a state of affairs in which unrestricted use leads to the degradation of resources. Common-property scholars argue that Hardin's "tragedy" is not inevitable; restricting rights to resources to particular user groups—licensed owners of commercial fishing boats, for example—and managing these rights—maximum fish catch, for example—can enable resources to be managed sustainably (Ostrom, 1990). CAAA policy attempts much the same thing, by restricting air use to permitted air users—from factories to cars—and by limiting the amount of pollution each of these users can emit.

Because both common-property scholars and political ecologists tend to look at the historical development of institutions, there are also significant overlaps with work in environmental history (see, in particular, recent work by Peluso and Vandergeest on the development of property institutions in South East Asia, 2001). In particular, political ecologists tend to share a great deal with the environmental history perspective of William Cronin, generally agreeing that there is "trouble" with wilderness as an idea of nature without people. Instead, political ecologists and environmental historians of Cronin's ilk tend to put society back into the history of the environment, particularly social, political, and cultural struggles between groups over access to resources.

To be sure, the right to air is not often a topic of study among political ecologists, although a few scholars have taken a look at air use from a common property perspective (Rose, 1994; see Farrell and Keating, 2000, for a critique). In part, this is due to the generally accepted understanding of air as a non-appropriable "public good." Yet, as some common-property scholars have noted, the relationship between public goods and common goods, while not identical, can be quite close under particular institutional conditions such as common law (Ostrom, 1990). As one commentator describes it: "Once provided by community agreement, public goods are like a commons, a shared resource that can be maintained or abused. In that sense, the problem of public nuisance [like pollution] is partly a problem of the commons and how it is managed so as to maximize collective wealth" (Yandle, 1992: 530).

The Ambiguities of Air "Ownership"

The ambiguities between environmental policy and resource property rights derive from two different, and somewhat contra-interpretable, parts of the Constitution.[1] The first is the Fifth Amendment in the Bill of Rights, which provides that no person shall, among other things, be deprived of certain rights, "nor be deprived of life, liberty, or property, without due process of law; nor shall private property be taken for public use without just compensation." This section of the Bill of Rights is commonly known as the Takings Clause. However, it also is the source of authority for the law of "eminent domain," which holds that states may take property, with compensation, if taking that property promotes the public interest. No court has attempted to put strict legal boundaries on the definition of "the public interest," and courts have generally held that environmental regulation is part of the public interest.

However, another U.S. legal tradition does, in fact, deal with the idea of states holding property rights "in trust" for the public. Most states, in their constitutions, originally adopted forms of Roman Justinian law. Justinian law held: "By the law of nature these things are common to all mankind: the air, running water, the sea, and consequently the shores of the sea." Yet even newer, more aggressively environmental state constitutions do not generally include air resources under the aegis of common property. In contrast, states often do claim water and coastal resources as under their ownership in trust for the public. As a result, most U.S. state law retains for the public only the shoreline and other waters, and with varying legal strengths. The trust nature of state waters is, perhaps more important, upheld in the Commerce Clause of the Constitution, with a long-standing body of law that upholds the State's interest in navigable waters as part of its authority to regulate interstate commerce. Therefore, a wide body of state law in most states maintains that waters and coastlines within State boundaries are held by states in public trust. However, a cursory review of state constitutions indicates that most do not include air, specifically, as held in trust by states. This makes sense, in that air does not contain itself to state boundaries, a fact that will become more important as we consider air pollution control regulation. However, a survey of U.S. state court cases up to 1986 found that twenty-nine state courts had expanded the Public Trust Doctrine beyond navigable waters to include trust applicability to areas such as non-navigable waters and non-aquatic resources (Lawler and Parle, 1989: 142).

Neither the Fifth Amendment nor any other part of the U.S. Constitution specifically gives any party property ownership to common-good resources. States hold regulatory authority through a separate set of legal precedents that do not specifically deal with the state ownership of public-good resources. The first of these is common law, which holds that state judiciaries are enabled to deprive property owners of certain "rights" if the use of these rights harm others; this is commonly known as "nuisance law." The second is state police power, which gives states the right to regulate the use of private property if those uses are contrary to the public interest. This right is protected under the Fourteenth Amendment to the Constitution.

On the other hand, common-property law also relies heavily on the principle known as "first possession," developed from precedent cases resolving disputes over the possession of wild animals in the case of hunting (in which more than one hunter "put labor into" tracking down an animal but only one killed it and took it). Under this principle, the courts have traditionally decided in favor of the individual who held the resource. The idea of first possession is important in environmental law, because it creates a rights claim to those who have been historically using these resources, namely, the polluters themselves. From a first possession point of view, air resources are already private property, owned by those who have used them. From this perspective, any attempt to remove that right is thereby considered a "taking" under the Fifth Amendment.

A comparison of the Clean Water and Clean Air acts reveals very different trust property claims. The Clean Air Act (CAA) begins by declaring that "air pollution control at its source is the primary responsibility of States and local governments" (CAA Section 101 [a][3]). The control over air resources within their boundaries is the responsibility of states. However, unlike water, state constitutions seldom explicitly hold these resources in trust for the public. The CAA is thereby following the legal tradition of American adoption of Justinian law (which restricted public trust resources to water, and that by states, not the federal government) and the Commerce Clause (which gives the federal government some say over the use of state waters but does not mention air). The history of the Clean Air Acts themselves are a story of how the boundaries between states and Congress were eventually negotiated, giving Congress powers due to "rapidly expanding metropolitan and other urban areas, which generally cross the boundary lines of local jurisdictions and often extend into two or more States" (CAA Section 101 [a][1]). Note that the interstate jurisdiction is based *not* on the fact that air pollution crosses state borders but on the fact that the *sources* of air pollution extend over state borders. Even in its interstate jurisdictional claims, Congress is not taking possession of what are deemed to be state resources.

In contrast, the "declaration of goals" that begins the Clean Water Act speaks specifically of the nation's waters and repeatedly declares improved water quality to be "national policy." This is despite the fact that states are the real holders of waters in the public trust. Federal law bases its authority on the interstate transport of waters. But, because states do not generally claim the ownership of air in the public trust, it is more difficult for federal law to claim a national trust in the same way. In its imposition of air quality standards, and national controls to meet those standards, it refers only to its police powers to protect against emissions that scientific evidence shows to produce "an adverse effect of public health and welfare" (CAA Section 108 [2][a][B]).

Interestingly, the major sanction that the federal government threatens to impose on states for not meeting clean air regulatory requirements is the withholding of federal highway monies, a sanction over which it has undeniable authority.

Is this difference really important? One answer is offered in Carol Rose's discussion of the relationship between governmental claims over property based on references to its police power and those based on references to the public trust doctrine. Her point, simply, is that they are mostly the same. "Nineteenth century jurists had a propensity to slide easily between police power and public property terminology," she states, making a close connection between "publicly created rents and public rights." She notes that the classic police power case, *Munn vs. Illinois*, relied greatly on water rights law, with the result that "[p]olice power regulation thus mirrored public property doctrine" (1994: 145). Both police power and public property "concerned a kind of 'easement' over things otherwise thought private—an easement to which the public is entitled and that cannot be bargained away to private individuals by governments or anyone else" (1994: 145). The publicness of the property had to do with the fact that "value in a sense is created by the very publicness of the practices in question" (1994: 145), such as is created by the easement of property to create railroad and electric systems.

Therefore, for both public trust and public interest/police power reasons, states act as if they have the legally constituted authority to hold the air in public trust, in ways similar to the doctrine of public trust ownership for water. As a result, despite weather flows, the air has come to be treated as state-managed "common property" within state boundaries.

How does the state become the manager of air resources without claiming absolute ownership? As Carol Rose has argued, property is "a kind of assertion or story, told within a culture that shapes the story's content and meaning. That is, the would-be 'possessor' has to send a message that others in the culture understand and that they find persuasive as grounds for the claim asserted" (1994: 25). Yet political ecologists' studies of forestry and other common-property resources show that these stories are sometimes contested, and that, under some circumstances, struggles over resources become conflicting messages about various groups' rights to use (Peluso, 1992; Vandergeest, 1995; Fortmann, 1995). As the following case study shows, the story of clean air regulation has been an attempt to bound the commons to a permitted set of users, to allocate the use of this bounded set of resources among various claims-makers, and to claim ultimate governmental rights over this resource. In this struggle, state police power and public trust authority do not, as Rose claims, simply mirror each other. Instead, differences between the two provide an "arena of institutional ambiguity" in which contested claims take place.

Air regulations treat industrial and other "stationary" sources as common-property users—through their emissions into the air—and have regulated them in ways that attempt to prevent these sources from creating a "tragedy of the commons" through overuse. Regions—usually metropolitan areas—where air pollution levels do not meet federal standards are switched into a non-compliance mode that makes air into a common-property resource with increasingly restrictive boundaries. Much like the ideal management of fisheries, the Clean Air Act Amendments of 1990 (CAAA) set a maximum amount of air that stationary sources can use (a "budget") in areas that are not "in attainment." This budget was capped first at a state's 1990 emissions and has been reduced over time according to various regulatory measures, as chosen by states. Included in this air use budget are the emissions from "mobile sources" (cars and other forms of transport), which together form the major air use activities that the state manages. In effect, the CAAA set the common property boundaries at various steps down from 1990 emissions (percent reductions in X years) and then leave the state to negotiate with various air users over exactly how much each user group will gain rights to use. The struggles to implement state laws mandated by the CAAA can be therefore seen as struggles over who will use the state's air commons, and how much.

The CAAA also set some initial limitations on air use. Primarily, the CAAA mandate the EPA to determine what technologies stationary and mobile sources must be required to use in order to be allowed into the commons. Sources that do not use these technologies are denied the right to emit into the air, either through denial of a pollution control permit or through the denial of a car registration.

Yet, for the most part, the EPA does not directly create the boundaries of air use. The agency sets the standards at which it deems air to be "safe" and then gives states the authority to create regulatory regimes, which include calculating the amount of pollution that sources can emit into the air while still meeting these standards. The states then, through modeling, create budgets of emissions that they predict will enable them to meet air standards.

However, the CAAA also allow states a great deal of flexibility in determining who will use their air resources and how. State regulatory processes thereby become arenas in which various stakeholders in the use of this resource make claims over their rights of use. State regulations are therefore "use rights regimes" that are a negotiated product of this claims-making process. As the following case study shows, the ambiguities in property law regarding air resources create the space for various rights claims over air use.

Case Study: Contesting ERCs in New York State

One air regulatory arena that has dealt specifically with the issue of air property rights is pollution control trading. There are a number of pollution control trading programs in Clean Air Act law and regulation. The most developed of these is the sulfur allowance trading program, created to provide a market-based solution to acid rain problems.[2] California's Reclaim Program is the most comprehensive, enabling sources to comply with regulations by trading both precursors to ground-level ozone: the nitrates of oxygen (NOx) and the volatile organic compounds (VOCs) that combine to produce smog. This case study involves another smaller trading program, the creation and trading of Emission Reduction Credits, also known as emission "offsets."[3] The offset program is part of the Clean Air Act known as New Source Review, the part of the program that considers permitting new, larger polluting facilities in a state. The offset program was created to deal with the creation of a "cap" on facility emissions in areas not in compliance with air quality standards for smog. CAA regulations put a cap on the emissions of the precursor pollutants from "stationary sources," basically industrial facilities and power plants. The cap on stationary source emissions, while numerically managed only from 1990 on, was set with the creation of the emission offsets regulations of New Source Review in the 1970s. In theory, each new large stationary source was required to find an offset—an equivalent reduction in the amount of emissions the source would add to the atmosphere—from an existing source.

Exactly how new large facilities seeking to site in states with non-attainment areas would go about finding these offsets was not spelled out for many years. Many states complained that these requirements posed unworkable siting requirements, thereby reducing economic development in non-attainment areas, which were often urban areas in need of new employment. In response, the Clean Air Act Amendments of 1990 called for states to set up certification programs for Emission Reduction Credits that would be legally acceptable to use as offsets to get new operating permits for new facilities.

The history of the creation, public review, and implementation of this program in New York State is an example of the negotiation on common-property "rights" in air at work. Citing the CAAA language of sulfur allowances, many states declared that Emission Reduction Credits were not a private property right but, as with allowances, "a limited authorization to emit" (42 U.S.C. 7651b). In other words, neither federal nor state law declares air use to be a specific property of the state, yet both declare that air use is not private property. As a related proposed rule on another form of air trading noted, Congress referred to allowances as a "limited authorization" to emit "to ensure that allowance holders understood that they were barred from claiming a government taking under the 5th Amendment of the U.S. Constitution."[4]

The extent to which the state could "limit authorizations to emit," however, was not infinite, as the history of Emission Reduction Credit policy in New York State illustrates. The first proposal for a revised Emission Reduction Credit Program was filed for public comment in September 1992.[5] This proposal took an expansive approach to the nature of state control over the Emission Reduction Credits that would be created under this program, including:

1. the retention by the state of 10 percent of all credits created;

2. the retention of all credits from sources creating reductions simply by shutting down the facility;
3. the reversion of credits not used to the state, after three years;
4. state use of a portion of these credits to distribute itself to certain categories of economically beneficial or disadvantaged sources. The state also reserved the right to use credits for meeting CAAA attainment requirements, if necessary.

In a memo to the Governor's Office environmental staff, Department of Environmental Conservation (DEC) Commissioner Thomas Jorling admitted that "[t]aking this position has certain legal and political risks. My position is based on the legal argument that offsets are permissions conferred by the State for a limited period of time and subject to certain restrictions, not a property right to pollute." However, he takes the counterargument seriously, that "CAAA offsets are property rights, and that any restrictions we place on them will be considered a taking for which the owner must be compensated. Courts have not ruled specifically on this issue, and EPA has waffled on it."[6]

The response of the Business Council of New York State—representing the majority of large industrial polluters and, therefore, potential ERC creators—was to "strongly oppose any state taking of emission offsets generated by the private sector."[7] The short letter to DEC used the word *taking* three times. Although the Business Council did not openly claim ownership of emissions reduction credits, the repeated reference to the idea of "takings" was a strategic threat to bring formal questioning of property issues into the public realm if the state proposal went forth with the retention and reversion provisions listed above.

The Business Council claim that retention of credits was a "taking" was based in the property argument of first possession. The very fact that existing facilities were grandfathered into the Emission Reduction Credit Program reflects an acceptance of the first possession claim. When the program started, facilities did not start at square one and have to find credits to run their facilities. Facilities with permits were given the potential to create credits based on the amount of pollution they already emitted. The polluters, in other words, were given the opportunity to create another valuable asset simply because of their history of polluting. Environmentalists, in response, have critiqued the program as giving "a license to pollute."

Not only environmentalists have found this first possession aspect of Emission Reduction Credits hard to swallow. Economists have argued that the grandfathering of existing facilities into the program is economically inefficient. As Robert Hahn and Roger Noll state:

> The current approach, which uses existing standards as the baseline from which trades can be made, is politically attractive because it grandfathers the wealth position of current permit holders. Unfortunately, simply to grandfather permits and to let polluters arrange trades is not the most efficient way to organize a market, because (1) it requires bilateral negotiations; (2) it does not incorporate a mechanism whereby transaction terms become matters of public record . . . (3) it can cause severe market structure problems. (1983: 74)

At the same time that the Business Council was stating its objections to the DEC, the New York State Senate introduced a bill that would have created property rights to pollute the air and would have prohibited the DEC from "confiscating" emission reduction credits.[8] The EPA responded forcefully in a letter to Commissioner Thomas Jorling, with a formal legal analysis of state rights over regulating air use.[9] In this letter, Acting Assistant Administrator Michael Shapiro expressed "strong opposition" to this bill as "inconsistent with the legal status traditionally accorded to air pollution." He argued that this body of law has established that air pollution is "not a property right" and that governments had the right to "abate it as a nuisance without compensation." Shapiro defended this ground based on "the State's police power to protect the health and safety of its citizens," as well as on "common law in interstate pollution disputes to hold that air and other pollution may be abated as a nuisance" (p. 2). He also cited a decision that held that rights created by governmental regulatory schemes were not property. While this letter formally addresses the property rights issue, the EPA begs the question of air as community property under public trust by addressing only the question of whether Emission Reduction Credits—air pollution rights specifically created by sources—are property.

Yet this does not avoid the prickly problem of air credits as property. On the one hand, Emission Reduction Credits fit the Lockean notion of property on which Western notions of property are based (Rose, 1994). A source creates an Emission Reduction Credit by investing in equipment that goes beyond federal technology standards. This action mirrors

Locke's idea of property as nature to which you add labor. Unlike the air a source pollutes, a source is creating clean air by over-controlling emissions. There is a strong Lockean argument, therefore, for the idea that cleaned air should be property. On the other hand, perhaps based on the right of first use, some states—including New York—allow for the creation of ERCs from shutdown facilities.

However, the notion of public trust entails, as noted earlier, "a kind of 'easement' over things otherwise thought private—an easement to which the public is entitled and that cannot be bargained away to private individuals by governments or anyone else" (Rose, 1994: 145). This inalienability of resources in the public trust makes any kind of air trading program questionable; while states can authorize sources to emit, can states allow the use of public trust resources to be sold, even if not declared official "property"?

Of course, industries prefer the argument about our Lockean property heritage, while environmentalists tend more toward the strong notion of public trust. But what does "public trust" mean? Does it include the creation of policies based on some notion of allocating public trust resources to private holders, for the sake of economic efficiency?[10] This somewhat contradictory heritage is part of what gives stakeholders "room" to contest air use rights. The state often finds itself in the middle.

In response to this political onslaught of claims making about air use property rights, state officials reversed their position and gave polluters (which include public sources such as public hospitals and prisons as well as industrial facilities) complete access to all the potential credits. The state neither retained percentages of credits for economic development or for meeting regulatory standards nor reverted credits to state ownership after three years.

Yet this emission offset requirement continued to be criticized as a "no growth" policy for industrial states with large urban unemployed populations. Northeastern states concerned about loss of employment and their inability to compete with southern and western states for new—and cleaner—industrial facilities were concerned that the offset requirements were just one more bullet competing states could use to out-compete them in the race for new industrial investment.[11] Contradictory state responsibilities for both clean air and a vibrant economy, especially for "good" factory jobs for a working-class population hard hit by the severe de-industrialization of New York State in the preceding three decades,

made state control over a certain proportion of credits extremely attractive. In addition, in the transition period when the ERC creation program
geared up, facilities with the potential for creating credits struggled to
figure out how to meet the regulatory standards of ERC creation, and
those that succeeded often hoarded credits for their own purposes. As a
result, the non-availability of credits, even with a state-run bank, was seen
as severely threatening industrial development.[12]

As a result, New York State economic development officials, once they
found themselves without credits available from state retention, scrambled
to create credits through certification of emission reductions caused by
shutdown of state facilities. Also during the retention struggle, the state
executive office transferred from a Democrat, Mario Cuomo, to a Republican, George Pataki, a candidate who ran on a promise to deal with the
state's foundering industrial economy.

Under Pataki, credits created from reduction by state facilities were
offered, for free, to a glass manufacturer, Guardian Glass, as part of an
package of incentives to attract the company to site a facility in the western part of the state. "We try to make it easier for manufacturers to move
into New York," a spokesperson for the Department of Economic Development explained. "It was a unique and innovative idea."[13] State officials
from the Department of Environmental Conservation agreed that this was
a legitimate use of state credits for state purposes. "We're reducing emissions from the state's own facilities at the same time that we're allowing
economic growth and job creation to occur," a spokesperson from the Department of Environmental Conservation explained.[14]

Environmentalists did not agree. "It's disturbing that the state would
turn around and give away pollution credits that it has accumulated by reducing its own pollution emissions," said a spokesperson for the state's
major environmental coalition. "The state should be retiring them for the
public health, not giving them to business."[15] In other words, the environmentalists challenged the movement of public credits to the private sector
on the basis of the state's public trust responsibilities.

In defending their position, New York State's economic development
officials claimed their own definition of public trust, which included state
responsibility to encourage the creation of high-wage jobs in the state. For
example, at the legislative hearings on the "Guardian ERCs," called by the
state's legislative democratic opposition, the state's economic development
director, Charles Gargano, attacked Richard Brodsky, the Westchester
County Democrat who called the hearing:

Chairman Brodsky, did we hear you speak to the concerns of the workers who packed up rental vans and left cities like Utica, Amsterdam, Jamestown, Binghamton and Buffalo and headed to a better future in states like Virginia, North Carolina, South Carolina and points south and west?[16]

The assemblyman, in response, agreed that the plant should be built, "but not at the expense of the air we breathe."[17] The rhetoric in the hearing set up a struggle over air use as one of workers versus breathers, with each political group representing themselves as speaking on behalf of one group of air users.

Rose (1994) has noted that the issue of the public trust is ambiguous: Does it mean the trust as managed by government officials, supposedly on behalf of public welfare? Or is there another kind of public trust, which belongs to the people themselves, and which the people defend, sometimes against the decisions of public officials? As this case shows, the ambiguity in which U.S. institutions define the ownership of air as public common property provides the discursive arena in which rights can be contested.

Conclusion

This discussion of use-claim struggles in this one small part of Clean Air Act regulation demonstrates the similarities between the struggles over the use of this common property and the struggles over the use of other, more conventional common property, such as fisheries, other coastal and water resources, and community forest resources. In each case, users are making a claim regarding their right to use a resource—or to manage a resource, in the case of government.

Challenges to these claims often work in the ambiguous and contradictory areas of ownership over the resource. The unresolved contradictions in U.S. property law, particularly as related to air resources, provide an "arena of institutional ambiguity" in which air use struggles take place. The case study on Emission Reduction Credits brought two of these ambiguous areas to light. The first pertains to whether air is explicitly in the public trust or whether common-law rules of "first possession" prevail. The second has to do with whether the definition of public trust makes government the final arbiter or whether "the public" owns resources in trust and can defend them even against government actions. The institutions around the use of this property have not stabilized, giving actors political space in which to make use claims.

Yet the fact that the ERC Program has functioned without much controversy over the last five years indicates that some institutional stability has taken place. ERCs are bought and sold; new facilities are permitted and built. In addition, the negotiation over claims resulted in some compromises that are not currently contested. Government officials withdrew their proposal to retain and revoke credits under threat of "takings" by the sources, who could have defended in court their rights to use by "first possession." In the case of the struggle over state give-aways of credits from state facilities, the state was challenged in its right to use credits from its own facilities for what it decided was the state's welfare. Since that time, economic development officials have not aggressively pursued the creation of more credits for economic development purposes, in part because potential credits are small but most likely also because they do not want to invite another political controversy. It is interesting to note that the previous Democratic administration was also prepared to offer credits for economic development purposes, but to do so with credits the state retained and revoked from industrial facilities, and only if they were not needed for attaining air quality.

New York State's struggle to meet CAA air quality standards has focused more recently on controversies with "upwind" states whose emissions enter over state borders. Because substantial emissions, particularly of large coal-burning power plants in the Midwest, affect New York State air quality, the state has sued upwind states for, essentially, using air resources within New York State jurisdiction. In other words, the struggle over air use goes on in many arenas, pitting different sets of air users against each other.

NOTES

1. The information provided here on the legal history of property rights in the United States relies to a great extent on Lawler and Parle (1989).

2. Title IV of the 1990 Clean Air Act Amendments.

3. As a policy analyst for the New York State Department of Economic Development, I was part of the development and implementation of the ERC program described here.

4. Proposed Open Market Trading Rule for Ozone (SMOG) Precursors, 8/3/95,

p. 33. *Federal Register* 60 (149) (August 3, 1995): 39668–39694; online via GPO Access waib.access.gpo.gov.

5. Public Hearing Proposal, November/December 1992, "Repeal 6 NYCRR Part 231 and Adopt New 6 NYCRR Part 231 'New Source Review in Nonattainment Areas and Ozone Transport Regions.'" Http://www.dec.state.ny.us/website/dar/reports/part231/text231.pdf.

6. Memo from Thomas Jorling, DEC Commissioner, to Joseph Martens, New York State Governor's Office, August 21, 1992, p. 3, author's files.

7. Letter from Business Council to Thomas Jorling, Commissioner, Department of Environmental Conservation, April 21, 1993, author's files.

8. S-4720–Skelos, "Prohibition of State Retention of Air Emissions Offsets."

9. Letter from EPA to Thomas Jorling, June 22, 1993, author's files.

10. The rationale for the creation of pollution trading systems has been economists' claims that more pollution would be reduced for less money.

11. Such opinions were expressed in the memo from Jorling to the Governor's Office (n. 6, above); memo, Air Management Advisory Committee, Stationary Source Subcommittee to Craig Wilson, April 22, 1993, author's files; Business Council to Jorling (n. 7, above); Thomas Jorling to the Air Management Advisory Committee, February 2, 1993; Department of Economic Development, "Comments of the New York State Department of Economic Development on Proposed 6 NYCRR Part 231 'New Source Review in Nonattainment Areas and Ozone Transport Regions,'" submitted April 22, 1994, author's files. However, earlier versions of New Source performance standard policy were criticized as being favorable to northeastern and midwestern states, which were "trying to slow the growth of the Sunbelt states" (Hahn and Noll, 1983).

12. See, for example, Matthew Wald, "Risk-Shy Utilities Avoid Trading Emission Credits," *New York Times,* January 25, 1993.

13. Raymond Hernandez, "New York Offers Pollution Permits to Lure Companies," *New York Times,* May 19, 1997.

14. Ibid.

15. Ibid.

16. Shannon McCaffrey, *Legislative Gazette: The Weekly Newspaper of New York State Government* 20 (22) (June 2, 1997): 1.

17. Ibid, p. 2.

REFERENCES

Cronin, William. 1983. *Changes in the Land: Indians, Colonists, and the Ecology of New England* (New York: Hill and Wang).

Farrell, Alex, and Terry J. Keating. 2000. "The Globalization of Smoke: Co-Evolution in Science and Governance of a Commons Problem." Presented at Constituting the Commons: Crafting Sustainable Commons in the New Millennium, the Eighth Conference of the International Association for the Study of Common Property, Bloomington, Indiana, May 31–June 4.

Fortmann, Louise. 1995. "Talking Claims: Discursive Strategies in Contesting Property." *World Development* 23 (6): 1053–1063.

Hahn, Robert W., and Roger G. Noll. 1983. "Barriers to Implementing Tradable Air Pollution Permits: Problems of Regulatory Interactions." *Yale Journal on Regulation* 63: 63–91.

Hardin, Garrett. 1968. "Tragedy of the Commons." *Science* 162: 1243–1248.

Hecht, Susanna, and Alexander Cockburn. 1989. *The Fate of the Forest: Developers, Destroyers, and Defenders of the Amazon* (London and New York: Verso).

Lawler, James J., and William V. Parle. 1989. "Expansion of the Public Trust Doctrine in Environmental Law: An Examination of Judicial Policy Making by State Courts." *Social Science Quarterly* 70 (1) (March): 134.

Ostrom, Elinor. 1990. *Governing the Commons: The Evolution of Institutions for Collective Action* (New York: Cambridge University Press).

Peet, Richard, and Michael Watts, eds. 1996. *Liberation Ecologies: Environment, Development, Social Movements* (New York: Routledge).

Peluso, Nancy Lee. 1992. *Rich Forests, Poor People: Resource Control and Resistance in Java* (Berkeley: University of California Press).

Peluso, Nancy Lee. 1996. "Fruit Trees and Family Trees in an Anthropogenic Forest: Ethics of Access, Property Zones and Environmental Change in Indonesia." *Comparative Studies in Society and History* 38 (3) (July): 510–549.

Peluso, Nancy Lee, and Peter Vandergeest. 2001. "Genealogies of the Political Forest and Customary Rights in Indonesia, Malaysia, and Thailand." *Journal of Asian Studies* 60 (3): 761–812.

Peluso, Nancy Lee, and Michael Watts, eds. 2001. *Violent Environments* (Ithaca: Cornell University Press).

Rose, Carol M. 1994. *Property and Persuasion: Essays on the History, Theory, and Rhetoric of Ownership* (Boulder, CO: Westview).

Tarr, Joel. 1996. *The Search for the Ultimate Sink: Urban Pollution in Historical Perspective* (Akron: University of Akron Press).

Vandergeest, Peter. 1995. "Territorialization and State Power in Thailand." *Theory and Society* 24 (3): 385–426.

Vandergeest, Peter, and E. Melanie DuPuis. 1996. Introduction to *Creating the Countryside: The Politics of Rural and Environmental Discourse,* ed. E. Melanie DuPuis and Peter Vandergeest (Philadelphia: Temple University Press).

Yandle, Bruce. 1992. "Escaping Environmental Feudalism." *Harvard Journal of Law and Public Policy* 15 (2): 516–539.

11

Air Pollution in Spain

A "Peripheral" Nation Transforms

Alexander Farrell

Energy and resource issues have become increasingly internationalized over the last several decades, which has changed how societies view the environment in many important ways. Naturally, this has had major effects on what societies do to protect the environment, and thus on environmental quality. This chapter looks at air pollution in Spain over the last half of the twentieth century, emphasizing the 1990s and, in particular, the roles of different levels of government (local, national, and international); the relative importance of energy, economic, and environmental policies; and the role of scientific research. In the telling of this story, overall political trends and macro-economic policy are shown to be far more important to Spanish air pollution policy than any concerns about air pollution itself, whether scientific or economic. Moreover, this study illustrates the important transformation of Spain from a so-called peripheral European nation to a fuller member of the international community.

The internationalization of environmental policy has occurred in part because the variety and scale of human activities have made us de facto managers of the environment at an international and even a global level, and in part because of the globalization of economic activities (Clark and Munn 1986). An important mechanism in the latter effect is the growing international trade, which tends to harmonize environmental standards for products, either toward the standards in the largest markets or the markets with the most stringent requirements (products sold there will be acceptable everywhere) or, increasingly, toward international bodies. Finally, the internationalization of the environment can also be driven by the need for nations to conform to international norms or rules, often connected to international organizations that are beneficial to belong to, such as trade blocs.

However, international approaches to environmental policy have been controversial. They stand accused of imposing inappropriately uniform standards across a wide variety of different environmental, economic, and political situations—what is appropriate for Bilthoven may not be right for Bilbao. They have also been accused of improperly empowering central governments at the expense of local and regional authorities.

Such internationalization is clear in Europe, where multi-lateral agreements on air pollution have been increasing in number (and possibly importance) for over twenty years. The best known is the 1979 Convention on Long-Range Transboundary Air Pollution (LRTAP) within the United Nations Economic Commission for Europe (UN-ECE) (Levy 1994; Wettestad 1997). Activities undertaken under the auspices of the European Union (EU) have been of growing importance in these issues as well (Bennett 1991; Farrell and Keating 1998).

Analyses of these processes have tended to focus on the main actors in northern Europe, especially Germany, Scandinavian countries, and the United Kingdom, which have been identified as either "leaders" or "laggards" in international environmental policy. In an effort to help fill the gap in representation, this chapter examines air pollution in Spain, which is a useful case study for two major reasons. First, Spain is sometimes considered a peripheral European nation, neither located in the heart of Europe nor important economically and politically (Baker et al. 1994; Castells and Ravetz 2001; VanDeveer forthcoming). Studying a "peripheral" European nation in detail is useful because, in fact, most countries in the world are more peripheral than powerful. Second, Spanish politics is very regionalized, and government functions are fairly decentralized, providing the opportunity to explore the meaning of international environmental regimes for this sort of state (in contrast to the highly centralized environmental regimes in northern Europe). This case study may thus be more relevant to other federalized nations.

Previous scholars have tended to be disappointed with environmental policy in Spain, seeming to hope that Spain would be more like the environmental leaders in northern Europe. Antonio LaSpina and Giuseppe Sciortino, for instance, lay out the case for a "Mediterranean Syndrome" that makes it difficult for southern European nations to provide public goods, including environmental quality (LaSpina and Sciortino 1993).

Their syndrome includes a civic culture that sanctions non-cooperative and non-compliant behavior, administrative structures and traditions that lead to weak regulatory enforcement, and legislative politics that are vicious and fragmented. LaSpina and Sciortino argue that this means Mediterranean nations will tend to have many of their domestic environmental policies created in response to external, international forces, while at the international level they will rarely propose or obstruct new environmental policies.

Susana Aguilar-Fernández focuses on the failure of Spain to implement and enforce EU directives, which she blames on a deeply rooted "statist institutional design" and powerful regional governments (Aguilar-Fernández 1994b). Ominously, she argues that these institutions (especially those that shape government-industry relations) are likely to be enduring, creating a barrier to the potential convergence of European environmental policies (Aguilar-Fernández 1994a).

Similarly, Xavier Villot notes that Spain is generally considered a "laggard" in environmental policy but notes that this may be explained by its relatively recent accession to the EU, its relatively low wealth, and the possibility of resentment within Spain to environmental policies designed mostly to respond to problems in northern Europe (e.g., acid rain) (Villot 1997). He emphasizes the role of regional (sub-national) government in environmental policy and finds little coordination between the national and sub-national levels. More seriously, Villot lists a series of factors that bode ill for air quality in Spain, notably: (1) the lack of official interest in the implementation of environmental policies; (2) the strong feeling in industry that environmental protection will make companies uncompetitive and should therefore be paid for by the national government; and (3) recent trends and future predictions for the "out-of-control" transport sector.

The preceding research focuses entirely on the politics and administration of environmental law and on pre-1990 data. This chapter attempts to look more broadly at political and economic forces as potential shapers of air quality and to update research on Spanish environmental policy to include some of the important economic and political changes in the last decade of the twentieth century. The research for this chapter was conducted as part of the Global Environmental Assessment project and consisted of literature reviews and extensive interviews with air pollution experts and policy-makers in Spain and elsewhere in Europe.

Setting the Stage

Air Pollution

Three types of air pollution were important in Spain during the last quarter-century: smoke, sulfur dioxide, and ozone (photochemical smog).

Smoke (or soot) is the traditional pollutant associated with industrialization and the use of coal as an energy source for industry, transportation (rail), and home usage. Smoke is a mixture of solids (ash and unburned coal) and gases (various unburned hydrocarbons). Historically, three approaches to solving the smoke problem have proved necessary: fuel substitution, combustion control, and ash collection. (Tall smokestacks have been used to disperse smoke, reducing local effects.)

In fuel substitution, oil, gas, and electricity replace coal. This switch tends to occur largely for convenience and technological reasons. The new fuels are easier for the users to deal with (e.g., no shoveling), and they enable new and better technologies (including internal combustion engines, turbines, electric lighting, and electronics). An important part of the added convenience of oil, gas, and electricity is that the users find them much cleaner than coal, improving conditions and requiring less work in the home or factory. This situation differs from traditional pollution problems, which generally refer to people other than the user suffering the effects of the pollution. Because users gained the benefits of fuel switching, and because of public pressures to reduce the pollution problems, the switch away from coal as a home and industrial energy source was relatively quick. It occurred in the United States in the 1940s and 1950s, and in most of Western Europe in the 1960s and 1970s. The same process took place in Spain from about 1975 to 1995, notably in the domestic sector as coal-fired central heating was replaced in all major Spanish cities with cleaner fuels.

However, fuel substitution only goes so far in solving the smoke problem, as electricity generation typically becomes the major use of coal and a significant source of smoke. Compared to homes and factories, power plants are few in number and often remote from population centers. However, their large size and the focus of owners on fuel costs enable the second approach, combustion control. Power-plant engineers and operators focused on coal preparation and handling in order to burn all of it and thereby lower costs. This often required expensive, specialized equipment that would pulverize coal to the consistency of talcum powder, enabling complete combustion. This technology is not feasible for small boilers in factories (powering steam engines) or home use, but the improved efficiency more than pays for the cost of capital at power plants, where fuel is the dominant operating expense. Here, as with fuel substitution, the air pollution benefit is something of a side note and somewhat partial—pulverized coal boilers emit virtually no unburned hydrocarbons, but since coals often contain a quarter or more unburnable material (e.g., silicates), ash remains a problem.

The third approach to smoke control, ash collection, is also made easier in large power plants. A large fraction (often more than half) of coal ash falls to the bottom of a coal boiler (bottom ash), where it is readily collected. The ash entrained in the exhaust gas (fly ash) is more difficult to gather, but filter systems (baghouses) and more efficient electrostatic precipitators have been developed. In the United States, fly ash control at power plants was accomplished from the mid-1960s through about 1980, and only a little later in most of Europe, essentially ending the smoke problem.

Acid deposition (e.g., acid rain) was first identified in the late 1960s but was not controlled in Europe until the late 1980s and 1990s. For the most part, acidification results from the deposition of sulfur on sensitive soils and water bodies, changing their chemistry and affecting plants and aquatic ecosystems. Sulfur is a contaminant in some fuels (notably coal) that is transformed into sulfur dioxide (SO_2) during the combustion process. It generally takes several days for the SO_2 to deposit on the ground, so it can travel great distances and lead to a transboundary pollution problem. Acidification has never been much of a problem in Spain because there is relatively little acidifying deposition except in the north, where soils are not very susceptible to acidification. For a long time, however, northern Spain suffered from a somewhat different problem due to the high-sulfur brown coal burned for electric power and industrial uses. The sulfur emissions were so great that plant life was directly assaulted, with emissions stunting growth and killing all vegetation in some areas. In addition, human eyes and lungs were irritated. These effects only occurred relatively near the sources of pollution, making this problem more like the traditional smoke problem and not a transboundary air pollution problem. These problems were never adequately addressed by air pollution policies in Spain but were eventually resolved by fuel switching accomplished for other reasons.

Emissions of SO_2 can be limited by switching away from high-sulfur fuels, by cleaning fuels prior to combustion, or by capturing the SO_2 from exhaust gases.

Ozone (or photochemical smog) is created in sunlight from emissions of hydrocarbons and nitrogen oxides (NOx). Spain is located at the southwestern corner of the continent; hence it has higher average temperatures and higher levels of insolation than northern Europe, leading to higher average temperatures and faster photochemical reactions. This tends to make ozone a worse problem in Spain than in the northern parts of Europe at similar emission levels. Spain's major cities exceed EU threshold values several times a year, especially in the Barcelona area (vanAalst 1998). However, diurnal recirculation over the Iberian peninsula tends to limit the buildup of ozone in urban areas, so photochemical smog is less of a problem in Spanish cities than might be expected but a worse suburban and rural problem. Thus crop and forest damage due to ozone may be some of the most important impacts, rather than human health problems.

Control of ozone is accomplished by reducing the two precursor emissions, hydrocarbons and nitrogen oxides (NOx), especially the latter. All combustion processes produce NOx, so lowering ozone to acceptable levels may require emission controls on power plants, industrial processes, and vehicles. Indeed, in many places, cars and trucks are the largest source of NOx emissions. In Europe, increasingly tighter NOx emission limitations have been imposed on these source categories since the late 1970s; however, the growth of economic activity and especially of vehicle use has offset these reductions to some degree, and photochemical smog remains a serious issue in many parts of Europe.

Most air pollution in Spain is due to Spanish sources, but the country is involved in significant transboundary flows. In 1993, Spanish SO_2 deposition was 237,000 metric tons per year, of which 87 percent is from Spanish sources, while the country exported 840,000 tons, 2.7 times as much it imported. Deposition of NOx was 867,000 metric tons annually, of which 68 percent is from Spanish sources, while exports were 348 tons, 1.27 times the amount it imported. Most transboundary flows are with France, followed by Portugal (OECD 1997, 163).

European Air Pollution Policy

In Europe, air pollution policy exists as a mixture of local, national, and international policies. The pattern of this policy varies greatly across the continent, but it is generally true that local and national air pollution policies were introduced first to deal with noxious odors, smoke, and toxic pollutants. By the 1950s, air pollution laws for at least some these pollutants existed in the United Kingdom, France, Germany, and the Netherlands (Avy 1955; Bennett 1991). Interest in international approaches to controlling air pollution did not emerge until the late 1960s, when researchers in Sweden began to claim (correctly, it turned out) that long-range transport of sulfur oxides (a new pollutant) from England, Germany, and other countries was causing acidifying deposition (acid rain) in Scandinavia.

These concerns led to a lengthy process of research and negotiation under LRTAP, a framework treaty among sovereign nations under which the language of individual *protocols* are developed. Member nations are then free to ratify the protocol or not. The original convention, signed in 1979, acknowledges transboundary air pollution as a problem and states the intention of the parties to reduce the magnitude of the problem but does not commit signatories to anything specific. The first protocol was signed in 1984 and established the European Monitoring and Evaluation Program (EMEP). The knowledge gained by research funded by EMEP has tended to confirm and expand the original Scandinavian claims of the importance of transboundary air pollution and has been absolutely critical to the successful development of subsequent protocols to control pollutants.

In contrast, concerns about local pollution and international trade motivated EU air quality policy, at least until the late 1980s. The EU began as an international trade bloc (the European Community), but that has grown into a more comprehensive supra-national system that has some aspects of a federal system and some aspects of an international regime (Richardson 1996; Baker 1997). In the EU, an elected parliament and national ministers share power with a strong bureaucracy, the European Commission. The principal policy mechanism of the EU is the *directive*, which obligates the member states to change their national legislation so that the outcomes defined in the directive are achieved. However, implementation and enforcement are left largely to national authorities, which has been lax in some cases. The Commission has increasingly brought member states before the European Court of Justice (ECJ), charging failure to implement or enforce EU legislation. However, individuals and non-governmental organizations (NGOs) do not have standing in the ECJ, and the citizen lawsuits seen in the United States are not pursued in Europe.

These twin tracks of international air pollution policy in Europe exhibited several key features. First, the LRTAP protocols have the appearance of forceful rules but actually function in a normative persuasive role (Levy 1994). They generally affirmed pre-existing trends and existing plans in the various signatories, pushing few, if any, nations to emissions controls beyond the expectations of domestic politics. Second, at least until 1988, EU directives nominally about air pollution were essentially designed to harmonize fuel and vehicle standards in order to increase trade and exports and were not centrally about improving the European environment (Boehmer-Christiansen 1989; Dietrich 1996). In contrast to LRTAP, this focus on trade led nations to accept standards that were *more stringent* than domestic laws, although the actual implementation and enforcement also lags (Bennett 1991; Ercmann 1996.) And third, national governments tend to seek common EU environmental standards as a means of protecting domestic industry (Dahl 1995). These features show up in the ways in which air pollution policy in Spain developed over the last thirty years.

Spain to 1990

The overarching theme of recent Spanish history is a recovery from the dictatorship of Francisco Franco (Arango 1995; Coates 1998). The Franco period lasted from the end of the Spanish Civil War in 1939 until the dictator's death in 1975. The root cause of the Spanish Civil War was the Spanish military's fear that the nation would disintegrate into the small, historical nationalities (e.g., Catalonia, Galicia, the Basque Province) that had allied in the fifteenth century and eventually rose to rule an empire, but which never fully integrated into a nation. Franco's regime suppressed these nationalities by banning their language and denying them any local political power.

The first twenty years of Franco's regime were marked by economic stagnation, a virtual end to foreign trade, and, for most of the period, severe political isolation. The regime might have fallen in the mid-1950s were it not for a sudden Cold War alliance with the United States in 1953, bringing both much-needed cash and political credibility. Economic reform did not occur until 1959, when the nation was near collapse. A 1959 Economic Stabilization Plan, more or less forced on Franco, handed over the central planning of the economy from political cronies to Western-educated professionals and led to rapid economic growth with low unemployment. But the nation remained relatively poor and largely centrally planned compared to the rest of Europe. Simultaneously, after the crisis of 1959 forced Franco to loosen his grip on the nation, regional forces became more vocal in their demands for recognition and power.

As elsewhere, economic growth brought increased air pollution, and environmental issues rose on the political agendas in the 1960s and 1970s; air pollution laws or regulations were created in 1961, 1972, 1974, and 1975. These rules focused on the role of the central government but featured weak emission control provisions and few enforcement mechanisms. Nevertheless, they do form the legal basis of current Spanish air quality regulation.

Everything changed in Spain after Franco's death in 1975. Fundamental political issues occupied the national stage almost completely as a new constitution was being written and new, democratic institutions were developed. The regions reasserted themselves in the writing of the constitution (adopted in 1978), which gave broad powers to seventeen Autonomous Communities, especially the historical nationalities. For instance, article 45 handed over authority (competence) for environmental policy from the central government to the regions.

This was a turbulent time for Spain. Democracy was somewhat fragile, solidifying only after masterful and courageous actions by King Juan Carlos to thwart a fascist coup in 1981. Further, these were the oil crisis years and Spain's economy suffered, especially in terms of unemployment, which reached persistent levels of 15 percent to 24 percent in the 1980s. This helped lead to the election of a new Socialist government in 1982, which turned its attention to economic reform and integration with Europe. It started privatizing state-owned firms, eliminating subsidies, and fostering competitive markets.

Two key parts of the 1980s reform of Spain's economy were the expansion of international trade and the accession to the EU. However, there was more to this effort than economic concerns; Spain (especially its elites) felt a very strong urge to "rejoin" Europe and re-establish the country's respectability among the world's nations, leaving the legacy of Franco's dictatorship behind. Thus Spain moved to join Western institutions as soon as possible, starting with the North Atlantic Treaty Organization (NATO) in 1982 and the EU in 1986 and proceeding into the European Monetary Union in 1996. The symbolism of these steps was so important that it is often noted that Spain did not really consider exactly what it was getting into, becoming modern and European was an unquestioned goal. The major impact in terms of air pollution policy was that

Spain was required to adopt (to approximate, in EU jargon) pre-existing EU directives at the time it joined and to continue to adopt subsequent ones, although it would participate in formulating and approving these.

Joining the EU had another consequence that, although essentially economic in nature, arguably had a larger impact on air quality policy—Spain began to receive EU development funds. The most important programs were the European Regional Development Fund and the Cohesion Fund. The regional funds have mostly been used to support industrial modernization, infrastructure development (i.e., telecommunications and transportation, primarily road construction), natural gas infrastructure, research, and some environmental improvements (mostly associated with water quality). The cohesion funds are specifically targeted at infrastructure and environment (emphasizing water quality). These were large infusions of cash. In 1996, for example, Spain received about $1.2 billion (almost 2 percent of its GDP) from the EU, of which 42 percent was spent on road construction, 36 percent on water projects, 12 percent on waste and brownfields, 8 percent on rail upgrades, and 2 percent on afforestation. Air pollution projects were not funded and were even ineligible for cohesion funds.

Given the enormous and fundamental political and economic changes underway in the last quarter of twentieth-century Spain, it is not surprising that just one piece of general scholarship on modern Spain (not counting books and articles that focus on the environment) mentions environmental policy at all. This is a work by Paul Heywood, who notes that "the later 1980s and early 1990s saw peace campaigners and environmental groups begin to make an impact on Spanish politics" (Heywood 1995, 186). He sees a move away from party machine politics and toward interest group politics in Spain, in which the rise of regional parties is seen as part of the response. Heywood also finds that "environmental groups have been able to identify a central issue of concern to many citizens, although the impact of such groups has tended to be limited on account of their fissiparous nature. Prior to the 1993 elections, nineteen such organizations—including groups of anarchist, Marxist, and nationalist provenance—came together to establish Los Verdes (The Greens)." Heywood does not believe this party wields any real power, but it is a political response to the inadequacy of the traditional parties on issues such as environmental protection. This general finding is supported by others—for instance, P. Norton, who finds that "in Spain . . . organized interests are not yet as developed as in some other countries" (Norton 1997). Moreover, water quality, waste disposal, and land degradation tend to be the most important for those in Spain who are interested on environmental issues at all. Thus, new air pollution policies were adopted without domestic pressure for them.

Transformations

In the 1990s, Spain remained a relatively poor member of the EU, with 1995 income per capita only about three-quarters of the EU average, but it experienced rapid growth (OECD 1998). The Spanish economy has a relatively low energy intensity, requiring only 0.19 tons of oil equivalent (toe) per $1,000 of GDP, compared with an average of 0.22 for all European OECD countries and 0.32 for the United States. However, it has a rather high "air pollution intensity," with disproportionately high SO_2 and NOx emissions (UN-ECE Economic and Social Council 1997).

This pattern can be partly explained by looking at fuel consumption. Spain's only domestic energy resources are low-grade (i.e., low heat content and high sulfur content) coal deposits located in the northern part of the country. This fuel is about 2 percent sulfur and sometimes as contains as much as 5 percent, very high levels compared to other fuels. It is also very uneconomical, costing approximately six times world coal prices. However, to maintain employment, the Spanish coal sector was supported from the 1960s through the 1980s by government policies, including direct subsidies (up to 0.3 percent of GDP), and requirements that the Spanish power sector use domestic coal. At the same time, however, government did not control emissions.

However, since 1990, energy and economic policies have tended to induce fuel switching and thus decrease Spanish air pollution. This process started with the publication of a *National Energy Plan* that focused on reducing consumption of expensive, domestic coal. This plan has been carried out over the last decade, which has seen deep cuts in the Spanish coal sector. In 1996 a new moderate-right government accelerated the shift away from central planning and government control and toward a market-based economy that was begun in 1982. This led to privatization and modernization in the refining, coal-mining, natural gas, and electricity sectors, which has further shrunk the Spanish coal industry. Further, the coal subsidies conflict with recent EU legislation, providing international pressure to reduce or eliminate them.

In comparison, natural gas provides a relatively small fraction of energy in Spain (7 percent, compared to 22 percent on average in the EU), and prices are high (about 20 percent higher than the average in the EU for electricity generation). However, EU funding has allowed Spain to increase natural gas transmission capacity (i.e., pipelines and port facilities) in the country. This effort, combined with the prospects of increased price competition between fuels and between companies in the energy sector and the availability of efficient gas generation technologies, has led to greater use of natural gas for electricity generation in Spain, reducing SO_2 emissions.

In contrast, NOx emissions have not decreased. The transportation sector is responsible for about 60 percent of NOx emissions in Spain, although this may be an underestimate (OECD 1997, 143). Several structural factors will tend to increase automobile and truck use in Spain in the future. In the mid-1990s the government introduced incentives for consumers to purchase cars, and changes to land use law will make it easier to zone rural land for urban uses (OECD 1998, 79). Further, the Spanish national government has given a preference to road-building programs over mass transit. These trends are consistent with observations that motorized transportation is rising consistently all over the world and tends to rise most quickly (in percentage terms) in poorer nations (Dargay and Gately 1997; Schafer and Victor 1997). Most analysts see little chance of stopping the trend toward greater mobility, especially through reducing the affordability of fuel, since the increase in price needed to reduce the demand for automobile driving is probably not politically feasible (JanKoopman 1997). Thus all the signs point toward especially rapid increases in automobile usage in Spain, which will tend to increase NOx emissions. Fewer data are available on hydrocarbon emissions, but these tend to come predominantly from the transportation sector. Taken together, these trends will likely worsen ozone pollution in Spain.

Importantly, experience has shown that the establishment of standards for new-vehicle tailpipe emissions is insufficient to ensure emissions reductions; generally, an in-use emissions inspection program is also required to ensure that poor maintenance, tampering, or simple wear and tear does not degrade the fleet's in-place emissions control technologies (Beaton et al. 1995; National Research Council 2002). It does not appear that inspection programs are in place in Spain.

Although there is not sufficient room here to explore the issue in depth, there is considerable evidence that air pollution research in Spain has been heavily supported and influenced by international organizations, in particular the EMEP and various EU bodies. Before 1980, there is virtually no research on air quality in Spain published in English (all LRTAP and EU documents are published in English, as well as other languages) and apparently none in Spanish either. Scientific papers and various reports that appear subsequently have two main features: they report on activities (e.g., data collection) that were begun after Franco's death, and they are virtually all funded by the EMEP or the EU. Further, interviews with Spanish researchers indicated that in the 1980s and 1990s, Spanish political leaders tended to become interested in environmental issues in large part due to their participation in LRTAP and EU activities (e.g., negotiations on policy). As with legislation, air pollution research in Spain increased in the 1990s, but it appears to have been driven by international (European), not domestic, interests and funding.

In 1997 the OECD noted that some steps had been taken toward the development of a coherent framework for environmental policy in Spain, that the country has moved to implement EU directives and other international requirements, and that the central government has supported consultative processes with many different groups interested in environmental policy (OECD 1997). However, officials interviewed for this research felt that Spain would never sign such an agreement if it did not think that it could honor the commitment at little or no cost. In many cases, it seems, that means the planned reduction would have to fit existing expectations of emissions in the future, mostly because of the expectation that cheap (and clean) natural gas would be substituted for expensive (and dirty) domestic coal in the power sector. This is a familiar pattern, occurring in the United Kingdom as well (Boehmer-Christiansen and Skea 1991).

The OECD also found deficiencies in the Spanish air quality management program, including overly lax standards, insufficient local capacity for implementing regulations, lax enforcement, and a lack of integration between environmental and other policies (e.g., industrial and transportation). Perhaps most fundamentally, this report finds a severe lack of air quality monitoring data, making it very difficult to understand what air pollution problems exist in Spain and how to characterize them.

Interestingly, the OECD report authors assume the normative position that Spain needs to converge with the rest of the EU in environmental protection (e.g., adopt identical environmental standards), just as it has begun to converge economically. Further, they assume that this convergence should be uniform across the nation, disallowing significant differences between the regions. The primary recommendation is that Spain must "effectively and efficiently implement environmental policies at the central government level." This assumption ignores potential differences in the need for environmental protection in different places, as well as more fundamental differences about politics and how the environment is viewed.

For instance, consider the implementation of the 1995 Access to Environmental Protection Act, which guarantees that all citizens should have access to the environmental information held by public authorities. Regions that have traditionally had air pollution problems and thus developed local government bodies to deal with them are implementing the new requirements with little problem, whereas those that have not dealt much with air pollution in the past do not appear to be implementing the law at all. It is not clear that regions without air pollution problems would serve their citizens by implementing an information program, and even less clear that this role should be given to the central government.

The roles of regional, national, and international governments in Spanish environmental policy became more complex in the 1990s. One step toward centralization was the establishment of a national environmental ministry in 1997, moving the regulators from various scattered locations into a single administrative body. Moreover, bodies like the EU and OECD (as seen above) tend to view nation-states as the essential political building block. Crispin Coates makes a good case for the argument that by joining the EU, Spain's strongest regions (the Basque country, Catalonia, and Galicia) lost power relative to the national government and relative to poorer regions in the south (Coates 1998, 265). This is partly because the regions don't really have strong relations with one another, mostly interacting through the central government. Francesc Morata sees this as a conundrum, arguing that "the ceding of [national] sovereignty to the EC has resulted in an implicit transfer of power to the central government at the expense of the regions. At the same time, these have assumed an essential role in the implementation of a large number of Community policies" (Morata 1995).

This conundrum extends to EU policies as well. For instance, the economic harmonization required for European monetary union forced the EU to develop linkages to all sub-national jurisdictions. Further, the Maastricht Treaty of European Union created a Council of the Regions (currently headed by the leader of the Catalan regional party), although its powers are quite limited. Another example is the Community Support

Frameworks, institutional subsidy programs of the EU that have benefited the regions substantially. More fundamentally, the general trend toward "subsidiarity" gives credibility to sub-national entities and institutionalizes the debate on the role of sub-national entities in the EU (Axelrod 1994; Farber 1997). It is hard to see an end to this debate or resolution of this conundrum; tensions between local and central governments may well be a permanent feature of politics, and therefore of air pollution policy (Jones and Keating 1995; Anonymous 1996; 1997). Perhaps the only obvious outcome is that Spain will see more government in this area.

Discussion

This research re-affirms some earlier analysis of Spanish environmental policy, such as that regarding the role of pan-European policies in driving domestic Spanish policy (if not actually changing behavior or air quality). However, some of the previous political analysis seems to be growing outdated. For instance, the "statist institutional design" that Aguilar-Fernández believed was deeply rooted in Spanish politics and would serve as a barrier to convergence of Spanish and European environmental policies seems to have at least started to change. The 1995 law on the disclosure of environmental information is one example of transformation; advances of regional power through the EU is another.

In addition, concerns that the relationship between industry and government would remain static and provide an additional barrier to this convergence do not seem to be supported by the evidence of the globalization of Spain's economy in the 1990s. Spanish industry has increasingly participated in air pollution research with both national and regional organizations. More important, Spanish firms often belong to pan-European trade groups that lobby and otherwise intervene in EU policy-making, largely to harmonize standards (i.e., to converge) so as to facilitate trade. Further, as the barriers to capital flow into Spain have come down and privatization has increased, many large Spanish firms have been acquired by (or merged with) transnational firms, such as the automaker SEAT, which is now owned by Volkswagen. This pattern of globalization, combined with the weakness of the central government's role in enforcing environmental regulation, makes Spain's past totalitarian government and statist economy seem less and less relevant

There seems to be some support for some aspects of the "Mediterranean Syndrome," including non-compliant behavior (due to poor enforcement of environmental laws) and the "follower" status in creating international environmental policy. However, Spanish politics has started to become more issue-oriented and less fragmented by parties. Moreover, it is not clear that the Mediterranean Syndrome can withstand the increasing trade and political linkages between Spain and the rest of the EU, which will tend to bring pressures for greater compliance with environmental policies.

Some of Villot's more recent analysis stands up better, notably the emphasis on regional governments and on the growth of transportation-related air pollution. However, lack of official interest in the environment and the belief by industry that government intervention is needed are both changing.

Overall, politically, it seems that Spain has achieved more change and become more like northern European countries than previous analysts had thought likely. This peripheral EU nation became more like a core country.

This research also provides further evidence for the importance of energy policies at both the domestic and international levels with regard to environmental policy and quality. And it shows how economic (i.e., development) policies can have a similarly important role. In addition, the endogenous movement away from (domestic) coal toward (imported) natural gas has been a major factor in improving air quality in industrializing economies. In fact, it appears that these forces have had a greater influence on air quality in Spain in the 1980s and 1990s than all specific environmental policies put together.

It is interesting to note how the importance of energy policy is demonstrated in the Maastricht Treaty of European Union. The relevant article (art. 130s) provided the EU with substantially more power over member states (by changing the voting rules from unanimity to qualified majority) in all areas of environmental policy save three: fiscal policy, land use, and energy.

There are four reasons why politicians are especially concerned about energy policy, and they are generally related to the fact that improvements in environmental protection generally induce a shift away from the only domestic energy resource in many nations—coal. First, reducing coal use puts miners out of work, creating a real political and economic problem for any government that does this. Second, cleaner energy supplies (oil and gas) tend to be imported, at least in part, in contrast to coal, which is a domestic resource for many countries. Thus switching away from coal affects a nation's trade balance and security concerns. The third reason is that energy use forecasts are closely tied to forecasts of future economic growth in many countries, and governments have a difficult time predicting any economic future except a rosy one, limiting the range of energy consumption scenarios that can be considered. The fourth reason is that environmental concerns can produce controversies over issues such as nuclear power, conservation, and renewables.

From the evidence gathered in this research, it appears that Spain has never been very interested in acid rain assessments or in making emission reductions to support European acid rain goals in any way other than opportunistically. That is, Spanish reductions in sulfur dioxide appear to be side benefits of either efforts to reduce local pollution problems, motivated by domestic politics, or fuel switching away from expensive, dirty (but domestic) coal in the electricity sector. Indeed, the Spanish interviewees pointed to domestic impacts in northern Spain as the rationale for all SO_2 emissions reductions. Government officials were sometimes quick to voice support for European efforts but just as quick to voice concerns about the burden emissions reduction places on a relatively poor nation such as Spain, often suggesting patience would be required.

Similarly, Spain has ratified several LRTAP protocols although the national government has little means of enforcing their provisions through environmental laws and the convention does not deal with sub-national governments. Nonetheless, the energy policies being developed in the late 1980s and early 1990s led the Spanish government to realize that they could meet these commitments at no cost (indeed, the substitution away from expensive domestic coal would *save* money).

It is interesting to note, however, that much of the analysis of Spanish environmental policy reviewed here contains an assumption that Spanish environmental policies *should* converge with "European policies." Generally, by "European policies" is meant policies of the European Union, which tend to be set by negotiations between power countries, in the role of environmental leaders, and laggards. In the case of air pollution, these policies tend to refer to emission levels or rates, not environmental effects. However, since different parts of Europe have different physical characteristics, different emission levels may not have equivalent environmental effects. This is generally ignored by a focus on emissions. Further, Spanish air quality policy *has* converged with the LRTAP protocols—perhaps for reasons different from those in northern Europe and perhaps opportunistically—and any theory of domestic and international environmental policy must account for this phenomenon.

REFERENCES

Aguilar-Fernández, S. 1994a. "Convergence in Environmental Policy? The Resilience of National Institutional Designs in Spain and Germany." *Journal of Public Policy* 14: 39–56.

————. 1994b. "Spanish Pollution Control Policy and the Challenge of the European Union." In *Protecting the Periphery: Environmental Policy in Peripheral Regions of the European Union,* ed. S. Baker, K. Milton, and S. Yearly, pp. 102–117. Portland, OR: Frank Cass.

Anonymous. 1996. "Spain's Regions: Me, Too." *The Economist* 16: 55, 56.

————. 1997. "Jordi Pujol: Regionalism, Far from Being Outdated, Is New and Dynamic." *IPI Report,* June/July: 9.

Arango, E. R. 1995. *Spain: Democracy Regained.* Boulder, CO: Westview Press.

Avy, A. P. 1955. "Air Pollution by Dust, Smoke, and Vapors." In *Problems and Control of Air Pollution: Proceedings of the First International Congress on Air Pollution,* ed. F. C. Mallette, pp. 264–272. New York: Reinhold.

Axelrod, R. S. 1994. "Subsidiarity and Environmental Policy in the European Community." *International Environmental Affairs* 6 (2): 115–132.

Baker, R., ed. 1997. *Environmental Law and Policy in the European Union and the United States.* Westport, CT: Praeger.

Baker, S., K. Milton, and S. Yearly, eds. 1994. *Protecting the Periphery: Environmental Policy in Peripheral Regions of the European Union.* Portland, OR: Frank Cass.

Beaton, S., G. Bishop, Y. Zhang, L. Ashbaugh, D. Lawson, and D. Stedman. 1995. "On-Road Vehicle Emissions: Regulations, Costs, and Benefits." *Science* 268: 991–993.

Bennett, G., ed. 1991. *Air Pollution Control in the European Community: Implementation of the EC Directives in the Twelve Member States.* International Environmental Law and Policy Series. Boston: Wolter Kluwer Academic Publishers.

Boehmer-Christiansen, S. A. 1989. "Vehicle Emission Regulation in Europe—The Demise of Lean-Burn Engines, the Polluter Pays Principle . . . and the Small Car?" *Energy and Environment* 1 (1): 1–25.

Boehmer-Christiansen, S., and J. Skea. 1991. *Acid Politics: Environmental and Energy Policies in Britain and Germany.* New York: Belhaven Press.

Castells, N., and J. Ravetz. 2001. "Science and Policy in International Environmental Agreements: Lessons from the European Experience on Transboundary Air

Pollution." *International Environmental Agreements: Politics, Law and Economics* 1: 405–425.

Clark, W., and R. Munn, eds. 1986. *Sustainable Development of the Biosphere.* New York: Cambridge University Press.

Coates, C. 1998. "Spanish Regionalism and the European Union." *Parliamentary Affairs* 51 (2): 259.

Dahl, A. 1995. "Environmental Actors and European Integration." *International Environmental Affairs* 7 (4): 299–320.

Dargay, J., and D. Gately. 1997. "Vehicle Ownership to 2015: Implications for Energy Use and Emissions." *Energy Policy* 25 (14–15): 1121–1127.

Dietrich, W. F. 1996. "Harmonization of Automobile Emission Standards under International Trade Agreements: Lessons from the European Union Applied to the WTO and the NAFTA." *William and Mary Environmental Law and Policy Review* 20: 175–221.

Ercmann, S. 1996. "Enforcement of Environmental Law in United States and European Law: Realities and Expectations." *Environmental Law* 26: 1213–1239.

Farber, D. A. 1997. "Environmental Federalism in a Global Economy." *Virginia Law Review* 83: 1283–1319.

Farrell, A. E., and T. J. Keating. 1998. "Multi-Jurisdictional Air Pollution Assessment: A Comparison of the Eastern United States and Western Europe." Cambridge, Massachusetts, Belfer Center for Science and International Affairs, Harvard University, GEA Working Paper 74.

Heywood, P. 1995. *The Government and Politics of Spain.* New York: St. Martin's Press.

JanKoopman, K. 1997. "Long-Term Challenges for Inland Transport in the European Union: 1977–2010." *Energy Policy* 25 (14–15): 1151–1161.

Jones, B., and M. Keating, eds. 1995. *The European Union and the Regions.* Oxford: Clarendon Press.

LaSpina, A., and G. Sciortino. 1993. "Common Agenda, Southern Rules: European Integration and Environmental Change in the Mediterranean States." In *European Integration and Environmental Policy,* ed. J. D. Liefferink, P. D. Lowe, and A. P. J. Mol, pp. 215–236. New York: Halsted Press.

Levy, M. A. 1994. "European Acid Rain: The Power of Tote-Board Diplomacy." In *Institutions for the Earth: Sources of Effective International Environmental Protection,* ed. P. M. Haas, R. O. Keohane, and M. A. Levy, pp. 75–132. Cambridge, MA: MIT Press.

Morata, F. 1995. "Spanish Regions in the European Community." In *The European Union and the Regions,* ed. B. Jones and M. Keating. London: Clarendon.

National Research Council. 2002. *Evaluating Vehicle Emissions Inspection and Maintenance Programs.* Washington, DC: National Academy of Science.

Norton, P. 1997. "Conclusion: Stronger Links, Weaker Support." *Parliamentary Affairs* 50 (3): 468–475.

Organization for Economic Cooperation and Development (OECD). 1997. *OECD Environmental Performance Reviews—SPAIN.* Paris: OECD.

———. 1998. *OECD Economic Surveys—SPAIN.* Paris: OECD.

Richardson, J. J., ed. 1996. *European Union: Power and Policy-Making.* New York: Routledge.

Schafer, A., and D. Victor. 1997. "The Past and Future of Global Mobility." *Scientific American,* October: 58–61.

UN-ECE Economic and Social Council. 1997. *Present State of Emission Data and Emission Database.* Geneva, Switzerland, United Nations Economic Commission for Europe. EB.AIR/GE.1/1997/3, June 24: 29.

vanAalst, R. M. 1998. *Topic Update Report 1997.* Bilthoven, Netherlands, European Topic Center—Air Quality, January.

VanDeveer, S. D. forthcoming. "European Politics with a Scientific Face: Framing, National Participation, and Capacity in LRTAP." In *The Design of Environmental Assessments,* ed. A. Farrell and J. Jaeger.

Villot, X. L. 1997. "Spain: Fast Growth in CO_2 Emissions." In *Cases in Climate Change Policy: Political Reality in the European Union,* ed. U. Collier and R. Loftstedt, pp. 147–164. London: Earthscan Publishers, Ltd.

Wettestad, J. 1997. "Acid Lessons? LRTAP Implementation and Effectiveness." *Global Environmental Change* 7 (3): 235–249.

12

Clearing the Air and Breathing Freely
The Health Politics of Air Pollution and Asthma

*Phil Brown, Stephen Zavestoski, Brian Mayer,
Theo Luebke, Joshua Mandelbaum,
and Sabrina McCormick*

The current asthma epidemic is one of the most important public health challenges. The increasing prevalence of asthma has led to much community organizing, especially among environmental justice groups. This epidemic is also a source of much contention among scientists, as well as between government regulators and corporate interests. The debate around the linkage of air pollution to the causation and exacerbation of asthma is set within a larger controversy regarding the science and politics of regulating air pollution in general. Scientists who study air quality are influenced both by regulatory disputes and by the growing activism around environmental causes of asthma. Air quality researchers have become more accessible to the environmental justice activists who are involved with asthma issues because of the growing debates around potential environmental links between air pollution and asthma.

Environmental justice approaches began as an effort to reduce toxic exposures that overly affected people of color and poor people. Environmental justice has grown to include racial and class disparities across a wide variety of societal structures and institutions, such as transportation and community development (Bullard 1994; Roberts and Toffolon-Weiss 2001).

This chapter examines the growing debate around environmental causes of asthma in the context of federal regulatory disputes, scientific controversy, and environmental justice activism. We argue that a multifaceted form of social discovery of the effect of air pollution on asthma has resulted from multi-partner and multi-organizational approaches and from intersectoral policy that deals with social inequality and environmental justice. More specifically, the multi-partner and multi-organizational component means that scientists, activists, health voluntary organizations, and some government agencies and officials have identified various elements of this asthma and air pollution connection. They have worked through a variety of collaborations and alliances to tackle these issues using a variety of strategies and tactics, including demonstrations and other direct action, lobbying and advocacy, lay-professional collaborative research, support for increased scientific research, and community empowerment through building community organization. The intersectoral nature of this action means that the actors have worked across different sectors of environmental regulation, public health, health services, housing, transportation, and community development.

As a result of the multi-partner, multi-organizational, and intersectoral policy approach, the regulatory disputes, scientific controversy, and environmental justice activism concerning asthma are inseparable. This interlinked science/policy/activism axis is emblematic of many other health-related matters, especially for what we term *contested illnesses*. Contested illnesses are illnesses that involve major scientific disputes and extensive public debates over environmental causes. They therefore include cancers; reproductive, immunological, and neurological disorders stemming from toxic waste sites; diseases from nuclear power and weapons; asthma and pulmonary diseases from air pollution; and diseases from military exposure to toxics.

First we present a brief introduction to the new asthma epidemic and the debates over potential causes and triggers of asthma. Following that, the first section explores the role of activist groups in discovering the increased rates of asthma in their communities and in framing asthma as a social and environmental issue. To address the social and environmental causes of asthma, these activist groups must sort out the current scientific controversies surrounding air quality research. The second section provides an overview of the current knowledge base regarding the link between air pollution and asthma and the controversies in science. Despite the strength of the scientific evidence linking air pollution to several negative health outcomes, there is much debate at the federal level over new regulations to address the new asthma epidemic. The third section situates the scientific knowledge in the regulatory debate and discusses the many challenges to the air quality researchers responsible for producing much of the science linking air pollution and health. The final section addresses the implications of the scientific and regulatory controversies over linking air pollution to increases in asthma. One important development has been the growth of community-based participatory research (CBPR) as an avenue for creating new scientific knowledge that incorporates local and professional knowledge. Through this process, the environmental justice activist groups are both creating and utilizing science in innovative new ways that allow them to make asthma a more prominent issue. We conclude with some theoretical contributions on the development of alliances between activists and scientists in the CBPR process and how these collaborations lead to new research strategies and innovations.

The New Asthma Epidemic

The number of individuals with asthma in the United States grew 75 percent between 1980 and 1994, making asthma one of the few diseases whose incidence and death rates continue to increase, despite broad-based medical advances in control and treatment (Pew Environmental Health Commission 2000). In the same period, hospitalizations for asthma rose 20 percent, with asthma responsible for 1.8 million emergency room visits in 1995. The estimated cost to society from asthma is greater than $11 billion a year (Pew Environmental Health Commission 2000). Mortality rates from asthma, which have risen across populations in the last twenty-five years, are higher for blacks than for whites. If current trends continue, deaths from asthma are expected to double to over ten thousand a year by 2020, out of a projected twenty-nine million people with asthma. What makes these figures even more notable is the contrast with the marked declines seen in asthma rates from 1960 to 1977 (Pew Environmental Health Commission 2000).

While the incidence and prevalence of asthma have increased dramatically in all segments of the U.S. population over the last twenty years, the effects on children are particularly staggering. Asthma is the number-one chronic childhood disease in the nation. The most rapid increase in asthma sufferers from 1980 to 1994 was among children under the age of four, at 160 percent. Among children ages five to fourteen, asthma sufferers increased by 74 percent (Pew Environmental Health Commission 2000).

In many low-income urban areas, especially minority communities, rates are significantly higher than the national average. While national prevalence of childhood asthma in 1997 overall was 7.8 percent for one- to six-year-olds and 13.6 percent for six- to sixteen-year-olds, black children and poor children were 15 to 20 percent more likely than average to have asthma (National Health Interview Survey 1997). Urban areas are particularly hard hit, with asthma hospitalization rates in New York City five times higher for minorities than non-minorities.

In response to these increases, asthma has become a public health priority for both medical and public health professionals and institutions, as well as for those affected by it. Medical and public health professionals and institutions have expanded treatment and prevention efforts. Some environmental groups and community activists have also made asthma a key focus. In several locales, coalitions have formed that include activist groups, academic research centers, health providers, public health professionals, and even local and state public health agencies.

Among the public health, scientific, governmental, and activist communities involved, there is widespread agreement that we do not know the causes of asthma but that a variety of environmental factors trigger asthma attacks. Most of these factors are part of the indoor environment, including animal dander, cockroach infestation, tobacco smoke, mold, and other allergens. The primary outdoor factor is air pollution, in the form of particulates, especially $PM_{2.5}$ (particles under 2.5 microns in diameter, which penetrate deeper into the lungs and are linked to asthma and other chronic respiratory symptoms, especially among children and the elderly).

Methods and Data

We focus on the activist-scientist collaborations of two community environmental justice organizations and their academic partners, Alternatives for Community and Environment (ACE) in Boston's Roxbury neighborhood and the Harvard University and Boston University Schools of Public Health, and West Harlem Environmental Action (WE ACT) and the Columbia University School of Public Health, wherein both partnerships organize around environmental factors in asthma and respiratory health as part of a broader program. We selected ACE and WE ACT because they are two of the country's leading community-based environmental justice groups that have a focus on asthma. Our methods include content analysis of government documents and scientific literature in medical, public health, and epidemiological journals; print media analysis; fourteen ethnographic observations of ACE and two of WE ACT; and nineteen interviews with ACE and WE ACT staff, public health practitioners, prominent air particulate researchers, and government officials. Unreferenced quotes and data come from our interviews and observations.

Environmental Justice and Asthma

Environmental justice organizations are finding asthma to be an excellent vehicle for addressing social and environmental hazards in their communities. Sources of air pollution such as automobile traffic, industrial emissions, bus depots, and waste storage facilities are predominantly located in poor and minority communities. Environmental justice organizations, with their focus on eliminating the disproportionate burden of environmental and social hazards in such communities, are capable of identifying the increased rates of asthma in their communities and linking those to the environmental hazards. Through teachers, families, and friends, these activists have been made aware of the sharp increase in childhood asthma rates, and they have rallied behind childhood asthma as a key example of the disproportionate burden of environmental health risks borne by their communities. This community realization has been most pronounced in poor urban areas with large minority populations. Environmental justice ideas circulating in many of these communities prompted people to consider asthma as another component of unequal environmental burden.

Because asthma is primarily a childhood disease, teachers and clinic workers were crucial in recognizing what appeared to be abnormally high rates of asthma. Teachers noticed a large number of their students using inhalers, coupled with high absence rates of children with asthma. Numerous asthma advocates and clinicians note that in some urban areas it is possible to find almost half a classroom suffering from asthma. Indeed, asthma accounted for over ten million missed school days nationally in 1995 alone, constituting the number-one reason for school absenteeism (Pew Environmental Health Commission 2000).

Health voluntary organizations play a key facilitative role in improving community environmental health. Medical and epidemiological knowledge is bolstered by research from the American Lung Association (ALA) and American Cancer Society (ACS), which support studies of air pollution and morbidity and mortality. While the ACS is not interested in asthma, their interest in lung cancer enables some relevant research support. The ALA specifically takes a strong stance on environmental factors in disease, especially air pollution (ALA 1996). These health voluntaries may seem to be part of the medical and scientific discovery, but the public education and advocacy work of these groups makes them a part of the public discovery process.

The activist groups included in our study, Alternatives for Community and Environment (ACE) and West Harlem Environmental Action (WE ACT), are two of the leading organizations in environmental organizing around asthma. ACE began in 1993 as an environmental justice organization based in the Roxbury-Dorchester area of Boston and has since become nationally recognized for its work. The organization is also active on issues involving brownfield cleanups, solid waste facilities, incinerators, and parking garages. ACE provides help from lawyers, public health professionals, and environmental consultants to other groups in Boston and, through the Massachusetts Environmental Justice Network, to groups around the state.

WE ACT was founded in 1988 in response to environmental threats to the community created by the mismanagement of the North River Sewage Treatment Plant and the construction of a sixth bus depot in northern Manhattan. WE ACT quickly evolved into an environmental justice organization with the goal of working to improve environmental protection and public health in the predominantly African-American and Latino communities of northern Manhattan.

As environmental justice organizations, ACE and WE ACT are influenced by the legacy of the civil rights movement and community organizing in the Saul Alinsky model. As a WE ACT staffer noted:

> I think one of the things that the environmental justice movement has learned from the civil rights movement is that . . . environmental degradation in communities like a place like northern Manhattan is linked in many ways to people's construct of race and quality of life and racism. You've got to fight that on many different fronts.

This model of organizing illustrates how ACE, as primarily an environmental and social justice activist organization, began to focus their efforts on asthma, a mainstream health issue. ACE's decision to focus its efforts on asthma came about through more than a year of talking with community residents. As one organizer recalled, ACE had expected at first to focus on issues such as vacant lots, but residents quickly established asthma as the number-one priority:

> And the one thing, the first thing that ever came out of their mouth was asthma. I mean, their mother was suffering from it, or their sister can't breathe or, you know, they got their inhaler but they're still suffering from asthma.

Like the public health professionals referred to above, ACE realizes that to tackle asthma requires addressing housing, transportation, community investment patterns, access to health care, pollution sources, and sanitation, as well as health education. "Everything we do is about asthma," said the same organizer. "Transportation is about asthma, development's about asthma."

ACE's conception of empowerment and education starts with community involvement in setting the organizational agenda and extends to the level of pressing government for change. At the micro level, this begins with people becoming involved in problem detection and small-scale actions. As part of a campaign to reduce air pollution in their neighborhoods, residents identified idling trucks and buses as a major source of particulate irritants. Working with ACE, community youth organized an anti-idling march and began giving idling buses and trucks educational fliers, disguised as parking tickets, that explained the health effects of diesel exhaust.

A key component of ACE's education and empowerment efforts is reflected in the Roxbury Environmental Empowerment Project (REEP). REEP teaches classes in local schools, hosts environmental justice conferences, and facilitates youth empowerment through its intern program. Classes designed to educate students about environmental justice use asthma as a focal issue. ACE staffers guide students through the process of building self-awareness of their community and in defining concepts and connections of environmental justice and correlations between physical conditions and health, especially asthma. Students, many of whom suffer from asthma, review both the biological mechanisms of asthma, through hands-on activities, and the underlying triggers of asthma attacks and high asthma rates (Loh and Sugerman-Brozan 2002).

WE ACT's Healthy Home Healthy Child campaign reflects a similar community empowerment approach to environmental justice issues. WE ACT works to address a broad range of issues and does not attempt to separate environmental issues from each other or from the community context. The Healthy Home Healthy Child campaign, developed in partnership with the Columbia Center for Children's Environmental Health, works to educate the community on a variety of risk factors including cigarettes, lead poisoning, drugs and alcohol, air pollution, garbage, pesticides, and nutrition. Educational materials, translated both from English into Spanish and from medical jargon into lay language, inform residents about the effects of risk factors and actions they can take to alleviate or minimize those effects (Evans et al. 2000). In the case of air pollution, one of the actions that residents can take is to contact WE ACT and become involved in their clean air campaign. However, WE ACT believes that focusing solely on air pollution can be a disservice to the community, and hence they address all the issues raised in the Healthy Home campaign. As with ACE's experience in identifying community issues, WE ACT's Healthy Home Healthy Child campaign began by focusing on specific asthma triggers but soon expanded to include residents' key concerns, such as drugs, alcohol, and garbage.

Scientific Controversy over Environmental Factors in Asthma

Activist groups' framing of environmental factors in asthma is situated in the medical and scientific controversy over the broader link between air pollution and health. Through their work on addressing environmental causes of asthma, these groups must address a long history of scientific air particulate research. The research on environmental causes and triggers of asthma within the larger literature on air quality is, however, a contested field. Activist groups often understand that the scientific process is conservative and time-consuming, and that there will always be political opponents to doing good science in a contested area. They understand that air pollution research has had a long history of controversy. Mary Amdur, a leading researcher in the 1950s, was fired from her university position for pursuing health effects research. Lester Lave and Eugene Seskin faced corporate attempts to discredit their work in the 1970s, and Douglas Dockery, Jack Spengler, and Richard Wilson faced similar challenges in the 1990s (Davis 2002: 75–77, 104–6, 120–22).

Scientific research tends to focus on health endpoints other than asthma because of several difficulties in measuring an increase in asthma (Pew Environmental Health Commission 2000). First, medical and public health science linking air pollution to asthma is hindered by a lack of good surveillance data. This lack of information feeds the debate around whether air pollution causes new cases of asthma or simply exacerbates current cases. This second difficulty in conducting environmental health research on asthma also leads to debate over the reality of the asthma epidemic. Finally, there are clear links between sources of indoor air pollution (i.e., mold, animal dander, or dust) and asthma exacerbation, but little evidence links sources of outdoor air pollution and asthma. Public health interventions are more likely to address indoor sources of pollution that are relatively easy to identify and remediate. The combination of these difficulties has led to a paucity of research on outdoor sources of air pollution and asthma. There is, however, a much more developed body of research on the relationship between particulate matter and health.

The research on the relationship between particulate matter and health has been at the center of much environmental health research but is also the focus of scientific controversy and regulatory debate. Current scientific thinking on particulates stems from the history of major air contamination crises. The association between air pollution and asthma was established as early as 1948, when 88 percent of asthmatics in Donora, Pennsylvania, had asthmatic exacerbations during a severe pollution episode (Amdur 1996). Thousands of deaths during the "London fog" of 1952, when particles reached 2,800 grams per cubic meter (a fourteen-hundred-fold increase over the EPA's current recommended limit), provided additional evidence (Wilson 1996). The exceptional nature of those episodes led scientists to believe there was a high threshold value of 500 g/m^3 for particulate-induced health effects. Yet mounting evidence indicated that a threshold does not exist for exposure to particulate matter. More recent research shows that, across various studies, the percentage of death from particulates increased from 5 to 16 percent (average = 8 percent) for every 100 g/m^3 increase (Schwartz 2000). Douglas Dockery's six-city study (Dockery et al. 1993) provided powerful longitudinal evidence of particulates' responsibility for pulmonary morbidity and mortality, and in 1997, the EPA established a new standard for smaller particles, $PM_{2.5}$, but did not implement it because of a court order.

Particulate researchers presented strong evidence in support of the new $PM_{2.5}$ standard, in part to counter attempts to halt enforcement through criticisms of scientific methods and findings. Scientists showed that cardiovascular hospitalization did not change when controlling for pollutants other than small particles (SO_2, CO, and ozone). They established that the dose-response curve is linear, without a threshold (Schwartz 2000). In response to objections that it would be impossible to know which types of particulates to regulate, researchers disaggregated sources of twenty-five substances and determined that all were associated with mortality (Schwartz 2000).

Critics also claimed that there was no plausible biological mechanism by which particulates could kill people. Joel Schwartz (1993) responded by pointing out that arrhythmia and myocardial infarction were the major causes of sudden death, and further, that low heart rate variability was the major risk factor in arrhythmia. Using heart monitors, researchers found people's heart rate variability was reduced as PM_{10} increased, and in a later study they found the same with $PM_{2.5}$ (Schwartz 2000). Critics then claimed the data were a spurious result of "harvesting" people who were about to die. If this were so, the excess of death in very sick people would be followed by fewer deaths, since the sickest would have already died. This trend, however, did not occur (Schwartz 2000). More refined research on mechanisms of injury by particulates has shown additional health effects: lung inflammation, increased neutrophils in blood, vascular injury, and direct toxicity to heart and lung tissue (Godleski 2000). In total, particulates are estimated to account for over one hundred thousand deaths annually, more than breast cancer, prostate cancer, and AIDS combined (Schwartz 2000).

The major studies involving particulates look at morbidity and mortality from severe lung and cardiovascular disease (Samet et al. 2000). There is less research on asthma, but the literature on air particulates as a trigger of asthma attacks and hospitalizations has grown. C. Arden Pope (1989) reported on a natural experiment where a Utah steel mill closed due to a strike, resulting in a dramatic drop in PM_{10} and in asthma. Another natural experiment showed that a 23 percent reduction in auto use due to traffic control at the 1996 Atlanta Summer Olympics led to a 42 percent reduction on asthma claims reported to the state's Medicaid program (Friedman et al. 2001). Schwartz and colleagues (1993) found that increases in PM_{10} led to more emergency room visits in Seattle. Averaging the health effects of studies in various countries, Dockery and Pope (1996) found an average 3 percent increase in asthma attacks per 10 $\mu g/m^3$ of $PM_{2.5}$.

Given the strength of the scientific literature linking air pollution to various health outcomes, many scientists and activists extrapolate the relationship between particulate matter and health to the relationship between air pollution and asthma. The search for a correlation between particulates and asthma rates, however, is plagued by what one researcher terms the "confounding curves": air quality has improved over time, while asthma rates have risen. But there are two potential explanations for this seeming lack of association. First, the urban areas, where asthma is concentrated, do not enjoy such improvements in outdoor air quality. Second, indoor air quality may have declined as a result of decaying buildings and less money for repair and maintenance, thus leading to a mixture of indoor and outdoor factors as an explanation for increased asthma rates.

For these reasons, environmental justice groups representing urban communities are beginning to enter the scientific arena to support and conduct research on outdoor sources of air pollution and their link to the increasing rates of asthma, in terms of both new cases and the exacerbation of existing cases. To generate new science and regulations to reduce air pollution, activists are faced with a political controversy similar to the debate around whether global warming actually exists, a situation in which a few professional "skeptics" join corporate interests and anti-regulatory elements of the government to fight against the broadly accepted science (Gelbspan 1997). The scientific controversy surrounding the research fuels the political debate and is often used as a tool by corporate interests to hinder the creation of regulations to address the increasing rates of asthma. Consequently, the political discovery of asthma generates further debate within science, making science that links air pollution and asthma a very controversial area of research.

Asthma, Air Pollution, and Regulatory Gridlock

Political discovery of asthma as a major public health problem has occurred in a variety of federal agencies. There is growing interest from various parts of the National Institutes of Health (NIH) on health inequalities, where asthma stands out as a prime example. The burgeoning research on health inequalities deals with race, class, and sex differences in disease, disability, and life expectancy (Wilkinson 1996; Berkman and Kawachi 2000). While most sociological and public health research on health inequalities centers on more serious diseases with high mortality rates, environmental justice proponents have found asthma to be an important component among these. Asthma has also emerged as an important impetus for promotion of environmental health tracking (Pew Environmental Health Commission 2000), which intersects with the Center for Disease Control's (CDC) efforts at improved health surveillance and has become more prominent as a political goal. Such tracking would collect data on many environmental hazards, as well as symptoms and diseases that might be attribute to environmental hazards. The Department of Housing and Urban Development (HUD) has targeted housing conditions as central to asthma problems and has funded research and interventions. The National Institute of Environmental Health Sciences (NIEHS) has been especially interested in asthma. NIEHS plays the lead role in its joint sponsorship with CDC and EPA of five Centers for Children's Environmental Health and Disease Prevention that include a focus on asthma, primary or otherwise, and that have major citizen participation components. One example of these centers is the Columbia Center for Children's Environmental Health in New York, which works in collaboration with the activist group WE ACT. NIEHS has created the "Environmental Justice: Partnership for Communications" program to support academic-community collaborations on research and education. Some of these address asthma and are mandated to include the community in their projects, and also sometimes involve lay partners in research (NIH 2000). The NIEHS effort on citizen participation is significant in rekindling this legacy from 1960s health and social services programs (Shepard et al. 2002).

The EPA is the primary government agency involved in the political discovery process, based largely on its regulatory mandate to analyze the National Ambient Air Quality Standards (NAAQS) every five years and to act on the basis of appropriate scientific knowledge. The growing literature on health effects of particulate matter has provided sufficient justification over the last thirty years for the EPA to move toward more stringent regulation, first with PM_{10} and later $PM_{2.5}$ In the 1970s, the EPA regulated large particles, "total suspended particulates," ranging in size from PM_{25} to PM_{45}, with a 260 g/m^3 twenty-four–hour average. In 1987, EPA moved to the smaller PM_{10} particulates, with a standard of 50 g/m^3 annual average or 150 g/m^3 twenty-four–hour average. In 1994 the American Lung Association sued the EPA for failing to have reset standards every five years, as required. In 1995–96, EPA scientists estimated that fifteen thousand deaths were attributable to particulates each year, and the agency sought to add

$PM_{2.5}$ standards of 15 g/m^3 on an annual average or 50 g/m^3 on a twenty-four–hour average (Greenbaum 2000). In November 1996 the EPA presented its proposals to tighten NAAQS air standards. The proposals followed a review of 185 health studies of ozone and 86 studies of PM_{10}, which determined that "current standards for these pollutants do not adequately protect sensitive populations, such as the sick, the young, and the elderly" (Brown 1997: 378). The November 1996 EPA proposal, which specifically addressed ozone and particulate matter, frightened many industries who feared the higher standards would necessitate the purchase of new equipment and be too expensive (Greenbaum 2000).

Opponents of the more stringent measures argued both against the costs and that this was "junk science," supported by "hidden data" unavailable to challengers. The EPA's response to the "junk science" charge was that there had been many peer reviews and that these data were very strong. In terms of costs, the EPA stuck to its belief that the law called for action based on public health considerations ("to protect the public health, with an adequate margin of safety"). According to the EPA, even with a cost-accounting, the cost of fifteen thousand deaths was higher than the critics' estimate of the costs of compliance. Finally, responding to the charge of "hidden data," the EPA asked for a reanalysis of the data by the Health Effects Institute, an organization jointly funded by the EPA and industry (Greenbaum 2000). That study affirmed the Dockery findings. As a result of this, on July 16, 1997, the EPA decided to retain the PM_{10} standards and adopt the $PM_{2.5}$ standards at 15 g/m^3 on an annual average or 65 g/m^3 on a twenty-four–hour average. But in a compromise, the EPA agreed to monitor $PM_{2.5}$ particulates, do more research, and not implement the actual $PM_{2.5}$ standards until the next five–year review in 2002. The outcome of this conflict was that thousands of monitors are now in place around the country, more research is strengthening the science, and the 2002 review is underway (Greenbaum 2000).

When the rules were signed into law in 1997, a series of lawsuits followed. On May 14, 1999, in its decision on one of these suits (*American Trucking Association, Inc., et al., v. United States Environmental Protection Agency*), the U.S. Court of Appeals for the District of Columbia agreed with the arguments that the EPA had construed sections 108 and 109 of the Clean Air Act so loosely as to render them unconstitutional delegations of legislative power. The court went on to note that "although the factors EPA uses in determining the degree of public health concern associated with different levels of ozone and PM are reasonable, EPA appears to have

articulated no 'intelligible principle' to channel its application of these factors; nor is one apparent from the statute" (Greenhouse 2001).

On May 20, 1999, EPA Administrator Carol Browner commented on
the court's decision in her testimony before the Senate Environment and
Public Works Committee:

> The court did not say that the air standards were based on bad science. Nor
> did the court find that the process that produced the standards were [sic]
> insufficient. In fact, the court explicitly recognized the strong scientific and
> public health rationale for tougher air quality protections. These proposals
> were based on a total of more than 250 of the best and most current scien-
> tific studies on ozone and PM—comprising thousands of pages—all of
> them published, peer-reviewed, fully-debated and thoroughly analyzed by
> the independent scientific committee. We stand by these standards. We
> stand by the science. We stand by the process. By finding this section of the
> Clean Air Act unconstitutional, the court has struck at the heart and soul of
> this legislation that is so critical to the health of our families. . . . To lose the
> ability to implement the new health standards for smog and soot would
> mean 125 million Americans—including 35 million children—are going to
> be placed at risk. (Browner 1999)

This exchange between the EPA and the Court of Appeals reflects what has
emerged as the most contested area of air pollution and public health impacts. Industries argue that meeting the new standards requires expenditures that far exceed potential savings in health care expenditures. But the
corporate argument on cost-benefit analysis lost out, and the Supreme
Court rejected the Trucking Association's position in early 2001 (Greenhouse 2001).

Another major political outcome of the research on particulates
stemmed directly from Dockery's six-city study. Industry asked the EPA to
provide the primary data, but Dockery refused to share that data for fear
that research subjects' confidentiality would be compromised. Senator
Richard Shelby (R-AL) added a provision to a 1999 appropriations bill
(P.L. 105-277) that instructed the Office of Management and Budget
(OMB) to revise Circular A-110 to ensure that all data produced with a
federal grant would be made available to the public through the Freedom
of Information Act (FOIA). (Circular A-110, which has been in effect since
1976, governs the management of federal grants by institutions of higher
education, hospitals, and other nonprofit agencies.) The provision was at-

tached to this appropriations bill without any public hearings, scrutiny, or comments. As one scientist indicated, the Shelby amendment could have significant impact on future research:

> I can no longer say to you, "I want you to participate in my study and keep what you tell me confidential." I can say to you, "I can keep your data confidential unless it's used by the EPA in rulemaking. Then anybody can request access to your data." . . . [It] changes the way we're going to have to do business in the future. I cannot give people the same assurances of confidentiality that I could in the past.

On January 6, 2001, H.R. 88 was introduced to repeal this provision by Representative George Brown (D-CA), with support of science and social science organizations that feared impingement on independent research. At the present time, the Shelby amendment on data access is in force. In fact, industry is asking that this be applied to past studies as well.

The Bush administration is also working to hinder research on environmental causes of disease. In 2002, the scientific advisory committees within the Department of Health and Human Services underwent major reorganization. Volunteer members of a committee who assess the effects of environmental chemicals on human health were almost entirely replaced. Some of the replacement experts have links to industries that produce the chemicals in question (Weiss 2002). These challenges to the science behind federal regulations have made linking air pollution to asthma more difficult for researchers to achieve.

The Future of the Science and Activism on Asthma

Without agreement on the scientific evidence linking air pollution to the increasing rates of asthma, the prospect of stricter regulations at the federal level is low. Community environmental justice groups choose to address air pollution at the local level, rather than wait for the political and scientific controversies to be settled. Through innovative collaborations in community-based participatory research, community groups are conducting their own science in conjunction with some of the foremost scientists in air pollution research. By choosing to conduct their own research with a focus on exposure rather than health effects, these environmental justice groups are assisting in the generation of evidence to create regulations at the local level. But activist groups such as ACE and WE ACT are not entirely committed to relying on science to provide absolute proof that air pollution causes new cases of asthma. Instead, they push for action based on the fact that their constituents are directly exposed to probable causes of air pollution and consider that this fact alone necessitates regulatory action. Thus the environmental justice groups involved in asthma activism push for more science but rely on political action to reduce the disproportionate burden of asthma in their communities. However, their political action and scientific advances have been met with much resistance.

The very strength of the science, the spread of public health action, and the growth of public advocacy have engendered powerful corporate opposition. Major companies find it important to counter the policy implications of air particulates research. For instance, ExxonMobil took out a large advertisement on the *New York Times* Op-Ed page that argued that air pollution was not a factor for asthma and that medications were the best we had to offer (ExxonMobil 2001). In the anti-regulatory regime under President George W. Bush, it will be less likely that the EPA will press forward with more stringent regulations. Still, the very strong science base, relative to other environmentally induced diseases, provides strong legitimacy to professionals and activists. The linkage of health with other social sectors creates an opening for a broad-based effort at improving health and democratizing society. The interest of federal agencies in multisectoral efforts that bring together activists, researchers, and providers offers a strong advance in collaborative, participatory models of health action.

The majority of participatory models of health intervention fail to address environmental causes of asthma. Given the extent of the asthma epidemic, it is understandable that many clinicians, social workers, and community activists want to get out and do front-line work on personal behaviors to clean up mold, mites, and roaches, and to use protective covers for bedding. They know that such measures are effective in reducing asthma suffering. But even if these programs reach a significant portion of inner-city residents, they cannot offer any protection against the outdoor air pollution that continues to trigger asthma attacks. Some activists believe that the focus on indoor environmental factors burdens people with individual responsibility for dealing with the triggers in their homes, rather than targeting broader-scale environmental factors that affect whole neighborhoods or cities. They note that there are still important players in the asthma world who do not address air pollution. For example, the Asthma and Allergy Foundation of America/New England Chapter (2000) puts out a sixty-two-item checklist for parents and providers, on which the only item concerning outdoor pollution is "outdoor fumes (such as from car exhaust, idling vans or buses, or nearby businesses) are prevented from entering the building through open windows or doors." Checklists in research literature are similar and often do not even mention vehicle exhaust.

Prior to the advent of academic and community scientific collaborations, community groups could only make requests for increased research on the link between air pollution and asthma. Through community-based participatory research, these groups can play a larger role in the political debate, as well as in the scientific controversy. Funding sources like the National Institute for Environmental Health Science are making CBPR a priority, and increasingly researchers in the environmental health field are finding community collaborations to be productive avenues for their research.

ACE's and WE ACT's uses of an environmental justice frame mean they are not wedded to the traditional procedures and science of public health. They prefer to focus on community building and environmental justice organizing, since they believe that other groups have gotten entangled organizationally in complicated epidemiology debates that can last many years. As one scientific collaborator with ACE noted:

[Community groups] are often very disappointed when . . . we cannot show in a scientific study that there is a direct linkage there. And usually it's an issue of having not enough numbers, weak associations, and you're never going to be able to say definitively that the bus station or the toxic waste site or whatever [is] the cause of the illness that is being observed in the community. So that can be very frustrating. ACE recognizes the weakness of epidemiology and so hasn't gone a long way down that path. And [ACE] has rather focused on what the environmental exposures are and trying to deal with just those on the basis of controlling exposures.

A researcher in partnership with WE ACT concurred:

Their agenda is not a scientific one as to discover the exact causes—it's more to identify causes that are known and that may be harming a community and actively doing something about it. So . . . it's a mixture of politics of discrimination and environmental kinds of things. But they do a very good job. . . . It's very hard in some sense to also answer the questions that WE ACT asks. You know, I sort of share their goal of thinking that diesel sources of point pollution are really a bad thing for people and that it's a good idea to have, either have them disappear altogether or at least have them more equitably distributed.

One WE ACT staffer expressed his frustration with the scientific process:

In the scientific arena, I think that the debate is always there about what's a definitive study. How is it proved beyond a reasonable doubt? Yet nothing in science is ever proved beyond a reasonable doubt but we're always looking for that definitive study in the scientific realm. You know, science, unlike any other social endeavor, places itself on this pedestal that says that, in essence, if it could speak as human being, "I am science and this is the end all and where with all." And if I don't have a definitive answer then there is no definitive answer. So there is that struggle within the scientific community. Is this the definitive study? Have we taken a large enough sample? Did we control for all the uncontrollable variables? Was it perfectly done? Of course it can't be perfectly done. And why are we waiting for "the definitive answer"?

Despite this frustration, ACE and WE ACT understand the need for scientific evidence and scientific legitimacy, recognizing the long-term importance of establishing links between air pollution and asthma. ACE's selectivity in working with science can be seen in its alliance with researchers at the Harvard and Boston University Schools of Public Health, and with local and regional public health and environmental agencies on the AirBeat project. AirBeat is designed to monitor local air quality and then analyze the relationship between air quality and clinic visits for asthma attacks and other respiratory ailments. As part of the AirBeat project, ACE was successful in requesting various government agencies and public health researchers to install a monitor at their Roxbury office. While ACE collaborates with scientists to produce quantifiable outcomes they hope will lead to greater understanding of air pollution and asthma links, AirBeat is useful in other ways as well. ACE derives political legitimacy from the involvement of government agencies and scientists in the process, such as the presence of Harvard scientists and the EPA Region 1 head at the press conference where they unveiled the air monitor. ACE is able to leverage media publicity from the project to forward their environmental justice approach and can, in turn, increase community awareness among a population that otherwise might not make such connections. Community members are also directly involved in the planning and implementation of these studies, as evidenced by the involvement of REEP students in identifying types of data to be collected from community clinics.

For scientists, ACE and WE ACT present opportunities to collaborate in the collection of community-level data and gain local political legitimacy and connections. While many of the scientists we interviewed and observed noted that this made the scientific inquiry process easier, they also expressed a sense of obligation to the localities in which their research occurred and to individuals with asthma. As one researcher noted:

> Connecting to people that are having real problems is very important. You just feel a lot of empathy for people that are suffering. And it's very important for us to get out of the academic world and have those connections to really ground our work.

Researchers working with both ACE and WE ACT emphasized the importance of joint decision making and goal setting, in part to avoid the perceptions of exploitation that have damaged other citizen-science alliances in other locations. They note that other alliances between citizens and scientists often do not achieve these goals:

> The ideal way that everybody describes the way community partnerships should develop is you should become partners. . . . You should really share agendas about what kind of work you want to do and then jointly reach decisions about what you are going to go after and then apply for money or support to do that. And that probably happens in about 5 percent of the cases [laughs].

The same researcher continued:

> One of the biggest difficulties for me, I mean I'm used to projects where I get the money. I hire the staff. They have to do everything that I say, basically. And it's not like that working with community groups. And in fact they know stuff that I don't know. I'm hopelessly naive in many ways related to how things will play out.

In addition to providing each other with a certain legitimacy, WE ACT's work with Columbia researchers has been both a learning and a teaching process, as an activist noted:

> [In] reaching out we haven't always come upon the most community-conscious people. And in the process of that relationship it has taken us a lot of work and time to educate those researchers, to give them a broader understanding of the complexities and the diversity of this community that they actually work in. And I think that overall I can say that has its rewards but it hasn't been all smooth and it hasn't been all easy. . . . I think that the relationship has also yielded for us an increase in our own sort of scientific knowledge and for them I think it's increased their knowledge of this community, its history, its complexity, its diversity. It's taught them how to be better communicators, how to be better neighbors in some ways.

Researchers and public health practitioners rely on groups like ACE and WE ACT to provide what one researcher called a "direct finger on the pulse of what's going on in the community from the health and environmental perspective." ACE and WE ACT are able to bring real-world community problems to the attention of academics and government, and to present them through an interface accessible to researchers and public officials. In turn, because of their trusted community role, they are valuable in translating and disseminating public health information about indoor and outdoor environmental asthma exposures.

Nevertheless, scientists, officials, and policy makers require a very different discovery process than community activists and community organizations such as ACE and WE ACT. For example, ACE does not wait for definitive scientific support for the impact of air pollution on asthma; instead, they act immediately. Because ACE chooses to work with science in a limited fashion, and often draws conclusions and benefits from the research beyond the actual findings, scientists and activists perceive their work with each other as problematic at times and occasionally become frustrated with each other's approaches:

> We had the launch of our air monitor and had an article in the [Boston] Globe, "New Tool in the Fight Against Asthma." And some of our partners were like "This is not necessarily the case." That's how we look at it, that's how a lot of residents look at it, but the folks like the DEP [Department of

Environmental Protection] and others, that's not necessarily why this air monitor is here, but that's the message that the media got.

That ACE staffer followed up:

> I know that we've been challenged even by our partners, like at the Harvard School of Public Health and the folks we worked with on the air monitor, who always are saying, you know, if you really want to deal with the asthma problem in Roxbury, it's more than diesel buses. . . . And we know that the problem is more than traffic and we know the problem is more than diesel buses. You know, it's housing, it's access to health care. There's a whole rubric of things. But, at the same time, clearly, you've got to start doing whatever you can and I think that folks know that even if science hasn't proven [it], people know that there's a link.

A researcher working with WE ACT noted a similar tension:

> Being affiliated with advocacy work . . . runs counter to the classic scientific process where the scientist approaches data in an impartial way and . . . takes whatever comes out of the data in a very balanced unbiased way. Whereas, from the community perspective, often they're going into a study with a particular bias about what the outcome will be and they're going to take the data and may sort of, they may be inclined to twist it or portray it in a way that supports their perspective, and that's something that scientists you know obviously are not that comfortable with. That hasn't been a real big problem for us. . . . When I publish results I just say what I think is justified. WE ACT can take those data and say whatever they want to say and that's okay with me. But it is an issue. I think it's a little bit of a friction that . . . just has to be worked out.

Such a response suggests that only researchers with some degree of commitment to environmental justice goals would be willing to work with these groups. Even if they are willing to work with the friction, they still must have an initial sympathy to the activists' goals.

ACE's and WE ACT's intent is to win public debates, not scientific ones, and they see no reason to place high stakes on controversial scientific opinions, since science is only one component of their overall approach. They see themselves as being trendsetters in the amalgamation of science, policy, politics, and community organizing, as formulated by a staff member:

> I think that the environmental justice movement has actually been a hybrid of . . . the idea of working from the grassroots but also recognizing that there is a power structure that you have to be sophisticated enough to affect and change. And I think that as WE ACT, we have sort of been right on the cusp of that hybrid or that synthesis, if you will, of working both within sort of the grassroots arena or the broader social arena yet at the same time recognizing that you've got to sort of be a strategic operator, political operator in order to move public policy. And that you pick from the best of both worlds in order to advance the goals.

This quote, especially in its use of the term *hybrid*, points to an interesting facet of environmental justice groups. By being hybrid groups that cross the boundaries of activism and science, they have an impact on both science and activism. They also build the capacities of their staff and constituencies by being so multifaceted.

Groups such as ACE and WE ACT choose to keep the focus of their work on their communities. As with other environmental justice organizations, they believe that if they become too nationally focused or involved in too many governmental and academic meetings, they would forsake their long-term local base. They are aware that even if there is national implementation of $PM_{2.5}$ standards, local injustices will remain, and hence local action will always be necessary.

Nonetheless, ACE's and WE ACT's local work does have national impact. Community-initiated citizen-science alliances with national-level research universities such as Harvard, Boston University, and Columbia have a cumulative national impact. In influencing the way this science is done, the organizations involved can influence research methods and techniques, how findings are presented, and, in some cases, the findings themselves. For example, WE ACT's institutionalized partnership with Columbia's Division of Environmental Health Sciences has led not only to useful studies on the health effects of diesel exhaust in northern Manhattan communities but to cooperation in the development of new methodologies for traffic counts, ambient air monitoring, and using biomarkers as a measure for an individual's exposure to diesel exhaust.

Additionally, limited national networking encourages replication of the contested illness approach to asthma. WE ACT in particular has been active in regional and national environmental justice coalitions, as members of the EPA's National Environmental Justice Advisory Council (NEJAC), the Environmental Justice Caucus, the Children's Environmental Health Network, and the Environmental Justice Fund. They have played a leadership role in regional environmental justice organizations, including the Northeast Environmental Justice Network and the Community-University Consortium for Regional Environmental Justice (CUCREJ). This high-profile role in the environmental justice movement has allowed WE ACT to exchange campaign ideas and help spread some of the more innovative campaigns and tactics to other organizations, and to pick up new tactics themselves. Such collaboration and sharing of tactics represents a pattern among community-based asthma groups. For example, ACE borrowed their "transit racism" campaign from the Bus Rider's Union in Los Angeles and WE ACT's current challenges to the Metropolitan Transit Authority's bus depot. Thus, strategies are shared, even if there is no single national organization.

Conclusion

The social discovery of asthma and its environmental correlates by lay, scientific, and political actors has been a unique example of action on environmentally induced disease, since there are so many shared points between the actors. As we have shown, a considerable amount of attention to the new asthma epidemic comes from empowered laypeople who are concerned with environmental triggers of the disease. Their intersectoral approach to asthma includes action in a number of social sectors, such as health services, public health, education, housing, transportation, and economic development, and is framed in environmental justice terms. Even among more mainstream progressive public health approaches to asthma, there is considerable intersectoral attention, as well as attention to the environmental justice perspective. But even though this progressive public health approach shares some beliefs with the environmental asthma activists, programmatic mainstream work is often based on indoor hazards. The environmental asthma activists focus their attention on political and economic action, addressing outdoor hazards, although they understand the need for the household level of attention.

ACE and WE ACT, as representative of this environmental asthma approach, define themselves as environmental justice organizations, with asthma activism only one part of their work. Even though they are not primarily health-oriented, they offer a sociologically informed approach to fundamental social causes of disease. These environmental justice groups have found creative ways to work alongside scientists, while not placing primary emphasis on research. The strengths of environmental asthma activism that we have addressed here offer lessons for future contested illnesses in terms of a combination of community organizing; social support for sufferers; creative political actions; and citizen-science alliances for treatment, prevention, and research.

Given our point that ACE and WE ACT emphasize community action rather than scientific research, we must ask why they began to work with scientists and why they continue to do so. In terms of starting to work with scientists, for both groups this was not an initial focus. They began their organizing work without emphasizing collaborations with medical and scientific professionals. But this type of collaboration developed, in part because a sufficient number of researchers were sympathetic to their environmental justice framework. It became clear that medical and scientific allies provide legitimacy for the aims of these environmental justice groups, allowing for the development of citizen-science alliances. Also, government typically wants a strong science base to justify action, and activists understand that connection. Additionally, activists understand that corporate opposition will continue, and that even current government support for environmental asthma connections may not be permanent. By allying with scientists, these groups can help the production of even further science to strengthen their case. They are also able to push their science collaborators to a greater support for citizen participation. In short, ACE and WE ACT have developed into "hybrid" organizations that are doing public health work and research, as well as engaging in community organizing. Through partnerships with university-based researchers, environmental justice groups maintain the option of being more science-oriented at some times, more activist-oriented at others.

The hybrid nature of academic-community partnerships also benefits professionals, who receive support from the people who are affected by the problems that researchers are working on. By becoming attuned to the value of lay involvement, researchers become more well-rounded, expand their repertoire of knowledge and research questions, and are able to compete for federal grants that require partnerships.

Because of the shared perspectives among actors, the hybrid nature of the environmental justice groups, and the significant successes in asthma research and particulate regulation, this case offers lessons in cooperation for action on other contested environmental diseases. While other diseases may have less solid science bases, the willingness of scientists and government to work collaboratively with lay organizations is crucial. Above all, the public's health has been improved by such action.

REFERENCES

Amdur, M. 1996. Animal Toxicology. In *Particles in Our Air: Concentrations and Health Effects,* ed. R. Wilson and J. Spengler, 85–122. Cambridge, MA: Harvard University Press.

American Lung Association (ALA). 1996. *Breathless: Air Pollution and Hospital Admissions/Emergency Room Visits in Thirteen Cities.* Washington, DC: American Lung Association.

Asthma and Allergy Foundation of America/New England Chapter. 2000. Asthma-Friendly Child Care: A Checklist for Parents and Providers. Washington, DC.

Berkman, Lisa, and Ichiro Kawachi, eds. 2000. *Social Epidemiology.* New York: Oxford University Press.

Brown, Kathryn S. 1997. "A Decent Proposal: EPA's New Clean Air Standards." *Environmental Health Perspectives* 105 (4): 378–82.

Browner, C. 1999. Remarks made to the United States Senate Environment and Public Works, Subcommittee on Clean Air, May 20. Available at http://www.epa.gov/ttn/oarpg/gen/cmbtest.html#remarks.

Bullard, Robert, ed. 1994. *Confronting Environmental Racism: Voices from the Grassroots.* Boston: South End Press.

Davis, Devra. 2002. *When Smoke Ran like Water: Tales of Environmental Deception and the Battle against Pollution.* New York: Basic.

Dockery, D., and C. A. Pope. 1996. Epidemiology of Acute Health Effects: Summary of Time Series Studies. In *Particles in Our Air: Concentrations and Health Effects,* ed. R. Wilson and J. Spengler, 123–48. Cambridge, MA: Harvard University Press.

Dockery, Douglas W., C. Arden Pope, Xiping Xu, John D. Spengler, James H. Ware, Martha E. Fay, Benjamin G. Ferris, and Frank E. Speizer. 1993. An Association between Air Pollution and Mortality in Six US Cities. *New England Journal of Medicine* 329: 1753–59.

Evans, David, Mindy Fullilove, Peggy Shepard, Cecil Corbin-Mark, Cleon Edwards, Lesley Green, and Frederica Perera. 2000. Healthy Home, Healthy Child Campaign: A Community Intervention by the Columbia Center for Children's

Environmental Health. Presentation at annual meeting of American Public Health Association, Boston, November 15.

ExxonMobil. 2001. Clearing the Air on Asthma. Advertisement, *New York Times,* November 15.

Friedman, Michael S., Kenneth E. Powell, Lori Hutwagner, LeRoy M. Graham, and W. Gerald Teague. 2001. Impact of Changes in Transportation and Commuting Behaviors during the 1996 Summer Olympic Games in Atlanta on Air Quality and Childhood Asthma. *Journal of the American Medical Association* 285: 897–905.

Gelbspan, Ross. 1997. *The Heat Is On: The Climate Crisis, the Cover-Up, the Prescription.* Cambridge, MA: Perseus.

Godleski, J. 2000. Mechanisms of Particulate Air Pollution Health Effects. Presentation at annual meeting of American Public Health Association, Boston, November 14.

Greenbaum, D. 2000. Interface of Science with Policy. Presentation at annual meeting of American Public Health Association, Boston, November 14.

Greenhouse, L. 2001. E.P.A.'s Authority on Air Rules Wins Supreme Court's Backing. *New York Times,* February 28, 1.

Loh, Penn, and Jodi Sugerman-Brozan. 2002. Environmental Justice Organizing for Environmental Health: Case Study on Asthma and Diesel Exhaust in Roxbury, Massachusetts. *Annals of American Academy of Political and Social Science* 584: 110–24.

National Health Interview Survey. 1997. NCHS Data Fact Sheet. January 1997.

National Institutes of Health (NIH). 2000. "Request for Proposals." Available at http://grants.nih.gov/grants/guide/rfa-files/RFA-ES-99–005.html, May 30, 2000.

Pew Environmental Health Commission. 2000. *Attack Asthma.* Baltimore: Johns Hopkins University School of Public Health.

Pope, C. A. 1989. Respiratory Disease Associated with Community Air Pollution and a Steel Mill, Utah Valley. *American Journal of Public Health* 79 (5): 623–28.

Roberts, J. Timmons, and Melissa M. Toffolon-Weiss. 2001. *Chronicles from the Environmental Justice Frontline.* Cambridge: Cambridge University Press.

Samet, Jonathan M., Francesca Dominici, Frank C. Curriero, Ivan Coursac, and Scott L. Zeger. 2000. Fine Particulate Air Pollution and Mortality in Twenty U.S. Cities, 1987–1994. *New England Journal of Medicine* 343: 1724–29.

Schwartz, J. 1993. Particulate Air Pollution and Chronic Respiratory Disease. *Environmental Research* 62: 7.

———. 2000. Fine Particulate Air Pollution: Smoke and Mirrors of the '90s or Hazard of the New Millennium. Presentation at annual meeting of American Public Health Association, Boston, November 14.

Schwartz, J., D. Slater, T. V. Larson, W. E. Pierson, and J. Q. Koenig. 1993. Particulate Air Pollution and Hospital Emergency Visits for Asthma in Seattle. *American Review of Respiratory Disease* 147: 826–31.

Shepard, P. M., M. E. Northridge, S. Prakash, and G. Stover. 2002. Preface: Advancing Environmental Justice through Community-Based Participatory Research. *Environmental Health Perspectives* 110 (2): 139–44.

Weiss, R. 2002. HHS Seeks Science Advice to Match Bush View. *Washington Post,* September 17, A01.

Wilkinson, Richard G. 1996. *Unhealthy Societies: The Afflictions of Inequality.* London: Routledge.

Wilson, Richard. 1996. Introduction. In *Particles in Our Air: Concentrations and Health Effects,* ed. R. Wilson and J. Spengler, 1–14. Cambridge, MA: Harvard University Press.

13

Invisible People, Invisible Places
Connecting Air Pollution and
Pesticide Drift in California

Jill Harrison

For decades, public health experts have recognized pesticide pollution as a problematic consequence of agricultural production. Pesticide drift is the latest version of these debates about the public health impacts of pesticide use and refers to situations in which pesticides move away from their target pest or crop and cause harm to people nearby.[1] The following two cases are examples of the type of drift incidents that received media attention in recent years:

In November 2000, at least thirty-five elementary school children and several teachers in Ventura County were hospitalized after a cloud of chlorpyrifos (Lorsban) drifted onto school grounds from a nearby lemon orchard. Chlorpyrifos is a neurotoxic organophosphate (OP) insecticide and has been classified as a suspected endocrine disruptor and possible developmental or reproductive toxicant. Chlorpyrifos was recently banned by the federal EPA for almost all residential uses but continues to be one of the most extensively used organophosphate pesticides in agriculture (PAN, 2003; Solomon, 2000).

In November 1999, 180 people were evacuated from the town of Earlimart in Tulare County after toxic vapors from the breakdown of metam sodium drifted from a nearby potato field. The soil fumigant drift sent at least twenty-four people to the hospital; most of the victims complained of acute effects, such as difficulty breathing, nausea, headache, and burning eyes and throat. Earlimart residents report that asthma and other respiratory ailments have increased since that incident. Metam sodium is listed by the state as a carcinogen, developmental or reproductive toxin, and possible endocrine disruptor (PAN, 2003).

Events such as these have put pesticide drift on the political agenda. For example, the U.S. Environmental Protection Agency (EPA) is currently debating new pesticide label requirements designed to help reduce spray drift accidents during application. Additionally, California's Department of Pesticide Regulation now has a Pesticide Drift Task Force, and the California EPA is currently aiming to reduce the incidence of drift by considering legislation that will restrict the conditions under which particular pesticide application methods may be used.

A number of public-interest research groups have also taken up the issue. Pesticide Action Network North America, Environmental Working Group, and Californians for Pesticide Reform are but three of the groups that have introduced campaigns to raise the visibility of the problem of pesticide drift and to argue for solutions that are more critical and substantial than those proposed by policymakers (Gray et al., 2001; Kegley et al., 2003; Reeves et al., 2002).

Furthermore, a variety of grassroots, community-based organizations have formed in response to local-level impacts of pesticide drift. Examples include Community and Children's Advocates Against Pesticide Poisoning (CCAAPP) in Ventura County, Farm Without Harm in Monterey County, Comité Para Bienestar de Earlimart in Tulare County, and the No Spray Action Network in Sonoma County (see CCAAPP, 2003; FWH, 2003; De-Anda, 2003a; NSAN, 2003)

In this chapter, I illustrate the ways in which policymakers and the mainstream media tend to frame the problem of pesticide drift—namely, as a series of isolated accidents in which pesticides drift through the air into nearby non-farm spaces, causing people to become seriously ill during or immediately after application. I will show that limiting the framing of the pesticide drift problem to the realm of "accident" in residential areas misrepresents the true scope of the problem. Namely, this conceptualization renders invisible and legitimizes exposures endured by farm laborers and excludes consideration of the "non-crisis," everyday exposures to pesticides endured by millions of Californians.

I also illustrate, on the other hand, that the problem of pesticide drift is currently being reframed in alternative spaces as an issue that *transcends* the few accidents that receive media attention. In particular, many researchers and activists are actively reframing pesticide drift as an *air pollution* problem. In contrast with the mainstream conceptualizations of the problem, this strategy brings out and problematizes the everyday nature of pesticide drift and creates an opportunity for making farm labor and daily pesticide exposures visible.

Mapping the Pesticide Drift Problem and Debates

Mainstream conceptualizations of pesticide drift render invisible some of the most significant impacts of pesticide pollution. These contradictions and invisibilities can be illustrated geographically by comparing (1) the spatial distribution of the problem throughout the state with (2) the spatial distribution of public attention to the problem. I illustrate in this section that while the problem of pesticide drift in California follows a particular pattern, that pattern contrasts significantly with the geographical dimensions of attention to the issue in the mainstream media.

Pesticide Action Network (PAN) created detailed maps illustrating the spatial distribution of pesticide use across the state of California, and these maps are available on the website of Californians for Pesticide reform (Osborne et al., 2001; see http://www.pesticidereform.org/datamaps .html.) These maps were derived from the State of California's Department of Pesticide Regulation (DPR) Pesticide Use Report (PUR) data and illustrate the distribution of agricultural pesticide use intensity (measured in pounds of active ingredients applied per square mile) across the state.

As illustrated, pesticide use intensity in general is the highest in the regions of greatest agricultural production: the Central Valley, the Salinas Valley, and the Imperial Valley. In addition, the State of California tracks pesticide exposure incidents through its Pesticide Illness Surveillance Program (PISP). PISP records indicate that the counties with the highest number of individuals poisoned by agricultural pesticides between 1997 and 2000 were Fresno, Kern, Kings, Tulare, and Monterey (see Table 13.1 below). This correlation is not surprising, given that these counties also lead the state in acreage devoted to agriculture and in pesticide use intensity.

However, while pesticide use and reported drift incidents follow one pattern (illustrated by the above map), public debate about pesticide drift follows a different, contradictory pattern. An analysis of media attention to pesticide drift is one way to compare the local public framings of this issue. A brief survey of newspaper articles on pesticide drift in California revealed spatially significant differences in media attention to and framing

TABLE 13.1
Pesticide Use and Drift Data for Selected California Counties[3]

County	# Reported Poisoning Cases (1997–2000)[a]	Acres Planted (# acres)[b]	Intensity of Pesticide Use lbs. chem. / acres planted[b]
Tulare	427	685,593	25.67
Fresno	221	1,331,327	29.27
Monterey	178	374,714	26.19
Kern	175	834,867	26.84
Kings	96	485,875	9.85
San Joaquin	73	472,362	28.59
Riverside	68	266,113	13.38
Madera	63	294,383	39.12
Merced	60	456,969	19.24
Imperial	57	570,787	15.97
Ventura	52	218,324	27.73
Stanislaus	42	306,439	22.15
Colusa	24	253,144	7.85
Santa Barbara	24	149,745	25.87
Yolo	21	274,247	11.39
Sacramento	21	128,619	30.56
Solano	14	156,845	10.39
Sutter	12	229,472	15.13
Glenn	12	200,093	13.06

[a] Reported Poisoning Cases data from DPR Pesticide Illness Surveillance Program (cited in Reeves et al., 2002) and represent agriculturally related poisonings; 44% of these cases are due to drift.
[b] Acres Planted data and Intensity of Pesticide Use data from Kegley et al., 2000, pp. 70–72; see also Appendix 1 for explanation of methodology. Intensity of Pesticide Use figures represent gross pounds of active ingredients per acre planted in 1998.

of the issue.[4] Specifically, the problem of pesticide drift is underrepresented in the inland areas of California. Only 26 percent of the collected articles addressed the problem of drift in the Central Valley. By contrast, 74 percent of articles on pesticide drift focused on the problem as it exists in more urban, coastal counties such as Ventura, Santa Barbara, Monterey, Santa Cruz, Sonoma, and Napa counties. Hence, although the problem of drift is most acute in the Central Valley, that region is relatively invisible to public attention to the problem.[5] Instead, attention to pesticide drift is clustered in the coastal and urban areas.

Additionally, most of the articles surveyed frame the pesticide drift problem as a series of "accidents," rather than as an air pollution problem.

Most of the few articles pertaining to drift in the Central Valley are limited to details of specific accidents; only *one* article was found to connect the problem of pesticide drift to the larger problem of air pollution in that region. In contrast, in the coastal areas, at least 50 percent of the articles utilized a discussion of a particular drift incident as a springboard for engaging in broader, more critical analysis of the adverse environmental and public health impacts of pesticides.

Current demographic trends in California may contribute to the shifting of public conceptualizations about the pesticide drift problem and therefore account for some of this variation. Increasing numbers of California residents are living in close proximity to pesticide-intensive farms and are raising concerns about the environmental and public health impacts of agricultural pesticide use (Coppock and Krieth, 1996; Sokolow and Medvitz, 1999). In coastal areas, these new rural residents are unlikely to work in agriculture, and they possess considerable social and political power and increasingly question the notion that pesticide drift is a tolerable or "natural" consequence of agricultural production. These demographic changes therefore contribute to increasing scrutiny of (and public debate about) the everyday presence of toxic chemicals in those regions of California.

As these demographic trends and pressures contribute to changes in public concern, media attention to drift in the coastal counties improves upon the accident-based discourse of the Central Valley articles. However, most of the coastal articles are still fairly constituency-based (for instance, focusing on effects of pesticide drift on children in schools, or on amphibians in the Sierras). Furthermore, only 18 percent of articles surveyed made any mention of farm workers. That is, in spite of workers' position as the group most intensively and consistently affected by pesticide drift, they have been quite thoroughly sidelined in public attention to the issue.

The significance of these exclusions from the problem framing should not be underestimated; by sidelining the Central Valley, farm laborers, and the conditions of farm work, these framings misrepresent the problem, tether the issue to the realm of "accident," and abstract pesticide drift from its everyday impact as an air pollution problem. As noted, pesticide drift and other types of air pollution are extremely severe in the Central Valley. Furthermore, drift incidents in the Central Valley frequently include very serious and explicit social injustices; when responding to large-scale drift incidents in Tulare County in 1999 and 2002, emergency crews failed to protect residents, mistreated and demoralized affected individuals, and dismissed their claims about the incident (DeAnda, 2003a). Additionally, media attention has focused almost exclusively on the occasional effects of pesticide drift on residents living in the coastal areas. Such characterizations privilege the health of residents over the health of workers, thereby obscuring the spaces in which people's bodies are affected most intensively on a regular basis. These framings inaccurately give the impression that pesticide drift is typified by the coastal anomalies that receive the most media attention and therefore abstract pesticide drift from its role as a daily air pollutant.

Accidents and Invisibilities

The origins of these invisibilities and contradictions are subtle, overlapping, and deeply rooted in the history of California's agricultural economy. While a thorough analysis of these explanations is beyond the scope of this chapter, a brief analysis of how the issue is typically framed helps explain the fragmented and insufficient attention to the problem of pesticide drift.

As described, policymakers and the mainstream media have tended to frame the problem of pesticide drift as a series of isolated incidents in which pesticides accidentally drift away from a farm and into another social space (such as a residential area or schoolyard). However, by limiting pesticide drift to the realm of isolated accidents, this discourse renders invisible the everyday nature of the problem, thereby effectively decoupling pesticide drift from its role in the larger problem of air pollution (for further discussion of "normal accidents," see Rajan, 1999; and Perrow, 1999). Indeed, the U.S. EPA explicitly excludes consideration of most types of drift, thereby removing them from the scope of policy, as illustrated in the following definition:

> EPA defines spray drift as the physical movement of a pesticide through air at the time of application or soon thereafter, to any site other than that intended for application (often referred to as off-target). EPA does not include in its definition the movement of pesticides to off-target sites caused by erosion, migration, volatility, or contaminated soil particles that are windblown after application. (U.S. EPA, 2002)

These mainstream conceptualizations of the problem limit drift incidents to residential or other off-farm areas, thereby removing workers from the debates. These definitions also suggest that official re-entry intervals (post-application intervals in which workers are not allowed to enter a field) are sufficient for protecting worker health and safety. However, new air monitoring data conducted by Californians for Pesticide Reform suggest that the established intervals do not always effectively protect the health of workers or nearby residents (Kegley et al., 2003). Farm workers' invisibility and exclusion from the problem's definition is troubling, because the intensity and consistency of exposure to toxins in the workplace frequently make workers the primary victims of chemical technologies; the workplace is also therefore the space in which researchers will most accurately understand the human health impacts of toxic chemicals (Brown and Froines, 1993).[6] Removing this important space from debates about pesticide drift therefore misrepresents the problem and suggests limited solutions. Pesticide drift debates cannot effectively confront the problem of pesticide poisonings if the actors *most* at risk are hidden from view and sidelined in discussion; farm workers' invisibility threatens the visibility of drift as an air pollution problem.

Framing the issue as a series of accidents, instead of as an air pollution problem, renders invisible the non-crisis, low-level exposures that have become so "naturalized" in agricultural workplaces and communities. These everyday circumstances are the events that no one would notice or report, for they include very subtle experiences, such as workers' dermal exposures in the field; workers' respiration of airborne pesticides; the transport of chemicals on clothing into workers' homes, and therefore to their spouses and children; and the low-level, unnoticeable aerial drift within and beyond the borders of agricultural communities. This is particularly problematic because public health research increasingly shows that these cumulative exposures to low levels of multiple environmental toxins cause some of the greatest long-term damage to the human body (Colburn et al., 1997; Moses, 2002; Solomon, 2000). As long as pesticide drift is tethered to the realm of "accident" or crisis, the everyday exposures remain invisible and normalized.

Additionally, the "accident" discourse artificially abstracts the poisonings from their institutional, structural supports. The structure of the agricultural labor market has historically posed special challenges to efforts aimed at increasing the visibility of problems endured by farm laborers. Carey McWilliams (1935) discussed the cyclical processes by which growers in California throughout the nineteenth and early twentieth centuries supported the development of new, profitable agricultural commodities by racializing and exploiting the most vulnerable ethnic-based migrant labor groups. As Carol Zabin, Michael Kearney, Philip Martin, and other researchers have shown, this process continues today—the Mixtecs of southern Mexico are the new "lowest group on the totem pole" and now comprise 5 to 10 percent of California's agricultural labor force. Their introduction unintentionally contributes to the further stratification of a labor force already divided along lines of legal status and nationality. Most important, these divisions further complicate the work of unions and other organizing efforts aimed at increasing the visibility of pesticide exposure issues faced by farm worker communities (see Kearney and Nagengast, 1989; Martin, 2001; Zabin, 1992; and Zabin et al., 1993).

This mainstream framing of pesticide drift portrays the problem as a strictly technical one, somehow distinct from socioeconomic issues. However, as many labor researchers have argued, there is a significant relationship between technology and justice in the workplace. Elaine Bernard (1993), William Friedland (1981), Margaret FitzSimmons (1990), and Miriam Wells (1996) have all argued persuasively that workplace structure and technology decisions are neither benign nor objective but, rather, are socially constructed processes imbued with ideology, power, and normative determinations of the distribution of risks.[7] Technological decisions are therefore not simply a function of technical efficiency but also are products of political, social, and financial *power.*

Furthermore, such discourse excludes discussion of agricultural pest management paradigms that prohibit the use of toxic synthetic pesticides (such as organic agriculture) or that permit only the use of least-toxic pesticides—and only as a last resort (such as Integrated Pest Management and Biointensive Pest Management; see, for example, Altieri, 1995; Benbrook, 1996; Gliessman, 1998).

Situating pesticide drift in the space of accident also obscures the inadequacies of the current pesticide risk assessment processes. While risk assessment can determine approximate lethal doses of immediate exposure, the system is unable to determine with any reasonable degree of certainty the synergistic impacts of exposure to low levels of multiple toxins over long periods of time (Brown et al., 2000; Thornton, 2000). However, as previously noted, these are precisely the types of exposure that characterize the agricultural workplace and communities and that pose some of the most significant threats to human health.

These limited conceptualizations of the problem therefore help explain the narrow scope of solutions that policymakers have proposed. Changes in labeling laws and restrictions on application methods at most will require growers to make minor adjustments to current practices, so as to reduce the incidence of accidents during or immediately following application. However, these technical adjustment recommendations will not reduce *post-application* drift, in spite of the fact that the bulk of off-site movement of pesticides occurs as the chemicals volatilize after application (Kegley et al., 2003). Not surprisingly, these policy recommendations make no indication that pesticide drift is an *everyday problem* impacting on the health and safety of all people in agricultural regions. Calls for increased enforcement of current regulations (the solution ubiquitously proposed by agency representatives), while necessary and overdue, perpetuate the illusion that drift is limited to accidental occurrences and fail to make visible the true nature of the problem.

It is important to note that some past efforts to define pesticide problems have suffered similar limitations. In *The Death of Ramon Gonzalez* (1990), Angus Wright shows that consumer-driven concerns in the 1960s and 1970s about pesticide residues on food prompted policymakers to implement restrictions on highly persistent organochlorine pesticides (such as DDT). In turn, these regulations prompted growers to shift to pesticides that were less persistent but that posed a much greater threat to people and wildlife in and near the site of application.

In this way, the solution for consumers became the problem for other, less visible people (such as workers). To reduce the incidence of residues on food crops, policymakers' limited definition of the problem transformed the social and environmental injustices of DDT into a technical issue. Thus the conditions of work and poisonings near the site of production continued to be rendered invisible.

Wright's work illustrates the importance of analyzing the conflicting ways in which different actors define the problem. Limited-scope technical solutions may provide relief for some people but may not provide a thorough or effective resolution to the problem.

Connecting Drift and Air Pollution

As long as the problem of pesticide drift is conceived as a series of accidents, the everyday exposures to pesticides remain invisible and naturalized. Alternatively, framing drift as an *air pollution* issue problematizes those everyday exposures and elevates their significance.

Indeed, some researchers and activists in California are starting to reframe the pesticide drift issue as an air pollution problem.[8] For example, in response to a serious drift incident that occurred in Tulare County in 1999, the United Farm Workers (UFW) joined forces with Californians for Pesticide Reform, the Center for Race, Poverty and the Environment, and several local community action groups.[9] These groups initially collaborated in order to protest the inhumane treatment of affected residents by local emergency response crews, and they are now actively engaged in reframing pesticide drift as an air pollution problem. At a conference on pesticide drift in February 2003, David Chatfield (representing Californians for Pesticide Reform) made the following statement in his opening comments: "We need to define the drift problem as an air pollution problem" (Chatfield 2003). Chatfield emphasized the importance of augmenting current attention to the acute symptoms of exposure with increased attention to asthma and other subtle, chronic effects of pesticides. Chatfield also suggested that conceptualizing pesticide drift as a pollution problem would highlight the ways in which all Californians are exposed. In this way, CPR's work unleashes pesticide drift from the confines of "accident" discourse and makes pesticide drift's role in the severe air pollution problems in California *visible*. This shift in meanings echoes the developments noted in other chapters in this book that discuss the emergence of air pollution as a visible phenomenon (for example, see the chapter by Harold Platt in this volume).

Californians for Pesticide Reform is not the only organization working to reframe pesticide drift as an air pollution problem. Comité Para el Bienestar de Earlimart is a grassroots community-based organization in Tulare County that formed in response to the Earlimart drift incident in 1999. Teresa DeAnda, president of the group, argues that pesticides are a central component of air pollution and that pesticide drift is a health and safety tragedy affecting all people in and near the San Joaquin Valley on a daily basis (for example, see DeAnda, 2000a, 2000b).

Re-making the meaning of drift in this way indicates that the problem is no longer bound to the realm of crisis or to the off-farm movement of chemicals. By framing the issue as one that affects all members of a community, this alliance brings workers back into the debates and therefore avoids some of the constituency-based problems caused by limited problem definitions that have hampered progress in past pesticide policy debates. Most important, these efforts have made progress toward unveiling the everyday nature of the problem.

By elevating awareness of the everyday exposures to pesticides, this recent "air pollution turn" may assist in democratizing the pesticide drift debates. When limited to the spheres of accidents, risk assessment, and regulation enforcement, discussion of toxics issues can be monopolized by experts and made inaccessible to the public. In these situations, lay knowledge is frequently sidelined and disregarded in favor of "expert" knowledge; claims about expertise, however, protect the assessment and allocation of risk from democratic discussion and obscure the ethical and value-laden circumstances of environmental issues (see Brown, 2000; Brown et al., 2000; and Brown et al., in this volume). In this way, the pesticide drift problem reflects the issues unveiled in other community anti-toxics movements such as those that emerged from the environmental tragedies at Love Canal and Woburn, Massachusetts (see Brown and Mikkelsen, 1997). Phil Brown shows that in-depth examinations of such debates raise questions about the distribution of risks associated with chemical technologies and about the appropriate spaces for determining acceptable risk levels. Increased contestation of boundaries suggests that environmental decisionmaking may benefit from increased democratic participation (Brown, 2000). Indeed, grassroots anti-drift organizations are actively confronting the monopolization of knowledge about local environmental issues by experts. As activist, drift victim, and Earlimart resident Teresa DeAnda argued at the recent CPR-sponsored Pesticide Drift Conference, "We need to educate the experts. . . . We *are* the experts! . . . We know what we're feeling and what we're going through" (DeAnda, 2003b).

The shift toward conceptualizing drift as an air pollution problem, therefore, implies that different political alliances can be made around these different meanings. That is, framing pesticide drift as an air pollution problem problematizes everyday exposures and, in turn, creates an opportunity for illustrating the connections between the various groups affected by pesticide pollution.

In this way, the innovative work on drift echoes many of the trends and innovative strategies that comprise the "multi-partner, multi-organizational, intersectoral" approach to linking air pollution and asthma illustrated by Phil Brown and his colleagues (in this volume). These connections are important, because engaging people in the community who are at risk with those people who are *most* at risk (in this case, agricultural workers) can raise the visibility of the conditions of farm labor, illustrate the intersection of labor and non-labor issues, and therefore contribute to solutions to the pesticide drift problem that are more comprehensive and socially just than those being proposed by state and federal agencies.

In recent history, connections have frequently been made between various groups affected by a common environmental problem. Laura Pulido (1996) shows that farm laborers (through the United Farm Workers) were responsible for some of the first pesticide reporting laws. In the late 1960s, the UFW used the tragedy of farm worker poisonings as part of a larger effort to improve farm workers' lives from all angles. These struggles were successful in large part because of the connections that the UFW made with other groups—in particular, with consumers and with people concerned about the risks that pesticides pose to residents of agricultural communities.

In spite of such achievements, many of the important connections that were established in the 1970s have withered in recent years. Patricia Allen and her colleagues (2003) note that although early alternative food initiatives developed strong associations with farm workers and shared a structural critique of existing agricultural practices, racism, and poverty, the neoliberal revolution of the 1980s and the rise of the political culture of entrepreneurialism weakened the connections between the civil rights movement, labor justice organizations, and alternative food movements.

Reframing pesticide drift as an air pollution problem presents a contemporary opportunity for overcoming those lost connections and making labor and everyday exposures more visible. Making labor visible will be a critical component of this process; making the agricultural workplace safer for farm workers will necessarily reduce the impact of pesticides on other residents of agricultural communities. This conceptual shift in the meaning of pesticide drift from accident to air pollution shows that drift damages the health of all people and wildlife in and near pesticide-intensive agricultural regions on a daily basis; highlights the intersections of various groups affected by pesticide pollution (i.e., children in schools, residents of farm communities, farm workers, amphibians, birds, beneficial insects, etc.); and creates space for new alliances that can strengthen the collective voice of hitherto distinct interests.

Conclusion

In this chapter, I have described the problem of pesticide drift and have shown that recent debates about the problem tend to conceptualize drift as a series of isolated accidents in which pesticides travel away from the site of production and cause harm to people in nearby off-farm spaces. I have argued that by limiting pesticide drift to the realm of "accident," these mainstream framings obscure the everyday nature of the problem and promote narrow and inadequate policy solutions. I have also shown, alternatively, that some activists and researchers are actively engaged in re-framing pesticide drift as an air pollution problem. This shift in the framing of the issue brings out and problematizes the everyday nature of the problem, thereby creating an opportunity to unveil the invisible everyday pesticide exposures historically and currently endured by all residents of California's agricultural regions. Effective solutions to the problem of pesticide drift will ultimately depend on the visibility of all spaces, actors, and exposures and on the reconceptualization of drift as pollution in public and policy discourse.

NOTES

1. Most effects that are reported are the *acute* health impacts that are experienced immediately after exposure—these include nausea, skin/eye irritation, and difficulty with breathing. However, there are numerous *chronic* health impacts that may not surface for years but pose significant detrimental consequences to human health. Chronic health effects refer to a chemical's long-term impacts on human health; these are obviously more difficult to determine precisely, typically take years to become evident, and are generally more severe than acute impacts. Known chronic health effects of agricultural pesticides include numerous types of cancer, birth defects, infertility, sterility, metabolic disorders, impaired neurological development, chronic fatigue syndrome, and behavioral abnormalities (see Solomon, 2000; Moses et al., 1993).

2. Californians for Pesticide Reform used DPR data to construct this map; this statewide map and county-level maps of greater resolution are available at http://www.pesticidereform.org/datamaps/maps.html.

3. This table has been limited to those counties in which at least ten cases of pesticide poisoning occurred between 1997 and 2000.

4. Newspapers surveyed included *Bakersfield Californian, Sacramento Bee,*

Fresno Bee, San Francisco Chronicle, Ventura County Star, and *Los Angeles Times.* Articles were included in the survey if they were published between January 1, 1998, and February 28, 2003, and if the words "pesticide" and "drift" occurred within five words of each other within the article. Of the thirty-nine articles that fit these parameters, ten dealt with drift in the Central Valley and twenty-nine dealt with drift in coastal counties.

5. The American Lung Association rates the ozone pollution of all counties in the nation and notes that California's Central Valley counties consistently top the charts. California has the five most ozone-polluted counties in the United States: "San Bernardino has been number 1 three years in a row; Kern, comes in at number 2 this year, after claiming the number 3 spot for the previous two years; Fresno moves up to number 3 after two years as the fourth-most polluted county, Riverside is number 4, after two years as the second-most polluted county; and Tulare, number five for the second year in a row. There is one bright spot on the California horizon: Salinas, which continues to rank among the least ozone-polluted cities in the nation" (ALA, 2003). In addition, as indicated in Table 13.1, nine of the top ten counties in terms of numbers of pesticide poisoning victims in recent years are located in the Central Valley.

6. Numerous researchers have provided documentation for the argument that farm workers and their families are not adequately protected from the health risks associated with exposure to agricultural pesticides (see, for example, Barnett, 1989; CHAMACOS, 2002; Mills and Kwong, 2001; Moses et al., 1993; Pulido, 1996; Reeves et al., 2002; Villarejo et al., 2000).

7. In *The Lie of the Land,* Don Mitchell similarly argues that agricultural landscapes in California are socially constructed relations of power: "The production of landscape is . . . a highly mystified, ideological project that seeks to erase the very facts of its (quite social) production" (Mitchell, 1996, p. 6).

8. As discussed at a Drift Conference sponsored by Californians for Pesticide Reform on February 8, 2003, in Fresno, California.

9. Notably, Comité Para Bienestar de Earlimart.

REFERENCES

ALA. 2003. American Lung Association. The State of the Air 2002 Report: Nationwide and Regional Analysis. February 26. Available at http://www.lungusa .org/air2001/analysis02.html#woes.

Allen, P., M. FitzSimmons, M. Goodman, and K. Warner. 2003. Shifting Plates in the Agrifood Landscape: The Tectonics of Alternative Agrifood Initiatives in California. *Journal of Rural Studies* 19 (1): 61–75.

Altieri, M. A. 1995. *Agroecology: The Science of Sustainable Agriculture.* Boulder, CO: Westview Press.

Barnett, P. G. 1989. *Survey of Research on the Impacts of Pesticides on Agricultural Workers and the Rural Environment.* Davis: California Institute for Rural Studies.

Benbrook, C. M. 1996. *Pest Management at the Crossroads.* Yonkers, NY: Consumers Union.

Bernard, E. 1993. Information Technology: Old Problems, New Tools, and New Possibilities for a Healthy Workplace. Chapter 2 in Brown and Froines, *Technological Change.*

Brown, M. P., and J. R. Froines. 1993. *Technological Change in the Workplace: Health Impacts for Workers.* Center for Occupational and Environmental Health, School of Public Health and Institute of Industrial Relations. Los Angeles: University of California.

Brown, P., and E. J. Mikkelsen. 1997. *No Safe Place: Toxic Waste, Leukemia, and Community Action.* Berkeley: University of California Press.

Brown, P. 2000. Popular Epidemiology and Toxic Waste Contamination: Lay and Professional Ways of Knowing. Chapter 21 in Kroll-Smith et al., *Illness and the Environment.*

Brown, P., S. Kroll-Smith, and V. J. Gunter. 2000. Knowledge, Citizens, and Organizations: An Overview of Environments, Diseases, and Social Conflict. Chapter 1 in Kroll-Smith et al., *Illness and the Environment.*

CCAAPP. 2003. Community and Children's Advocates Against Pesticide Poisoning. See http://nice2people.com/organizations/ccaapp.htm.

CHAMACOS. 2002. Center for Health Analysis of Mothers and Children of Salinas. See http://ehs.sph.berkeley.edu/chamacos/.

Chatfield, D. 2003. Presentation at Pesticide Drift Conference, sponsored by Californians for Pesticide Reform, February 8, Fresno, California.

Colburn, T., D. Dumanoski, and J. P. Myers. 1997. *Our Stolen Future.* New York: Penguin.

Coppock, R., and M. Krieth. 1996. *Farmers and Neighbors: Land Use, Pesticides, and Other Issues.* Davis: Agricultural Issues Center, University of California.

DeAnda, T. 2003a. President of Comité Para Bienestar de Earlimart. Personal conversation with author, February 7.

DeAnda, T. 2003b. Presentation at Pesticide Drift Conference, sponsored by Californians for Pesticide Reform, February 8, Fresno, California.

DeAnda, T. 2000a. Our Valley Air. Our Community/Nuestra Communidad Newsletter 1. October.

DeAnda, T. 2000b. Letter to San Joaquin Valley Air Pollution Control District on behalf of Comité Para el Bienestar de Earlimart. September 15.

FWH. 2003. Farm Without Harm. See http://www.amesti.santacruz.k12.ca.us/farmwithoutharm.html.

FitzSimmons, M. 1990. The Social and Environmental Relations of US Agricultural Regions. In P. Lowe, T. Marsden, and S. Whatmore, eds. *Technological Change and the Rural Environment.* London: David Fulton.

Friedland, W. H. 1981. *Manufacturing Green Gold.* New York: Cambridge University.

Gliessman, S. R. 1998. *Agroecology: Ecological Processes in Sustainable Agriculture.* Chelsea, MI: Ann Arbor Press.

Gray, S., Z. Ross, and B. Walker. 2001. Every Breath You Take: Airborne Pesticides in the San Joaquin Valley. Environmental Working Group. Available at http://www.ewg.org.

Kearney, M., and C. Nagengast. 1989. *Anthropological Perspectives on Transnational Communities in Rural California.* Davis: California Institute for Rural Studies.

Kegley, S. E., A. Katten, and M. Moses. 2003. Secondhand Pesticides: Airborne Pesticide Drift in California. San Francisco: Pesticide Action Network, California Rural Legal Assistance Fund, and Californians for Pesticide Reform.

Kegley, S., S. Orme, and L. Neumeister. 2000. *Hooked on Poison: Pesticide Use in California, 1991–1998.* San Francisco: Pesticide Action Network North America.

Kroll-Smith, S., and H. H. Floyd. 1997. *Bodies in Protest: Environmental Illness and the Struggle over Medical Knowledge.* New York: New York University Press.

Kroll-Smith, S., P. Brown, and V. J. Gunter. 2000. *Illness and the Environment: A Reader in Contested Medicine.* New York: New York University Press.

Martin, P. 2001. Labor Relations in California Agriculture. Chapter 5 from 2001 *State of California Labor* report from the Institute for Labor and Employment. Berkeley: University of California.

McWilliams, C. 1935. *Factories in the Fields: The Story of Migratory Farm Labor in California.* Berkeley: University of California Press.

Medvitz, A. G., A. D. Sokolow, and C. Lemp. 1999. *California Farmland and Urban Pressures: Statewide and Regional Perspectives.* Agricultural Issues Center–Division of Agriculture and Natural Resources. Davis: University of California.

Mills, P. K., and S. Kwong. 2001. Cancer Incidence in the United Farm Workers of America (UFW), 1987–1997. Cancer Registry of Central California. Accessed on the United Farm Workers Web site: http://www.ufw.org.

Mitchell, D. 1996. *The Lie of the Land: Migrant Workers and the California Landscape.* Minneapolis: University of Minnesota Press.

Moses, M. 2002. Presentation at annual conference of Californians for Pesticide Reform, December 7, Sacramento, California.

Moses, M., E. S. Johnson, W. K. Anger, V. W. Burse, S. W. Horstman, R. J. Jackson, R. G. Lewis, K. T. Maddy, R. McConnell, W. J. Meggs, and S. H. Zahm. 1993. Environmental Equity and Pesticide Exposure. *Toxicology and Industrial Health* 9 (5): 913–959.

Osborne, W. J., S. E. Kegley, and s. Orme. 2001. 1999 California Pesticide Use Maps. San Francisco: Pesticide Action Network. http://www.pesticidereform.org/datamaps/datamaps.html.

NSAN. 2003. No Spray Action Network. See http://www.freestone.com/nospray/.

PAN. 2003. Pesticide Action Network Pesticides Database. Available at http://www.pesticideinfo.org/index.html.

PANUPS. 2002. Latino Farm Workers Face Greater Risk of Cancer. Pesticide Action Network Updates Service, July 19. See http://www.panna.org.

Perrow, C. 1999. *Normal Accidents: Living with High-Risk Technologies.* Princeton, N.J.: Princeton University Press.

Pulido, L. 1996. *Environmentalism and Economic Justice.* Tucson: University of Arizona Press.

Rajan, S. R. 1999. Bhopal: Vulnerability, Routinization, and the Chronic Disaster. In A. Oliver-Smith and S. Hoffman, eds., *The Angry Earth: Disaster in Anthropological Perspective.* New York: Routledge.

Reeves, M., A. Katten, and M. Guzmán. 2002. Fields of Poison 2002: California Farmworkers and Pesticides. Pesticide Action Network. Available at http://www.panna.org.

Sokolow, A. D., and E. G. Medvitz. 1999. The California Scene. Introduction to Medvitz, Sokolow, and Lemp, *California Farmland and Urban Pressures.*

Solomon, G. 2000. *Pesticides and Human Health: A Resource for Health Care Professionals.* Physicians for Social Responsibility. San Francisco: Californians for Pesticide Reform.

Thornton, J. 2000. *Pandora's Poison: Chlorine, Health, and a New Environmental Strategy.* Cambridge, MA: MIT Press.

U.S. EPA. 2002. Spray Drift of Pesticides. U.S. Environmental Protection Agency Office of Pesticide Programs. July 2. Available at http://www.epa.gov.pesticides/citizens/spraydrift.htm.

Vargas, M. 2001. Labor and Community Collaboration. Chapter 16 from 2001 *State of California Labor* report from Institute for Labor and Employment. Berkeley: University of California.

Villarejo, D., D. Lighthall, D. Williams, A. Souter, R. Mines, B. Bade, S. Samuels, and S. McCurdy. 2000. *Suffering in Silence: A Report on the Health of California's Agricultural Workers.* Davis: California Institute for Rural Studies.

Wells, M. 1996. *Strawberry Fields: Politics, Class, and Work in California Agriculture.* Ithaca, NY: Cornell University Press.

Wright, A. 1990. *The Death of Ramon Gonzalez: The Modern Agricultural Dilemma.* Austin: University of Texas Press.

Zabin, C. 1992. *Mixtec Migrant Farm Workers in California Agriculture: A Dialogue among Mixtec Leaders, Researchers, and Farm Labor Advocates.* Davis: California Institute for Rural Studies.

Zabin, C., M. Kearney, A. Garcia, D. Runsten, and C. Nagengast. 1993. *Mixtec Migrants in California Agriculture: A New Cycle of Poverty.* Davis: California Institute for Rural Studies.

14

Notes from the Field

Air Pollution Engineering as Cultural Experience

Roger K. Raufer

I was recently asked to make a presentation at a workshop designed to encourage the development of combined heat and power (CHP) systems in
Pennsylvania, sponsored by the U.S. Department of Energy and the State
of Pennsylvania's Department of Environmental Protection. I had spent a
period of eight years working on the Grays Ferry Cogeneration project, a
150-megawatt combined-cycle facility located in downtown Philadelphia,
and had obtained a number of air quality permits that allowed that facility
to be constructed and operated. What was most unique about the experience in my mind was that I had three bosses—the developer, the steam
host, and the electric utility—all of whom were partners in the facility. I
often found that the most difficult permit negotiations encountered were
among these three partners. If I could get them to agree on a position,
then the negotiations with the air pollution regulatory agency were usually
quite cordial in comparison.

I prepared the presentation during a trip to China and happened to be
reading the Chinese classic by Luo Guanzhong, *Three Kingdoms* (Luo
1999). This is the story about the turbulent period following the breakup of
the Han dynasty at the turn of the third century A.D. I immediately recognized the electric utility in my downtown Philadelphia project as the powerful Wei Kingdom; the steam host as the opportunistic Wu Kingdom; and
the small, verging-on-bankruptcy independent developer that had hired
me as the embattled Shu Kingdom. I cast myself as Kongming, the crafty
and cunning adviser to the Shu leader, who sought to use whatever means
were available to unite the warring kingdoms and capture the permit.

I offered this version to my Chinese colleagues, who seemed convinced it was all brought about by a rather severe case of jet lag. It was better received at the CHP conference, however, and it did get me thinking about some of the similarities and differences that we encounter in performing air pollution engineering work around the globe.

I don't pretend to be an anthropologist or sociologist, and it might be considered a bit presumptuous to label such anecdotes "cultural experience." But I've used Mary Douglas and Aaron Wildavsky's work on risk and culture (Douglas and Wildavsky 1982), as well as the illuminating follow-up work by Michiel Schwarz and Michael Thompson (Schwarz and Thompson 1990), in a previous effort (Raufer 1998) and have found they offer a useful way of thinking about environmental situations in other countries.

A Cultural Model

Briefly, Schwarz and Thompson looked at the strategies that ecologists employ when managing ecosystems and then mapped social groupings onto these strategies. From the ecologists they found that management strategies followed one of the four "myths of nature" shown in terms of a ball in a landscape in Figure 14.1. *Nature benign* is a forgiving world; the ball always returns to the bottom of the basin, and nature maintains its equilibrium. *Nature ephemeral* is almost exactly the opposite, with the world always on the brink of catastrophic collapse. *Nature perverse/tolerant* is forgiving within a normal range but is vulnerable if conditions go outside the norms. Finally, *nature capricious* is a random world, and all one can do is cope with erratic events. The researchers attached social relationships to these myths of nature, using two well-known archetypes in the social science literature (individualists and hierarchists) and adding two less recognized groups: egalitarians, who have a critical rationality and a communal viewpoint; and fatalists, who suffer whatever happens. The result of this mapping is also shown in Figure 14.1.

Environmentalists are clearly in the egalitarian grouping, fearful that the least environmental change will bring about disaster. Market-oriented economists are just as clearly individualists, living in a *nature benign* world. Their laissez-faire beliefs tend to admit few unintended impacts outside the direct actions of the market. Hierarchists are the police, lawyers, EPA government officials, and municipal environmental engi-

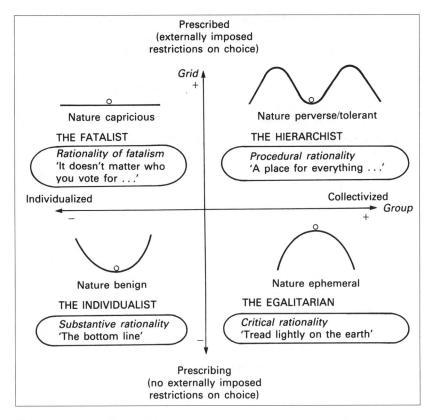

FIGURE 14.1

neering staffs who keep things functioning normally, within a proper operating range. As long as things stay within this range, the situation will be fine. And finally, there are the fatalists—most citizens, who go about their everyday business with very little thought about air quality, pollution concerns, or environmental threats.

Schwarz and Thompson suggest that from any quadrant, people in the other quadrants appear to be irrational; that there is constant conflict among the three "active" quadrants, with all three trying to influence the passive fatalists; that no single viewpoint ever permanently triumphs over the others; and that no quadrant's viewpoint is viable on its own—it needs the others. Collective wisdom—a sort of "meta-understanding of the inchoate" (Schwarz and Thompson 1990)—comes from the constant tensions, clashes, and interactions among these viewpoints. The strength of countries like the United States is to be found in the institutional arrangements that allow, foster, and politically accommodate such differences. Hence the title of their work: *Divided We Stand.*

Much of my work has involved the formerly centralized, planned economies, and it is interesting to note Schwarz and Thompson's view on their demise. These economies essentially tried to eliminate the two lower quadrants, the market-oriented individualists and the complaining egalitarians, leaving behind only the administrative-oriented hierarchists (e.g., the police, the army, and the bureaucrats) and the long-suffering fatalists. Although the long-lasting reign of one "active" quadrant caused considerable environmental harm, even that was not permanent, and the other active quadrants are now making their come-back.

My own experience abroad has fallen almost exclusively within the upper right and lower left quadrants of this figure. I don't deal very often with the egalitarians, and in countries such as China, their role is still quite limited. The Chinese government no doubt noticed how environmental non-governmental organizations (NGOs) served as a vehicle for political dissent in the former Soviet Union and Central Europe, and I suspect that it is not anxious to repeat that experience. Nor do I tend to deal with the fatalists, the everyday citizens who go about their everyday matters with little direct consideration about environmental concerns. They certainly hold views about these issues, and the danger of assuming a "top down" view of environmental management is well documented (Khator 1984, 105–112). But, admittedly, my work doesn't provide much insight into these quadrants.

So with these caveats in mind, let us turn to the upper-right quadrant, the hierarchists.

Hierarchists

Schwarz and Thompson suggest that "the situation [in that quadrant] cries out for hierarchy: sober, expert, and, above all, enduring" (Schwarz and Thompson 1990, 10). It is the governmental officials in this quadrant who set environmental goals (typically in the form of ambient standards), gather environmental data, and ensure that appropriate pollution control strategies are developed to address air quality concerns.

Air Quality Goals

Perhaps the most surprising element in air quality engineering abroad is that the air quality goals are so readily adapted from the U.S. experience. The U.S. has both primary and secondary ambient standards, with the former designed to protect public health and the latter addressing welfare. The control effort is heavily oriented toward the primary, health-based standards—yet U.S. citizens spend less than 10 percent of their time outside. Total exposure assessment analyses have documented that a much greater impact is caused by indoor air quality, and this is affected by such factors as tobacco smoke and household chemicals.

The U.S. EPA has focused its attention on industrial emissions, but these typically have a much smaller effect on health than the localized, indoor sources. James Roumasset and Kirk Smith have estimated, for example, that on a mass-quantity emissions basis, sidestream tobacco smoke represents only about 4 percent of the total particulate emissions from coal-fired power plants. Yet tobacco smoke is about seventeen hundred times more effective in causing exposure than the power plant emissions. If a regulatory agency could get a 2 percent reduction in tobacco smoke exposure, it would be equivalent to eliminating all of the health impacts from the power plants (Roumasset and Smith 1990).

This idea gains particular force when applied in developing countries, where respiratory diseases are a principal cause of death and illness, and where the need for efficient environmental spending is particularly critical. One of the major sources of indoor pollutant exposure is the primitive cookstove, often burning dung and other poor-quality fuels. The authors compared two potential programs in India—one designed to improve power plant control of particulate emissions, and another to improve cookstoves. Following an emissions approach such as that of the U.S. EPA, the power plant option is clearly the best strategy: it is almost twenty times more cost effective on a rupees/ton basis than cookstoves. Yet, if exposure is considered—something any health-based approach ought to do—the same degree of exposure reduction could be obtained from cookstoves at one-ninth the cost (Roumasset and Smith 1990).

The situation in China is very similar, with high risks associated with indoor particulate emissions and a dramatic increase in cigarette smoking in recent years (Chu 1999). Yet the government has followed a path that focuses on ambient emissions from industrial emission sources. This is not to argue that industrial sources should be ignored. But if public health improvements due to respiratory concerns are truly the goal, there are certainly more direct paths than the current air quality regulatory process in either India or China.

Air Quality Data

Knowing how close we are to achieving air quality goals depends on ambient monitoring. In the United States, it is routinely accepted that one should site monitors to measure the maximum impact of a facility or the area of the cities likely to have the highest ambient concentrations. I've been involved in a number of power plant programs where both pre- and post-construction monitoring was performed, and the monitor site selection process has been audited by the regulatory agency. It is a bit difficult to convey the obsessive focus in the United States to document such "worst-case" conditions. I've helped to develop analytical techniques that would assure that such monitoring sites are exactly targeted (Noll et al. 1977), and in one project we even employed mobile monitors to capture every worst-case condition (Raufer, Courtney, and Noll 1979). At another facility, we agreed to test for three chemicals not even emitted in the power plant's plume—the neighbors simply wanted to have a better idea about what was going on at a nearby chemical factory down the street.

Such worst-case monitoring is not necessarily the norm in other parts of the world. It tends to be relatively expensive, and many urban areas simply do not have the resources or number of monitors necessary to pick out all of the "hot spots." Even given these constraints, however, it tends to come as a surprise to U.S. engineers that the environmental agency in another country might not be particularly interested in finding such worst-case concentrations. Certainly, the distribution of ambient monitoring sites in some cities is "selective," even given resource constraints. This may also be the case with related public health data. One country I worked in turned down offers of technical assistance to sample blood lead levels in children, and in another we were not allowed to obtain data concerning the exposure of traffic police to carbon monoxide concentrations. One gets the sense that some governmental environmental agencies do not necessarily want to know worst-case conditions in their cities, nor even "typical" conditions, if such information might require some significant governmental response.

Other Environmental Data

Air quality data are not the only kind of information required, of course, and environmental regulatory officials must gather data about emissions of various pollutants, stack heights, exhaust gas conditions, meteorology, and so forth. They usually face a daunting job in doing so, especially in countries where information is not readily shared or where environmental management does not have a particularly high governmental status.

It is thus not unusual to find large "gaps" in databases. Some gaps might be intentional (in one case, for example, I found that a whole class of industrial activity was missing from a regional emissions inventory, by administrative fiat; those emission sources were treated differently and hence were simply not included in the regular database). More often, however, the gaps are the result of a lack of resources on the part of the environmental regulator or simply of the poor quality of the data collection effort itself. Emissions are often based on crude mass balance estimates, or rough emissions factors applied to questionable fuel statistics. (In China, however, we found through data quality checks that emissions estimated by such crude means were sometimes overstated as well as understated [Raufer, Zhuang, and Tang 2000, 12].)

Environmental agencies themselves are often reluctant to share such data with "outsiders," and the agencies often now request funds for access to such data. Some data are particularly sensitive (e.g., the amount of non-compliance fees collected by the government or how such fees were spent), and there is often little transparency in such matters.

These data issues create a particular problem when the environmental agency tries to make the linkage between the air quality goal (i.e., the ambient standard) and what is actually happening in the region (e.g., the emission sources, their operating conditions, meteorology, etc.). This linkage is usually accomplished through physical modeling, and in most developing countries this can present a rather difficult task. The dispersion models are often computationally complex, trying to represent the atmospheric chemistry, transport, and dispersion occurring over regions that often have uniquely complex terrain features. The regulatory personnel might have the intellectual resources to tackle the job, and they often have considerable interest in doing so—but the exercise might well be compared to having an expensive, finely tuned race-car but no gasoline to run it. The crude input data are simply no match for the sophisticated tasks for which they are being employed.

Control Strategy Development

When the air quality problem is understood, then the next and fundamental step in air quality management is to do something about it. There are, of course, many facets to such a complex and difficult chore, but the hierarchists must typically deal with at least two key parameters: (1) the technology to be employed and (2) the institutional setting.

The technology itself usually takes the form of so-called end-of-pipe controls (e.g., electrostatic precipitators, scrubbers, etc.) or pollution prevention (e.g., energy conservation, clean production, etc.). In the United States, old-time air quality engineers like myself tend to feel more comfortable with the end-of-pipe approaches, since we've always assumed that the market would take care of the latter. If energy or resource efficiency were economically warranted, then the facility would simply have gone ahead and done it. Even "clean production" in the United States represents a "post-end-of-pipe control" strategy—when the marginal costs of pollution control became too high, then it began to make more economic sense to get rid of the pollutant.

But the situation is exactly the opposite in the formerly centralized economies. Their facilities did not operate in such a market context, and market-oriented resource efficiency never played a role in reducing pollution. There are still plenty of low-cost opportunities there (i.e., fix the steam trap, insulate the hot water pipe, etc.), and so the latter types of engineering skills are more urgently needed. When these have been employed, there will still be a need for the end-of-pipe types. But the more pressing need is for the efficiency types.

Necessary end-of-pipe controls do face one considerable obstacle when applied in developing countries: they cost money to operate. And one of the most frustrating aspects of performing engineering work in such countries is observing what happens to pollution control technology when there is little (or no) willingness to use it. In one country, I observed an expensive fabric filtration system that was supposed to collect lead dust from a secondary lead smelter. The facility was causing considerable environmental damage to nearby residents, and a European country had donated equipment to mitigate the problem. But when I saw it, the device was filled from flange to flange with lead dust—and a new exhaust pipe had been added to simply bypass the control device. Similar devices in the facility's operating plant (which were part of the production process and captured valuable product) were operating as designed, however. To the plant manager, the former units represented an unwanted cost, the latter a valuable economic investment—but the nearby community was paying a very heavy price for such views.

In another country, I saw a similar device that was not filled with dust but nevertheless did not operate. The plant manager there found it less expensive to pay the pollution penalty fee than to operate the control equipment. The plant manager was happy to reduce his production costs, and the local environmental agency was actually pleased as well, since their incoming revenue increased. No national environmental authority stepped in to address this situation.

Since the "demand" for air pollution control comes through the government, it is perhaps not surprising that institutional issues almost always play a crucial role in air quality management. And it is difficult to summarize experience in this area, since the institutional component in every country is different. In no other area does the "cultural" context take on greater meaning, and the experience of U.S. engineers becomes quite atypical.

There are at least three general areas in which the hierarchists must deal with institutional concerns. The first is in the sheer complexity of the air quality issue. There are many different pollutants, interacting in various ways, coming from many different types of emission sources, in different locations, with different control options, and so on. Some are best handled at the national level (e.g., emissions from new motor vehicles), others at the local level (e.g., street sweeping for dust control), with a wide range of institutional interaction in between. Environmental officials at the local level often do not have the financial resources or the technical expertise to deal with tough pollution problems, and in many cases, one of the most valuable roles of an outsider is to convince officials that such problems are not intractable.

At the second level is the complexity of institutional motivations. In many countries, local environmental authorities seem much more concerned about economic development than about their own environmental protection purview.[1] Their own job performance might be evaluated in exactly such terms, and their career advancement, community status, and perks often depend on it. Sun Guodong has noted that the local environmental agency director's position in China is "lucrative and attractive for bureaucrats" (Sun 2000) because the director judges the emission source's degree of environmental compliance and decides the negotiable pollution fee; as such, the director has to "satisfy the mayor's expectations" (Sun

2000). But clearly, environmental officials operate within a hierarchical framework (the very point of the quadrant's label) and pursue broader goals than just air quality.

Finally, there is the complexity of the hierarchists' own views, and especially their perception of their own government. Judith Shapiro has pointed out that after decades of public exhortations for collective good, the Chinese people have been left with a deep cynicism about state-promoted values in any form (Shapiro 2001, 204). Comparable frustration is evident in many other countries, where regulators may view even their own agencies as inept or corrupt or perhaps both.

Environmental regulators are also often left to fend for themselves in a harsher market-oriented world, leading them to try to "sell" services that we in the United States would consider a blatant conflict of interest. In addition to selling emissions or ambient monitoring data, agency personnel might prepare environmental impact assessments (EIAs) or design pollution control equipment—and then, as the regulator, sit in judgment about their adequacy.

But that harsh new market-oriented world also offers a brand new environmental vision for those persons in the bottom left quadrant, the individualists.

Individualists

> Economists are technicians, who explain how goals might be achieved, while supposedly remaining indifferent to the goals themselves. This indifference to goals makes economics a favoured political tool. (Milton 1996, 72)

The transformation of environmental thinking to incorporate economics is a topic I discussed rather extensively in a previous work (Raufer 1998). I suggested that over recent centuries, a general regulatory framework has evolved that is quite compatible with the engineering (and hierarchical) worldview, as shown in Figure 14.2. Governments set environmental goals, typically in the form of environmental quality standards, to protect society from excessive pollutant levels. The goals are typically set by analyzing scientific knowledge about public health impacts, damage to ecosystems, and so forth, and then choosing a level that will provide, to use the words of the Clean Air Act of 1970, "an adequate margin of safety." These goals are then generally accomplished by instituting prohibitions and/or tech-

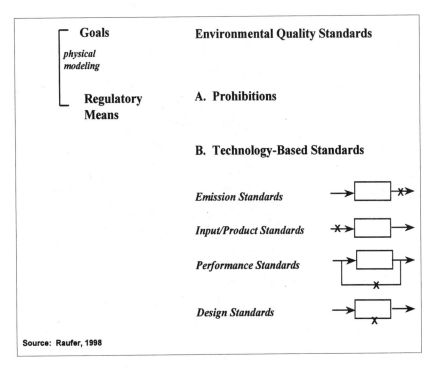

FIGURE 14.2. Command/Control Regulation

nology-oriented requirements (emission standards, design standards, etc.) that will achieve and maintain the desired pollutant levels. As noted earlier, the linkage between the environmental goals and the regulatory means is physical modeling.

In recent decades, however, economists have offered an alternative to this regulatory approach. In this approach, governments would set environmental goals at the point where marginal costs (MC) equal marginal benefits (MB), instead of setting ambient standards. Theoretically, at least, all the concerns about public health, ecosystem damage, visibility, and so on could be incorporated into these curves.

Economists also offer different regulatory means to accomplish their environmental goals. It would be nice if there was an "invisible hand" that would guide society to the singular point where MC = MB, as happens with supply and demand. But this is not the case, so economists offer two approaches to reach that point, one based on prices and the other based

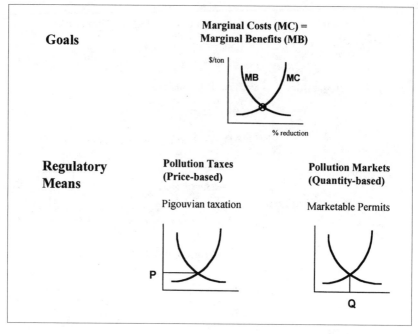

FIGURE 14.3. Economic Regulatory Approach

on quantities. The price mechanism was developed by the English economist Arthur Pigou in his classic text *The Economics of Welfare* in 1920, and pollution taxes are referred to as Pigouvian taxation (Pigou 1920).

The quantity approach was outlined by Professor John Dales of the University of Toronto in 1968, in his book titled *Pollution, Property and Prices* (Dales 1968). These price and quantity mechanisms in Figure 14.3 are really different sides of the same coin, but there are important differences in their application, particularly in the political arena.

In the United States, Figure 14.2 has not been replaced by Figure 14.3, and the economists' approach does not eliminate the hierarchists' goal setting, data collection, and institutional problems discussed earlier. In many cases, it actually requires an even more sophisticated institutional response from government. But the individualist ideas inherent in this latter figure are nonetheless beginning to have a significant effect on the regulatory process. In the mid-1970s, the EPA adopted the Emissions Trading Program, which grafted an economic mechanism allowing marginal cost thinking onto the traditional system shown in Figure 14.2. Then, in 1990,

Congress adopted Dales's quantity-based approach to control the acid rain caused by the total loading of sulfur dioxide from electric utilities. In the late 1990s, the same quantity-based mechanism was employed to tackle the problem of tropospheric ozone, through the NOX Budget and similar city and regional markets.[2]

This transition did not occur because of the goal-setting ideas detailed in Figure 14.3, in which marginal costs are set equal to marginal benefits. Kay Milton (1996) suggests that economists remain indifferent to how environmental goals are set—but I believe that the real problem for goal-setting economists is the difficulty in operationalizing their theories. The tools they have (contingent valuation, hedonic pricing, etc.) are no match for the task demanded, and as economists move farther and farther from "use" values and into "non-use" terrain, such as sympathy for other species and bequests to future generations, these tools become increasingly clumsy and blunt.

But while their goal-setting approach might be suspect, the power of the economic regulatory means in Figure 14.3 is a completely different story. These have some extremely useful properties: they allow the government to focus on setting environmental targets, rather than dictating stack-by-stack means; they are economically efficient; this efficiency can, in turn, influence "real-world" goal setting, allowing us to purchase more environmental protection; and pollution always bears a cost, leading polluters continuously to seek means of reducing it.

The New Markets

From the perspective of a U.S. air quality engineer, what is perhaps most surprising is the speed with which these new individualist mechanisms (and in particular the idea of employing environmental markets) have become internationally accepted. This is no doubt part of a broader movement recognizing the limits of governmental command/control mechanisms and the new market-oriented view from the "commanding heights" (Yergin and Stanislaw 1998). But individualist thinking is now evident over a broad range of environmental topics (Hahn 2000), and its influence is increasing. It is perhaps not surprising that the whole framework for the Kyoto Protocol follows such an economics approach, and that carbon trading is now a hot topic in Ukraine, China, and Ecuador.

This has occurred despite the fact that there is still a general lack of understanding about how such markets operate; that the markets themselves are artificial, with "demand" coming from governmental coercion; and that, as noted earlier, there remain considerable institutional difficulties associated with their implementation. The powerful properties of the economic instruments—governmental focus, economic efficiency, aggressive protection, and costs for pollution—all rely on that regulatory, institutional base.

I recall attending a conference about market-oriented environmental management in what was then still the Soviet Union, and after three days of hearing about "markets, markets, markets," I decided to use my scheduled time to present a somewhat "reactionary" viewpoint. I noted that in the 1960s the United States had a sophisticated market system, but it still had a lot of pollution; that it cleaned up using command/control measures; and that market-oriented thinking became important only as the society began to climb the marginal cost curve. In the early stages of the program, when we didn't know much about who was emitting the pollution, where, or how much, it was important to develop a workable regulatory, technology-oriented framework. Given that marginal costs were probably relatively low and marginal benefits relatively high, such actions were more important than economic efficiency. Today's sophisticated market-oriented programs still rely on that base. Some of my non-engineering colleagues put more emphasis on the economics, suggesting that if one can get prices right, then everything else will follow. But I must confess to remaining somewhat skeptical.

Price versus Quantity

More interesting, perhaps, from a cultural viewpoint is the important distinction between price (P) and quantity (Q) mechanisms. Most of the world has tended to focus on the price-based Pigouvian tax approach, in which the government sets the tax, collects the money, and then, one hopes, does environmentally admirable things with the collected revenue. In the United States, there has never been political support for such price-based mechanisms, and the economic systems that have evolved follow the quantity-based approach. These are more closely attuned to the American political characteristics of property rights, markets, and minimizing wealth transfers to the public sector. Years ago, when I was approached by Michael Dukakis's campaign to put together a position paper on acid rain, they only wanted to hear about Q-based approaches; there was simply no political interest in using taxes for such purposes.

When I lectured about U.S. quantity-based programs in Europe in the 1980s and talked about emissions brokers and similar attributes of the quantity-based approach, the idea was met with considerable disdain. Such crass capitalist thinking would never find favor in Europe, I was told, because it was simply uncouth to consider buying and selling pollution. Even the economists swallowed hard. Robert Nelson has noted the support of environmental economists for Pigouvian taxation over quantity-based approaches and suggests:

> In part, this seems to have been a case of simply picking the wrong horse. But it is also likely that professional economists in the environmental field were aware of at least some of the practical advantages of a market permit system, but simply could not accept its ideological implications. (Nelson 1987, 70)

Today, of course, many of these price-based countries are enthusiastic supporters of the Kyoto Protocol's quantity-based approach, and the European Union plans to introduce a carbon-trading scheme in 2005. Individual European countries have already adopted emissions trading programs,[3] and others are closely studying the idea. Even price-based countries such as China are now paying attention (Fernando et al. 1999; Raufer 2000).

Market Simulations

One very useful tool for teaching about quantity-based instruments is the Electric Power Research Institute's SO_2 Emissions Trading Simulator (Niemeyer et al. 1991). This multi-media training program was developed in 1991 to help teach power plant operators how the market-based acid rain control approach in the Clean Air Act Amendments of 1990 would work. Participants spend the morning with video instruction, learning how to use software that lets them operate five power plants in an electric utility system, with various fuels and pollution controls. In the afternoon, they buy and sell electricity and pollution allowances to each other in a full-scale market simulation, under progressively tighter pollution constraints. We know their starting and finishing costs and can tell how well each participant did (compared with an optimum trading scenario) in the power sector marketplace.

I've now run this program in a number of countries, for European, Russian, Ukrainian, Chinese, and developing country participants (as well as for a wide range of students at the University of Pennsylvania). There is almost universal fascination with the fundamental economic ideas and with the manner in which abstract ideas about pollution control marginal costs and such can be translated into real-world choices and operating decisions.

There were also interesting cultural differences (although the sample sizes here are admittedly minuscule). The Ukrainian session was the most unruly, bordering at times on anarchy. The Europeans tended to be appreciative, the Chinese skeptical. Most developing-country participants seemed convinced that, while the concept might be interesting, it had absolutely no relevance for the non-American/European world.

In the Russian session (conducted in the early 1990s, shortly after the Soviet breakup), the market ideas themselves seemed quite strange. I remember quizzing one participant, who appeared reasonably comfortable with the software and technical data but who just sat staring at his computer. When queried, he replied: "Well, no one has come to me with any deals." When I suggested that he might be able to formulate his own deals and take the initiative in a prospective transaction, it was almost as if the proverbial light bulb appeared over his head: "Yes, I suppose I could do that," and off he went.

It may well be that the chief value of the Kyoto Protocol lies in exactly this area, bringing doubting developing-world participants and newly converted centralized economies into the environmental marketplace, through project-oriented Clean Development Mechanism and Joint Implementation "flexibility" mechanisms. In addition to their market characteristics, such mechanisms introduce both transparency and environmental accountability into project development. They might at least be considered a start in a task that will require decades, and probably centuries. And, just maybe, the country that is the chief proponent of such quantity-based approaches will ultimately see its value and decide to join the venture as well!

Conclusions

"Sustainable development" in most of the developed world is viewed almost exclusively within an "environmental" context, but such is not the case in the developing world. There, the term has important economic and social components as well, and any hope of achieving air quality goals must be cognizant of these differences. Air quality engineers, like other technical specialists, find that there are considerable cultural components embedded in their views about how the world works.

This chapter describes some of these factors for a U.S. engineer working in other countries, relying on a "cultural theory" model that posits important roles for government-type "hierarchists" and market-oriented "individualists." Both have played an important role in achieving air quality goals in the United States, and both are likely to play an important role in other countries as well. Environmentalist-type "egalitarians" are also active participants, and all three active groups try to influence the passive "fatalists"—although these latter groups are not addressed in this chapter.

Hierarchists set the environmental standards, gather the environmental data, and ensure that the appropriate pollution control strategies are developed and implemented. Like their U.S. counterparts, other countries have typically developed an air pollution regulatory process more attuned to tackling emission source problems than to directly accomplishing public health or other environmental goals. They must wrestle with poor data, but there sometimes appears to be a reluctance to target environmental data if these, in turn, will necessitate a strong governmental response. Hierarchists must also wrestle with institutional problems, and the complexity of air pollution problems, the motivations of environmental actors, and their individual viewpoints all affect control actions.

Individualists have fostered a new way of thinking about environmental regulation and have been quite successful in the United States in introducing market-based economic instruments. These still have many of the same data and institutional problems as the hierarchists' approach but offer some powerful properties, including both governmental focus and economic efficiency. They are now spreading worldwide, at a very rapid rate—despite the fact that much of their U.S. success has rested on an existing command/control regulatory base. Following the U.S. lead, there has also been a noticeable shift from price- to quantity-based instruments, despite (or perhaps because of) their ideological trappings. European countries and China are now readily exploring such approaches, and the Kyoto Protocol is taking such markets worldwide.

NOTES

1. See, for example, H. S. Chan, K. K. Wong, K. C. Cheung, and J. M. Lo, "The Implementation Gap in Environmental Management in China: The Case of

Guangzhou, Zhengzhou, and Nanjing," *Public Administrative Review* 55 (July/August 1995): 4.

2. See Raufer 1998 for a discussion of these programs and comparable figures.

3. Denmark launched a power sector emissions trading (ET) program on July 1, 2000; the United Kingdom launched an ET program on August 14, 2001.

REFERENCES

Chu, H. 1999. "Cigarette Toll Rising among Men in China." *International Herald Tribune,* November 11.

Dales, J. H. 1968. *Pollution, Property and Prices.* Toronto: University of Toronto Press.

Douglas, M., and A. Wildavsky. 1982. *Risk and Culture: An Essay on the Selection of Technological and Environmental Dangers.* Berkeley: University of California Press.

Fernando, P., et al. 1999, *Emissions Trading in the Energy Sector: Opportunities for the People's Republic of China.* Manila: Asian Development Bank. September.

Florig, H. 1997, "China's Air Pollution Risks." *Environmental Science and Technology* 31 (6): 274–279.

Finkelman, R., H. Belkin, and B. Zheng. 1999. "Health Impacts of Domestic Coal Use in China." *Proc. Natl. Acad. Sci. USA* 96 (March): 3427–3431.

Hahn, R. 2000. "The Impact of Economics on Environmental Policy." *Journal of Environmental Economics and Management,* 39 (3): 375–399.

Khator, R. 1984. "Environment as a Political Issue in Developing Countries: A Study of Environmental Pollution in India—A Viewpoint." *International Journal of Environmental Studies* 23: 105–112.

Luo, G. 1999. *Three Kingdoms.* Beijing: Foreign Language Press; Berkeley: University of California Press.

Milton, K. 1996, *Environmentalism and Cultural Theory: Exploring the Role of Anthropology in Environmental Discourse.* London: Routledge.

Nelson, R. 1987. "The Economics Profession and the Making of Public Policy." *Journal of Economics Literature* 25 (1): 49–91.

Niemeyer, V., et al. 1991. SO_2 *Emissions Trading Simulator.* Palo Alto, California, EPRI AP-100276. November.

Noll, K. E., T. L. Miller, J. E. Norco, and R. K. Raufer. 1977. "An Objective Air Monitoring Site Selection Methodology for Large Point Sources." *Atmospheric Environment* November 11 (11): 1051–1059.

Pigou, A. C. 1920. *The Economics of Welfare.* London: Macmillan & Co.

Raufer, R. 1998. *Pollution Markets in a Green Country Town: Urban Environmental Management in Transition.* Westport, CT: Praeger.

———. 2000. "Economic Tools in Air Pollution Abatement: The Increasing Role of Quantity-Based Instruments." Paper presented at International Conference on Engineering and Technological Sciences, Beijing, October.

Raufer, R., Y. Zhuang, and X. Tang. 2000. *Urban Air Pollution Control in China: A Sector Review Report.* UNDP and CICETE. Beijing: China Science and Technology Press. October.

Raufer, R. K., A. O. Courtney, and K. E. Noll. 1979. "Air Monitoring Network Design to Meet PSD Requirements." *Power Engineering* February 83 (2): 63–65.

Roumasset, J., and K. Smith. 1990. "Exposure Trading: An Approach to More Efficient Air Pollution Control." *Journal of Environmental Economics and Management,* 18 (3): 276–291.

Schwarz, M., and M. Thompson. 1990. *Divided We Stand: Redefining Politics, Technology and Social Choice.* Philadelphia: University of Pennsylvania Press.

Shapiro, J. 2001. *Mao's War against Nature: Politics and the Environment in Revolutionary China.* Cambridge: Cambridge University Press.

Sun, G. 2000. "An Integrated Study of China's Air Pollution Management: Effectiveness, Efficiency, and Governance." Diss., Carnegie Mellon University.

Yergin, D., and J. Stanislaw. 1998. *The Commanding Heights: The Battle between Government and the Marketplace That Is Remaking the Modern World.* New York: Simon and Schuster.

15

The Social and Political Construction
of Air Pollution
Air Pollution Policies for Mexico City, 1979–1996

José Luis Lezama

According to official data, more than 2.5 million tons of pollutants are discharged into the Mexico City's atmosphere annually. Official environmental standards are violated over 320 days a year, 150 days a year in the case of suspended particles. The problem is compounded by the fact that, apart from the substances that are officially acknowledged and regularly monitored, there is also a group of pollutants known as toxic substances that are virtually ignored by official programs. A number of specialists agree that the latter constitute the greatest risk for the population, not only because of their high degree of toxicity but because of the lack of public awareness of their existence and dangerousness.

Advances in knowledge, both at the international level and in case studies undertaken in Mexico City, have yielded increasingly precise evidence of the scope of the damage to human health caused by air pollution. Studies have shown that women, children, and the elderly are particularly sensitive to acute exposure to these pollutants.

Government policies have started to systematically address Mexico City's air pollution problem. However, these policies have failed to eliminate or significantly reduce pollution. From 1979 to 1996, three official programs have been executed. After the implementation of the first program, data show an actual increase in the volume of substances discharged into the atmosphere. Subsequent programs implemented in 1990 and 1996 have achieved a partial reduction of substances such as sulfur dioxide and carbon monoxide yet have failed to decrease ozone, suspended particulates, and hydrocarbons. Despite achievements, the situation continues to be severe. The severity of the problem has sparked interest in the scientific community. Fairly detailed studies have been undertaken of the chemical composition of the substances, their reactions and synergistic effects on the atmosphere, and the geographic and meteorological conditions that exacerbate and in some cases disperse pollutants, together with major sources of emissions, particularly sectoral contributions by industry, transportation, and services. Significant progress has also been made in the study of the effects on human health caused by air pollution.

Nevertheless, these studies have focused on the physical, chemical, and technical aspects of air pollution. They have ignored the social aspects of pollution. In this study, interviews with Mexican scientists, academics, environmental activists, and government officials show that air pollution is a socially contested issue and that air pollution policy is socially and politically constructed.

As the chapters in this book argue, there is a social dimension to environmental problems that has the same reality status as that of their physical dimensions. From this perspective, environmental problems depend on a process of social construction and are identified by their perception and public recognition. A problem may have a physical existence, but unless it is socially perceived and assumed as such, the physical facts become socially irrelevant.

The social perspective does not deny the physical existence of air pollution, which it uses as its starting point. Nevertheless, it emphasizes the analytical need to separate the social existence of problems from their chemical and physical existence, thereby giving rise to disciplinary study from the perspective of the social sciences. The authors who have reflected on the social dimension of environmental problems seek to explain the social mechanisms that at times enable certain aspects of reality to acquire a special meaning and significance, enabling them to emerge on the public scene.

In this context, certain communities regard air pollution as a more important problem than others. In other societies they are not even regarded as such. For some authors, it is society that gives meaning and importance to the ranking of problems, regardless of their intrinsic importance. But apart from these ideological and social factors, there are also political factors that influence or bias the selection of what is risky and what is safe. In Matthew Crenson's classic work *The Un-politics of Air Pollution*, subtle mechanisms of power and social conflict management determine the success or failure of certain problems to reach the public scene. Analyzing two case studies, Crenson (1974) describes a concrete policy-making process, emphasizing the specific way in which air pollution policies were designed as a result of the interplay of social, ideological, and political forces. What Crenson is interested in discovering is the social mechanism that explains the emergence of air pollution in or its concealment from the public arena. He asks a very simple question: Why is there no agreement between the size of an environmental problem and the degree of public alarm? It is necessary, according to Crenson, for a social scientist to ask why certain problems that should be a matter of concern are not.

Crenson carried out his study on air policies in two cities in the United States: Gary, Indiana, and East Chicago. In Gary, the presence of a large steel company, the dominance of a single political party, the lack of a diverse productive plant, and the reputation of power inherent in the steel company were decisive factors that helped prevent the air pollution issue from being brought to the political scene as an important civic claim. The steel company did not always have to exert direct pressure on the local political institution to defend its interests, since many other people took it upon themselves to do so. No one wished to prevent the company from providing jobs and prosperity for the community.

East Chicago was not economically dependent on a single large company, nor was it dominated by a single political party, and its occupational structure was fairly diverse. As a result, air pollution problems had more opportunities to become an *issue*. This city could promote a more aggressive air pollution policy earlier. In both cases, social, economic, and political features determined the presence or otherwise of an air pollution policy. The severity of the air pollution problem was not the main factor behind the emergence of air pollution as a political *issue*. Although both cities had the same level of air pollution, their economic, social, and political characteristics were different, meaning that air pollution was treated differently.

In this context, some sociologists emphasize the separation often observed between the scope of problems and their emergence as an object of interest for both the general public and those who reflect on them analytically. After comparing countries with severe environmental problems to others where they are less acute, Ulrich Beck (1995) and other authors suggest that countries with the most critical problems appeared to be less concerned about environmental deterioration. Conversely, countries with fewer environmental problems appeared to be the most concerned. In this author's view, cultural standards and the will to perceive certain problems constitute decisive factors in the emergence of awareness about high-risk situations and the establishment of what society defines as acceptable or unacceptable damage. Beck suggests that there is not a mechanical relationship between ecological damage and consciousness; both aspects are mediated by cultural standards and the will to perceive certain problems as such.

The natural environment and ecological damage also appear in Maarten Hajer's (1995) perspective as something that is shaped by images and discourses. Nature emerges as the result of perceptions, and these are the products of experiences, language, images, and fantasies. Some societies have an image of nature as something fragile, while others perceive it as robust and able to resist disturbances. People have different ideas regarding the ecological crisis, and consequently, they have different solutions for what they have perceived and defined in different terms. Nature and environment mean different things for different societies.

What is important for the purposes of this research is to analyze how some authors reflect on the way environmental problems undergo the transition from being regarded as a purely physical to a social condition, in order to become a matter of public recognition and of government intervention. According to Hajer, the developments in environmental politics critically depend on the specific social construction of environmental problems. For this author, the policy-making process cannot be thought of only as a mechanism to find solutions to preconceived environmental problems but must also be considered as a practical way for modern societies to regulate latent social conflicts, such as those produced by the environmental crisis. The policy-making process is thought of as a process of redefining the problems to be addressed and finding solutions according to a set of socially accepted practices. Hajer perceives the policy-making process as something that takes place in a context of and through fragmented and contradictory discourses, not only within but also outside the environmental sphere. The policy-making process has to do with the creation of problems to be handled institutionally by means of *ad hoc* solutions. In this context, he affirms:

> Policies are not only devised to be able to solve problems. Problems also have to be devised to be able to create policies. (Hajer, 1995: 15)

Hajer suggests using discourse analysis as a method to uncover the social and cognitive basis of the way problems are constructed. He analyzes the interaction between social processes that make actors' mobilization possible and those ideas that permit people to share similar understanding and common environmental goals. Political decision making takes place in disputed scenarios of competing social constructions of environmental problems. In this public domain, characterized by conflicting points of view, some consensual images of what is good or bad and of what is risky or safe are constructed. It is in this scenario of fragmented and contradictory discourses that decisions are taken.

In modern societies, the process of regulation, according to Hajer, carries out three tasks. The first has to do with what he calls "discursive closure," which means to suggest certain definitions of problems to give the policy making a proper target. The second is to find ways to contain social conflicts, and the third is to provide a "problem closure," to offer a remedy to what was defined as a problem. An important clarification made by Hajer regarding these tasks of regulation is that they do not necessarily have a mutually supportive character. On some occasions, one task can contradict another. For example, technical solutions insensitive to the common-sense social construction of a problem can result in a regulatory failure. It is also possible that a solution based in a consensual social construction could aggravate a problem in spite of achieving great social support.

The regulatory function of government environmental institutions is dependent on the discursive construction of problems. It is not the physical crisis of environment that provokes social change, nor the destruction of certain valued social assets, but the creation of images, identifiable emblems that allow people from different positions and perspectives to share a common image of what can be considered a problem. These emblems permit the creation of discursive coalitions that make it possible to construct a dominant vision of what the problems are. In the discursive process, the meaning and the importance of some problems are susceptible to change, and the positions and interest of people can also be transformed.

Government policies appear in Hajer's perspective as a socially accepted set of measures to deal with what has previously been defined as the problem. But what can be considered factual reality or an objective problem is rather the subjective result of social interaction. These sets of facts are not the same as those empirically defined as the physical facts associated with environment; instead, they emerge as socially constructed.

There is a social construction of environmental problems, and there is a process of selection of what can be considered risky and safe. That process takes place in a symbolically constructed world and is carried out by means of language, words, and discourses. Ideological factors and political forces are mobilized and displayed in this constructed world made possible by human interaction.

It is not the logic of scientific knowledge that dominates in the policy-making process but that of political and ideological negotiation around some meanings, perceptions, hopes, fantasies, and interests. As Beck (1992) points out, rather than being based on objective scientific foundations, decisions are taken guided by moral and political principles. This does not mean that science is irrelevant in the policy-making process. What it mean is that scientific findings have to be considered as a relative body of truths, and public attitudes toward science have to change from faith to doubt and criticism. In a terrain dominated by contradictory and ambivalent scientific findings, it is not possible to base government intervention on a non-existent body of irrefutable truths. It is not only environmental claims that are contested but also the available knowledge on crucial environmental problems. Many decisions have to be taken in a scenario where uncertainties play an important role.

The Case of Mexico City

In interviews carried out with a group of people closely involved with Mexico City's air pollution (academics, political party representatives, green activists, entrepreneurs, government officials, etc.), air pollution emerges as a debated and contested issue. The social construction of air pollution appears in the way actors define the emergence, the severity, the magnitude, the government capacity to solve the problem, and the role of science in the policy-making process, and also in the possibilities, obstacles, and solutions the actors suggest for Mexico City's air pollution problem. Actors viewed the emergence of air pollution as a matter for concern, reflection, and government intervention in a contested way. It is not just the damage inflicted on nature and people but also the public appearance of a new attitude, the diffusion of alternative values and principles, and the repercussions of the international environmental movement that are thought by some actors to trigger air pollution consciousness.

The majority of the actors interviewed acknowledged the importance of air pollution as a real source of concern. This acknowledgment reflects a certain degree of agreement between what the data describe as a significant objective problem and what people perceive about it. However, two important analytical aspects must be emphasized. First, the relative general agreement on the importance of air pollution is not unanimous. There are significant differences among the actors over the accepted degree of air quality degradation that makes air pollution socially relevant. For example, academics and government officials generally acknowledged the importance of the problem. However, they did not share the almost apocalyptic view of green activists and political parties of the damage and deterioration caused by poor quality of Mexico City's air. Contrasting sharply with the green activists' and political parties' perceptions was the entrepreneurs' denial of the importance of air pollution. For the former, air pollution was a problem of survival for Mexico City's inhabitants. For the latter, the extent of air pollution damage was heavily exaggerated by environmental groups and politicians. In terms of existing data, both positions are extreme, and both contain a broad subjective variability. In this respect, both positions differed considerably from what existing data describe as the physical dimension of air pollution. Both reflected a clearly social dimension of the air pollution problem.

On the other hand, the social actors interviewed understood the emergence of environmental and air pollution problems in different ways. One group of actors thought that air pollution had emerged in the public awareness as a result of the degree of environmental degradation and because of the damage inflicted on people. In their view, social and cultural mediation was unnecessary for the recognition of a severe problem. Another set of actors did not think that the magnitude of the problem or the attendant damage was the only reason behind the emergence of air pollution as a matter of public concern. It had more to do with changes in values, cultural and social changes that determined what was tolerable or intolerable. In this case, academics and green activists held opposing views. The former cited social facts and values as triggering recognition of a problem as a social threat. The latter believed that the magnitude of the problem itself automatically led to an awareness of air pollution damage. Most of the remaining actors' positions fluctuated between these two extremes.

In this context, when the actors interviewed for this research answered the question on the factors explaining the emergence of air pollution as a matter of social concern, they mentioned factors linked to one or the other of these two perspectives. Academics and green activists expressed two extreme positions. The former attributed environmental awareness to a changing perception of problems in the modern world, which meant that at some point environmental issues became relevant for different social groups, first in the developed world and then throughout the rest of the world. For the latter, consciousness had emerged as a result of the severity of the problem and because many of them had begun to notice that their health was being affected. No social or symbolic mediation was required for consciousness to emerge; the degree of damage alone sufficed.

Not all the actors interviewed can be classified into one of these two positions, but their respective perceptions expressed different degrees of agreement or disagreement with them. The social construction of these air pollution perceptions were expressed through the different social conditions that led the groups to focus on certain trigger factors, such as the physical nature and damage caused by pollution, in the extreme case of the green activists, and the more cultural and social elements, in the case of the academics. For academics, the explanatory possibilities were broader, since they included different disciplines and approaches. Conversely, green activists had to focus on a narrower range of factors. Describing the extent of the damage and the threat due to the physical magnitude of a problem was better suited to their role as claim-makers.

But it is not only in the appreciation of the triggering factors of the public emergence of air pollution that actors interviewed show their divergence; it is also in the way they qualify the severity of air pollution in Mexico City. What separates actors in this specific issue is how they present their argument to define either the harmful or the harmless character of air pollution problem. Some actors transmit an image of urgency, while others argue that the problem is overemphasized by extremist positions.

The interviewees' answers reflected these contrasting perceptions of the issue. At one extreme of this perceptual spectrum, government and entrepreneurial representatives held that air pollution was a significant problem but not as serious as some groups declared. At the other end of the spectrum were the rest of the social actors—the academics, the green activists, the political parties, and the international representatives—who expressed their concern over the severity of air pollution. Yet these extreme positions did not mean that all those within a particular position shared the same reasons and arguments. For example, government officials and the entrepreneurial sector gave different reasons for their denial of the severity of air pollution. For the former, the main reason was government's success in reducing pollution. For the latter, the problem's severity was exaggerated. However, both insisted on exonerating themselves from responsibility for the problem.

The rest of the social actors, in the opposite position, included more diversity in their answers. The green activists and academics gave the strongest arguments to explain the severity of air pollution. However, while the greens regarded government and the entrepreneurial sector as the main culprits with regard to air pollution, the academics used more social groups and more social explanations to explain the reasons for bad air quality. The academics insisted that it was not only the government's and entrepreneurs' responsibility to clean up the environment; it was also a general societal obligation. In their view, the rest of society was reluctant to perceive the severity of the problem and to become more involved in the search for solutions. For the greens, both government and the entrepreneurial sector were involved in a conspiracy to pollute while the greens, armed with certain confidential official documents, were trying to show the population the true facts to raise their awareness and achieve greater public involvement in the solution.

The social construction of air pollution, particularly its severity, was borne out by the wide range of perceptions. However, even more important were the possibilities of observing some of the ideological dimensions that define an environmental ideological political construction (EIPC), such as those used in this research. For example, some of the answers given by government and the entrepreneurial sector reflected a need to express their own institutional or group perspective, thereby proving their particular point; in other words, ideology in these circumstances works as a legitimizing mechanism to reproduce the status quo. In contrast, the academics' inclusion of more social factors to account for the severity of air pollution not only reflected their greater analytical scope, due to their use of more rigorous methods, but also exemplified one of the ideological dimensions used in this research, a dimension that operates as a constitutive element of social life.

Air pollution also emerged as a social problem through the way in which actors compared it with other environmental issues. Most actors agreed over the magnitude of the air pollution problem. However, they disagreed over the relative importance given to air pollution. Water, sewage, hazardous waste, and soil erosion competed with air pollution for the role as Mexico City's major environmental problem. With the exception of political party representatives, who unanimously cited air pollution as the most worrying problem in the city, each of the sectors interviewed gave a range of different answers. There was relative consensus in some sectors, but in most of them, the other environmental problems mentioned above were regarded as more important. However, air and water were usually considered the main problem. There were, however, some distinct differences in the various actors' social constructions. For example, government was more interested in prioritizing problems and selecting just one to focus on, be it air or water. Instead of emphasizing the range of problems, academics were more concerned with explaining the conditions that ensured that a particular problem was socially accepted as the most significant. In describing the importance of both air and water, government emphasized the physical aspects of these problems that had made them an object of social concern. Academics, in contrast, acknowledged the importance of considering all the environmental problems in the city, attributing the wider recognition of air pollution to knowledge and communication of the latter to the general population. In their view, government, as well as the general public, was biased toward air pollution. Among the rest of the social actors, air and water vied for consideration as the main environmental problem of the city.

The general agreement over the magnitude of the air pollution problems reflected the shared feeling that, according to the actors, was present at the societal level. In this respect, EIPCs revealed their socially constitutive dimension. However, ideological influence can also be viewed as a means of reproducing group and institutional perspectives. This is the case in terms of government's need to prioritize environmental problems so as to focus its planning activities on a socially acknowledged object of concern, namely, air pollution. The need to legitimate its actions is a plausible explanation for the government's bias toward air pollution issues. The academic sector did not attempt to prioritize the problems. In their view, all of them deserved the same analytical attention. They were more interested in explaining the social reasons behind the emergence of environmental problems. Finally, the political parties cited air pollution as the city's main environmental problem. The fact that this coincided with the view of the general public fit in with their need for public support.

Finally, the actors also showed a variety of conceptions and ideas on how to face and solve air pollution problems. Most actors shared a general optimism over the possibilities of solving the problem. However, differences began to emerge when the actors specified the conditions required for the problems to be solved. Government officials emphasized their institutional perception of the problem. Solving the problem would require streamlining the institutional structure, raising awareness among all the government officials in the different areas of public administration, and creating a sort of intersectoral team to work together on the environment. Government intervention was depicted as a central factor in solving the problem. Government officials mentioned a wide range of obstacles to decision making, including social, economic, and political problems. They also referred to more concrete obstacles, such as budgetary restrictions, vehicular and population concentrations, and proposed highly specific measures for improving the transport system.

For most of the other actors, particularly for academics, the problem could be solved, although radical measures would have to be taken, which would mean affecting powerful economic and political interests. Yet, while academics mentioned the need for both societal and government commitment to the environmental cause, the rest of the non-governmental actors, particularly the green activists and the political parties, attributed the entire responsibility for the problem to government failure to enforce regulations and poor environmental performance on the part of the entrepreneurial sector.

All the social actors perceived at least some of the social elements that either helped or hindered the improvement of air quality. According to some perceptions, government actions appeared to be influenced or shaped by economic and political forces. According to others, government was paralyzed by these political forces. However, in their own perception, government officials depicted themselves as an independent body that would be able to provide a solution through the more efficient use of their technical and human resources. However, while all the actors were clear about the obstacles to improving air quality, most of them experienced difficulties in proposing solutions. The proposals they made were either general, such as changing the development model, or concrete and isolated, such as building special tracks for public buses or improving fuel quality.

The various aspects of EIPCs analyzed here reflect the presence of a social construction of air pollution. Actors agree or disagree over central issues related to the nature of air pollution: its magnitude, its importance in relation to other environmental problems in the city, the role of scientific knowledge in the planning process, the obstacles and solutions created by other actors, and the role of values and social, economic, and political forces in the policy-making process. There was some consensus over certain issues, but there were also disagreements. Air pollution emerged as a hotly disputed and frequently debated and contested issue. This scenario of broad subjectivity reflected the social construction of the problem that this research sought to prove.

In analyzing the air pollution constructions of various actors, this research shows the various ideas, conceptions, and interpretations that can be used to reconstruct a relevant social dimension of air pollution involving values, economic factors, political forces, and ideological meanings. According to some actors, the issue of air pollution is not restricted to its physical-chemical and technical aspects but is also the result of the dynamic interplay of actions and reactions among social actors. These actors participate in the air pollution scenario as the embodiment of various kinds of knowledge, ideological principles, particular interests, social principles, and demands that must be claimed for the benefit of society as a whole. The conceptualization of air pollution in the policy-making process constitutes another reality, different from yet complementary to the physical nature of this problem. This reality has its own legitimacy not only from an analytical perspective but also with regard to the needs of the planning process. Its inclusion in the policy-making process could enhance the efficiency of air pollution policies.

Air pollution program officials did not regard air pollution as the result of social factors, despite the fact that some of the most important social actors involved in the issue had a social perspective of the problem. While the latter experienced, perceived, and constructed air pollution as a dynamic, contested, and debated problem, subject to social subjectivity, and as a reality resulting from values, different kinds of knowledge, ideology, economy, and politics, official programs failed to understand the non-physical, non-technical nature of air pollution. While social actors disagreed over the need to include non-governmental factors and actors as necessary components of the policy-making process, governmental programs regarded government as the main forum for programmatic intervention in air pollution issues. Most social actors did not consider obstacles and solutions to air pollution purely on the basis of technical decisions. Likewise, social actors did not view environmental decisions and solutions as solely determined at the level of knowledge and the will to make decisions but rather as the result of different social dynamics in which scientific knowledge was a necessary, albeit insufficient, condition for decision making. These different social dynamics appeared in the general discourse of some actors, as the result of the interplay between economic, political, and ideological factors. Air pollution as an issue also appeared to be the result of awareness and the will to perceive it. It was not solely determined by its magnitude or by the damage it caused but was a socially constructed problem. This constitutes the social dimension of air pollution that the official programs failed to incorporate when analyzing the problem and attempting to solve it.

The incorporation of the social construction of environmental problems in government programs, and its use to educate the general population, can be a crucial element of social support for stricter political measures to attack air pollution, particularly in a deteriorated environment such as Mexico City's air. This recognition could be used to design educational programs to educate people on environmental problems. This will help them make the connections between environmental problems such as air pollution and human or personal health. A community well informed and more involved in air pollution issues could be a source of social support to propose programs and actions to a cleaner environment.

REFERENCES

Beck, Ulrich. 1992. *Risk society: towards a new modernity.* Newbury Park, Calif.: Sage Publications.
————. 1995. *Ecological enlightenment: essays on the politics of the risk society.* Atlantic Highlands, N.J.: Humanities Press.
Crenson, Matthew. 1974. *The un-politics of air pollution; a study of non-decision-making in the cities.* Baltimore: Johns Hopkins University Press.
Hajer, Maarten. 1995. *The politics of environmental discourse: ecological modernization and the policy process.* New York: Oxford University Press.

Afterword

Joel A. Tarr

This collection's creative title, *Smoke and Mirrors*, aptly describes the scholarly articles in this volume that explore issues relating to air pollution in historical, contemporary, and cross-national perspectives. The articles examine air pollution issues at different times and in different locations, but with a common perspective: that air pollution and its abatement policies need to be viewed as "social artifacts," rather than "scientific facts" or "economic values" alone. This perspective reflects the current thrust in historical and social science studies to study phenomena from a wider cultural and social perspective, rather than from a narrow political, policy, or technological focus. It therefore borrows its conceptual apparatus from bodies of scholarship related largely to social "constructionism." This perspective, applied to the environment and, in this case, specifically to issues of air quality, promises to broaden our understanding of how we have dealt with such questions in the past and suggests possibilities for future studies and strategies. I would like to point out, however, some of the risks associated with such an approach. In particular, I am concerned that the critique of the centrality of scientific "fact" will lead to an analytical blind spot that ignores the importance of scientific knowledge in environmental policymaking.

I will try to illustrate my comments with the following Pittsburgh vignette.

As I sit at my computer desk writing this "Afterword," I notice a scattering of black particles that has accumulated on my desktop and threatens to dirty my white pages; perhaps, when airborne, they would invade my bronchial tubes. The presence of this "dirt" (defined as "matter out of place") brings to mind several memories. Twenty-five years ago I would have identified the black particles as pollution stemming from the large integrated steel mill that sat on the shores of the Monongahela River about two and a half miles from the university. The mill closed down in 1983, however, so I must search elsewhere. Ten years ago I might have blamed the particles on the byproduct coke oven (coke ovens are notorious polluters) that stood close to the blast furnaces, supplying them with the coke necessary to make iron in Pittsburgh and elsewhere. But then I remember, the source could not possibly be the coke plant, which closed in 1997.

The mill was eventually replaced by a shiny new technology park, with only a plaque and a picture of the former mill (the "Eliza" furnaces) to remind us of what had been. Gone were the columns of black smoke that issued from its lofty chimneys over many years. It is as if the mill had never existed, nor the eight to ten thousand jobs it provided to the region's industrial working class. The coke plant survived for about fourteen years longer than the mill, and today its partially cleared site awaits the outcome of discussions about its future between various stakeholders, including community residents, city and county officials, and the Pittsburgh foundations that now own the property. In the meantime, the site qualifies as a major eyesore, and the several thousand workers whom the mill employed have gone elsewhere, usually to lower-paying jobs. Also gone are the plumes of white smoke, smelling of sulphur, that would periodically issue from the plant as each load of red hot coke was quenched.

Understanding who was responsible for the pollution generated by the steel mill and the coke plant is more difficult than one might assume. Certainly, fumes and particles came from the plants, but by 1960 a county air pollution control bureau existed that supposedly was responsible for regulating this pollution. Should blame for the pollution fall on the public agency that was unwilling to push the industry to control its pollution? Perhaps, but are we sure the technology was available to make complete control possible? And at what cost? Should the air pollution control bureau have been willing to engage in a technology-forcing policy? Not very likely, given the power of the industry in the region. But even if the steel mill itself had been willing to modernize, controlling emissions from the coke plant was a more difficult task. In other words, both the science—questions about the effectiveness of the technology—and the politics—questions about the mobilization of economic and social interests—came into play in the creation of this particular pollution.

Eventually, some reduction came about, primarily because of the activities of a citizens group called the Group Against Smog and Pollution (GASP), composed primarily of a group of middle-class women, many of whom were housewives, plus some academics and professionals. Provided with stature by the county variance code, the citizens' organization successfully demanded its right to participate in county variance board hearings and brought enough pressure to force the variance board to enforce and tighten the county code against the mills. Now the mills are gone, and so is the pollution they generated. And while there are several explanations as to why the mills closed, there are those who will tell you that it was primarily because of the cost of environmental controls.

Yet, I still have not answered the question that I began with—where did the particles on my desk originate? The steel mill and the coke plant are gone, although certainly other sources of pollution remain. And GASP is still actively watching over the quality of the air in Pittsburgh. The pollution that continues is indeed a much smaller problem than that which existed twenty-five years ago, when the mill and the coke plant operated day and night, filling the air with fumes, odors, and particles. For this we can largely thank several factors—the coming into the city (unexpectedly) of clean natural gas in 1946–47 (eventually largely driving out coal as well as the regional coal mining industry) and a strong smoke control law; and, somewhat later, the collapse of the regional steel industry. These events brought Pittsburgh and its region cleaner air and water but cost it many thousands of good-paying industrial jobs. These costs are reflected in the boarded-up storefronts and decayed neighborhoods that mark the mill towns where the steel plants had been located.

When one queries the residents of these towns and neighborhoods about whether they are happy to see the mill gone, one gets different answers—some bemoan the loss of valued jobs, while others are thankful that the pollution generated by the mills is no more. Clearly, the industry itself bears much of the responsibility for its own demise, but possibly not all. For environmentalists not living in the immediate area of the former mill, however, the environmental gains are palpable.

This brief vignette typifies the complexity that surrounds many air pollution issues. First of all, there is the question of defining the problem or question—are we addressing a scientific problem of air pollution and its abatement, or is it a larger issue that relates to the nature of the social and economic structure of the society? Then there is the economic issue— could the mills have afforded to install the most modern pollution control technology, given the foreign competition they were meeting, or would they have fallen even if they had modernized? For whom was the pollution a problem that demanded action? The population most affected by the smoke and fumes were those living closest to the mills, but these people were also largely employed in the mills and lost their jobs when the mills closed. Members of GASP also benefited from the cleaner air, but they also largely retained their jobs. If pollution was identified as problematic and as an issue for policy to address, how was it measured and what indictors were used? How were the thresholds for action set? Did the policy enacted and implemented solve the problem? Did it transfer it somewhere else? Or was it only a superficial response that left the problem largely untouched? Scientific knowledge, while not enough, could certainly play a role in answering these questions.

Scholars approaching these questions often use a model, either explicit or implicit, to organize their writing. While historians are much less self-conscious than social scientists about the use of models, they employ them nevertheless. What themes of analysis scholars choose to emphasize often shapes the character of the outcomes. Working a problem backward rather than forward in time, for instance, can provide the analyst with different perspectives and insights. With both approaches there is always the danger that the writer may project backward on his or her materials the values and scientific and medical knowledge of the writer's own time. Identifying health effects from various pollutants may be possible today but was not necessarily possible given the state of medical knowledge in the past. This does not mitigate the severity of the issue but does shed light on the evolution and character of policies to regulate pollution.

As we try to understand the development of air pollution policy, the question often arises about its origins. Do air pollution policies reflect the long-term accumulation of scientific knowledge about the injurious effects of various emissions, or are they a sudden response by a governmental body jolted by a crisis, usually related to the public health? How far has science advanced in helping us comprehend the problem's origins and consequences? What relationship do policies have to the capabilities of technology to deal with the issue? Were firms that were identified as responsible for problem generation reluctant to make necessary innovations and changes because of costs? Would a policy, therefore, that followed a technology-forcing strategy be doomed to failure?

Certainly, the role of culture in a larger sense enters into the picture. How do we evaluate its effects? The middle-class women who organized

GASP were unlikely participants in Pittsburgh air pollution battles, but they played a critical role. Why hadn't Pittsburghers, newly victorious over smoke pollution a few years earlier, organized quickly against industrial pollution? Were the power configurations of the area against it? In the case of the steel industry, the economic implications of such regulations were much greater. In addition, was it possible that the new and cleaner technology was so expensive that the industry could not afford to make the investments?

There is the critical issue of whose "culture" and values are involved. A citizen's group largely organized and run by middle-class women led the drive against industrial pollution; but what of other social groups? There are often many stakeholders involved in environmental issues, with varying degrees of investment, and it is not always easy to sort them out. Industrial workers both suffered and benefited from the existence of a large plant—suffered in terms of their exposure to potentially harmful fumes and particles and benefited because of the availability of industrial jobs. Some workers became environmentalists, but others, especially after the mills had closed down, questioned the cost of clean air.

As scholars explore these questions, enlarging our understanding of the issues surrounding air pollution, it is predictable that a number of alternative approaches or models will be utilized. Some of these approaches—social constructivism in particular—are more critical of science than others. In the process, the most important factor to be aware of is the necessity of making our values and scholarly approaches clear and to understand that the issues we are dealing with are often multi-faceted. While it is fashionable in social constructionism to challenge the validity of science and science indicators, it is important not to dismiss their usefulness but rather to question what they are measuring and not measuring, and where thresholds for action are set.

And, by the way, where do those black particles on my desk actually come from, do they do more than dirty my papers, and who will pay the price in this zero-sum game to get rid of them? Answering this question will require *both* scientific and constructivist knowledge.

Contributors

A graduate of the Chemistry Department of the University of Auckland, *Peter Brimblecombe* is now Professor in Atmospheric Chemistry at the School of Environmental Sciences, University of East Anglia. Active on air pollution matters within working parties in the European Commission and the European Science Foundation, he is also Senior Executive Editor of *Atmospheric Environment* and on the boards of *Chemosphere, Environment and History, Idojaras, Journal of Cultural Heritage,* and *Environmental International.* His research work (on solubility of atmospheric gases, thermodynamics of atmospheric electrolytes, air pollutant damage to materials, history of air pollution) is widely published in academic books and journals (roughly two hundred articles). These include two books on air pollution history: *The Big Smoke,* Methuen, London (1987); and, with Christian Pfister, *The Silent Countdown. Essays in European Environmental History,* Springer Verlag, Heidelberg (1990).

Phil Brown is Professor of Sociology and Environmental Studies at Brown University. He is currently examining disputes over environmental factors in asthma, breast cancer, and Gulf War–related illnesses, as well as toxics reduction and precautionary principle approaches that can help avoid toxic exposures. He is the co-author, with Edwin Mikkelson, of *No Safe Place: Toxic Waste, Leukemia, and Community Action*; co-editor of a collection, *Illness and the Environment: A Reader in Contested Medicine*; and editor of *Perspectives in Medical Sociology.*

Joshua Dunsby is Postdoctoral Fellow with the Institute for Health Policy Studies and the Center for Tobacco Control Research and Education at the University of California, San Francisco, where he is researching the politics of indoor air pollution and the shaping of scientific debate surrounding environmental tobacco smoke. He completed his Ph.D. in Sociology and Science Studies at the University of California, San Diego. His doctoral dissertation, "Clarifying Smog: Expert Knowledge, Health, and the Politics of Air Pollution," concerns the public health response to smog in Southern California from its inception until the late 1960s and considers the ways in which smog was constructed as a moral, scientific, medical, and political object. He has published on the politics of air toxics risk assessments in *Science, Technology, and Human Values* and has collaborated on a article, published in *Social Studies of Science,* on public commentary regarding the Food and Drug Administration's proposed tobacco control regulation.

E. Melanie DuPuis is Associate Professor in the Department of Sociology at the University of California, Santa Cruz. Her work focuses on the political sociology of the environment, both urban and rural. She is the author of *Nature's Perfect Food: How Milk Became America's Drink* (New York University Press, 2002), the co-editor of *Creating the Countryside: The Politics of Rural and Environmental Discourse,* and a number of articles on rural land planning, urban consumer politics, and the political economy of agriculture.

Alexander Farrell is Assistant Professor in the Energy and Resources Group at the University of California, Berkeley. His research focuses on energy and environmental technology, economics, and policy. He has published numerous articles on the use of technical information in policy-making, market-based environmental regulation (i.e., emissions trading); the environmental impacts of energy; the application of sustainability in decision making; security in energy systems; and alternative transportation fuels. Alex has a B.S. in Systems Engineering from the U.S. Naval Academy and a Ph.D. in Energy Management and Policy from the University of Pennsylvania. His prior experience has been with Carnegie Mellon University, Harvard University, the American Association for the Advancement of Science, Air Products and Chemicals, and the U.S. Navy.

Angela Gugliotta is Lecturer and Research Associate in Environmental Studies and Humanities at the University of Chicago. She is completing her dissertation "'Hell with the Lid Taken Off': A Cultural History of Air Pollution: Pittsburgh before 1942" at the University of Notre Dame, under the direction of Christopher Hamlin. She has published articles in *Environmental History,* in the *Journal of the History of Medicine and Allied Sci-*

ences, and in the forthcoming collection *Pollution and Redemption in the Smoky City: The Environmental History of Pittsburgh and Its Region,* edited by Joel Tarr.

Jill Harrison is a doctoral candidate in Environmental Studies at the University of California, Santa Cruz. Her dissertation research examines the public health and ecological impacts of agricultural pesticide use in California. She has recently been awarded a Dissertation Fellowship from the University of California's Institute for Labor and Employment.

Theo Luebke teaches Biology and Environmental Science at Mohave High School in Bullhead City, Arizona. In addition to the traditional course of study, his curriculum focuses on ethical considerations in science and public health, as well as southwestern debates over land, water, and property. Continuing research interests include uses of scientific knowledge in environmental health disputes, asbestos-related disease in South Africa, and the evolution of social movements among military veterans.

José Luis Lezama is the head of the Center for Demographic and Urban Development Studies, El Colegio de Mexico. Dr. Lezama earned a Ph.D. in Environmental Policy from University College, London, and was a Visiting Professor at the Massachusetts Institute of Technology, coordinating the Air Pollution Chapter of the Mexico City Air Quality Project that was coordinated by the Nobel laureate Dr. Mario Molina. He is a sociologist specializing in environmental policy. He is the author of the following books: *Divided Air: Criticism of the Air Pollution Policy in the Valley of Mexico* (1990); *Social Theory, Space and City* (2002); *The Environment Today: Crucial Issues in the Contemporary Debate* (2001); *The Social and Political Construction of Environment* (2003).

Joshua Mandelbaum is Policy Adviser to Iowa Governor Tom Vilsack. He is a graduate of Brown University and a Harry S. Truman Scholar. His areas of interest include environmental sociology, social movements, and urban/regional planning.

Brian Mayer is a doctoral student in the Sociology Department at Brown University. His interests include environmental and medical sociology, as well as science and technology studies. His recent projects include an investigation of the growth of the precautionary principle as a new paradigm among environmental organizations and a study of social movements addressing environmental health issues.

Sabrina McCormick is a doctoral student in the Department of Sociology at Brown University. She is a Henry Luce Foundation Fellow through the Watson Institute of International Studies. Her main interests are environmental sociology, medical sociology, and the politics of development. As a Luce Fellow, she is engaged in comparing environmentally based movements in the United States and Brazil. Additional special interests include the social contestation of environmental illness, the insertion of lay knowledge into expert systems, and the role of social movements in these struggles. Sabrina has recent publications by *Ms.* magazine and the National Women's Health Network related to these areas.

Stephen Mosley is Lecturer in History at the School of Education, University of Birmingham, United Kingdom. He is the author of *The Chimney of the World: A History of Smoke Pollution in Victorian and Edwardian Manchester*. His research interests are in urban culture and environmental history.

Matthew Osborn received his Ph.D. in Modern European History from the University of California, Santa Cruz, in 1997. He is an Assistant Professor of History and Environmental Studies at Green Mountain College in Poultney, Vermont. His dissertation, "Land, Community and the Industrial Transformation: An Environmental and Social History of the Early Industrial Revolution in Oldham, England, 1750–1820," is being revised for publication.

Harold L. Platt is Professor of History at Loyola University of Chicago. He is the author of *City Building in the New South: The Growth of Public Services in Houston, Texas, 1830–1920* (Philadelphia, 1983); *The Electric City: Energy and the Growth of the Chicago Area, 1880–1930* (Chicago, 1991); and *Shock Cities: The Environmental Transformation and Reform of Manchester, U.K. and Chicago, U.S.A.* (forthcoming, Chicago, 2004).

Sudhir Chella Rajan is Senior Scientist at Tellus Institute, a non-profit research organization based in Boston that works on environment and resource strategies. He was previously Director at an international energy and development NGO in Bangalore and member of the engineering staff at the Mobile Source Division of the California Air Resources Board. He is the author of *The Enigma of Automobility: Democratic Politics and Pollution Control* (University of Pittsburgh Press, 1996) and has written numerous academic and popular articles on environment, politics, and development. He has a doctorate in Environmental Science and Engineering from UCLA. He is currently working on a long-term project exploring connections among environment and energy, politics, poverty, and the claims of global citizenship.

Roger K. Raufer, an environmental engineer with more than twenty-five years of experience, joined the Division for Sustainable Development at the United Nations in 2001. He had previously served as a consultant to the United Nations addressing environmental issues in China since 1990 and has also been a consultant to the World Bank and USAID in numerous countries around the world. He holds a Ph.D. in Energy Management and Policy from the University of Pennsylvania and taught there as an adjunct faculty member for eighteen years. He also holds degrees in chemical engineering, environmental engineering, and political science and is a registered Professional Engineer in a number of U.S. states. He has written two books on the role of economic mechanisms in environmental management.

Joel A. Tarr is the Richard S. Caliguiri Professor of Urban and Environmental History and Policy at Carnegie Mellon University. His main research interests are in the history of urban environmental pollution and urban technological systems. His latest book is *Devastation and Renewal: An Environmental History of Pittsburgh and Its Region* (editor, University of Pittsburgh Press, 2003).

Peter Thorsheim is Assistant Professor of History at the University of North Carolina at Charlotte. He is a British historian specializing in environmental history and the history of science, technology, and medicine. He is the author of a forthcoming book on coal smoke and perceptions of the environment in Britain during the nineteenth and twentieth centuries.

Frank Uekoetter is currently research assistant at the University of Bielefeld. His book titled *From the Smoke Question to the Environmental Revolution: Controlling Air Pollution in Germany and the United States, 1880–1970* was recently published by Klartext Verlag, Germany.

Stephen Zavestoski is Assistant Professor of Sociology at the University of San Francisco. His current research examines the role of science in disputes over the environmental causes of unexplained illnesses, the use of the Internet as a tool for enhancing public participation in federal environmental rule making, and citizen responses to community contamination. His work appears in journals such as *Science, Technology and Human Values, Journal of Health and Social Behavior,* and *Sociology of Health and Illness,* and in the book *Sustainable Consumption: Conceptual Issues and Policy Problems.*

Index

Access to Environmental Protection Act (Spain, 1995), 254

ACE. *See* Alternatives for Community and Environment

Acid, changing ecology of High Moorlands, 88–91

Acid deposition, 79–80, 91–92, 245. *See also* Acidification; Acid rain

Acidification, 87–88, 89, 95. *See also* Acid deposition; Acid rain

Acidity: attempts to regulate, 79; decrease in rainfall, 95; from mine drainage and run-off, 82–88; recognized as global issue, 94; recovery from, 93–94

Acid rain: difference in urban/rural approaches to, 27; effects on High Moorlands, 78, 80–82; improvements relating to, 92; market-based solution to problem, 231; studies in mid–nineteenth century, 31, 32; threat of, 80; vehicular influence on, 93. *See also* Acid deposition; Acidification

Aguilar-Fernández, Susana, 243

Ainsworth, Ed, 197n. 25

Air: ambiguities of "ownership," 226–31; common-property users, 230; disagreement over state regulation of, 234; negotiation over use as struggle over property rights, 225; political dominance over, 1; as public good, 223, 224, 226, 229–30

Air and Rain (Angus Smith), 80

AirBeat, 278

Air credits, as property, 234–36

Air Hygiene Foundation, 103–4

Air pollution, 177; broadening approach to, 102–3; changing perceptions about, 29; characterizing pesticide drift as, 289–90, 292–93, 296–99; conditions in Spain, 244–46; difficulty in defining and measuring, 110; earlier terms for, 196n. 14; early historical examples of, 15–16; effects of in nineteenth-century U.K., 22; effects on plants, 113n. 8; human effects in late-nineteenth-century Manchester, 34, 35; during industrialization, 15–16; in late-nineteenth-century cities, 18–20; linking to asthma, 269–71, 275; in Mexico City, 324–25, 329–36; monitoring networks for, 18–19; moral beliefs about, 177; policy about, 9–10; respiratory disease related to, 164–65; social and artistic implications, 22–24; social and political approaches to, 2; social aspects of, 325; source of class conflict, 34–35

Air pollution control: debate over rationales for, 137–38; inattention to automobile exhausts, pre-1945, 120; political economy of regulation, 215–18

Air pollution engineering, cultural experience of, 305–21

Air pollution policies, questions of origin, 340

Air quality: complexity of issue, 313; data, 310; foreign approach to engineering, 309; institutional motivations for addressing, 313–14

Aitken, John, 157

Alkali Acts of 1863, 19, 20

Allen, Patricia, 299

Altadena Property Owners' League, 187

Alternatives for Community and Environment (ACE), 264, 266–67, 277–84

Ambient monitoring, 310

Amdur, Mary, 268

Ancoats, mortality rates vs. suburbs, 39–41

Andrews, Thomas, 66

Angus Smith, Robert, 19, 31, 32, 33, 80, 87

Anthracite Institute, 103, 104

Anthramatic, 115n. 17

Anti–Air Pollution Committee (Pasadena, Calif.), 191

Aquatic life, harmed by acidic run-off, 84–85

Architecture, threat to, 22, 23–24, 67–68

Armstrong, William, 62

Arnott, Neil, 62

Art, pollution's implications for, in nineteenth-century England, 23

Asthma: checklist for parents and providers, 276–77; controversy over environmental factors, 268–71; corporate opposition to research on, 276; environmental factors contributing to, 264; environmental justice groups focusing on, 265–68; epidemic of, 263–64, 265; failure of participatory models to address environmental causes, 276; future of science and activism on, 275–83; growing debate around causes, 261–63; individual responsibility for addressing, 276–77;

political discovery as public health problem, 271–75; unique example of action on environmentally induced disease, 283

Atmospheric Pollution Research Committee (U.K.), 160

Automobile exhaust: failure to control, 119; German government reaction to, 132–36; noninfluence on policy, 120; public view of, 128–31; as research topic, 121–28; U.S. governmental reaction to, 131–32. *See also* Automobile pollution

Automobile pollution: cause and development of, 205; consumer tampering to overcome controls, 208; in-use controls, 210–14, 252; need to regulate, 206. *See also* Automobile exhaust

Automobile regulation: citizen participation, 208, 209; disallowing federal aid for state highway construction, 209; emissions control technology, 206; technical solutions preferred over behavioral, 207, 208. *See also Emissions listings*

Automobilism: contested nature of rise of, 120; early social costs of, 128–29

Automobility, 204–5, 207, 219

Back-to-nature movement, 179

Bacteriology, 29, 35, 41, 42

Bailey, G. H., 39

Baines, Richard, 55–56

Banham, Reyner, 206, 207

Barlow, Walter Jarvis, 181

BASF, 136

Baur, John E., 178, 179, 180

Beaver, Hugh, 161, 165

Beaver Committee, 161, 164–65

Beck, Ulrich, 326–27

Bell, Michelle L., 163

Bellasis, Mrs. E. J., 54–55

Benzol, 136
Berry, D. M., 180
Black's Guide to Manchester, 59–60
Bone, William, 69
Boulton-Watt steam engine, 83–84
Brodsky, Richard, 236–37
Brown, Phil, 298
Browner, Carol, 274
Buildings. *See* Architecture, threat to

CAAA. *See* Clean Air Act Amendments of
    1990 (CAAA) (U.S.)
California: addressing pesticide drift, 289;
    Inspection/Maintenance Program for
    automobiles, 211–13; political paralysis
    in, 217–18; reduction achieved in auto
    emissions, 213; regulatory response to
    automobile pollution, 204; reputation
    as pioneer in pollution regulatory
    field, 204; *See also* California, South-
    ern
California, Southern: air purity legend
    collapsing, 183–84, 192–93; location for
    health-seekers, 177–83; response to
    smog, 193–94; smog in, 172, 174. *See
    also* Los Angeles
California Air Resources Board (CARB),
    208, 209, 214, 215–17
California Energy Commission, 220n. 4
California Motor Vehicle Pollution Con-
    trol Act of 1960, 210
California Motor Vehicle State Bureau of
    Air Sanitation, 206
Californians for Pesticide Reform, 297
Carbon dioxide, 94
Carbon monoxide, 124–26; civic activism
    nonexistent against, 130–31; German
    approach to, 135
Carbon pollution standards, 217
Carbon trading, 317, 319
Car ownership, offsetting industrial pol-
    lution progress, 92–93

Carpenter, Edward, 64
Center for Disease Control, 272
Centers for Children's Environmental
    Health and Disease Prevention, 272
Central economies, pollution control
    strategy development, 312
Chadwick, Michael, 86
Chandler, Dorothy, 188, 197n. 25
Chandler, Norman, 188, 197n. 25
Chatfield, David, 297
Chemical climatology, 31
China, 8, 308; addressing air quality im-
    provement, 309–10; citizen's cynicism
    about state-promoted values, 314
Chlorpyrifos, 288
Cities, gender-based characterization of, 4
City beautiful movement, 179
Clarke, Allen, 69
Class conflict, resulting from air pollu-
    tion, 34–35
Class divisions, environmental injustice
    underscoring, 39–41
Clausius, Rudolph, 62
Clean Air Act (U.K.): 1956, 78, 80; 1968, 92
Clean Air Act (U.S.), 209, 213, 229
Clean Air Act Amendments of 1990
    (CAAA) (U.S.), 223; air use budgeted,
    230; air use limitations, 230–31; Emis-
    sion Reduction Credits, 232; state im-
    plementation of, 224–25
Clean Water Act (U.S.), 229
Climate change, "supertanker" issue, 95
Climatic therapy, 177, 178–79, 182
Climatology, 196n. 21
Coal, 6–7; arsenic in, 86; British national
    preference for fires from, 69; contra-
    dictory meanings of, 109; decline's
    effect on Pittsburgh, 101; fog related to
    smoke from, 157; as necessity of life,
    70; squandering of reserves, 61–62;
    usage in nineteenth-century Man-
    chester, 30

Coal gasification, 109–10
Coates, Crispin, 254
Cohesion Fund, 250
Coke, perceived as fuel of poverty, 57
Columbia Center for Children's Environmental Health, 272
Comité Para el Bienestar de Earlimart, 297
Common-good resources, ownership of, 227–28
Common-property regimes, 224, 225–26
Community action, addressing pesticide drift, 297. *See also* Environmental justice
Contested illnesses, 262
Control strategy development, 312–14
Convention on Long-Range Transboundary Air Pollution (LRTAP) (1979), 94, 242, 247, 248, 257
Cooke, A. S., 80
Cookstoves, 8, 309
Cost-benefit analysis, 10–11n. 3, 61, 273, 274
Cradle Will Rock, The, 105, 108
Crenson, Matthew, 1, 325–26
Cronin, William, 226
Cronon, William, 51–52
Crossing the Smog Barrier: A Factual Account of Southern California's Fight against Air Pollution (LACAPCD), 192
Culture, influence on pollution issue, 340–41

Dales, John, 316
Davis, Devra Lee, 163
DeAnda, Teresa, 297, 298
Death of Roman Gonzalez, The, 296
Derain, André, 23
Deutch, I. A., 184
Deutsche Saduyn-Gesellschaft, 122, 134
Dex Voeux, H. A., 157
Dickens, Charles, 60, 155–56

Didion, Joan, 206–7
Discourse analysis, 328
Dispersion models, 311
Divided We Stand (Schwarz and Thompson), 308
Dockery, Douglas, 268, 269
Douglas, Mary, 155, 166, 173, 306
Dry deposition, 79, 91
Durkheim, Emile, 173

Ecological economics, 3–4
Ecology, strategies for managing ecosystems, 306–8
Economics of Welfare, The (Pigou), 316
Egalitarians, 306, 307, 308, 321
Egerton, Lord of Tatton, 63
Electric vehicles, 216–17
Emission control, 91–93, 206–8, 210
Emission offset requirements, 235
Emission Reduction Credits, 223, 231–38
Emissions brokers, 319
Emissions inspection, 252
Emissions Trading Program, 316
End-of-pipe controls, 312–13
Energy, efficiency of, 41
Energy policy, politicians' concerns about, 256–57
Energy research, linking human body, city, and environment, 38
Environmental cleanup, contradictory process of, 4–5
Environmental data, gaps in, 311
Environmental health tracking, 272
Environmental history, 226
Environmental issues: factors related to reaction to, 326–29; frameworks for discussing, 1–2; social dimension to, 325–27
Environmental justice, 261, 265; community building and organizing, 277; groups as hybrid between science and activism, 282, 284–85; groups per-

forming own research, 275–76; shared strategies among groups, 282–83

Environmental policy: cultural approach to regulation, 321; economics approach to, 2–3, 314–17; internationalization of, 241–42; price and quantity mechanisms for regulation, 318–19; set by hierarchists, 308; social and political approaches to, 3

Environmental problems, possible responses to, 203–4

Environmental Protection Agency (U.S.), 209, 211–14, 228, 229, 272–74, 283, 289; defining "spray drift," 293; focus on industrial emissions, 309

Environmental quality standards; command/control regulation, 315; economic regulatory approach, 316–17

Estcourt, Charles, 35–36

Europe, air pollution agreements in, 242, 247–48

European Monitoring and Evaluation Program, 247, 253

European Regional Development Fund, 250

European Union, 247, 250, 251–52, 253, 254–55, 257

Evelyn, John, 63

Exhaust gases: ambivalent attitude toward, 123; cleaning, 122–23, 134–35; no presumed ill health effects, 123–24

Exhaust Gas Recirculation, 208

Exposure standards, 103

Fatalists, 306, 307, 308, 321

Federal Air Pollution Control Act (U.S., 1955), 206

Fifth Avenue Association, 129–30

Fireplace, central place in domestic life, 57–58

First possession, 228, 233

Flury, Ferdinand, 123, 124, 130

Fog: changing ideas about, 155–56; connotations of, 156; deaths related to, 154, 156; distinguishing natural and unnatural, 165; effects of, 22, 23–25; fear of, 41; frequency of reports, 20; opinions regarding health risks, 164–65; perceived as antithetical to civilization, 155; prompting need for reform, 29; smoke and sulfur dioxide related to, 157. *See also* London, 1952 fog disaster

Ford, Anson, 170

Fossil fuel, 7; exponential increase in consumption, 42; invisible gases considered harmful (1857), 31; invisible gases related to consumption of, 95

Foster, Reginald Le Neve, 58

Franco, Francisco, 148

Frankland, Edward, 157

Fry, G. L. A., 80

Fuel-celled vehicles, 218

Fuel reserves, realizing finite nature of, 62

Fuel substitution, 244–45

Gargano, Charles, 236

Gas, tool in Manchester environmental reforms, 37

Germany: Bureau of Public Health, 128; Department of Transportation, 128; governmental reaction to automobile exhaust, 132–36

Germ theory of disease, 35, 176, 182

Gesler, Wilbert M., 174

Gilbert, Roy O., 188–89

Globalization, 241–42, 255

Global pollution control, 5–6

Gothenburg protocol, 94

Government: policies of, socially accepted response to problems, 328–29; role of, 8

Graham, Eleanor, 105–6

Graham, John W., 43

Graham, William, 41

Greater Manchester Acid Deposition Survey, 95
Greenhouse gas standards, 217
Grindon, L. H., 89–90
Griswold, S. Smith, 191
Gross emitters, 214, 215
Group Against Smog and Pollution (Pittsburgh), 339

Haagen-Smit, Arie, 193, 197n. 27
Haggard, Howard, 125
Hahn, Robert, 233–34
Hajer, Maarten, 327–28
Harris, Ora, 212
Hart, Ernest, 68
Health Effects Institute, 273
Health inequalities, 271–72
Health-seeker movement, 172, 177–83, 192
Health voluntary organizations, 265–66
Healthy Home Healthy Child, 268
Henderson, Yandell, 125, 126
Heron, Joseph, 68
Heywood, Paul, 250
Hierarchists, 306–7, 308, 321
High Moorlands, 77–79, 88–91
Hirsch, Julius, 129
Holland, Robert, 36
Horsfall, Thomas, 71
Houldsworth, Henry, 61
Houldsworth, W. H., 63
Hygienically pure air, 103

Imperialism, threatened by ill health effects of pollution, 67
Individualists, 306, 307, 314–20, 321
Indoor air quality, 271
Indoor pollutants, 309
Industry, pressures on in nineteenth-century U.K., 21–22
Invisible gases, 5, 27, 31, 33, 36, 38, 95

Jevons, W. Stanley, 62
Jones, Billy M., 178
Jones, George, 71
Jorling, Thomas, 233
Justinian law, 227, 228

Kalman, Sumner M., 137
Kehoe, Robert Arthur, 127, 137, 138
Kellogg, J. H., 179
Knight, Goodwin, 189, 190, 205–6
Korff-Petersen, A., 124
Kyoto Protocol, 317, 319, 320

Laborless fuels, 110
Lancashire, sulfur dioxide threat in, 80–81
Lancashire Smoke Abatement League (LSAL), 41
Larson, Gordon, 190, 197n. 27
LaSpina, Antonio, 242–43
Lave, Lester, 268
Leigh, John, 29, 32, 33
Lewis, John L., 109, 110
Lichens, as pollution indicator, 89–90
Liesegang, Wilhelm, 121, 124, 130
Lime industry, 98n. 34
Lipietz, Alain, 1
Livestock, effect of smoke on, 22
Logan, W. P. D., 163
London, 1952 fog disaster, 78, 269; compiling data about, 161–63; death toll, 154, 159–60, 162–63; delayed reaction to, 159; health effects virtually unmentioned during, 157–58; political disputes relating to, 159, 160–61; questions regarding, 155; rise in health problems during, 159; seeping indoors, 158–59; social effects of, 158–59; sulfur dioxide levels during, 86; visual interest of, 157–58
Long, Haniel, 101
Long duree view, 6

Los Angeles: advertised as smokeless city, 179; controlling visible pollution sources, 187–89; 1964 smog attack, 189–91; smoggy conditions first gaining attention, 185–86, 192

Los Angeles County Air Pollution Control District, 188, 191, 192

Los Angeles Times, 190

Low-Emission Vehicle and Clean Fuels Program (CARB), 216

LRTAP. *See* Convention on Long-Range Transboundary Air Pollution (LRTAP) (1979)

Luckin, Bill, 155, 166

Maastricht Treaty, 254, 256

Macleod, Iain, 159

Macmillan, Harold, 160

Manchester (U.K.), 16; Air Pollution Advisory Board, 61; air pollution reform in, 28–30; air quality in the 1990s, 45n. 4; antipollution activists, 31–33, 60; antismoke societies, 60, 61; center of study for pollution's effects, 30–33; civil responses to pollution offenses, 16, 17; contradictory reports of smoke pollution, 52; economic fears in, 58; effects of environmental reform, 42–45; enforcing smoke-abatement laws, 33–34; environmental setting exacerbating pollution problems, 29–30; local perceptions of downside of technology, 30; mortality rates in, 63–64; pollution's ill effects on architecture, 67–68; public perceptions of smoke pollution, 51–73; public reaction to smoke pollution, 51–52; smoke-abatement exposition (1911), 41, 44; smoke-abatement reform groups formed, 30; smoke related to prosperity in, 53–60; smoke's negative effects in, 60–73; status in nineteenth century, 52–53; threatened by degeneration of urban populace, 66, 67; urban/suburban mortality rates, 39–41

Manchester and Salford Noxious Vapors Abatement Association (MSNVAA), 34, 35–37, 60, 71

Manchester and Salford Sanitary Association (MSSA), 33–34, 37

Manchester Association for the Prevention of Smoke (MAPS), 51, 60

Manchester Field Naturalist Society (MFNS), 37–41

Manchester Guardian, 68

Manchester Literary and Philosophical Society, 31, 32

"Manchester's Improving Daily" (Baines), 55–56

Market-oriented environmental management, 312, 316, 317–18, 319–20

Market simulations, 319–20

Markino, Yoshio, 23

Maybach, Wilhelm, 122

McAdam, Douglas, 195n. 7

McWilliams, Carey, 184, 194–95

Medical climatology, 178, 181–82

Medical Climatology: Climatic and Weather Influences in Health and Disease (Mills), 182–83

Mediterranean Syndrome, 242–43, 256

Meller, Herbert, 101, 103, 108, 110–11, 113–14n. 12, 115n. 16

Mellon family, 107

Mellon Institute, 102–4, 107, 108

Metal pollution, 84–85

Metam sodium, 288–89

Mexico City: air pollution as social concern, 330–31, 332–33, 334–36; approach to air pollution problems, 333–34, 335–36; perceptions of air pollution problems in, 329–32; pollutants in, 324

Miasma, 176
Middle Ages, responses to pollution, 16
Middle-class reform groups, 9
Mills, Clarence A., 182–83
Milton, Kay, 317
Mining, acidity from, 83–84
Molesworth, John, 51, 63
Monet, Claude, 23
Monrovia (Calif.), 180–81
Moorgrime, 87
Moors, 77–78, 89
Moral environmentalism, 176
Moral reform, 176–77
Morata, Francesc, 254
Mortality rates, from respiratory disease,
    63–64
Moss, C. E., 81
Motor Vehicle Pollution Control Board
    (Calif.), 211
Mukerji, Chandra, 195n. 6
Multicriteria assessment, 3–4
Mumford, Lewis, 106–7
Munn vs. Illinois, 229

National Ambient Air Quality Standards,
    272
National Expert Group on Transbound-
    ary Air Pollution, 94
National Institute of Environmental
    Health Sciences, 272
Nature: perceptions of, 327; promoted as
    source for synthetics, 108; related to
    industry and technology, 101
Nature benign, 306, 307
Nature capricious, 306, 307
Nature ephemeral, 306, 307
Nature perverse/tolerant, 306, 307
Nelson, Robert, 319
Neotechnic ideology, 106; among Pitts-
    burgh's business leaders, 110; posing
    threat of dislocation, 108
Newcomen steam engine, 83

New Source Review, 231–32
New York state, Emission Reduction
    Credits program in, 232–38
Nitrogen oxide, 92, 94, 246, 252
Noll, Roger, 233–34
Non-governmental organizations, 308
Nye, David, 44

Occupational health research, 104
Office of Air Pollution Control (Los An-
    geles), 188, 189
Oldham: acidic run-off in, 82–83; coal
    smoke influence on rainfall in, 81;
    reservoirs in, 89
Organic life, threat of acid rain to, 32
Organization for Economic Development
    and Cooperation, 253
Our Mutual Friend (Dickens), 155–56
ozone, 246
Ozone pollution, 301n. 5

PAHs, 85–86
Parkes, Louis, 157
Particulate research, 269–71, 272–73,
    274–75
Pasadena (Calif.), 180, 190
Pataki, George, 236
Pax toxicologica, 148n. 57
Peat, 77, 87, 90–91
Pennines, 77–79; change in lichen flora,
    90; importance of rain in, 88–89
Percy, John, 62
Pesticide Action Network, 290
Pesticide drift, 288–89; attention to,
    290–93; characterizing, 289–90,
    293–96; connecting with air pollution,
    289–90, 292–93, 296–99; health im-
    pacts, 300n. 1; incidents of, 290–91; re-
    sponse to, 292–93
Pesticide Illness Surveillance Program,
    290
Phenols, 84

Philips, Herbert, 34
Physical modeling, 315
Pigou, Arthur, 316
Pigouvian taxation, 316, 318, 319
Pillsbury, R. Cree, 137–38
Pittsburgh, 337–41; desire for transformation in, 104–6; pollution investigations in, 102–4; Renaissance, 110–11; smoke abatement in, 101–2; smoke ordinance (1941), 108, 110; social criticism in 1930s, 104–6; transformation expected, 109–10, 111n. 1; transformation narratives, 100
Pittsburgh, 108–9
"Pittsburgh 1932" (Graham), 105–6
Planned economies, 308
Platt, Harold, 80
Police, role in controlling automobile exhaust, 121–22
Police power, 228–29
Policy formation studies, 5
Political ecology, 223–24; approach to use rights, 225; overlap with environmental history, 226
Pollution, 177, 196n. 15; absence of single prevailing view, 72; conversation about, 7–8; cultural analysis applied to, 173–74; cultural effects, 166; determining limits of regulation, 103; displacing, 61; emerging public perception of, 8–9; financial cost in Manchester, 61–62; leading to moral degeneration, 66; problem emerging from context of human interactions, 3; racial hierarchy of exposure to, 7; reform mirroring social inequalities, 6; reform movements in late nineteenth and early twentieth centuries, 175–83; relations between Los Angeles society and, 172; social and cultural context for, 174–75; social perception of, 15; threat to social order, 173, 174, 192–93; working population's views about, 70–72
Pollution control: global, 5–6, 8; policy setbacks, 211; policy successes, 4; role of polluters in conversation, 7
Pollution control trading, 231
Pollution prevention technology, 312–13
Pollution, Property and Prices (Dales), 316

Polycyclic aromatic hydrocarbons, 85–86
Popular culture, praising pollution for its accompanying benefits, 54–56
Positive Crankcase Ventilation (PCV), 206
Pottenger, Francis M., 181
Precautionary principle, 119–20, 137–40
Property, Lockean approach to, 234–35
Property law, ambiguity in, 224
Property rights, 227, 318
Public action, 8
Public Health Act of 1872/1875 (U.K.), 17–18
Public health movements, 172–73
Public relations, 103–4, 107–8, 191, 192
Public trust, defining, 235–37
Public trust doctrine (U.S.), 227, 228, 229
Pulido, Laura, 299

Race, related to pollution exposure, 7
Radkau, Joachim, 120
Ransome, Arthur, 64, 66
Reach, Angus, 58
Reclaim Program (Calif.), 231
Reform, paradox of, 31, 36, 43–44
Regulation, tasks of, in modern society, 328–29
Republican Party (U.S.), 3
Rickets, 96–97n. 13
Risk and Culture (Douglas), 173
Risk assessment, 173–74
Roberts, Robert, 70
Rome, Adam W., 177

Rose, Carol, 229–30
Roumasset, James, 309
Rowbottom, William, 85
Roxbury Environmental Empowerment
    Project, 267, 279
Royal Sanitary Institute, 165
Royce, Stephen, 188
Russell, Rollo, 61, 62, 156, 157
Russell, W. J., 19

Scandinavia, 92, 94
Schramm, E., 27
Schultz, Stanley, 176
Schwartz, Joel, 270
Schwarz, Michiel, 306, 307–8
Science-based regulatory state, interac-
    tion between experts in, 119, 136–37
Scientists, as part of social context, 2
Sciortino, Giuseppe, 242–43
Scott, Fred, 34–35, 67
Seeder-feeder enhancement of rainfall, 89
Select Committee on Smoke Nuisance
    Abatement, 68–69
Self-regulation, 131
Sellers, Christopher, 127
Seskin, Eugene, 268
Seventh-Day Adventism, 179
Shapiro, Judith, 314
Shapiro, Michael, 234
Sierra Madre (Calif.), 180
Simon, Shenna, 28
Simpson, Henry, 35
Sisson, L. B., 103
Sleigh, A. W., 70
Smith, Kirk, 309
Smith, R. A., 89
Smog, 157, 165, 177; awareness about
    affecting public policy, 206; contexts
    for in Southern California, 172, 174;
    cultural analysis of, 174–75; explana-
    tions for, 171–72; fear of, 194–95n. 5;
    growing problem in Los Angeles,

170–71; initial response to, in Southern
    California, 184–85; local feature of, 193;
    locating context for, 174; 1964 Los An-
    geles attack, 189–91; problem of cul-
    tural boundaries, 173, 174; reform
    movement in Southern California,
    171–72; Southern California's response
    to, 193–94; transforming meaning of
    landscape, 193; *See also* London, 1952
    fog disaster
Smog reformer movement (1940s), 195n.
    7
Smoke: beneficial aspects of, 52, 53–60,
    69, 70, 72, 177; competing narratives
    about, 64–73; connecting with wasted
    resources, 60, 61–63; health damage
    from, 63–67; methods of control,
    244–46; public meeting against, 71;
    subject of transformation stories in
    Pittsburgh, 100–101
Smoke abatement: encouraging greater
    energy consumption, 31, 36; in nine-
    teenth-century United Kingdom,
    17–22; in Pittsburgh, 101–2; presumed
    positive effects of, 69; programs for,
    complementing neotechnic ideology,
    106; technology for, contributing to
    ash problem, 113n. 10
Smoke Abatement Exhibition, 34
Smoke Abatement Exposition (1881–82),
    29
Smoke-abatement movement; elevating
    engineers' status, 195–96n. 12; emer-
    gence of, 63
Smoke and Fumes Commission (Los An-
    geles), 187
Smoke control, shifting emphasis of,
    176–77
Smoke-control movement, postwar pre-
    dictions, 109
"Smokeless Chimney, The" (Bellasis),
    54–55

Smokeless City, utopian fantasy of, 44

Smokestacks, height of, 5, 44, 91–92

SO_2 Emissions Trading Simulator, 319–20

Social constructionism, 337, 341

Socialized individualism, 205

Social relations, embedding in physical objects, 195n. 6

Society of Residents of the Lower Friedrichstadt, 129

Society, pollution's implications for, in nineteenth-century England, 23

Soldiers, unfit because of health problems, 67

Soot-fall studies, 102–3

Spain, 242; air pollution in, 244–46; air pollution policies, 251; air pollution research in, 252–53; domestic energy resources, 251; Economic Stabilization Plan, 248–49; environmental policy in, 250–51, 253–56; fuel consumption in, 251–52; National Energy Plan, 251; political and economic environment, 248–51; scholars' disappointment with environmental policies, 242–43; transportation sector, 252

Spence, Peter, 31, 32, 33

Spencer, Reuben, 59

Spengler, Jack, 268

Spitta, Oskar, 135

State laws, treatment of air resources, 227–28, 229–30

Stationary source emissions, control of, 231–32

Steam engine, 16, 83–84

Sulfates, diseases related to overexposure to, 86–87

Sulfur, deposition of, 94–95

Sulfur allowance trading program, 231

Sulfur dioxide, 80–81, 86–87, 245–46; effect on southern Pennines, 90; during London fog disaster, 154

Sulfuric acid, 36, 79–80

Sun Guodong, 313

Sunlight levels, 40; absence of, 66; reduced because of pollution, 82; rickets as indicator of, 96–97n. 13

Sustainable development, 320

Synthetics, problems related to, 107–8

Takings, 233

Talking claims, 225

Tarr, Joel, 109

Tatham, John F. W., 39

Taylor, William Cooke, 54

Technics and Civilization (Mumford), 106

Technology, worship of, 44

Temple of Science (Pittsburgh), 107

Tetraethyl lead, 126–28, 130–31; effects on health, 137–38; German approach to, 135–36; U.S. approach to, 132

Therapeutic landscape, 174, 175

Thompson, Michael, 306, 307–8

Three Kingdoms (Luo), 305

Tobacco smoke exposure, 309

"Toddlin' Whoam" (Waugh), 57

"Tragedy of the commons," 225–26, 230

Transboundary air pollution, 245–47

Tucker, Raymond, 188

Tucker Report, 188

UN Conference on the Human Environment, 94

United Kingdom: effects of pollution, 22; nineteenth-century responses to pollution, 17–22; social and artistic implications of pollution, 22–24. *See also London, Manchester, listings*

Unleaded gasoline, 130

Un-Politics of Air Pollution, The (Crenson), 2, 325–26

Urban environment, moral reform of, 176–77

Urban environmental reform movement,
172
Urban fogs, 155, 156
Urban reform movements, interconnec-
tions among members, 48
Urban sanitary reform, unique solution
proposed, 47n. 11
U.S. Bureau of Mines, 103
U.S. Constitution, 224, 227, 228
U.S. Department of Housing and Urban
Development, 272

Use rights, 225–26
U.S. Surgeon General's Ad Hoc Committee on Tetraethyl Lead, 127–28

Vegetation, pollution's threat to, 67–68
Vehicle manufacturers, target of auto
emissions regulation, 215
Victorian cities: effects of pollution
on, 22–25; environmentalists in,
27–29
Vielhaben, Fritz, 129, 133
Villot, Xavier, 243

Water supply, threatened by mining, 83–84
Waugh, Edwin, 57
WE ACT. *See* West Harlem Environmen-
tal Action
Weidlein, Edward, 102
West Harlem Environmental Action, 264,
266–68, 277–84
Wet deposition, 79–80
Wildavsky, Aaron, 306
Wilkins, E. T., 163, 165
Wilmont, Sarah, 42
Wilson, Richard, 268
Wolff, Georg, 122, 131
Woman's Municipal League, 129–30
Women: emerging as professionals in
pollution abatement, 18; leading
urban reformers, 176
Worst-case conditions, 310
Wright, Angus, 296
Wright, Mrs. A. Romley, 56–57

Zangger, H., 127
Zernik, Franz, 123, 124, 130
Zero-Emitting Vehicles, 216–18